Hong Kong's Governance Under Chinese Sovereignty

As a hybrid regime, Hong Kong has been governed by a state–business alliance since the colonial era. However, since the handover in 1997, the transformation of Hong Kong's political and socio-economic environment has eroded the conditions that supported a viable state–business alliance. This state–business alliance, which was once a solution for Hong Kong's governance, has now become a political burden – rather than a political asset – to the post-colonial Hong Kong state.

This book presents a critical re-examination of the post-1997 governance crisis in Hong Kong under the Tung Chee-hwa and Donald Tsang Administrations. It shows that the state–business alliance has failed to function as an organizational machinery for supporting the post-colonial state and has also served to generate new governance problems. Drawing upon contemporary theories on hybrid regimes and state capacity, this book looks beyond the existing opposition-centred explanations of Hong Kong's governance crisis. By establishing the causal relationship between the failure of the state–business alliance and the governance crisis facing the post-colonial state, Brian C. H. Fong broadens our understanding of the governance problems and political confrontations in post-colonial Hong Kong. In turn, he posits that, although the state–business alliance worked effectively for the colonial state in the past, it is now a major problem for the post-colonial state, and suggests that Hong Kong needs a realignment of a new governing coalition.

Hong Kong's Governance Under Chinese Sovereignty will enrich and broaden the existing literature on Hong Kong's public governance, while casting new light on the territory's political developments. As such, it will be welcomed by students and scholars interested in Chinese politics, Hong Kong politics and governance.

Brian C. H. Fong is Assistant Professor in the Department of Asian and Policy Studies, Hong Kong Institute of Education.

Routledge research on social work, social policy and social development in Greater China
Series editors: Angelina Woon-ki Yuen-Tsang, Ben Hok-bun Ku and Ngai Pun
Hong Kong Polytechnic University

This series focuses on issues related to the rapid social change in contemporary Mainland China, Hong Kong, Macao and Taiwan. Comprising contributions from diverse disciplines, the series will explore and respond to the impacts of marketization, globalization, urbanization, modernization, migration, technological change, consumerism, dualism and disasters on people's livelihoods, well-being and social life in Chinese societies.

1   **Mobile Communication and Greater China**
    Edited by Rodney Wai-chi Chu, Leopoldina Fortunati, Pui-lam Law and Shanhua Yang

2   **Hong Kong's Governance Under Chinese Sovereignty**
    The failure of the state–business alliance after 1997
    Brian C. H. Fong

Hong Kong's Governance Under Chinese Sovereignty
The failure of the state–business alliance after 1997

Brian C. H. Fong

LONDON AND NEW YORK

First published 2015
by Routledge
2 Park Square, Milton Park, Abingdon, Oxon OX14 4RN

and by Routledge
711 Third Avenue, New York, NY 10017

Routledge is an imprint of the Taylor & Francis Group, an informa business

© 2015 Brian C. H. Fong

The right of Brian C. H. Fong to be identified as author of this work has been asserted by him in accordance with sections 77 and 78 of the Copyright, Designs and Patents Act 1988.

All rights reserved. No part of this book may be reprinted or reproduced or utilized in any form or by any electronic, mechanical, or other means, now known or hereafter invented, including photocopying and recording, or in any information storage or retrieval system, without permission in writing from the publishers.

Trademark notice: Product or corporate names may be trademarks or registered trademarks, and are used only for identification and explanation without intent to infringe.

British Library Cataloguing in Publication Data
A catalogue record for this book is available from the British Library

Library of Congress Cataloging in Publication Data
Fong, Brian C. H.
Hong Kong's governance under Chinese sovereignty: the failure of the state–business alliance after 1997/Brian C.H. Fong.
  pages cm. – (Routledge research on social work, social policy and social development in greater China; 2)
  Includes bibliographical references and index.
  1. Hong Kong (China)–Politics and government–1997. 2. Business and politics–China–Hong Kong. 3. Representative government and representation–China–Hong Kong. 4. Dong, Jianhua, 1937. 5. Tsang, Donald, 1944– I. Title.
  JQ1539.5.A91F66 2015
  320.95125–dc23   2014008101

ISBN: 978-0-415-73828-6 (hbk)
ISBN: 978-1-315-81747-7 (ebk)

Typeset in Times New Roman
by Wearset Ltd, Boldon, Tyne and Wear

Printed and bound in Great Britain by
CPI Group (UK) Ltd, Croydon, CR0 4YY

This book is dedicated to everyone who cares about Hong Kong

Contents

List of figures	xii
List of tables	xiii

PART I
Governance under hybrid regimes: the case of Hong Kong

1

1 Governance crisis in post-1997 Hong Kong: in search of a new theoretical explanation

3

The politics of hybrid regimes: the case of Hong Kong 3
The mainstream explanation of legitimacy deficit: the
challenges of the democratic opposition under the hybrid
regime 18
Going beyond the mainstream explanation: from
opposition-centred explanation to a critical analysis of
governing coalition building 27
Synthesis of the argument and its theoretical implications: a new
theoretical explanation on Hong Kong's governance 32
The research design of this book 37
Conclusion 40

2 Governance and the state: revisiting the concepts and theories of state capacity

50

The capacity of the state to govern: state capacity
defined 50
State capacity as political autonomy 55
State capacity as embedded autonomy 58
State capacity as governed interdependence 59
State capacity as state–society synergy 61
State capacity as forging coalitions 64

viii   *Contents*

*An integrated conceptual framework: state capacity as governing
   coalition building 65*
Conclusion 69

PART II
**The legacy of state–business alliance: from the colonial
time to the transitional period**   71

**3   Reinterpreting governance and state capacity in colonial
     time: the colonial state–business alliance**   73

*The nature of the colonial state: an administrative state dominated
   by bureaucrats 73*
*The making of the capitalist class: the emergence of British and
   Chinese merchants 76*
*State–business relations in colonial times: the formation and
   evolution of the state–business alliance 79*
*Governing coalition building in colonial times: how did the
   state–business alliance contribute to the effective governance
   in colonial Hong Kong? 82*
Conclusion 97

**4   The crafting of the post-1997 state–business alliance:
     Beijing's governing strategy after 1997**   103

*The politics of transition and the crafting of the post-1997 political
   order 104*
*The making of the post-1997 state–business alliance:
   the convergence of interests between Beijing and the local
   capitalist class 106*
*The rise of a new China-centred state–business alliance:
   the co-option of the business sector by Beijing since the
   1980s 112*
Conclusion 115

Contents ix

PART III
Missing link between state, business and society: the growing erosion of the intermediary role of business elites after 1997 119

5 **The missing link between state and business: the fragmentation of agents of business interests** 121

The end of the traditional business representation system: the changing configuration of the economic and political structures since the 1980s 122
Who can represent the business sector in the post-1997 political-economic order? The underdevelopment of business-oriented political parties 131
Implications of the fragmentation of agents of business interests: the paradox of "strong business representation, weak political support" 142
Conclusion 154

6 **The widening gap between state and society: the growing disconnection of the business sector from the local community** 160

The dominant representation of business elites in the advisory bodies after 1997: old wine in a new bottle 160
New challenges for the state–business alliance: the rise of civil society activism 162
Implications of the growing disconnection of the business sector: the widening gap between the post-colonial state and the society 168
Conclusion 174

PART IV
Uneasy partnership between state and business: the rising power leverage of the business sector in post-1997 Hong Kong 181

7 **Institutionalization of business power under the HKSAR political system: Chief Executive Election Committee and functional constituencies** 183

The constitutional design of the post-1997 political system: the making of the state–business alliance 183

x   *Contents*

Chief Executive Election Committees: institutionalization of business power in the executive branch 185

Functional constituency electoral system and voting-by-group system of the Legislative Council: institutionalization of business power in the legislative process 196

Implications of the institutionalization of business power under the HKSAR political system: the unprecedented power bases for the business sector 201

Conclusion 205

8   The business sector's direct access to the sovereign state: the close partnership between Beijing and the local capitalists   210

The business sector's institutionalized access to the sovereign state: the National People's Congress and the National Committee of Chinese People's Political Consultative Conference 211

Political co-option of the business elites by the local agent of the sovereign state: the united front work of the Central Liaison Office 213

Business sector's increased economic links with the Mainland authorities: Mainland–Hong Kong economic integration and its political implications 218

Implications of the business sector's direct access to the sovereign state: the circumvention activities by the business elites 221

Conclusion 225

PART V
Rethinking Hong Kong's governance under Chinese sovereignty: from an opposition-centred explanation to a critical analysis of governing coalition building   231

9   Conclusion: rethinking the governance crisis in post-1997 Hong Kong   233

A new theoretical explanation on the governance crisis in post-1997 Hong Kong: the failure of the state–business alliance 234

Rethinking Hong Kong's governance crisis under Chinese sovereignty: legitimacy deficit or failure of governing coalition building? 243

*The way out for Hong Kong's governance: in search of a new
    political order 248*
*Comparing Hong Kong with other East Asian hybrid regimes:
    lessons from the case of Hong Kong and future research
    agenda 253*
Conclusion 256

**Epilogue: Hong Kong's governance in the aftermath of the
2012 Chief Executive election: governing coalition built on
sand**   261

Appendix: interview guidelines   268

Index   270

Figures

1.1	A fourfold typology of political regimes	6
1.2	The level of public dissatisfaction towards the Hong Kong government (half-yearly average) (1997–2012)	15
1.3	The number of people participating in the 1 July protest rally (2003–2012)	16
1.4	The number of social demonstrations (1997–2012)	16
1.5	The level of public trust toward the Hong Kong government (half-yearly average) (1997–2012)	17
5.1	Percentage of equity of British capital, local Chinese capital, Mainland capital and other capital in the total market capitalization of the Hang Seng Index (1978–2003)	124
5.2	Market capitalization of major British business groups in the Hong Kong stock market in 1979	127
5.3	Market capitalization of major local Chinese business groups in Hong Kong stock market (both main board and growth enterprise market) in 2003	128
5.4	Number of regional headquarters in Hong Kong by country (2012)	140
5.5	Number of regional offices in Hong Kong by country (2012)	141
6.1	Number of civil society organizations (1997–2012)	167
6.2	The development of a public discourse against the business sector in the post-1997 period	171
8.1	Hong Kong's total trade with Mainland China (1981–2012)	219
8.2	Inward direct investment in Hong Kong by major countries at market value (1998–2011)	219
8.3	Outward direct investment of Hong Kong by major recipient country at market value (1998–2011)	220
8.4	Percentage of assets hold by Hong Kong conglomerates in the Mainland	220
E.1	Comparison between the public ratings of Tung Chee-hwa, Donald Tsang Yam-kuen and Leung Chun-ying	264
E.2	The level of public dissatisfaction towards the Leung Chun-ying Administration (July 2012–December 2013)	264
E.3	The level of public trust towards the Leung Chun-ying Administration (September 2012–December 2013)	265

Tables

1.1	Number of "partly free" hybrid regimes (1972–2012)	4
1.2	Legislative success rate of the Hong Kong government since the handover (1998–2012)	10
1.3	The sluggish implementation of business regulatory initiatives under the Donald Tsang Administration	12
1.4	Public perceptions on government–business relations	18
1.5	Hong Kong people's views on social harmony	19
1.6	Hong Kong people's views on "real estate hegemony"	19
1.7	Comparing Hong Kong's economic performance with public support for the Hong Kong government (1997–2012)	20
2.1	Theoretical approaches to state capacity	66
3.1	Unofficial members in the Executive Council and Legislative Council (1965–1986)	84
3.2	List of unofficial members of the Executive Council (1896–1941)	86
3.3	Composition of Legislative Council (1843–1983)	89
3.4	Hong Kong's total trade with United Kingdom (1972–1997)	91
3.5	Evaluation of performance of the colonial administration	96
3.6	The level of public trust toward the Hong Kong government (1992–1997)	97
4.1	Background analysis of members of China-appointed bodies in the 1990s	114
5.1	Number of interlocks per company (1982–2004)	125
5.2	Multiple directorships held by individual directors (1982–2004)	126
5.3	Composition of Legislative Council (from 1984–2008)	130
5.4	Income and expenditure accounts of the Liberal Party and Hong Kong Progressive Alliance	138
5.5	Distribution of small and medium enterprises (as of June 2011)	142
5.6	Business associations in Hong Kong	143
5.7	Background analysis of pro-business Legislative Councillors (1998–2012)	145
5.8	Interlocking directorships of the Liberal Party and four major business associations (1997–2010)	146

xiv *Tables*

5.9	Representation of business interests in the Executive Council (1998–2010)	150
6.1	Background analysis of unofficial members in the Executive Council (1998–2011)	163
6.2	Background analysis of unofficial members in the commission on strategic development (2005–2009)	163
6.3	Background analysis of part-time members in the Central Policy Unit (2003–2011)	165
6.4	Community networks of major political parties	170
6.5	Public perceptions of business leaders	171
6.6	Public perceptions on the political discourse of economism	172
7.1	Composition of the Chief Executive Election Committee	187
7.2	Register of electors for Chief Executive Election Committee subsectors: an illustration of the 2011 Chief Executive Election Committee	188
7.3	Background analysis of members of the 1996 Chief Executive Selection Committee	191
7.4	Background analysis of members of the 2000 Chief Executive Election Committee	192
7.5	Background analysis of members of the 2006 Chief Executive Election Committee	193
7.6	Background analysis of members of the 2011 Chief Executive Election Committee	194
7.7	Distribution of registered electors by functional constituencies in 2011	198
7.8	Background analysis of legislative councillors returned by functional constituencies	200
7.9	Number of motions rejected by functional constituencies under the voting-by-group system	201
7.10	List of motions rejected by functional constituencies under the voting-by-group system	202
8.1	Background analysis of Hong Kong Deputies to the National People's Congress (1998–2012)	212
8.2	Background analysis of Hong Kong members of the National Committee of the Chinese People's Political Consultative Conference (1998–2012)	213
8.3	Background analysis of members of the Presidium of Preparatory Committee of Hong Kong Compatriots in celebration of the founding anniversary of the People's Republic of China (1998–2011)	216
8.4	Number of Hong Kong delegations to Beijing (1998–2011)	224
8.5	State officials visited by business delegations (1997–2011)	225
8.6	Selected circumvention activities by the business sector after 1997	226
9.1	State–business alliance before and after 1997	244

		Tables xv
9.2	A brief comparison of the hybrid politics in Hong Kong, Singapore and Malaysia	255
E.1	Background analysis of political officials under the Leung Chun-ying Administration	262
E.2	List of unofficial members of the Executive Council appointed by Leung Chun-ying in 2012	263

Part I

Governance under hybrid regimes

The case of Hong Kong

1 Governance crisis in post-1997 Hong Kong

In search of a new theoretical explanation

The politics of hybrid regimes: the case of Hong Kong

The growing scholarly attention on hybrid regimes

In recent years there have been increasing academic discussions and debates in the field of comparative political studies about "hybrid regimes", which by definition combine both democratic and authoritarian elements (e.g. Diamond, 2002; Levitsky & Way, 2002; Schedler, 2002). This new wave of scholarly attention is attributable to the fact that the "third wave of democratization" as advocated by the renowned American political scientist Samuel Huntington in the 1990s has already come to a halt in recent years. Instead, there is unprecedented growth in the number of hybrid regimes in the world and experts predicted that these intermediate regimes will likely remain in the "political grey zone" between full democracies and outright authoritarianism over a long period of time (Diamond, 2002).

According to the Freedom House's "Freedom of the World 2013", which provided comparative assessment of global political rights and civil liberties,[1] 58 out of the 195 countries around the globe could be considered as "partly free" hybrid regimes in 2012, representing 30 per cent of the world's countries and covering about 23 per cent of the world population (Table 1.1). Countries falling into this category have been on an increasing trend in recent decades and now include Albania, Bolivia, Colombia, Ecuador, Georgia, Libya, Malaysia, Mexico, Paraguay, Singapore, Turkey, Ukraine and Venezuela. According to the studies of the Freedom House, these "partly free" hybrid regimes are usually characterized by limited respect for political rights and civil liberties, under which an incumbent dominates the political landscape while tolerating a certain degree of pluralism (Freedom House, 2013).

As a consequence of the growing importance of these hybrid regimes in the contemporary political map, it was not surprising that there has been a great deal of comparative political studies in recent years which aimed at accounting for the nature and characteristics of hybrid regimes (e.g. Brownlee, 2007; Case, 2005, 2008; Levitsky & Way, 2010; Slater, 2010).

Clearly, the increasing scholarly attention on the notion of hybrid regimes is built upon the understanding that competitive election is the necessary condition – but

4   *Governance under hybrid regimes*

Table 1.1 Number of "partly free" hybrid regimes (1972–2012)

Year	Total number of countries	Free countries		Partly free countries		Not free countries	
		Number	%	Number	%	Number	%
2012	195	90	46	58	30	47	24
2011	195	87	45	60	31	48	24
2010	194	87	45	60	31	47	24
2009	194	89	46	58	30	47	24
2008	193	89	46	62	32	42	22
2007	193	90	47	60	31	43	22
2006	193	90	47	58	30	45	23
2005	192	89	46	58	30	45	24
2004	192	89	46	54	28	49	26
2003	192	88	46	55	29	49	25
2002	192	89	46	55	29	48	25
2001	192	85	44	59	31	48	25
2000	192	86	45	58	30	48	25
1999	192	85	44	60	31	47	25
1998	191	88	46	53	28	50	26
1997	191	81	42	57	30	53	28
1996	191	79	41	59	31	53	28
1995	191	76	40	62	32	53	28
1994	191	76	40	61	32	54	28
1993	190	72	38	63	33	55	29
1992	186	75	40	73	39	38	21
1991	183	76	42	65	35	42	23
1990	165	65	40	50	30	50	30
1989	167	61	37	44	26	62	37
1988	167	60	36	39	23	68	41
1987	167	58	35	58	35	51	30
1986	167	57	34	57	34	53	32
1985	167	56	34	56	34	55	33
1984	167	53	32	59	35	55	33
1982–1983	166	52	31	56	34	58	35
1981–1982	165	54	33	47	28	64	39
1980	162	51	31	51	31	60	37
1979	161	51	32	54	33	56	35
1978	158	47	30	56	35	55	35
1977	155	43	28	48	31	64	41
1976	159	42	26	49	31	68	43
1975	158	40	25	53	34	65	41
1974	152	41	27	48	32	63	41
1973	151	44	29	42	28	65	43
1972	151	44	29	38	25	69	46

Source: Freedom House, 2013.

Governance crisis in post-1997 Hong Kong 5

not the sufficient condition – for democracy, and thus political regimes should not be classified as democracies simply because they hold regular multiparty elections on the basis of universal suffrage (Diamond, 2002; Schedler, 2002). For scholars of hybrid regimes, modern democracies should not only be defined as a system of holding regular multiparty elections, but should also encompass the relaxation of controls on political activities and the recognition of basic civil rights. Following renowned political scientist Robert Dahl's classical theories of polyarchies, comparative theorists considered competitive elections and civil liberties as the two basic dimensions of modern democratic systems, and only when both of these two dimensions of democracy are present can such a political regime be categorized as "full democracy"; a political regime should be classified as "full authoritarianism" when neither dimension exists (Case, 2008). Between these two poles of full democracy and full authoritarianism, conceptually there are two typical forms of hybrid regimes, namely "liberal authoritarianism" (also known as "semi-authoritarianism") and "electoral authoritarianism" (also known as "semi-democracy" or "competitive authoritarianism").

Under liberal authoritarianism, while civil liberties are to a large extent respected and the activities of interest groups and opposition parties are generally recognized, popular election for the national chief executive is absent and opposition forces' access to government power are basically denied. In contrast, under electoral authoritarianism there are regular multiparty elections for the national chief executive operated on the basis of universal suffrage, but civil liberties are largely suppressed by the government in order to prevent the opposition forces from mobilizing against the authoritarian incumbents and endangering its continued hegemony (Case, 1996, 2008; O'Donnell & Schmitter, 1986). This scheme of classification results in the fourfold typology shown in Figure 1.1, which broadly captures the four ideal types of political regimes that can be found in contemporary societies.

For much of the existing studies of democratization, hybrid regimes were described by political scientists as unstable and transitional regimes (Levitsky & Way, 2010, p. 1). By combining both democratic and authoritarian elements within a single political regime, hybrid regimes, no matter whether they are liberal authoritarianism or electoral authoritarianism, were said to be experiencing endless political conflicts between the incumbent and the opposition. In the eyes of many political scientists, hybrid regimes are an unstable form of government and are more vulnerable to different kinds of governance problems and political instability than full democracies and full authoritarianism (Goldstone et al., 2005).

For liberal authoritarian regimes, the trend of political liberalization will often stimulate people's desire for a greater pace of democratization and also provide important fertile ground for opposition parties and civil society organizations to mobilize their supporters against the authoritarian incumbents. Motivated by civil liberties to participate in politics but denied real access to government power through democratic elections, opposition forces under liberal authoritarian regimes may eventually seek political reforms through anti-establishment

6 *Governance under hybrid regimes*

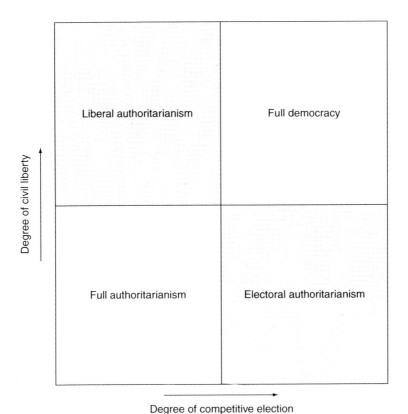

Figure 1.1 A fourfold typology of political regimes (source: adapted from O'Donnell & Schmitter, 1986 and Case, 2008).

behaviours. Intense political pressures and tensions are therefore continuously placed upon the political system, paving the way for pushing towards a full democratic transition (Case, 2008; Huntington, 1991).

Similarly, under electoral authoritarian regimes, the incumbents' attempts to maintain their political powers through manipulation of elections and suppression of civil society's activities will usually stir up confrontations with opposition forces. In this connection, authoritarian rulers are always situated in a "nebulous zone of structural ambivalence", swinging from imposing tighter control on elections and civil society but at the cost of intensifying domestic conflicts and inviting international isolation, to tolerating the challenges of opposition parties but at the expense of regime uncertainties. Comparative theorists have observed that these political dilemmas and persistent rivalries have brought about political crisis in many hybrid regimes like Mexico in 1988, Russia in 1993 and Albania in 1997 (Levitsky & Way, 2002; Schedler, 2002).

Hong Kong as a hybrid regime and its governance crisis after 1997

In the context of comparative political studies, Hong Kong is an interesting case of hybrid regime. Since the colonial era, the British colonial government had put in place a liberal authoritarian regime in the city-state: while political powers were concentrated in the hands of the colonial administration headed by the Governor and the people of Hong Kong were denied the rights to choose their own government though democratic elections, a high level of civil liberties, independence of judicial courts and rule of law that were on a par with that of many well-developed Western democratic regimes had been in place for many decades. In this regard, the establishment of the Hong Kong Special Administrative Region (HKSAR) on 1 July 1997 did not change Hong Kong's liberal authoritarian regime, because various civil liberties have been generally guaranteed under the Basic Law. On the other hand, while the process of democratization had already been started in the mid 1980s, Hong Kong is still far away from developed into a full-fledged democracy due to its limited electoral franchise. Nowadays, half of the seats in the Legislative Council are selected by popular elections, and the Chief Executive, who replaced the colonial Governor as the executive head after 1997, remains handpicked by an election committee controlled by the Beijing government and could not be held accountable to the legislature or people of Hong Kong (Lau & Kuan, 2002).

By maintaining the high degree of civil liberties and incorporating some limited elements of democratic elections, Hong Kong's experience is quite unusual in comparative political studies and could be considered as a particular type of hybrid regime: the post-1997 Hong Kong is fundamentally a liberal authoritarian regime featuring some electoral authoritarian elements[2] (Case, 2008). The academics questions here are whether Hong Kong, as a particular type of hybrid regime, experiences the same inherent risk of instability and political conflicts commonly found in other hybrid regimes. If Hong Kong is considered to experience crisis of governance, are these problems closely connected to the territory's hybrid regime or contributed by other factors? Was Hong Kong's experience unique in any sense?

Comparative political studies indicate that hybrid regimes usually encounter political confrontations between the authoritarian governments and the opposition forces, and it is not uncommon for them to experience serious political instabilities and conflicts like revolutionary wars, adverse regime changes, collapse of state power, ethnic conflicts and genocides (Goldstone *et al.*, 2005). Obviously, unlike other hybrid regimes, Hong Kong so far has not experienced this kind of serious political turmoil or violent conflict. In fact, since the handover of sovereignty the post-colonial state has managed the day-to-day administration of the society quite effectively; thanks to the highly efficient and clean civil service, independent judiciary and sound rule of law system, Hong Kong has been successful in preserving its political stability, maintaining efficient delivery of public services and ensuring law and order.[3] Most importantly, given Hong Kong's status as an autonomous region under Chinese sovereignty, Beijing

8 *Governance under hybrid regimes*

performed as an important force for blocking democratic change and preserving overall political stability in the territory, making its hybrid regime more persistent than other similar polities (Case, 2008). Although Hong Kong's overall political situations are clearly much more stable than many other hybrid regimes, it does not mean that the territory is free from political confrontations and governance problems. Since the handover of sovereignty in 1997, "governance crisis" has become the most popular term used by local politicians, commentators and academics to describe the political situation in post-colonial Hong Kong. From time to time, the post-1997 governance crisis has been described by different scholars as "institutional incompatibility" (Cheung, 2005a, 2005b), "hollowing-out of executive power" (Cheung, 2007), "disarticulation of the political system" (Scott, 2000), "political decay" (Lo, 2001) or "institutional incongruity" (Lee, 1999). In the eyes of many local political scientists and researchers, Hong Kong has been trapped in a governance crisis after 1997 and there seems to be no clear prospect of improvement in the foreseeable future.

But what are the nature and characteristics of the so-called "governance crisis" in the post-1997 Hong Kong? Conceptually, there is no universally accepted definition of "governance crisis" in political science literature and its manifestation differs greatly across societies; thus the substance and seriousness of the governance crisis in Hong Kong can only be understood in the specific political contexts of the territory (Lau, 1994). From this perspective, when compared with its colonial predecessor, the post-colonial state has been facing an unprecedented governance crisis since 1997. Such a governance crisis has been expressed on three major fronts. First, the post-colonial state is facing growing challenges in re-embedding itself with major socio-economic actors and it is struggling to forge societal acceptance for delivering policy changes. Second, the post-colonial state's relative autonomy is facing growing challenges from the business sector and therefore it struggles to maintain its role as the arbitrator of class interests. Third, the post-colonial state is facing a political quagmire of pervasive public discontent and public distrust and the popular support base of the HKSAR political order is in danger of collapse.

The first indicator of the governance crisis is that the post-colonial state is facing growing challenges in re-embedding itself with major socio-economic actors and it is struggling to forge societal acceptance for delivering policy changes. In contemporary political science literature, "governance" has been defined by some academics as "the capacity of government to make and implement policy" (Pierre & Peters, 2000, p. 1) and the state has been considered as playing a pivotal role in the governance process by steering and making policy changes (Pierre & Peters, 2006). In the British colonial era, Hong Kong's system of governance was widely described as an "executive-dominant governance system" by which most of the decision-making power was concentrated in the hands of the executive and the colonial Governor, and his senior officials held a dominant position in directing policy-making (Li, 2007). In this connection, the close linkages between the colonial state and the business sector, as well as its immunity from the challenges of a weak civil society, both served to strengthen the capacity of the colonial Governor and his senior officials to deliver policy changes (Cheung, 2007).[4]

Although it was the grand strategy of the Beijing leaders to preserve the executive-dominant governance system after 1997, and such a system was adopted as the basic model of the HKSAR constitutional system under the Basic Law,[5] the post-handover political developments indicated that the post-colonial state has all along been suffering from weakening of policy-making capacity. In the policy process, both the Tung Chee-hwa Administration and the Donald Tsang Administrations have been exposed to political challenges from all fronts, including its traditional business allies and those newly emerged civil society groups, and there is a widening political gap between the post-colonial state and the major socio-economic constituents (Lui & Chiu, 2009). Facing serious challenges in gaining the cooperation of major socio-economic constituents, quite a number of policy initiatives proposed by the post-colonial state were either shelved and withdrawn due to strong opposition, or only achieved a pyrrhic victory after prolonged battles of political attrition. The "legislative success rates" of the post-colonial state after 1997 was strong, measurable evidence of its growing difficulties in delivering policy changes. In the first 15 years of the HKSAR era, the post-colonial state failed to put into practice many planned legislative initiatives and its legislative success rates on average only stood at 56.05 per cent. In particular, the statistics showed that on many occasions the post-colonial state was inclined to stay away from controversy and it had shelved and postponed over 40.04 per cent of legislative initiatives that were originally planned in its annual Policy Address and Legislative Programme (Table 1.2).

The second indicator of the governance crisis is that the post-colonial state's relative autonomy is facing growing challenges from the business sector and therefore it struggles to maintain its role as the arbitrator of class interests. As pointed out by Neo-Marxists such as Nicos Poulantza and James O'Connor, although under modern capitalist systems the state must serve the interests of the bourgeoisie by facilitating capital accumulation, it needs to maintain a certain degree of relative autonomy from the capitalist class. The relative autonomy of the state shall allow it to go against the immediate interests of the bourgeoisie and pursue policies that create better conditions for fostering class harmony and maintaining long-term sustainability of the capitalist order, such as the provision of social welfare and labour protection (O'Connor, 1973; Poulantzas, 1978). In the British colonial era, despite its political alliance with the big capitalists, it was notable that the colonial state had maintained a considerable degree of relative autonomy vis-à-vis the business sector and it had been quite effective in performing its role as an arbitrator of different class interests (Chiu, 1994; Scott, 1989, pp. 58–59) by pursuing policy reforms that were not welcomed by the business elites.[6]

However, the post-1997 developments showed that the post-colonial state's impartiality in relation to the business sector have become increasingly untenable. Unlike its colonial predecessor, the post-colonial state is not quite capable of mitigating social contradictions and encounters greater difficulties in

Table 1.2 Legislative success rate of the Hong Kong government since the handover (1998–2012)

	1998– 1999	1999– 2000	2000– 2001	2001– 2002	2002– 2003	2003– 2004	2004– 2005	2005– 2006	2006– 2007	2007– 2008	2008– 2009	2009– 2010	2010– 2011	2011– 2012	Tung Chee-hwa Administration (1998–2005)	Donald Tsang Administration (2005–2012)	Total
(a) Government bills proposed	70	57	73	44	38	17	39	26	28	20	31	26	27	16	338	174	512
(b) Government bills shelved or postponed	32	21	30	23	9	5	12	15	10	7	14	10	10	7	132	73	205
(c) Government bills tabled	38	36	43	21	29	12	27	11	18	13	17	16	17	9	206	101	307
(d) Government bills passed	38	27	42	21	24	8	27	11	18	13	17	16	16	9	187	100	287
(e) Government bills not passed	0	9	1	0	5	4	0	0	0	0	0	0	1	0	19	1	20
Government bills shelved and postponed [(b)/(a)] (%)	45.71	36.84	41.10	52.27	23.68	29.41	30.77	57.69	35.71	35.00	45.16	38.46	37.04	43.75	39.05	41.95	40.04
Legislative success rate [(d)/(a)] (%)	54.29	47.37	57.53	47.73	63.16	47.06	69.23	42.31	64.29	65.00	54.84	61.54	59.26	56.25	55.33	57.47	56.05

Source: Author's own research based on the information available on the website of the Policy Address (www.policyaddress.gov.hk) and the Legislative Council (www.legco.gov.hk).

Note
The legislative success rate for each legislative year is calculated according to the following steps. First, I ascertain the number of bills proposed by the HKSAR government during a particular legislative year by conducting a content analysis of the Chief Executive's Policy Address (including the Policy Agenda and relevant Legislative Council panel papers) and the Legislative Programme provided by the HKSAR government to the Legislative Council. A policy statement is counted as *"Government bills proposed"* if the HKSAR government expressed a clear plan to introduce such a bill into the Legislative Council. Second, I trace the status of each government bill proposed in the respective legislative year. If a government bill was tabled in that legislative year as originally proposed in the Policy Address and/or Legislative Programme, it is counted as *"Government bills tabled"* and further action is taken to trace whether the bill was finally passed by the Legislative Council (if it is found that the government bill was finally passed by the Legislative Council within its four-year term, it is counted as *"Government bills passed"*; otherwise, it is counted as *"Government bills not passed"*). If a government bill was not tabled in that legislative year as originally proposed in the Policy Address and/or Legislative Programme, it is counted as *"Government bills shelved or postponed"*. Third, on the basis of the information gathered I calculate the *"Legislative success rate"* and *"Percentage of government bills shelved and postponed"* for that legislative year.

Governance crisis in post-1997 Hong Kong 11

overcoming business opposition in pursuing policy reforms. The experiences of the Donald Tsang Administration in recent years are illustrative. After assuming the office of Chief Executive in 2005, Donald Tsang was not unaware of the aggravation of social contradictions and people's growing dissatisfaction with the monopoly of big businesses in Hong Kong. Thus the Donald Tsang administration had tried to reduce public discontent by pursuing reforms on labour and consumer protection. In his maiden Policy Address in 2005, Donald Tsang pledged to "uphold equity in its governance" and in order to foster social harmony his Administration would support the introduction of cross-sector competition law and statutory minimum wage – the two major policies that had been long rejected by the government in the past (Tsang, 2005). In his 2008 Policy Address, in response to the growing public dissatisfaction with unfair sales practices in the property market and retail sector, Donald Tsang pledged to step up the government's regulation on the sales of new residential properties and to introduce a more comprehensive consumer protection law (Tsang, 2008). While all these policy measures had received general support within the community, the Donald Tsang Administration's policy agenda met with strong opposition from the business sector, who put up staunch resistance against all these regulatory initiatives. As a consequence of the strong opposition from the business sector, these policy initiatives were in gridlock for a long period of time and were implemented only when substantial modifications were made in favour of business interests (Table 1.3).

The last indicator of the governance crisis is that the post-colonial state is facing a political quagmire of pervasive public discontent and public distrust and the popular support base of the HKSAR political order is in danger of collapse. Throughout the colonial period, the public were generally satisfied with the governance of the colonial state (Lau, 1994). Even on the eve of transition of sovereignty, the majority of Hong Kong people were still in favour of the continued governance of the colonial state and also harboured a high regard for its performance[7] (Lau, 1999b). In addition, the colonial state had commanded a decent level of public trust even in the final years of its colonial rule.[8] It was seen by most of the public as conducting government affairs by and large fairly[9] (Lau & Kuan, 1995) and people generally believed that colonial officials had formulated policies in an impartial manner with the public interest in mind (Lau, 1997, p. 32). Obviously, the success of the colonial state in fulfilling people's expectation of an effective and fair government (Tsang, 2004, p. 206) was built upon on its capacity to maintain both policy-making effectiveness (to deliver policy changes) and an acceptable order of resources distribution (to function as an arbitrator of class interests).

However, as noted above, the post-colonial state is facing a political quagmire of pervasive public discontent and public distrust, and the popular support base of the HKSAR political order is in danger of collapse. Opinion surveys indicate that the number of people who were dissatisfied with the overall performance of the post-colonial state clearly outnumbered those who were satisfied for most of the time since the handover[10] (Figure 1.2). In particular, the

Table 1.3 The sluggish implementation of business regulatory initiatives under the Donald Tsang Administration

Policy name	Original plan of the HKSAR government	Source	Results/progress
Cross-sector competition law	In view of grave public concerns about the monopoly and anti-competitive behaviours of big business conglomerates, Donald Tsang proposed to set up a Competition Policy Review Committee to consider the introduction of a cross-sector competition law.	Policy Address 2005–2006 (para. 35–37)	The business sector strongly resisted the Donald Tsang Administration's plan to introduce a cross-sector competition law. The government conducted two rounds of public consultation exercise in 2006 and 2008 but it still failed to reach a consensus with the business sector on the enactment of the competition law and its scope of application. The Donald Tsang Administration pledged in its 2008/2009 Legislative Programme to introduce the Competition Bill into the Legislative Council but the bill was finally postponed. After more than five years of postponement, the Competition Bill was only submitted to the Legislative Council for scrutiny in the 2010/2011 legislative year. While the business sector did not publicly oppose the Competition Bill, the pro-business legislators and major business associations queried and challenged all the critical provisions of the bill. In October 2011 the government made concessions by imposing "de minimis arrangements", reducing maximum penalties, adopting a warning notice for non-serious anti-competitive behaviours and eliminating the right of private action. The Competition Bill was finally passed by the Legislative Council in June 2012, but there has been doubt as to the effectiveness of the bill in promoting market competition.

Statutory minimum wage	In response to growing public demand for implementing a minimum wage for addressing the poverty problem, Donald Tsang for the first time endorsed this idea by entrusting the Labour Advisory Board to study the question of implementing minimum wage by legislation.	Policy Address 2005–2006 (para. 53)	The Donald Tsang Administration's plan met with strong opposition from the business sector. In 2006 the HKSAR government decided to put on hold the legislative plan of the minimum wage and introduced a "Wage Protection Movement" to encourage business corporations to provide minimum wages to employees in the cleansing and guarding services sectors on a voluntary basis. This implementation of this charter movement and postponement of the legislative plan were widely regarded as a concession made by the Donald Tsang Administration in response to strong resistance from the business sector. After prolonged debates and postponement, the Minimum Wage Bill was finally submitted to the Legislative Council for scrutiny in June 2009 but the business sector still tried to set the minimum wage at a lower level. Although the Minimum Wage Bill was subsequently passed in July 2011, all the bill amendments proposed by legislators to strengthen the protection for workers (e.g. annual review of the level of minimum wage) were rejected by pro-business legislators under the voting-by-group system and also the first statutory level of minimum wage has been set at the relative low level of $28 per hour.
Monitoring the sale of first-hand flats	In the face of increasing public dissatisfaction with the inaccurate information contained in the sale brochures and advertisements of first-hand residential flats and other unfair sale practices in the property market, Donald Tsang promised to step up the regulation regime by requesting property developers and property agent industries to provide more standardized and accurate information to home buyers.	Policy Address 2008–2009 (para. 56 and 57)	Since 2008 the Donald Tsang Administration requested the Real Estate Developers Association of Hong Kong (REDA) to enhance the clarity and accuracy of the information in the sales brochures and promotional materials of first-hand residential properties. However, the REDA only agreed to issue several sets of guidelines for voluntary compliance by private property developers and the non-compliance of these guidelines would not in itself give rise to any statutory prosecution or penalty. In view of the growing public criticism on this issue, Donald Tsang finally announced in his 2010/2011 Policy Address that a steering committee would be set up to discuss specific issues on regulating the sale of first-hand flats by legislation and the committee would put forward its recommendations within one year. In his last 2011/2012 Policy Address, Donald Tsang pledged to put in place a statutory regulation regime and sought to have the legislation enacted in the 2011/2012 legislative year. The Residential Properties (First-hand Sales) Bill was finally passed in June 2012 after four years of postponement. *continued*

Table 1.3 Continued

Policy name	Original plan of the HKSAR government	Source	Results/progress
Review of consumer protection legislation	In response to growing public concerns about the unfair and misleading sales practices in the retail sector, Donald Tsang pledged to review the existing consumer protection legislation.	Policy Address 2008–2009 (Policy Agenda, page 50)	The Consumer Council conducted a review of consumer protection and it proposed the enactment of a cross-sector legislation for prohibition of unfair trade practices in all goods and services. The business sector opposed the enactment of such cross-sector legislation as it would greatly enhance their operating cost, while the Donald Tsang Administration also found the Consumer Council's proposal too wide-ranging and complex. In the 2009–2010 Policy Agenda, the Donald Tsang Administration pledged to draft legislative proposals on consumer protection. Finally the government decided not to introduce a comprehensive consumer protection law as proposed by the Consumer Council and it would only tackle the unfair trade practices by amending the Trade Descriptions Ordinance. It also proposed to limit the scope of the regulation regime by excluding financial services products and residential properties and dropping the idea of imposing mandatory cooling-off arrangements. The Donald Tsang Administration included this bill in the Legislative Programme for 2010/2011 but the bill was finally postponed. The Trade Descriptions (Unfair Trade Practices) (Amendment) Bill was finally passed by the Legislative Council in July 2012 after four years of postponement.

Source: Author's own research based on the annual Policy Addresses (various years).

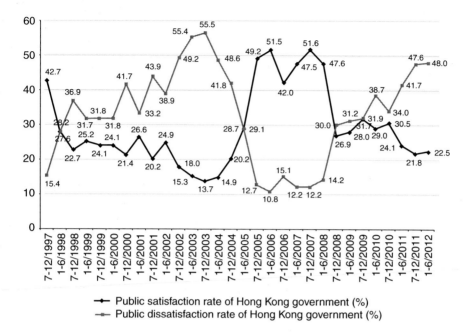

Figure 1.2 The level of public dissatisfaction towards the Hong Kong government (half-yearly average) (1997–2012) (source: University of Hong Kong's Public Opinion Programme (http://hkupop.hku.hk)).

Note
The above figure excluded respondents who answered "Half–half" and "Don't know/Hesitate to say".

pervasive public dissatisfaction with the performance of the post-colonial state has not only been evident by opinion polls, it also has been reflected in the rising number of social protests against the government. Since the explosion of the historical 1 July protest rallies in 2003 and 2004, the number of people participating in this annual protest has become the barometer for measuring the level of public discontent. Although the number of protesters in the 1 July rallies has not reached the historical high levels in 2003 and 2004 again, a critical mass of protesters have participated in mass protests every year to voice their discontent towards the policy failures of the post-colonial state (Figure 1.3). Apart from the 1 July protest rallies organized every year, the number of social protests against the post-colonial state have also increased rapidly since the handover. In 2012 the number of protests had increased to a record level of 7,529, amounting to more than 20 protests and rallies organized every day (Figure 1.4).

There is also serious deterioration in the level of public distrust towards the post-colonial state. Surveys show that public trust in the post-colonial state has stayed at the low level of less than 50 per cent for most of the post-1997 period and in recent years the number of people who distrust it has been generally increasing[11] (Figure 1.5). In particular, people's distrust toward the post-colonial

16 *Governance under hybrid regimes*

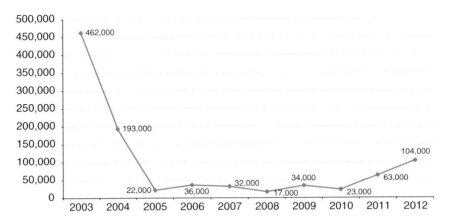

Figure 1.3 The number of people participating in the 1 July protest rally (2003–2012) (source: University of Hong Kong's Public Opinion Programme (http://hkupop.hku.hk)).

Note
The above figure excluded respondents who answered "Half–half" and "Don't know/Hesitate to say".

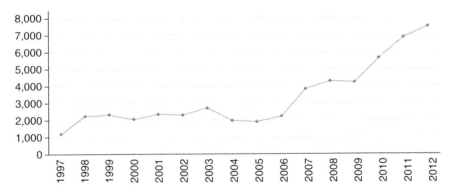

Figure 1.4 The number of social demonstrations (1997–2012) (source: data obtained from the Hong Kong Police Force).

Note
The number of demonstrations refers to the total sum of notified public meetings/processions and unnotified public meetings/processions.

state has been expressed in terms of growing public suspicion of "government–business collusion" and declining public confidence in the impartiality of government officials. For example, the impartiality of the post-colonial state has been challenged by the public in a number of controversial incidents, such as construction of the Cyberport,[12] development of the West Kowloon Cultural District[13] and post-retirement employment of senior civil servant Leung Chin-man,[14] to name only a few. In light of these controversial incidents there are growing public suspicions that leaders of big business now exercise more and more

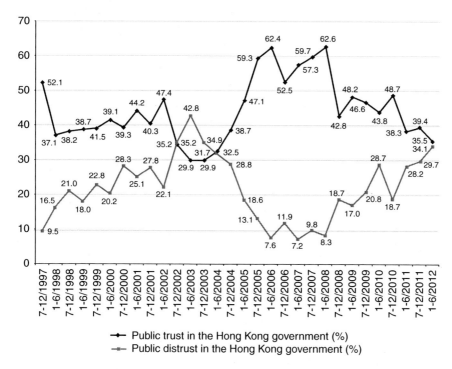

Figure 1.5 The level of public trust toward the Hong Kong government (half-yearly average) (1997–2012) (source: University of Hong Kong's Public Opinion Programme (http://hkupop.hku.hk)).

Note
The above figure excluded respondents who answered "Half–half" and "Don't know/Hesitate to say".

influence over government affairs, and the illicit "transfer of interests" between the government and the business sector has also become very serious (Table 1.4). In recent years the increasing public suspicions of government–business collusion and the accusations of transfer of interests have already sparked off anti-business and anti-rich sentiments within the community. Various opinion polls have indicated that the contradiction between the poor and the rich and the contradiction between the people and the big business corporations are widely considered by the public as the two most important factors that hinder social harmony in Hong Kong. In addition, there is growing public dissatisfaction against the dominance of "real estate hegemony"[15] in both the political and socio-economic arenas (Tables 1.5 and 1.6). Without doubt, public trust in the impartiality of the post-colonial state has fallen to a record low.

The above discussions suggest that the governance crisis facing the post-colonial state is unprecedented and such a governance crisis has been lingering, and even worsening, in the first 15 years of the HKSAR era. Why does the post-colonial state fail to consolidate the support of major socio-economic

18   *Governance under hybrid regimes*

Table 1.4 Public perceptions on government–business relations

Question	Percentage of respondents	
	2006 survey	*2011 survey*
(1) Public opinion on the statement "Do you think business leaders have any influence over the affairs of government?".		
Very big influence or big influence	**66.2**	**69.7**
Moderate	28.5	26.5
Little influence or very little influence	5.2	3.9
(2) Public opinion on the statement "Do you agree that business leaders have undue influence over the political affairs in Hong Kong?".		
Strongly agree or agree	**59.0**	**62.3**
Moderate	31.5	27.5
Disagree or strongly disagree	9.4	10.2
(3) Public opinion on the statement that "Is there any transfer of interests between the HKSAR government and the business sector?".		
Yes	**82.4**	**82.9**
No	17.6	17.1
(4) Public opinion on the statement "How serious is the problem of transfer of interests between the government and the business sector?".		
Serious	**44.0**	**66.3**
Moderate	49.1	28.8
Not serious	6.9	4.9
(5) Public opinion on the statement that "The government is no longer effective in balancing the interest conflicts among business leaders".		
Strongly agree or agree	**46.7**	**69.9**
Moderate	27.6	14.5
Disagree or strongly disagree	25.7	15.6

Source: Wong & Zheng, 2006; Zheng & Wan, 2011a, 2011b.

constituents when steering policy changes? What are the reasons behind the erosion of the role of the post-colonial state as arbitrator of class interests? How do these factors undermine the popular support base of the HKSAR political order and plunge the post-colonial state into a political quagmire of persuasive public discontent and public distrust?

The mainstream explanation of legitimacy deficit: the challenges of the democratic opposition under the hybrid regime

Is the governance crisis the result of poor economy or poor political leadership?

Over the years there have been three popular explanations for the post-1997 governance crisis, which could be described as *economic thesis*, *political leadership explanation* and *legitimacy deficit thesis*. The *legitimacy deficit thesis*, which is

Table 1.5 Hong Kong people's views on social harmony

Question	Percentage of respondents			
	2006 survey	2008 survey	2010 survey	2012 survey
(1) Public opinion on the statement "Do you agree that Hong Kong is a harmonious society?".				
Strongly agree or agree	37.8	37.5	26.5	23.8
Moderate	39.4	41.4	47.1	45.7
Disagree or strongly disagree	**22.3**	**20.3**	**26.2**	**29.7**
(2) Public opinion on the major factors that affect Hong Kong as a harmonious society.				
Contradiction between people and big businesses	**50.3**	**48.4**	**56.8**	**68.1**
Contradiction between the poor and the rich	**61.9**	**61.9**	**64.4**	**67.6**
Contradiction between people and government	34.6	31.0	56.0	67.6
Political disputes	49.2	38.5	59.2	55.3
Lack of tolerance within the society	38.2	36.9	39.8	42
Family disputes	40.4	44.1	43.4	35.1
Contradiction between employees and employers	32.3	33.2	28.0	27.7

Source: Chinese University of Hong Kong, 2012.

Table 1.6 Hong Kong people's views on "real estate hegemony"

Question	Percentage of respondents
Public opinion on the statement that "Do you think 'real estate hegemony' really exists in Hong Kong?"	
Yes	**77.9**
No	14.3
Don't know/Difficult to say	7.8
Public opinion on the statement that "Do you think 'real estate hegemony' is serious in Hong Kong?"	
Serious	**73.3**
Moderate	22.7
Not serious	3.3
Don't know/Difficult to say	0.7

Source: Chinese University of Hong Kong, 2011.

widely held to be correct by local political scientists, explains the governance crisis due to the nature of the HKSAR political system and will be the focus of our discussion in the next section. In this section, we will first discuss the notions of the *economic thesis* and *political leadership thesis*.

The *economic thesis* argues that the post-1997 governance crisis is mainly attributable to the economic downturn since the handover and has nothing to do with "politics". According to this explanation, Hong Kong has experienced many economic crises after 1997, including the Asian Financial Crisis in 1998, the outbreak of Severe Acute Respiratory Syndrome (SARS) in 2003 and the Financial Tsunami in 2008, which inflicted a number of economic problems such

20 Governance under hybrid regimes

as salary reduction, unemployment and negative equity upon the Hong Kong people. The economic explanation implied that the waves of political challenges and public anger facing the post-colonial state are mainly the result of these economic sufferings and therefore the governance crisis could be dealt with by improving the economic situation.

However, developments in recent years have showed that the *economic thesis* has limited explanatory power. The poor economic performance in the first years of the post-1997 period did coincide with the erosion of public satisfaction and public trust in the Tung Chee-hwa Administration, but it failed to explain the situations under the Donald Tsang Yam-kuen Administration. Thanks to the implementation of the Individual Visit Scheme, the signing of the Closer Economic Partnership Arrangement (CEPA) and rapid development of the financial services and banking industries, Hong Kong's economy has strongly rebounded since 2004. Nevertheless, Table 1.7 shows that although the local economy has been experiencing rapid growth and the employment rate has also fallen to a very low level from 2008 to 2012, they do not help sustain high levels of public

Table 1.7 Comparing Hong Kong's economic performance with public support for the Hong Kong government (1997–2012)

	GDP year-on-year % change (at current market prices)	Unemployment rate (not seasonally adjusted) (%)	Public satisfaction rate of Hong Kong government (year-end figures) (%)	Public trust in Hong Kong government (year-end figures) (%)
Tung Chee-hwa era				
1997	11.2	2.2	41.7	43.0
1998	−4.7	4.7	28.8	38.8
1999	−1.7	6.2	32.6	35.9
2000	4.0	4.9	23.1	41.0
2001	−1.2	5.1	20.2	44.1
2002	−1.8	7.3	16.9	36.3
2003	−3.1	7.9	16.7	31.8
2004	4.8	6.8	21.5	39.2
Donald Tsang era				
2005	7.2	5.6	48.8	58.9
2006	6.5	4.8	34.3	43.9
2007	9.8	4.0	44.9	50.8
2008	3.4	3.5	22.5	42.2
2009	−2.8	5.3	32.3	48.3
2010	7.1	4.3	28.9	44.4
2011	9.0	3.4	21.7	35.3
2012	5.5	3.3	19.9*	34.8*

Source: The GDP and unemployment figures are obtained from the website of the Census and Statistics Department at www.censtatd.gov.hk. The public satisfaction rate and trust in the Hong Kong government are obtained from the website of the University of Hong Kong's Public Opinion Programme at http://hkupop.hku.hk.

Note
* Figures as of June 2012 when the Donald Tsang Administration's term of office was about to end.

satisfaction and public trust in the post-colonial state and, ironically, these indicators have even fallen to new lows. All these figures show that the *economic thesis* is far from a comprehensive and sensible answer to the governance problems facing the post-colonial state, and the post-1997 governance crisis could not be adequately explained by economic factors.

Another popular explanation for the post-1997 governance crisis is the *political leadership thesis*. This explanation argues that the governance crisis experienced by the post-colonial state is the result of the limited governing experiences and poor political skills of the first HKSAR Chief Executive Tung Chee-hwa. As a former business tycoon who spent most of his career in the shipping industry, Tung Chee-hwa was widely criticized for having limited skills and experiences in running the complex government machinery. According to this explanation, the governance crisis and the various policy failures are the direct result of the poor performance and incompetency of Tung Chee-hwa as Chief Executive.

However, the political developments in the post-Tung period proved that the *political leadership thesis* is also not a comprehensive answer to the post-1997 governance crisis. In 2005 Tung Chee-hwa resigned from office and was succeeded by the Chief Secretary Donald Tsang. The appointment of Tsang as Chief Executive was widely seen as a solution to the governance crisis. As a former civil servant who had served in the government for more than 40 years, many people believed Donald Tsang could make use of his rich governing experience and political skills to restore effective governance. Nevertheless, the discussions in the preceding paragraphs have showed that the replacement of Tung Chee-hwa by Donald Tsang as the Chief Executive has had a very limited impact on improving the governance crisis facing the post-colonial state. Both the Tung Administration and Tsang Administration experienced the same difficulties in making policy changes and the legislative success rates of both governments stood at similar levels – 55.33 per cent and 57.47 per cent, respectively (Table 1.2). The arbitration role of the post-colonial state had also deteriorated under the Donald Tsang Administration, and people's trust in the impartiality of government officials had fallen to new levels (Tables 1.3–1.7). When the stock of political goodwill enjoyed by Donald Tsang was rapidly depleted after 2008, his Administration experienced the same problem of pervasive public discontent and public distrust as the Tung Administration (Figures 1.2 and 1.6). Therefore, the lingering of the governance crisis in the post-Tung period pointed to the fact that the crisis does not simply stem from the leadership qualities of the Chief Executive, but is attributed to structural problems arising from the HKSAR political system.

The legitimacy deficit thesis: the challenges of the democratic opposition under the hybrid political regime

The limited explanatory powers of both the *economic thesis* and *political leadership thesis* pointed to the conclusion that the post-colonial state has been structurally trapped in a governance crisis since the handover of sovereignty in 1997,

22   *Governance under hybrid regimes*

and such a crisis could not be simply explained by economic factors or leadership qualities. In other words, the crisis of governance is the result of systemic failures and should be explained by examining the structural defects of the HKSAR political system.

When accounting for the relationship between the HKSAR political system and the post-1997 governance crisis, the leading theoretical explanation adopted by most of the political scientists in Hong Kong is the *legitimacy deficit thesis*. The *legitimacy deficit thesis* is theoretically connected to much of the existing studies of democratization as discussed in the preceding paragraphs. It emphasized that the post-1997 governance crisis actually stems from the challenges of the democratic opposition under Hong Kong's hybrid political regime, under which the post-colonial state is falling into a legitimacy crisis and struggling to accommodate the rising public demand for democracy. As a consequence, the post-colonial state does not have the necessary political legitimacy and governing authority to consolidate its governance and to steer policy-making. Therefore, the argument goes, the most appropriate way forward is to elect the Chief Executive and all members of the Legislative Council by means of universal suffrage, because only by doing so could the post-colonial state rebuild its political legitimacy and strengthen its governing capacity. This theoretical explanation has been commonly shared by academics and political commentators in Hong Kong when accounting for the post-1997 governance crisis. Our discussion in the forthcoming paragraphs will, however, indicate that while this theoretical approach has its merits, it has important weaknesses in terms of explanatory power. The discussion of the limitations of this mainstream explanation is of great importance because it points to the need to develop an alternative theoretical perspective for understanding the governance problems in post-1997 Hong Kong.

The *legitimacy deficit thesis*, adopted by the majority of local political scientists, is the most popular explanation for Hong Kong's crisis of governance after the handover (e.g. Cheung, 2005a, 2005b, 2010; Li, 2001; Ma, 2007a; Scott, 2005, 2007; Sing, 2001, 2003, 2009; Tang, 2008). According to this theoretical perspective, the problem of legitimacy deficit, which stems from the challenges of the democratic opposition under the hybrid regime, is the fundamental cause of the post-1997 governance crisis: since the handover, the post-colonial state has been trapped in a structural deficit of political legitimacy[16] under the present hybrid political regime, and the resultant political confrontations and tensions within the political system have severely undermined the governing capacity of the Chief Executive and his governing team.

This theoretical explanation is firmly based on the existing studies of democratization, as Western political scientists long recognized that it was quite common for liberal authoritarian regimes to encounter difficulties in legitimating their governance in the process of democratic transition. O'Donnell and Schmitter, for example, had pointed out in their seminal study, *Transitions from Authoritarian Rule: Tentative Conclusions about Uncertain Democracies*, that intermediate regimes such as liberal authoritarianism are usually trapped in

Governance crisis in post-1997 Hong Kong 23

legitimacy crises because "they are regimes that practice dictatorship and repression in the present while promising democracy and freedom in the future". In this connection, liberal authoritarian governments as "transitional powers" could only justify their autocratic rule by trying to shift people's attention from democratic reforms to other immediate and substantive policy accomplishments such as social peace and economic development. This creates a structural problem for the liberal authoritarian governments to maintain a stable level of political legitimacy over the long run and from time to time prompts the opposition forces to press for the replacement of the authoritarian governments by democratic regimes (O'Donnell & Schmitter, 1986, p. 15). Various governance problems and political conflicts are therefore structurally inherent within this kind of hybrid regime, and it is very difficult for the incumbent governments to fend off the pressure and demands for full democratization over a long period of time (Case, 1996).

For many local political scientists, Hong Kong is a typical case to illustrate the above structural vulnerability of hybrid regimes (Ma, 2007a, p. 226). Under its present hybrid system, the post-colonial Hong Kong state is by nature undemocratic because the Chief Executive was "elected" by an election committee dominated by pro-China politicians and appointed by the Central People's Government (CPG) in Beijing.[17] On the other hand, the HKSAR Legislative Council was partially elected by means of universal suffrage, under which half of the legislators were elected by one-person–one-vote through geographical constituencies and another half by functional constituencies with limited franchise. Most importantly, the coexistence of this largely appointed executive and partially elected legislature is theoretically a transitional arrangement only, because Articles 45 and 68 of the Basic Law, respectively, state that the Chief Executive and the Legislative Council will ultimately be elected by means of universal suffrage[18] (Ma, 2007a, p. 226).

According to the theories of legitimacy deficit, the coexistence of a largely appointed executive branch with a partially elected legislature and the transitional nature of the present constitutional arrangements under the Basic Law have created a structural problem of legitimacy for the post-colonial state on the executive–legislative front. As a consequence of the quasi-appointed nature of the Chief Executive, the post-colonial state could not obtain the consent of the people through election. But the worst thing is that this non-popularly elected executive had to deal with a partially elected Legislative Council in the process of governance and policy-making, which is the most representative political institution in the territory under the present hybrid political system (Ma, 2007a, pp. 129–131). Because the Legislative Council enjoys a higher political mandate than the executive branch, legislators, particularly those directly elected members from the pro-democracy camp, are increasingly hostile to the non-popularly elected Chief Executive. Therefore the Chief Executive and his senior officials often struggle to command respect, trust and acceptance from the Legislative Council for their policy proposals and initiatives. The post-colonial state is handicapped by this "mis-matching of the operational logic within the new

24 *Governance under hybrid regimes*

HKSAR constitutional arrangements", and the resultant confrontations and tensions between executive and legislature have frustrated many of the policy initiatives introduced by the Chief Executive and his governing team (Li, 2001).

The political confrontation in the HKSAR era are fully embodied in the endless controversies surrounding the pace of constitutional reforms,[19] as well as the politics of delegitimation practised by the democratic camp. In this connection, although the democratic opposition remains a minority in the legislature under the present electoral systems,[20] most of the legislators in the camp are popularly elected. Justifying themselves as the "representative of public opinion", the democratic opposition could usually better mobilize public opinion support and command more political legitimacy than the post-colonial state, as well as those pro-government legislators returned by functional constituencies. Therefore, although the pro-government legislators from time to time form the majority in the Legislative Council and the post-colonial state could get through its bills and initiatives in the legislature with the support of these political allies, it does not necessarily have the majority support in society and usually enjoys less political legitimacy and public opinion support than the pro-democracy legislators. In this regard, the democratic opposition will often strive to delegitimize the government actions by criticizing controversial public policies, exposing the weaknesses of the government and its allies in the legislature and mobilizing public opinion against government misdeeds. By doing so the democratic opposition could not only prove their value, but also justify the pressing need to implement further democratic reforms. The existence of such a vocal opposition camp in the legislature has definitely worsened the problems of inherent legitimacy deficit and incessant public distrust for the post-colonial state, adding fuel to the post-1997 governance crisis (Cheung, 2010; Ma, 2007a, pp. 132–133).

In short, theorists of legitimacy deficits emphasized that under the present hybrid political regime, the whole society is embroiled in a constant political struggle over the pace of democratization. In this connection, the post-colonial state's legitimacy is under continuous challenge from the democratic opposition in the post-1997 period, by which the democrats will stage opposition campaigns against the Chief Executive and his governing team, both inside and outside the legislature (Ma, 2007a, p. 227). If legitimacy is defined as the government holding and exercising political power with legality, justification and consent from the standpoint of its citizens (Gilley, 2009, p. 11), then the undemocratic post-colonial state is destined to be trapped in a structural crisis of legitimacy because it falls short of the moral expectations and strong demands for democratic reforms of the Hong Kong people.

For theorists of legitimacy deficit, this structural crisis of legitimacy has severely undermined the post-colonial state's capacity to govern: as a result of the problem of legitimacy deficit, the process under which policy decisions are made by the post-colonial state is usually attacked by the democratic opposition as illegitimate, and the strong opposition by democrats has on many occasions forced the government officials to postpone, withdraw or modify their policy proposals. This has seriously eroded the post-colonial state's capacity to forge

Governance crisis in post-1997 Hong Kong 25

policy consensus within the society and command public trust, and every concession will contribute to a downward spiral of weakening governing authority of the Chief Executive (Cheung, 2010; Scott, 2007). An example usually quoted by theorists of legitimacy deficit is the prolonged delay of the West Kowloon Cultural District project, in which the post-colonial state was forced to postpone the project in the face of the continuing public criticism that the process by which decisions have been made is illegitimate and involves government–business collusion (Scott, 2007). Weak legitimacy also constrained the ability of the post-colonial state to build support for its urban planning projects, because stakeholders usually felt they were insufficiently consulted and their strong opposition often forces the administration to delay the projects (Lai & Loh, 2007, p. 133). Hindered by the problem of legitimacy deficit, many theorists argue that the post-colonial state has increasingly tended to shy away from boldly confronting the long-term challenges facing Hong Kong, like an ageing population, healthcare financing and public sector reforms (Sing, 2009).

To sum up the arguments of those theorists of legitimacy deficit, the crisis of legitimacy, which is induced by the inherent struggles over democratization under the existing hybrid regime, is the fundamental reason behind the post-1997 Hong Kong's governance crisis. For these theorists, the present political system can no longer help to resolve the various policy issues and challenges facing the territory, and the Hong Kong people have already paid the price in good governance (Lai & Loh, 2007, p. 169). Unless the election of the Chief Executive is fully democratized, the legitimacy crisis and governance problems currently faced by the post-colonial state will persist in a vicious cycle (Lo, 2001, p. 300; Tang, 2008). Following this line of reasoning, these theorists go on to argue that universal suffrage for the Chief Executive and the Legislative Council elections should be introduced as early as possible, because popular election is the ultimate solution that could fundamentally get Hong Kong out of its present legitimacy crisis and help rebuild the post-colonial state's governing capacity (Scott, 2007). Ma (2007a) provided a good summary analysis of this *legitimacy deficit thesis* as follows:

> Hong Kong, as a hybrid regime in this sense, is going to witness struggles over democratization for a long period of time.... The SAR government is also afraid of challenge from civil society and the pro-democracy minority for want of legitimacy of the regime.... The promise of democracy invites constant challenges from the democrats for an early implementation of full democracy.... Hong Kong will be embroiled in a constant political struggle over the pace of democratization and its government form, and the legitimacy problem will continue to trouble SAR governance for years to come.
>
> (Ma, 2007a, p. 227)

Simply put, in accordance with this popular explanation of legitimacy deficit, full democratization will be the most appropriate way forward to restore the legitimacy and governing capacity of the post-colonial state. Without full-scale

26 *Governance under hybrid regimes*

democratic reforms, it is inconceivable that the Chief Executive and his ruling team could be able to climb out of the present mess of governance crisis and rebuild its governing capacity in the foreseeable future.

Limitations of the legitimacy deficit thesis

Obviously, this mainstream argument of legitimacy deficit has provided a very reasonable and logical explanation for the governance crisis experienced by the post-colonial state. It highlighted the importance of the concepts of hybrid regimes and political legitimacy in accounting for the governance problems of Hong Kong, and also offered a very convincing case on the urgent need to implement universal suffrage in the territory as a solution to the problem of policy-making impasse. Nevertheless, this mainstream explanation is not without problems and its limitations have called into question its comprehensiveness in explaining Hong Kong's governance crisis after 1997.

The first important limitation of this theoretical paradigm is that it has over-emphasized the implications of legitimacy and democratization on Hong Kong's governance. What has been implied in this theoretical perspective is that the level of political legitimacy should be the most significant factor, if not the only factor, that determines the governing capacity of the post-colonial state. Without doubt, the level of political legitimacy will have implications for the governing capacity of any government, because political leaders equipped with higher legitimacy will certainly have stronger authority to command respect and acceptance from different policy stakeholders, and vice versa (Coicaud, 2002). However, it is also important to note that governance process in modern societies is quite a complicated phenomenon and it will be overly simplistic to examine the governing capacity of the post-colonial state solely based on the notion of legitimacy. In fact, the contemporary governance literature has pointed out that in modern pluralistic societies whether a government could maintain effective governance depended very much on its abilities to forge institutionalized cooperation and coalitions with those major socio-economic constituents (Pierre & Peters, 2000, pp. 98–100). From this perspective, the mainstream theorists' over-reliance on the *legitimacy deficit thesis* in explaining the post-1997 governance crisis may have missed something very important: the changing dynamics between the post-colonial state and the major socio-economic constituents in the wider political contexts and their implications on a territory's governance are generally ignored by theorists of legitimacy deficit.

The second limitation is that it has overstated the role of the democratic opposition in accounting for the post-1997 governance crisis. The theories of legitimacy deficit are clearly based upon the contention that the continuous political challenge from the democratic opposition is the fundamental factor that has undermined the political legitimacy and governing authority of the post-colonial state. While it is important to analyse the role of the democratic camp, its actual influences should not in any way be overstated. First, the policy influences of democrats in the Legislative Council have in practice been significantly

Governance crisis in post-1997 Hong Kong 27

constrained not only by its minority status, but are also limited by Article 74 of the Basic Law[21] and voting-by-group system[22] (Ma, 2007a). Second, the post-1997 democratic movement was marked by internal fighting and loss of direction as a result of the fading away of the anti-communist sentiments, the constitutional straitjacket on the pace of democratic reforms as imposed by the Basic Law, the implementation of the proportional representation electoral system and the abolition of Municipal Councils (Ma, 2007b). The cohesiveness of the democratic opposition has suffered from another heavy blow in the 2010 constitutional reform saga, when the whole pro-democracy camp was split into moderates and radicals fighting against each other (Ma, 2011). In view of their limited policy influences and internal division, the problems facing the democratic opposition are actually no less than the post-colonial state. From this perspective, theorists of legitimacy deficit have certainly over-emphasized the power of democratic opposition in challenging the governance of the post-colonial state, and they have somehow underestimated that the post-1997 governance crisis is actually contributed by political forces other than the democratic opposition.

The above discussion points to the conclusion that we could not solely rely on the *legitimacy deficit thesis* to explain the governance crisis facing the post-colonial state. Given that most of the existing literature on the post-1997 governance crisis focused too much on the notions of legitimacy and democratization, there is a pressing need for us to construct an alternative theoretical perspective with a view to broadening our understanding on the political dynamics in contemporary Hong Kong.

Going beyond the mainstream explanation: from opposition-centred explanation to a critical analysis of governing coalition building

The organizational power of the incumbent: a new perspective for examining the politics of hybrid regimes

Much of the existing literature on hybrid regimes put great emphasis on discussing the role of the opposition forces in challenging the governance and stability of authoritarian incumbents (e.g. Beissinger, 2002; Bratton & van de Walle, 1997; Collier, 1999; Diamond, 1999; Fish, 1995; Wood, 2000). The theorists of legitimacy deficit put forward by Hong Kong's political scientists, as discussed in the previous paragraphs, have largely followed this line of thought by focusing on examining how the political challenges of the democratic opposition have brought about the post-1997 governance crisis. In other words, the *legitimacy deficit thesis* is by nature an opposition-centred explanation to the governance crisis in post-1997 Hong Kong.

The latest comparative studies on hybrid regimes, however, indicated that putting too much emphasis on the role of the opposition forces is just like looking on one side of the coin only, while largely overlooking the other side of

28 Governance under hybrid regimes

the coin – the existing literature on hybrid regimes has basically ignored the considerable variation that exists in the capacity of authoritarian states in accommodating and resisting opposition challenges. In their latest comparative studies, *Competitive Authoritarianism: Hybrid Regimes After the Cold War*, Levitsky and Way (2010) examined the trajectories of 37 hybrid regimes in the post-Cold War period and they found that hybrid regimes did not uniformly democratize as assumed by much of the existing literature. Rather, Levitsky and Way's empirical studies on the 37 hybrid regimes indicated that these authoritarian governments have followed three board regime pathways: 14 of the hybrid regimes covered by their studies have been democratized (the authoritarian regimes had been removed and democratic regimes were firmly established, such as Mexico, Peru, Serbia, Bulgaria, Croatia, Slovakia and Taiwan), 12 of them are considered as unstable authoritarianisms (authoritarian incumbents had been removed from power but were replaced by new authoritarian rulers, such as Albania, Georgia, Haiti and Senegal) and the remaining 11 cases are stable authoritarianisms (the authoritarian regimes have remained stable and effective in resisting the challenges of opposition forces, including Armenia, Cambodia, Cameroon, Malaysia, Russia and Zimbabwe).

According to the cross-national empirical studies conducted by Levitsky and Way, such diversity of regime outcomes should be explained by the varying capacity of authoritarian incumbents in accommodating and resisting opposition challenges[23] (Levitsky & Way, 2010, p. 54). Quoting the old story of "Three Little Pigs" to illustrate their arguments, Levitsky and Way said if the wolf represents the opposition forces, then the pigs are the autocratic incumbents and their houses are the authoritarian regimes. When the wolf (democratic opposition) puffs at the three houses (authoritarian regimes), the houses of straw and sticks collapse quickly, while the house of bricks remains intact. Levitsky and Way went on to point out that such differences in regime outcomes do not lie in the strength of the wolf (power of the democratic opposition), but rather in the differences in the strength of the houses (the varying capacity of the authoritarian regimes to resist opposition challenges).

By highlighting the importance of the varying capacity of authoritarian states in resisting opposition challenges, Levitsky and Way articulated an innovative perspective to understanding the politics of hybrid regimes. Unlike autocratic rulers in full authoritarian systems, authoritarian states in hybrid regimes are required to manage and control a number of actors that may challenge their governance, including opposition parties, media, judges and civil society groups in the different arenas of contestation (election, legislatures and judicial courts). To sustain their regimes, Levitsky and Way argued that authoritarian states need to put in place an organizational machinery, usually in the form of a governing party or governing coalition, for managing and resisting different political challenges. In this connection, the empirical studies conducted by Levitsky and Way showed that where the authoritarian states are supported by strong governing party organization, the autocratic incumbents are more likely to enhance elite cohesion, win elections and maintain control over legislative process even amid

Governance crisis in post-1997 Hong Kong 29

vigorous opposition challenges; where the authoritarian states lack organizational tools and the governing parties are generally weak, the authoritarian incumbents will be more likely to fall in spite of relatively weak opposition movements. Levitsky and Way concluded that strong states supported by well-organized governing parties or coalitions could enhance authoritarian incumbents' capacity to maintain effective governance and to overcome the inherent instabilities within hybrid regimes (Levitsky & Way, 2010, pp. 54–68).

Examining the robustness of the post-colonial governing coalition: Lau Siu-kai's theory and its limitations

Levitsky and Way's comparative studies on hybrid regimes have been illuminating to our understanding of the governance crisis in post-1997 Hong Kong. To use the words of Levitsky and Way, the *legitimacy deficit thesis* is basically an opposition-centred explanation which focuses on examining the role of the democratic opposition in undermining the governing capacity of the post-colonial Hong Kong state. Theoretically speaking, such a mainstream explanation has certainly overstated the power of the democratic opposition in challenging the governance of the post-colonial state, while ignoring the facts that the democrats in Hong Kong generally lack the organization and resources to sustain a robust democratic movement.

The above discussion revealed that in order to have a more comprehensive understanding of governance crisis in post-1997 Hong Kong, we need to go beyond the opposition-centred explanation as currently suggested by theorists of legitimacy deficit and concurrently examine why the post-colonial state has been dragged into governance crisis despite a relatively weak democratic movement. To put Levitsky and Way's studies into Hong Kong's context, several questions will arise: Does the post-colonial state have any organizational machinery to support its governance? If so, is this governing organization strong or weak? For Levitsky and Way, the governing organizations of authoritarian incumbents usually take the form of a single political party, but on certain occasions they are little more than a loose coalition of political elites (Levitsky & Way, 2010, pp. 377–378). In Hong Kong's contexts, while the formation of a governing party is prohibited under the present political system (Ma, 2007b), the territory has been governed by a state–business alliance since the British colonial time (Ngo, 2000). The remaining question is therefore: Is there any causal relationship between the governing coalition building and the governance crisis in post-1997 Hong Kong?

In this regard, the *governing coalition thesis* put forward by political sociologist Lau Siu-kai should be relevant to our discussion (Lau, 2000, 2002b), because it is the only explanation in the existing literature that examined the internal weaknesses of the post-colonial state. According to Lau, although a wide range of constitutional powers is conferred upon the Chief Executive under the Basic Law, the executive-dominant governance system could only function smoothly if the post-colonial state is supported by a strong and broad-based

30 *Governance under hybrid regimes*

governing coalition. Lau argued that a viable governing coalition should have two characteristics. First, this governing coalition should comprise leaders of major political and socio-economic groups, so that the Chief Executive could make use of this coalition as a mechanism for balancing and reconciling the interests of major political forces. Second, members of this governing coalition should enjoy broad social support and command extensive political resources so that the Chief Executive could mobilize their support for implementing his policy agenda. Lau reckoned that in a pluralistic society like Hong Kong, the executive-dominant political order could only be put into practice with the support of a viable governing coalition (Lau, 2000).

Lau pointed out that the governance problems experienced by the first Tung Chee-hwa Administration from 1997 to 2002 were attributable to his failure to construct such a "strong governing coalition". Lau found that when Tung Chee-hwa assumed the office of Chief Executive in July 1997 he encountered much difficulty in building a broad social support base for his administration. First, as a former business tycoon who spent most of his life running his family business, Tung Chee-hwa was undoubtedly a newcomer to Hong Kong's political scene and had limited political experience and networks. When he came to the post of Chief Executive, Tung was definitely a political loner and had few political allies. As a result, Tung Chee-hwa faced difficulties in establishing a strong and extensive political alliance to mobilize sufficient support for his administration and could only rely on a few trusted friends from the business sector and personal aids for support. Second, because Beijing leaders were generally sceptical about the democratic activities and anti-communist sentiments of Hong Kong's society, they would not tolerate the Chief Executive to broaden his social support base by co-opting political forces that were unfriendly and hostile to the CPG. This had enforced a political straitjacket upon the autonomy of the post-colonial state, making it difficult for Tung Chee-hwa to engineer a governing coalition that was firmly embedded in the society. Third, top civil servants, being the pillar of the colonial state and an important stabilizing force during the transitional period, were retained by Beijing as Tung Chee-hwa's principal officials after handover as a move to maintain public confidence in Hong Kong's transition in the early years of the HKSAR. These top officials, led by the Chief Secretary for Administration Anson Chan Fang On-sang, generally adopted a laissez-faire thinking and "Hong Kong first" mind-set and they did not share Tung's political values or policy agenda on restructuring Hong Kong's economy and society. Given their suspicion of communism and vigilance over any possible intervention from the Beijing leaders, the bureaucratic elites were also distrustful of Tung Chee-hwa, who was answerable and loyal to the CPG, and they generally kept a wary eye on business elites and pro-Beijing politicians who might pose a challenge to their dominant position in the governing process. This unavoidably created tensions and rivalries between the top civil servants and the Chief Executive and his political aides, undermining the solidarity and cohesiveness of the top management of the Tung Chee-hwa Administration (Lau, 2002b).

Governance crisis in post-1997 Hong Kong 31

As a result of the above factors, Lau Siu-kai observed that Tung Chee-hwa, in his first term of office, could only rely on a narrow-based and divided governing coalition to maintain governance. In the eyes of Lau, the governing coalition crafted by Tung was no more than a loose collection of incongruent political groups including top civil servants, pro-Beijing figures and business elites, under which these different groups shared no common political ideals and interests and could not be bound together to form a stable and durable political alliance. In particular, the Executive Council, which was supposed to be the Chief Executive's "inner cabinet", comprised politicians from different backgrounds and did not function as a cohesive team. Most of these Executive Councillors were by and large detached from the main population of Hong Kong and did not have the political networks to mobilize popular support for Tung's policy initiatives (Lau, 2002b). Lau found that such a narrow-based and divided governing coalition was unable to furnish the Tung Administration with the necessary cohesive political leadership for maintaining effective governance. In the first place, the internal rivalries within the governing team resulted in ineffective formulation and implementation of public policies. Also, this governing coalition suffered from the lack of organizational means to reconcile the different interests of its members and to aggregate the various social demands into workable policy programmes. Last but not least, this governing coalition did not have the political machinery to mobilize political and societal support to Tung's policy agenda, making it difficult for his Administration to sustain political legitimacy by producing substantive policy outputs (Lau, 2002b).

Based on the above observations and analysis, Lau concluded that the absence of a strong and broad-based governing coalition is the fundamental reason why the executive-dominant governance system existed only in the constitutional sense but not in reality after the handover (Lau, 2002b). In order to strengthen the executive-dominant political order and to address the governance problems, Lau recommended that a strong governing coalition with a broad social support base should be constructed as the central vehicle of the Tung Chee-hwa Administration (Lau, 2000).

Lau Siu-kai's *governing coalition thesis* was an important contribution to the literature on Hong Kong's governance. Unlike the theorists of legitimacy deficit who mainly attribute the governance crisis to the opposition challenges and struggles over democratization, Lau raised a significant question of how to improve governance by reforming the governing coalition of the post-colonial state. To use the words of Levitsky and Way, Lau Siu-kai's *governing coalition thesis* enables us to move beyond the existing opposition-centred explanation of mainstream theorists and rethink the organizational strength of the post-colonial state.

While Lau's *governing coalition thesis* was theoretically inspiring, the weaknesses of his theory are also obvious. First, Lau's analysis looks like a folk theory rather than a formal and internally consistent theory. In his work, Lau failed to provide a clear conceptualization of his notion of "governing coalition" by specifying what social classes and political groups could form the base of

32 *Governance under hybrid regimes*

such a coalition, what policy could be introduced to secure broad social support and how the political elites with different backgrounds and interests could reach consensus within the governing coalition. Without a clear conceptualized framework it will be very difficult to see how the post-colonial state could build a viable governing coalition capable of earning support from different stakeholders under the present political system (Lui & Chiu, 2007; Ma, 2007a, p. 78). Second, Lau ignored the fact that a state–business alliance had existed and functioned effectively during colonial times and he failed to examine why this political alliance no longer worked after 1997. Local literature has long recognized that the existence of a strong state–business alliance was the foundation of effective governance in the colonial days (e.g. Lui & Chiu, 2007; Ngo, 2000; Rear, 1971). From this perspective, Lau overlooked several important questions: Why does the state–business alliance, which furnished the colonial state with strong governing capacity, fail to work effectively after 1997? Do the political and socio-economic changes after 1997 contribute to the failure of this state–business alliance? How does the failure of the state–business alliance undermine the governing capacity of the post-colonial state? All these are important questions that are unanswered in Lau's notion of governing coalition.

To conclude, apart from the mainstream explanation of legitimacy deficit, Lau's *governing coalition thesis* has the theoretical potential to further develop into an alternative perspective to the post-1997 governance crisis by underlining the importance of examining the organizational strength of the post-colonial Hong Kong state vis-à-vis opposition challenges, but such a perspective should be more specifically defined within a comprehensive conceptual framework. This research is going to fill this gap by reconstructing the *governing coalition thesis* within a more sophisticated analysis of changing state–business relations and state–society relations in post-1997 Hong Kong.

Synthesis of the argument and its theoretical implications: a new theoretical explanation on Hong Kong's governance

State capacity and governance: the theoretical foundations of this book

The above discussions clearly stated that the existing explanations on post-1997 Hong Kong's governance crisis did contain important limitations and were far from comprehensive and exhaustive answers to the territory's governance problems. In order to more fully grasp the governance crisis after 1997, we need to go beyond the opposition-centred explanation as put forward by the theorists of legitimacy deficit and explore an alternative theoretical perspective that could broaden and enrich our understanding of Hong Kong's governance. In this regard, the theories and concepts of "state capacity" should provide a useful theoretical foundation in the development of a new perspective to explain the post-1997 governance crisis. In contemporary political science literature, the notion of state capacity is an important and popular theoretical construct that has been widely applied by political scientists to account for the modern governance issues. From the perspective of state theorists, the state is the central agent that steers socio-economic changes and thus the capacity of the state is of paramount importance to maintaining effective governance in modern societies (e.g. Brodsgarrd & Young, 2000; Evans, 1995; Pierre & Peters, 2000; Weiss, 1998). Francis Fukuyama, a renowned political scientist in the United States, has highlighted the key role of the state in modern governance as follows:

> the chief issue for global politics will not be how to cut back on stateness but how to build it up. For individual societies and for the global community, the withering away of the state is not a prelude to utopia but to disaster. A critical issue facing poor countries that blocks their possibilities for economic development is their inadequate level of institutional development. They do not need extensive states, but they do need strong and effective ones within the limited scope of necessary state functions.
>
> (Fukuyama, 2004, p. 120)

The theories of state capacity should be useful in shedding new insight to the governance problems in post-1997 Hong Kong. According to the literature, state capacity, which can be defined as the "ability of the state to get things done in pursuance of state-defined objectives and goals", is the basis for effective governance (Cheung, 2008). For state theorists, the capacity of the state to govern and steer policy-making is shaped by the interactions between the state and the major political and socio-economic actors. In this connection, a number of theoretical perspectives were constructed by state theorists in the past few decades to conceptualize and account for the essential conditions that endow state capacity.

One of the important theoretical perspectives in the discussion of state capacity is the orthodox notion of "political autonomy". Tracing back to the Marxist theories of "relative autonomy" of the state, the notion of political autonomy rested on the contention that the insulation of the state from the pressures of powerful socio-economic actors is the institutional foundation for effective governance. According to theorists like Eric Nordlinger and Theda Skocpol, only a politically autonomous state could muster sufficient capacity to translate its own policy preferences into authoritative actions and to appropriately balance the different interests in the society (Nordlinger, 1981; Skocpol, 1985):

> States conceived as organizations claiming control over territories and people may formulate and pursue goals that are not simply reflective of the demands or interests of social groups, classes or society. This is what usually meant by "state autonomy". Unless such independent goal formulation occurs, there is little need to talk about states as important actors.
>
> (Skocpol, 1985)

Another important theoretical foundations of state capacity was the concept of "embedded autonomy" put forward by Peter Evans, which highlighted that the governing capacity of modern states is not only dependent on its autonomy from

34   *Governance under hybrid regimes*

external pressure – its embeddedness and connectedness with influential societal actors should be given equal emphasis in the discussion. From the perspective of Evans (1995), the effectiveness of modern developmental states in pursuing collective objectives depended very much on its ability to achieve two apparently contradictory missions: To combine "Weberian bureaucratic insulation" (autonomy) with "intense connection to the surrounding social structure" (embeddedness):

> This "embedded autonomy" ... is the key to the developmental state's effectiveness. "Embedded autonomy" combines Weberian bureaucratic insulation with intense connection to the surrounding social structure.... Given a sufficiently coherent, cohesive state apparatus, isolation is not necessary to preserve state capacity. Connectedness means increased competence instead of capture. How autonomy and embeddedness are combined depends, of course, on both the historical determined character of the state apparatus and the nature of the social structure.
>
> (Evans, 1995, p. 50)

Linda Weiss (1998) similarly pointed out that an effective state should be able to preserve its autonomy from undue special interests on the one hand, while on the other hand maintaining an institutionalized relationship of negotiation and political exchange with the dominant economic and societal actors so as to ensure the achievement of state-defined goals. Weiss described such a style of governance as "governed interdependence":

> Governed interdependence (GI) refers to a negotiated relationship, in which public and private participants maintain their autonomy, yet which is nevertheless governed by broader goals set and monitored by the state. In this relationship, leadership is either exercised directly by the state or delegated to the private sector where a robust organizational infrastructure has been nurtured by state policies. GI is intended to convey a reality in which both state and dominant economic groups are "strong": i.e. the state is well insulated and industry is highly organized and linked into the policy-making framework via a robust negotiating relationship.
>
> (Weiss, 1998, p. 38)

Evans (1997) broadened the scope of discussion by highlighting the role of civil society in the governance process. For Evans, the governing capacity of modern states is not only dependent on fostering state–business cooperation over economic development projects, as highlighted by the notions of "embedded autonomy" and "governed interdependence", a cooperative state–society relation and the construction of "state–society synergy" should be given equal emphasis in the discussion of state capacity. Modern states could scale-up existing social capital in the society for effective formulation and implementation of development projects by putting in place a "competent and engaged set of public institutions":

The value of synergistic strategies is evident. Creative action by government organizations can foster social capital; linking mobilized citizens to public agencies can enhance the efficacy of government. The combination of strong public institutions and organized communities is a powerful tool of development ... synergy involves concrete ties connecting state and society which make it possible to exploit complementarities.

(Evans, 1997)

Jon Pierre and Guy B. Peters (2000) also recognized that the capacity of the state to govern and steer policy-making is determined by its abilities to forge coalitions and elicit cooperation with powerful socio-economic actors. For Pierre and Peters, the strength of the state is more a matter of building coalitions across a wide range of interests so that its policies could command broad societal acceptance: "Governance implies, slightly paradoxically perhaps, softer and more subtle means of steering society.... Institutional strength, in this view, is more a matter of entrepreneurial and networking skills than the exercise of regulatory or any other traditional governmental capability" (Pierre & Peters, 2000, pp. 98–99).

Although the analytic focuses of the above theorists are not exactly the same, they share the common perspective that the capacity of the state to govern and steer public policy-making is shaped by the interactions between the state and major socio-economic constituents. From this perspective, the different notions of "state autonomy", "state embeddedness" and "governing coalition building" should be considered as the important foundations for modern states to develop and muster sufficient capacity for maintaining effective governance.

State embeddedness, state autonomy and governing coalition building: a new state-centric perspective to governance crisis in post-1997 Hong Kong

On the basis of the above theories of state capacity, this book aims at going beyond the existing mainstream explanation of legitimacy deficit and developing an alternative theoretical perspective to reinterpret the governance crisis in post-1997 Hong Kong. Drawing inspiration from the contemporary governance and state capacity theories, the overarching argument of this book is that the post-1997 governance crisis is not simply the consequence of the problem of legitimacy deficit facing the post-colonial state under the hybrid regime, but it is also the result of the failure of the state–business alliance after 1997. Unlike the British colonial era, the state–business alliance as engineered by the Chinese government has been operated in completely different political and socio-economic environments after the handover, and therefore it fails to live up to its original function in providing a strong political support base for consolidating the governing capacity of the post-colonial Hong Kong state. The major arguments pursued in this research can be summarized as the following theoretical propositions:

36 *Governance under hybrid regimes*

- *Crisis of state embeddedness.* While the business sector enjoys over-representation in the HKSAR political establishment, the fragmentation of agents of business interests means that there is a vital missing link between the post-colonial state and the business sector. Thus the post-colonial state is facing growing difficulties in mediating between major business interests and consolidating business support for its policies. On the other hand, because the business sector has become increasingly disconnected from the community, the co-opted business elites are generally powerless in mediating the challenge of civil society and there is a widening gap between the post-colonial state and society. As a result of the erosion of the intermediary role of co-opted business elites between the state, business and society, the post-colonial state is facing growing challenges in re-embedding itself with major socio-economic actors and therefore it struggles to forge societal acceptance for delivering policy changes.
- *Crisis of state autonomy.* The institutionalization of business power in the HKSAR political system (Chief Executive Election Committee and functional constituencies of the Legislative Council) and the business sector's direct access to the sovereign state (the closer political and economic partnership between the Chinese government and the business elites) were both deliberately designed by Beijing leaders to perpetuate the state–business alliance after 1997. But instead of consolidating business support to the Chief Executive, these rules of engagement have only equipped the business sector with considerable power leverages vis-à-vis the post-colonial state. As a result, the post-colonial state's relative autonomy is facing growing challenges from the business sector and therefore it struggles to maintain its role as the arbitrator of class interests.
- *Failure of the state–business alliance.* Under the combined effects of crisis of state embeddedness and crisis of state autonomy, the enabling conditions that endowed a viable state–business alliance during the colonial time have been seriously eroded after the handover. As a result, the post-colonial state is neither embedded nor autonomous and it is facing severe governance challenges on two major fronts. Because of the crisis of state embeddedness, the post-colonial state fails to consolidate the support of major socio-economic constituents for steering policy changes; and because of the crisis of state autonomy, the post-colonial state bears the notoriety of collusion with the business sector and it can no longer hold the proper balance between business interests and public interests. The failure of the state–business alliance after 1997 has undermined the popular support base of the HKSAR political order, plunging the post-colonial state into a political quagmire of pervasive public discontent and public distrust.

To sum up, this book will offer a new perspective on Hong Kong's governance by arguing that the post-1997 governance crisis is not simply the result of a legitimacy deficit, but also the consequences of the failure of governance coalition building. By going beyond the opposition-centred explanation as widely held by theorists of legitimacy deficit in the local existing literature, this book project will provide an alternative understanding on the erosion of the governing capacity of the HKSAR government and will offer novel interpretations of Hong Kong's governance crisis after 1997. Such theoretical developments, which mainly focus on the concepts of governing coalition building and their implications on governance, have been overlooked in the existing literature on Hong Kong politics. From this perspective, this book will certainly enrich and broaden the scope of existing literature on Hong Kong's public governance and should be useful in shedding new insight on the territory's political developments.

The research design of this book

Objective of the research

This book is a critical re-examination of the governance crisis in post-1997 Hong Kong. By drawing upon the contemporary literature on governance and state capacity, this book aims to go beyond the existing theoretical explanations and to articulate a new conceptual framework for re-examining the post-1997 governance crisis. Arguing for the causal relationship between the failure of the state–business alliance and the governing crisis facing the post-colonial state, this book not only broadens our understanding of the governance problems after 1997, but also compensates the limitations of the existing opposition-centred explanations on Hong Kong's governance. Specifically, this book project intends to answer the following research questions:

- The existence of a viable state–business alliance was widely considered by local political scientists as the foundation of effective governance in colonial Hong Kong. What were the structural and contextual factors that contributed to the effective functioning of this governing coalition during the British colonial time?
- It was the grand strategy of the Chinese government to maintain the state–business alliance after 1997. Why does this state–business alliance not work as effectively as in the colonial past? What are the political and socio-economic changes that have resulted in the failure of the state–business alliance in the post-1997 period? How does the failure of the state–business alliance eventually undermine the capacity of the post-colonial state to maintain effective governance and to resist the challenges of the democratic opposition?
- The implementation of universal suffrage for Chief Executive and Legislative Council elections has been widely seen by local political scientists and researchers as the ultimate solution to the post-1997 governance problems. If it is established that the lingering of the governance crisis in the post-1997 period is not only the result of a legitimacy deficit but also the consequences of failure of governing coalition building, apart from the introduction of popular elections what else could be done to address the HKSAR governance crisis?

38 *Governance under hybrid regimes*

Scope of the study

This book mainly covers Hong Kong's governance under the first two HKSAR Chief Executives, Tung Chee-hwa and Donald Tsang, in the period of 1997 to 2012. It aims at making certain broad generalizations about the patterns of public governance in the first 15 years of HKSAR governance.

While the core theme is to analyse the governance crisis in post-1997 Hong Kong by conducting a critical analysis of governing coalition building, we have largely confined our discussion within the scope of changing state–business relations and state–society relations. While the post-1997 governing coalition was usually considered as a loose alliance of business elites, bureaucratic elites and pro-Beijing leftists (Lau, 2002b), it is difficult to provide a thorough analysis of the roles of these three major groups of players on HKSAR governance within a single book. In order to keep the arguments and analysis of this book to a manageable level, this project will primarily focus on the unique role of the business sector, having regard to the fact that the business elites form the majority of the HKSAR political establishment and they are the predominant players under the post-1997 governing coalition. The political roles played by bureaucratic elites and pro-Beijing leftists in post-1997 Hong Kong's governance will be generally excluded from analysis.

Research strategy and methods

In the world of political science there are many different kinds of research approaches, including behaviouralism, structuralism, institutionalism, rational choice theory, feminism, interpretive theory and Marxism. Each of these approaches represents a different set of attitudes, concepts and practices that guides a particular way of studying political science (Stoker & Marsh, 2002). In this connection, structuralism is a longstanding research approach in the field of political studies. This research approach states that the "social reality is governed by the complex interaction of economic, political and ideological structures which have their own relative autonomy from one another" (McAnulla, 2002). From the perspectives of structuralists, structural variables, which are rooted in long-term historical processes and cannot be easily changed by individual leaders, play the central role in shaping political outcomes and explain most of the political phenomenon.

The arguments of this research are structuralist and we will basically follow a structural research approach, i.e. this book project is designed to examine the various structural and contextual factors that have shaped the functioning of the state–business governing coalition in post-1997 Hong Kong, including the political structures, economic environment and social developments. In other words, this research study will explore explanations that go beyond the utilitarian calculations of individual political actors and focus on structural variables whose origin lie in the long-term historical processes that cannot be easily changed by individual behaviours. In order to examine the structural and contextual factors that have brought about the post-1997 governance crisis in Hong Kong, we have to collect evidence as to how the structural contexts have shaped the interests, behaviours and strategies of different political actors and organizations.

In accordance with the structural research approach, this book project has adopted both qualitative and quantitative research methods with a view to generating solid empirical findings to support our theoretical propositions and arguments. In this connection, the information, data and evidence have been obtained through the following research methods:

- *Quantitative analysis.* Tabulations have been compiled to discern the striking empirical patterns that underline the nature and the functioning of the state–business alliance both before and after 1997. The original data set was mainly obtained from open information sources such as government publications and company financial reports, etc.
- *Qualitative interviews.* In order to gain primary understanding of the functioning of the state–business alliance before and after the handover, qualitative interviews were conducted with influential political players, including senior government officials, legislators, business leaders, academics and experts, etc. The interview guidelines have been set out in Appendix I.
- *Documentary studies.* Scholarly publications and newspaper reports are our important sources of secondary information. Official documents such as government papers and official record proceedings of the Legislative Council meetings are supplementary information sources.

The plan of this book

The book is divided into ten chapters as follows:

- Chapter 1: Governance crisis in post-1997 Hong Kong: in search of a new theoretical perspective
- Chapter 2: Governance and the state: revisiting the concepts and theories of state capacity
- Chapter 3: Reinterpreting governance and state capacity in colonial time: the colonial state–business alliance
- Chapter 4: The crafting of the post-1997 state–business alliance: Beijing's governing strategy after 1997
- Chapter 5: The missing link between state and business: the fragmentation of agents of business interests
- Chapter 6: The widening gap between state and society: the growing disconnection of the business sector from the local community
- Chapter 7: Institutionalization of business power under the HKSAR political system: Chief Executive Election Committee and functional constituencies
- Chapter 8: The business sector's direct access to the sovereign state: the close partnership between Beijing and the local capitalists
- Chapter 9: Conclusion: rethinking the governance crisis in post-1997 Hong Kong
- Epilogue

40 *Governance under hybrid regimes*

Chapters 1 and 2 represent the theoretical overview of this book project. Chapter 1 provides a theoretical foundation for the whole book by discussing in what theoretical contexts this book project has been developed. Chapter 2 reviews the contemporary literature on governance and state capacity and articulates a new conceptual framework for re-examining the governance crisis in post-1997 Hong Kong.

Chapters 3 and 4 trace the political legacy of the state–business alliance in Hong Kong from the British colonial time to the transitional period. Chapter 3 offers a background analysis by examining the functioning of the state–business alliance in colonial Hong Kong. Chapter 4 reviews the Chinese government's grand strategy to maintain a state–business alliance after the handover and its united-front work during the transitional period.

Chapters 5 and 6 examine how the increasing erosion of the role of intermediaries of business elites after 1997 has resulted in the widening gap between the post-colonial state and the major socio-economic constituents. Chapter 5 argues that because of the underdevelopment of business-oriented political parties after 1997, there is a general lack of encompassing agents of business interests to fill in the missing link between the post-colonial state and the business sector. Chapter 6 argues that the co-opted business elites have been increasingly disconnected from the local community after 1997 and therefore are generally powerless in bridging the widening gap between the post-colonial state and society.

Chapters 7 and 8 examine how the rising power leverages of the business sector have enabled it to capture the post-colonial state. Chapter 7 argues that the business sector has developed unprecedented power bases as a result of the installation of the Chief Executive Election Committee and functional constituencies and there is a shift in the balance of power between the post-colonial state and the business sector. Chapter 8 argues that business elites gained direct access to the sovereign state after 1997 and there is a growing tendency of the business sector to influence local politics by directly lobbying the Mainland authorities.

Chapter 9 is the conclusion of the book. This chapter summarizes the central arguments of the book by articulating an alternative perspective to the post-1997 Hong Kong governance crisis. This chapter examines how the failure of the state–business alliance has brought about the various governance problems for the post-colonial state. It also highlights the theoretical implications of this research study by discussing its original contribution to literature and the future research agenda.

Conclusion

Since the handover, the post-colonial state has been stuck in a crisis of governance under which it is experiencing great difficulty in steering policy changes and is also suffering from serious erosion of its role as the arbitrator of class interests. Many important policy initiatives introduced by the post-colonial state fail to secure the support of the major political and socio-economic constituents and class divisions have already reached an unprecedented high. In this connection,

Governance crisis in post-1997 Hong Kong 41

the existing theoretical perspective for the post-1997 governance crisis is the *legitimacy deficit thesis*, which is basically an opposition-centred explanation examining how the challenges of the democratic opposition have undermined the governing capacity of the post-colonial state. Although such a theoretical perspective is a popular explanation commonly adopted by most of the local political scientists, it is far from a comprehensive and exhaustive answer to Hong Kong's governance problems after 1997.

The theoretical discussions in this chapter demonstrate the genuine need for the development of a new intellectual project that can move beyond the existing literature. This book therefore aims at offering a new interpretation of Hong Kong's governance crisis after 1997, arguing for another plausible theoretical explanation rested on the concepts of governing coalition building and state capacity. Such an alternative theoretical perspective is built upon the contention that the significant political and socio-economic changes have resulted in the failure of the state–business alliance after the handover, and this is the fundamental reason behind the declining governing capacity of the post-colonial state after the handover of sovereignty.

Notes

1 The Freedom House's "Freedom of the World" survey provides an annual comparative assessment of global political rights and civil liberties. This annual survey measures freedom of countries around the globe according to two broad categories, namely political rights and civil liberties. For Freedom House, political rights ratings are based on an evaluation of electoral process, political pluralism and participation and functioning of government, while civil liberties ratings are based on an evaluation of freedom of expression and belief, associational and organizational rights, rule of law and personal autonomy and individual rights (Freedom House, 2013).

2 According to Freedom House, Hong Kong is classified as "partly free" territory. Hong Kong scores high marks on "civil rights" but its score on "political rights" is low, reflecting its status as liberal authoritarianism with some electoral authoritarian elements (Freedom House, 2013).

3 Hong Kong's high level of political stability and efficient day-to-day administration of its society have been reflected in the Worldwide Governance Indicators conducted by the World Bank. This survey assessed the state of governance of 212 countries and territories according to six indicators: "voice and accountability", "political stability", "government effectiveness", "regulatory quality", "rule of law" and "control of corruption". According to this survey, Hong Kong has been at the forefront of the world on most of the dimensions of governance (World Bank, 2009).

4 For more analysis on the colonial state's close linkages with the business sector and its immunity from the challenges of civil society, see Chapter 3.

5 There were two major considerations behind the CPG's decision to extend the executive-dominant system in the post-1997 era. First, in the eyes of Beijing leaders, the executive-dominant system had been doing a fine job in maintaining stability and effective governance for many decades. To secure Hong Kong's political stability after 1997 and to provide a higher degree of institutional continuity, the CPG intended to retain this key feature of the colonial governance system (Ma, 2007b, p. 58). Second, the executive-dominant system could facilitate Beijing's ultimate control over Hong Kong. For Beijing's leaders there were always misgivings about the rise of anti-communist political forces in Hong Kong, and in particular they did not want to

42 *Governance under hybrid regimes*

see the existence of an influential elected legislature which could function as a platform for those anti-China political parties or hostile foreign forces (Lau, 1999a). Thus Beijing's leaders were inclined to marginalize the influences of the legislature and to preserve the colonial executive-dominant government. By concentrating power in the hands of the Chief Executive and principal officials who are appointed by the CPG and are directly answerable to it under the Basic Law, Beijing could maintain its political control over the HKSAR and prevent it from taking any action which would go against its interests (Lau, 2000). Against this background, an executive-dominant government headed by the Chief Executive was adopted as the basic model of the post-1997 political order and the distribution of power under the Basic Law was obviously in favour of the executive rather than the legislature.

6 For more analysis on the relative autonomy of the colonial state and its role as arbitrator of class interests, see Chapter 3.

7 For example, an opinion poll conducted in 1996 found that 66.5 per cent of respondents said the colonial administration had done a good job in governing Hong Kong for the past 150 years (Lau, 1999b).

8 According to surveys carried out by the University of Hong Kong, the level of public trust towards the colonial government ranged between 56.9 per cent in 1992 and 63.2 per cent in 1997 (http://hkupop.hku.hk).

9 For example, a 1992 survey found that 51.4 per cent and 23.5 per cent of people gave an average score or a high score to the colonial government in conducting government affairs fairly (Lau & Kuan, 1995).

10 The major exception was the period of 2005–2007 when Donald Tsang still enjoyed his political honeymoon. But the stock of political goodwill enjoyed by the Tsang Administration has depleted very rapidly since 2008 as a result of a series of policy blunders and controversial incidents.

11 Similar to the trend of public satisfaction, public trust toward the HKSAR government had enjoyed a short rebound from 2005 to 2007 when Donald Tsang was in his political honeymoon.

12 In 1999 the Financial Secretary Donald Tsang announced in his Budget Speech that a Cyberport would be constructed. This project aimed at providing an ultramodern office and residential complex with a view to fostering the growth of innovation and technology industry in Hong Kong. However, this project was finally awarded to the Pacific Century Group, the high-technology flagship company owned by tycoon Li Ka-shing's son Richard Li, without going through any open tendering process. The granting of the Cyberport project to the Li family gave rise to concerns of growing cronyism between the post-colonial state and large capitalists (Ngo, 2002).

13 In 1999 Tung Chee-hwa announced the government's plan to build an arts and cultural performance centre in West Kowloon. In 2003 the government announced that a single development approach would be used in the development of the West Kowloon Cultural District, by which a 50-year land grant would be awarded to a single business consortium for financing, constructing and managing all the cultural, commercial and residential facilities in the entire site. The government's plan stirred up public concerns that the single development approach would only benefit big property developers and effectively turn the whole West Kowloon Cultural District into a developer's colony (Ng, 2005).

14 In 2008 Mr. Leung Chin-man, the former Director of Building Services, retired from the civil service and his application for post-retirement employment in the New World China Land (a subsidiary company of property giant New World Development) was approved by the Civil Service Bureau. It was well known that Leung during his service in the government had made the "wrong decision" in the sale of the Hunghom Peninsula development project that led to millions of extra profits for New World Development, and the public severely criticized the Civil Service Bureau's approval and considered this incident a prominent example of government–business collusion

Governance crisis in post-1997 Hong Kong   43

by which Leung was rewarded by a generous employment contract for the favours he had provided to the New World Development during his service as Director of Building Services (Ma, 2009).

15 The notion of "real estate hegemony" comes from a popular book called *Di Chan Ba Quan*. This book examined the dominance of property giants in Hong Kong's economic arena (Poon, 2010).

16 In political science literature, legitimacy can be defined as the "rightfulness of a regime" (Heywood, 2002, p. 210), or more clearly the "recognition of the right to govern" (Coicaud, 2002, p. 10). In the eyes of political scientists, political leaders must obtain sufficient legitimacy in order to command respect, obedience and acceptance from its citizens for the government's actions and policies. Max Weber, the German political sociologist of the nineteenth century, offered the most classical classification of the major sources of legitimacy, including traditional authority, charismatic authority and legal-rational authority (Heywood, 2002, pp. 211–212). Huntington (1991, pp. 46–58) provided an updated theory of legitimacy by refining the concepts of "procedural legitimacy" and "performance legitimacy". For Huntington, in modern times authoritarian regimes could no longer justify rule by means of tradition, religion or divine right of kings. As a result, "performance legitimacy" in the form of economic growth and prosperity has increasingly become the principal justification for personal or one-party dictatorship in many societies. For democratic regimes, elected political leaders could achieve "procedural legitimacy" by means of regular popular elections, which function as a mechanism either for the incumbents to renew their legitimacy through re-election or for the new leaders to come to power with new promises and policies for the future. However, Huntington observed that performance legitimacy is not a stable source of government legitimacy when compared with procedural legitimacy, because under authoritarian regimes any policy failures not only undermine the legitimacy of the rulers but also the legitimacy of the whole political system.

17 Under the present constitutional system, the Chief Executive is elected by an election committee dominated by pro-Beijing figures and is appointed by the CPG. In accordance with Annex I of the Basic Law, the present 1,200-member Chief Executive Election Committee is composed of members from the following four sectors, each of 300 members: (1) industrial, commercial and financial sectors; (2) the professions; (3) labour, social services, religious and other sectors; and (4) Legislative Council members, representatives of district organizations, Hong Kong deputies to the National People's Congress, representatives of Hong Kong members of the National Committee of the Chinese People's Political Consultative Conference (Li, 2007). For more details about the Chief Executive electoral system, see Chapter 7.

18 Article 45 of the Basic Law promised that "the ultimate aim is the selection of the Chief Executive by universal suffrage" while Article 68 stipulated that "the ultimate aim is the election of all members of the Legislative Council by universal suffrage".

19 The politics of the constitutional reforms have dominated Hong Kong's political agenda since the handover, because the democrats have all along pressed for the early implementation of universal suffrage for the Chief Executive and Legislative Council elections. In April 2004 the Standing Committee of the National People's Congress (NPCSC) reached a verdict stating that the elections of the 2007 Chief Executive and 2008 Legislative Council would not be returned by universal suffrage, thereby defeating the democrats' appeal for full democracy for 2007/2008. In 2005 the Donald Tsang Administration announced its blueprint for reforming the 2007/2008 election methods, but the proposals were voted down by the democrats. In December 2007, the NPCSC ruled that the Chief Executive may be elected by universal suffrage in 2017, and that after the Chief Executive is selected by universal suffrage, the election of the Legislative Council may also be implemented by means of universal suffrage. The introduction of this "timetable" for universal suffrage, however, does not

44   *Governance under hybrid regimes*

completely resolve the constitutional reform issue, because the democrats now request the CPG and the Chief Executive to provide a concrete "roadmap" for the implementation of full democracy.

20 In order to promote strong executive-dominant governance after 1997 it was the strategy of Beijing's leaders to install a stable pro-government majority in the post-1997 Legislative Council so that legislators would not pose serious challenges to the executive branch (Lau, 2000). Such a pro-government majority was achieved through a tactfully designed electoral system for the post-1997 Legislative Council. First, Annex II of the Basic Law provides that not more than half of the 60-strong Legislative Council is made up by directly elected members in the first ten years of post-1997 Hong Kong, while another half will be elected through functional constituencies. Such a composition of the legislature is to make sure the Chief Executive receives stable support from those conservative business and professional legislators returned by functional constituencies (who share similar political perspectives and policy orientations with the Chief Executive and are groomed and co-opted by Beijing as the post-colonial state's political allies in the governing of Hong Kong) (Lau, 2002a). Second, the electoral system for direct elections in the geographical constituencies was also reformed after the handover to restrict the political space of the pro-democracy activists. This referred to the replacement of the "single-member constituency first-past-the-post system" by "proportional representation" as the electoral formula for direct elections in geographical constituencies since the 1998 Legislative Council election. The rationale behind this reform was that the more popular pro-democracy candidates would not be able to win a great majority of directly elected seats in geographical constituencies while the less popular pro-China candidates would be decently represented with their minority vote (Lau, 1999a, 2002a). With the combined effects of the proportional representation electoral system and the existence of functional constituencies, it is anticipated that a stable pro-government majority will be installed and engineered in the post-1997 Legislative Council while the pro-democracy opposition will be condemned into a minority position (Ma, 2007a).

21 Article 74 of the Basic Law forbids legislators from proposing any private member's bill that is related to public expenditure, political structure and operation of the government. For bills that relate to government policies, written consent of the Chief Executive must be obtained. These restrictions have greatly hindered democratic legislators from introducing their own legislative bills (Ma, 2007a).

22 Annex II of the Basic Law stipulates that while all government bills and amendments need only a simple majority to pass the Legislative Council, all bills, amendments and motions proposed by individual members require separate majorities among both geographical constituency and functional constituency members. This voting arrangement makes it difficult for pro-democracy legislators to pass substantial and controversial motions and has therefore weakened motion debates as a policy-influencing tool. It also makes it difficult for the democratic opposition to influence policy-making by proposing amendments to government bills (Lui, 2007; Ma, 2007a).

23 Apart from the strength of the authoritarian regimes in resisting opposition challenges (domestic variable), Levitsky and Way found that the different regime trajectories could also be explained by the regimes' linkages with the West (international variable). According to Levitsky and Way, "Western leverage" (the power of the West to use threat, conditionality and other forms of pressure to punish the authoritarian regimes) and "linkages to the West" (political, economic, technocratic, social and diplomatic ties and cross-border flow of capital, people, information, goods and services) will raise the cost of maintaining the authoritarian regimes and the authoritarian incumbents will be more likely to cede power and agree to democratic reforms. Levitsky and Way's research revealed that when ties to the West were less extensive, international pressure for democratization are weaker and the domestic variable (capacity of the authoritarian incumbents) will be weighted more heavily (Levitsky & Way,

Governance crisis in post-1997 Hong Kong 45

2010). Because Hong Kong as a Special Administrative Region is directly supervised by the Chinese government under the framework of "one country, two systems" and Western countries have largely restrained from directly intervening in the affairs of the territory, the international variable as outlined by Levitsky and Way is not relevant and politics in post-1997 Hong Kong is primarily shaped by the domestic variable. As a result, here we only focus on discussing the domestic variable, which is more closely relevant and applicable to Hong Kong's contexts.

References

Beissinger, M. R. (2002). *Nationalist mobilization and the collapse of the Soviet State.* New York: Cambridge University Press.

Bratton, M., & van de Walle, N. (1997). *Democratic experiments in Africa: Regime transitions in comparative perspective.* New York: Cambridge University Press.

Brodsgarrd, K. E., & Young, S. (2000). Introduction: State capacity in East Asia. In K. E. Brodsgarrd, & S. Young (Eds.), *State capacity in East Asia: Japan, Taiwan, China and Vietnam* (pp. 1–16). New York: Oxford University Press.

Brownlee, J. (2007). *Authoritarianism in an age of democratization.* New York: Cambridge University Press.

Case, W. (1996). Can the "halfway house" stand? Semidemocracy and elite theory in three Southeast Asian countries. *Comparative Politics, 28*(4), 437–464.

Case, W. (2005). Southeast Asia's hybrid regimes: When do voters change them?. *Journal of East Asian Studies, 5*(1), 215–237.

Case, W. (2008). Hybrid politics and new competitiveness: Hong Kong's 2007 Chief Executive Election. *East Asia, 25*(4), 365–388.

Census and Statistics Department. (2012). The GDP and unemployment figures. Retrieved 1 January 2013 from: www.censtatd.gov.hk.

Cheung, A. (2005a). Hong Kong's post-1997 institutional crisis: Problems of governance and institutional incompatibility. *Journal of East Asian Studies, 5*(1), 135–167.

Cheung, A. (2005b). The Hong Kong system under one country being tested. In J. Y. S. Cheng (Ed.), *The July 1 protest rally: Interpreting a historic event* (pp. 41–68). Hong Kong: City University of Hong Kong Press.

Cheung, A. (2007). Executive-dominant governance or executive power "hollowed-out": the political quagmire of Hong Kong. *Asian Journal of Political Science, 15*(1), 17–38.

Cheung, A. (2008). The story of two administrative states: State capacity in Hong Kong and Singapore. *The Pacific Review, 21*(2), 121–145.

Cheung, A. (2010). In search of trust and legitimacy: The political trajectory of Hong Kong as part of China. *International Public Management Review, 11*(2), 38–63.

Chiu, S. W. K. (1994). *The politics of laissez-faire: Hong Kong's strategy of industrialization in historical perspective.* Hong Kong: Hong Kong Institute of Asia-Pacific Studies, Chinese University.

Coicaud, J. M. (2002). *Legitimacy and politics: A contribution to the study of political right and political responsibility.* Cambridge: Cambridge University Press.

Collier, R. B. (1999). *Pathways toward democracy: The working class and elites in Western Europe and Latin America.* New York: Cambridge University Press.

Diamond, L. (1999). *Developing democracy: Toward consolidation.* Baltimore, MD: Johns Hopkins University Press.

Diamond, L. (2002). Thinking about hybrid regimes. *Journal of Democracy, 13*(2), 21–35.

46 *Governance under hybrid regimes*

Evans, P. B. (1995). *Embedded autonomy: States and industrial transformation*. Princeton, NJ: Princeton University Press.

Evans, P. B. (1997). Government action, social capital, and development: Reviewing the evidence on synergy. In P. Evans (Ed.), *State–society synergy: Government and social capital in development* (pp. 178–209). Berkeley, CA: University of California at Berkeley.

Fish, M. S. (1995). *Democracy from scratch: Opposition and regime in the new Russian revolution*. Princeton, NJ: Princeton University Press.

Freedom House. (2013). *Freedom in the world 2013: The annual survey of political rights & civil liberties*. New York: Rowman & Littlefield.

Fukuyama, F. (2004). *State-building: Governance and world order in the 21st century*. Ithaca, NY: Cornell University Press.

Gilley, B. (2009). *The right to rule: How states win and lose legitimacy*. New York: Columbia University Press.

Goldstone, J. A., Bates, R. H., Epstein, D. L., Gurr, T. R., Lustik, M. B., Marshall, M. G., Ulfelder, J., & Woodward, M. (2005). *A global forecasting model of political instability*, Paper prepared for Annual Meeting of the American Political Science Association. Retrieved 1 January 2013 from http://globalpolicy.gmu.edu/pitf/PITF global.pdf.

Heywood, A. (2002). *Politics* (2nd ed.). Basingstoke: Palgrave.

Hong Kong Institute of Asia-Pacific Studies. (2010). *Public opinion survey on Hong Kong's social harmony*. Retrieved 1 January 2013 from www.cuhk.edu.hk/hkiaps/CSP/download/Press_Release_20100408.pdf.

Hong Kong Institute of Asia-Pacific Studies. (2011). *Public opinion survey on real estate hegemony*. Retrieved 1 January 2013 from www.cuhk.edu.hk/hkiaps/tellab/pdf/telepress/11/Press_Release20110810.pdf.

Huntington, S. P. (1991). *The third wave: Democratization in the late twentieth century*. Norman: University of Oklahoma Press.

Lai, C., & Loh, C. (2007). *From nowhere to nowhere: A review of constitutional development, Hong Kong*. Hong Kong: Civic Exchange.

Lau, C. K. (1997). *Hong Kong's colonial legacy*. Hong Kong: Chinese University Press.

Lau, S. K. (1994). Hong Kong's "ungovernability" in the twilight of colonial rule. In Z. L. Lin, & T. W. Robinson (Eds.), *The Chinese and their future: Beijing, Taipei, and Hong Kong* (pp. 287–314). Washington, DC: AEI Press.

Lau, S. K. (1999a). The making of the electoral system. In H. C. Kuan, S. K. Lau, T. K. Y. Wong, & K. S. Louie (Eds.), *Power transfer and electoral politics: The first legislative election in the Hong Kong Special Administrative Region* (pp. 3–35). Hong Kong: Chinese University Press.

Lau, S. K. (1999b). The rise and decline of political support for the Hong Kong Special Administrative Region government. *Government and Opposition, 34*(3), 352–371.

Lau, S. K. (2000). The executive-dominant system of governance: Theory and practice. In S. K. Lau (Ed.), *Blueprint for the 21st century Hong Kong* (pp. 1–36). Hong Kong: Chinese University Press (in Chinese).

Lau, S. K. (2002a). Hong Kong's partial democracy under stress. In Y. M. Yeung (Ed.), *New challenges for development and modernization: Hong Kong and the Asia-Pacific region in the new millennium* (pp. 181–205). Hong Kong: Chinese University Press.

Lau, S. K. (2002b). Tung Chee-hwa's governing strategy: The shortfall in politics. In S. K. Lau (Ed.), *The first Tung Chee-hwa administration* (pp. 1–39). Hong Kong: Chinese University Press.

Lau, S. K., & Kuan, H. C. (1995). Public attitudes toward political authorities and colonial legitimacy in Hong Kong. *Journal of Commonwealth & Comparative Politics, 33*(1), 79–102.

Lau, S. K., & Kuan, H. C. (2002). Between liberal autocracy and democracy: Democratic legitimacy in Hong Kong. *Democratization, 9*(4), 58–76.

Lee, E. W. Y. (1999). Governing post-colonial Hong Kong: Institutional incongruity, governance crisis and authoritarianism. *Asian Survey, 39*(6), 940–959.

Levitsky, S., & Way, L. A. (2002). The rise of competitive authoritarianism. *Journal of Democracy, 13*(2), 51–65.

Levitsky, S., & Way, L. A. (2010). *Competitive authoritarianism: Hybrid regimes after the Cold War.* New York: Cambridge University Press.

Li, P. K. (2001). The executive–legislature relationship in Hong Kong: Evolution and development. In J. Y. S. Cheng (Ed.), *Political development in the HKSAR* (pp. 85–100). Hong Kong: City University of Hong Kong.

Li, P. K. (2007). The executive. In W. M. Lam, P. L. T. Lui, W. Wong, & I. Holiday (Eds.), *Contemporary Hong Kong politics: Governance in the post-1997 era* (pp. 23–37). Hong Kong: Hong Kong University Press.

Lo, S. H. (2001). *Governing Hong Kong: Legitimacy, communication, and political decay.* New York: Nova Science Publishers.

Lui, P. L. T. (2007). The legislature. In W. M. Lam, P. L. T. Lui, W. Wong, & I. Holiday (Eds.), *Contemporary Hong Kong politics: Governance in the post-1997 era* (pp. 39–58). Hong Kong: Hong Kong University Press.

Lui, T. L., & Chui, S. W. K. (2007). Governance crisis in post-1997 Hong Kong: A political economy perspective. *The China Review, 7*(2), 1–34.

Lui, T. L., & Chiu, S. W. K. (2009). *Hong Kong: Becoming a Chinese global city.* London: Routledge.

Ma, N. (2007a). *Political development in Hong Kong: State, political society and civil society.* Hong Kong: Hong Kong University Press.

Ma, N. (2007b). Democratic development in Hong Kong: A decade of lost opportunities. In J. Y. S. Cheng (Ed.), *The Hong Kong Special Administrative Region in its first decade* (pp. 49–74). Hong Kong: City University of Hong Kong Press.

Ma, N. (2009). Reinventing the Hong Kong state or rediscovering it? From low intervention to eclectic corporatism. *Economy and Society, 38*(3), 492–519.

Ma, N. (2011). Hong Kong's democrats' divide. *Journal of Democracy, 22*(1), 54–67.

McAnulla, S. (2002). Structure and agency. In D. Marsh, & G. Stoker (Eds.), *Theory and methods in political science* (pp. 271–291), (2nd ed.). New York: Palgrave Macmillan.

Ng, M. K. (2005). Governance beyond government: Political crisis and sustainable world city building. In J. Y. S. Cheng (Ed.), *The July 1 protest rally: Interpreting a historic event* (pp. 469–499). Hong Kong: City University of Hong Kong Press.

Ngo, T. W. (2000). Changing government–business relations and the governance of Hong Kong. In R. Ash, P. Ferdinand, B. Hook, & R. Porter (Eds.), *Hong Kong in transition: The handover years* (pp. 26–41). New York: St. Martin's Press.

Ngo, T. W. (2002). Money, power, and the problem of legitimacy in the Hong Kong Special Administrative Region. In F. Mengin, & J. L. Rocca (Eds.), *Politics in China: Moving frontiers* (pp. 95–117). New York: Palgrave Macmillan.

Nordlinger, E. A. (1981). *On the autonomy of the democratic State.* Cambridge, MA: Harvard University Press.

O'Connor, J. (1973). *The fiscal crisis of the state.* New York: St. Martin's Press.

48 *Governance under hybrid regimes*

O'Donnell, G., & Schmitter, P. C. (1986). *Transitions from authoritarian rule: Tentative conclusions about uncertain democracies*. Baltimore, MD: Johns Hopkins University Press.

Pierre, J., & Peters, G. (2000). *Governance, politics and the state*. New York: St. Martin's Press.

Pierre, J., & Peters, G. (2006). Governance, government and the state. In C. Hay, M. Lister, & D. Marsh (Eds.), *The state: Theories and issues* (pp. 209–222). Oxford: Oxford University Press.

Poon, A. (2010). *Di chan ba quan (Land and the ruling class in Hong Kong)*. Xianggang: Tian Chuang Chu Ban She You Xian Gong Si (Hong Kong: Enrich Publishing) (in Chinese).

Poulantzas, N. A. (1978). *Political power and social classes*. London: Verso.

Public Opinion Programme, University of Hong Kong. (2012). The public satisfaction rate and trust. Retrieved 1 January 2013 from: http://hkupop.hku.hk.

Rear, J. (1971). One brand of politics. In K. Hopkins (Ed.), *Hong Kong: The industrial colony – a political, social and economic survey* (pp. 55–139). Hong Kong: Oxford University Press.

Schedler, A. (2002). The menu of manipulation. *Journal of Democracy, 13*(2), 36–50.

Scott, I. (1989). *Political change and the crisis of legitimacy in Hong Kong*. Hong Kong: Oxford University Press.

Scott, I. (2000). The disarticulation of Hong Kong's post-1997 political system. *The China Journal, 43*, 29–53.

Scott, I. (2005). *Public administration in Hong Kong: Regime change and its impact on the public sector*. Singapore: Marshall Cavendish International.

Scott, I. (2007). Legitimacy, governance and public policy in post-1997 Hong Kong. *Asia Pacific Journal of Public Administration, 29*(1), 29–49.

Sing, M. (2001). The problem of legitimacy for the post-1997 Hong Kong government. *International Journal of Public Administration, 24*(9), 847–867.

Sing, M. (2003). Legislative–executive interface in Hong Kong. In C. Loh, & Civic Exchange (Eds.), *Building democracy: Creating good government for Hong Kong* (pp. 27–34). Hong Kong: Hong Kong University Press.

Sing, M. (2009). Hong Kong at the crossroads: Public pressure for democratic reform. In M. Sing (Ed.), *Politics and government in Hong Kong: Crisis under Chinese sovereignty* (pp. 112–135). Hong Kong: Hong Kong University Press.

Skocpol, T. (1985). Bringing the state back in: Strategies of analysis in current research. In P. B. Evans, D. Rueschemeyer, & T. Skocpol (Eds.), *Bringing the state back in* (pp. 3–37). Cambridge: Cambridge University Press.

Slater, D. (2010). *Ordering power: Contentious politics and authoritarian leviathans in Southeast Asia*. Cambridge: Cambridge University Press.

Stoker, G., & Marsh, D. (2002). Introduction. In D. Marsh, & G. Stoker (Eds.), *Theory and methods in political science* (2nd ed.). New York: Palgrave Macmillan.

Tang, J. (2008). Hong Kong's continuing search for a new order: Political stability in a partial democracy. In C. McGiffert, & J. T. H. Tang (Eds.), *Hong Kong on the move: 10 years as the HKSAR* (pp. 18–36). Berkeley, CA: University of California at Berkeley.

Tsang, S. (2004). *A modern history of Hong Kong*. Hong Kong and New York: I.B. Tauris.

Tsang, Y. K. (2005). *Strong governance for the people: The 2005–06 Policy Address*. Retrieved 1 January 2013 from www.policyaddress.gov.hk/05-06/eng/index.htm.

Tsang, Y. K. (2008). *Embracing new challenges: The 2008–09 Policy Address*. Retrieved 1 January 2013 from www.policyaddress.gov.hk/08-09/eng/policy.html.

Weiss, L. (1998). *The myth of the powerless state: Governing the economy in a global era*. Cambridge: Polity Press.

Wong, S. L., & Zheng, H. T. (2006). *Guan Shang Gou Jie: Xianggang Shi Min Yan Zhong De Zheng Shang Guan Xi (Government–business collusion: Public perception of government-business relations in Hong Kong)*. Hong Kong culture and society programme occasional paper series no. 3. Hong Kong: The University of Hong Kong.

Wood, E. J. (2000). *Forging democracy from below: Insurgent transitions in South Africa and El Salvador*. New York: Cambridge University Press.

World Bank (2009). *Governance matters VIII: Aggregate and individual governance indicators, 1996–2008*. Washington, DC: World Bank.

Zheng, H. T., & Wan, P. S. (2011a, August 8). Public perception of government–business relations in Hong Kong. *Hong Kong Economic Journal*. P15 (in Chinese).

Zheng, H. T., & Wan, P. S. (2011b, September 14). Public perception of the changing business environment in Hong Kong. *Ming Pao*. A24 (in Chinese).

2 Governance and the state
Revisiting the concepts and theories of state capacity

In contemporary political science literature, governance has been defined as the process of making authoritative collective decisions. In this regard, while the state plays an important and irreplaceable steering role in the governance process, its governing capacity will depend very much on its power to bond different state institutions and major socio-economic actors together in the pursuit of collective interests. As a result of the growing importance of non-state actors such as business sector and civil society in the governance process, modern governance is not simply the imposition of control and directive from above, it is about managing the interaction between state and different socio-economic constituents. From this perspective, understanding modern governance means understanding the nature of the relationship between the state and major societal actors in the pursuit of collective interests.

In this chapter, we will first provide readers with a general picture of the concepts of state and the various dimensions of state capacity. We will then draw upon contemporary governance studies to discuss the importance of managing the interactions between the state and major socio-economic constituents in the process of governance. Then we will introduce the various theoretical approaches to state capacity and examine the important enabling conditions that shape the capacity of the state to govern, including "political autonomy", "embedded autonomy", "governed interdependence" and "state–society synergy" and "forging coalitions". On the basis of these theoretical discussions, we will articulate a new conceptual framework which argues that the capacity of modern states to govern largely hinges on its ability to forge a stable and broad-based governing coalition on the political foundations of state autonomy and state embeddedness. All in all, the theoretical discussions on governance and state capacity in this chapter will provide a solid foundation for the development of a new theoretical perspective for re-examining the post-1997 Hong Kong governance crisis in the next chapter.

The capacity of the state to govern: state capacity defined

[S]tate and society are bonded together in the process of creating governance. If anything, the state actually may be strengthened through its interactions with society. The state may have to abdicate some aspects of its nominal control over policy, especially at the formulation stage of the process. On the other hand, it tends to gain substantial control at the implementation stage by having in essence coopted social interests that might otherwise oppose its actions. The ultimate effect may be to create a government that understands better the limits of its actions and which can work effectively within those parameters.

(Pierre & Peters, 2000, p. 49)

In the field of political studies, the concept of the state is, of course, not new and can be traced back to the nineteenth century, when German political sociologist Max Weber authoritatively defined the state as a political organization exercising monopoly on the legitimate use of violent forces within a given territory. From the perspectives of Weber, the monopolization of physical forces is the very foundation of the state in making and implementing authoritative binding decisions within the society (Weber, 1947). Following the footsteps of Weber, most of the political scientists would now agree that the state is a political entity that establishes sovereign jurisdiction within well-defined territorial borders and exercises its binding authority to govern the people through a set of government and political institutions (Heywood, 2000, p. 39). From this perspective, the modern state could be considered as including such institutions as armed forces, police, legislature and judicial courts, with political executive and bureaucracy as its core components.

The power to make authoritative decisions is undoubtedly central to the nature of the state, but there is no universal definition of "state capacity" and this concept has many different dimensions in existing political literature. For example, in their classical book *Comparative Politics: A Developmental Approach*, Gabriel A. Almond and G. Bingham Powell (1966) identified several functions that states could perform through the political system, including extractive capability (the capacity to extract resources from the society), regulative capability (the capacity to control behaviours of individuals and groups), distributive capability (the capacity to allocate goods and services to individuals and groups), symbolic capability (the capacity to pursue measures that symbolize statehood in the society) and responsive capability (the capacity to convert various inputs to the political systems into appropriate and effective policy outputs). Michael Mann provided another classical theory of state capacity in his work *The Sources of Social Power*, by which he defined despotic power and infrastructural power as the two major types of state capacity: the former refers to the capacity of the state to take actions without "routine negotiations with civil society groups", while the latter refers to the capacity of the state to penetrate into socio-economic life by implementing logistically political decisions throughout the territory (Mann, 1993, p. 59). All these classical theories on state capacity have inspired subsequent academic discussions on the role and functions of modern states, paving the way for the examination of different dimensions of state capacities by various political scientists in their studies (e.g. Painter & Pierre, 2005; Polidano, 2000).

52 *Governance under hybrid regimes*

For the purpose of this book, state capacity has been specifically defined as "the capacity of the state to govern", i.e. the capacity of the state to make authoritative collective decisions by managing its interactions with socio-economic actors (Kooiman, 1993, 2003; Pierre & Peters, 2000; Stoker, 1998), and in this regard under what "enabling conditions" could the state muster such a capacity is the primary focus. This research defined state capacity in this sense because it is most relevant to its research theme: the post-1997 governance crisis facing Hong Kong is the result of changing state–business and state–society relations and the overriding objective of this book is to employ state capacity theories in accounting for the declining governing capacity of the post-colonial Hong Kong state.

Such a definition of state capacity – the capacity of the state to make authoritative decisions by managing its interactions with major socio-economic actors – was actually drawn from the contemporary studies on modern governance. In recent decades, the concept of "governance" has become popular within academia and has taken a central place in political sciences debates (Pierre & Peters, 2000, p. 1). In this connection, governance has been defined by political scientists as the process through which the state steers the economy and society,[1] and more specifically, about the establishment of collective objectives and the development of the means for achieving those collective objectives by the state (Pierre & Peters, 2006).

"Traditional" governance theories are top-down in perspective, which mainly focuses on the dominant role of the state throughout the governing process. Such a theoretical perspective assumes that the political mandate or formal authority of the state should provide it with an adequate basis to govern effectively and enforce its decisions (Cheung, 2009). However, in recent decades the "modern" governance literature has paid greater attention to the interaction between the state and various socio-economic constituents. It emphasizes that the studies of governance should go beyond institutions and actors within government and adopted a much broader perspective in accounting for the role and functions of the state in the governing process through interacting and collaborating with major socio-economic constituents (Pierre & Peters, 2000, 2006).

Such a shift from the traditional top-down perspective of governance to a modern interactionist theory of governance has largely reflected the efforts of Western political scientists in searching for a new theoretical paradigm to reconstruct the role of the state in dealing with various contemporary governance challenges. In this connection, many political science literatures indicated that the traditional top-down commanding role of the state has been changed in recent decades and it is now subject to various new challenges as a consequence of significant transformations on both global and domestic fronts (Pierre & Peters, 2006).

The first challenge facing the state is the growing trend of economic globalization and multi-level governance under the globalized world.

Economic globalization, which can be defined as the intensification of all different kinds of economic activities such as production, distribution, finance and management across the borders, has brought about significant transformation in the economic arena, including the growing interconnectedness among national economies of the world, the rising power of transnational corporations, increasing influences of various regional economic blocs such as the Asia-Pacific Economic Co-operation Forum and emergence of global economic norms and standards. All these economic changes imply that the state has to develop a new way of regulating and managing the national economy and to interact with a wider range of private companies, groups and organizations (Sørensen, 2006). Apart from economic aspects, the trend of globalization also brings about profound political implications. Because different economic and social activities have been increasingly undertaken not merely within national boundaries but elsewhere as well, there is a greater demand for political cooperation across borders. This certainly gives rise to the emergence of multi-level governance in recent decades, which takes the form of inter-state cooperation and collaboration through various international organizations, as well as transgovernmental cooperation through the dense web of policy networks among executive agencies of different countries. Such political changes imply that the state can no longer govern on its own within the well-defined territorial borders, and governance has increasingly become an international, transgovernmental and transnational activity involving many different levels of government agencies (Sørensen, 2006).

The modern state is also facing growing challenge on the domestic front as a result of the growing influence of various autonomous societal actors.

The public sector reforms in Western countries since the 1980s have brought about far-reaching changes to the relationship between state, business and society. On the one hand, the roles of many Western governments have gradually shifted from direct provider of a wide range of public services to regulators of private provision; on the other hand, many public and social programmes are now increasingly implemented through cooperative arrangements between the state and not-for-profit civil society organizations (Pierre & Peters, 2000, pp. 29–33). Apart from public sector reforms, society in general also demands greater participation in the governing process and socio-economic constituents from both ends of the political spectrum ask for greater involvement in government decisions (Pierre & Peters, 2006). In this regard, improvements in education, urbanization and industrialization, proliferation of mass media and information technology have all inspired greater demands for political participation and citizen engagement in many Western countries. All these structural changes have certainly opened up government for greater influence from both private and civil society actors, while limiting the capacity of the state to impose control and directive from above through the traditional top-down approach (Pierre & Peters, 2006).

While the changes on global and domestic fronts imply that modern societies have become increasingly complex and multi-interest and the state can no longer maintain effective governance by unilaterally taking command and imposing order as in the traditional top-down governance perspective, it is not the case that the state has lost its power to govern. Governance has undoubtedly been

54 *Governance under hybrid regimes*

changed in recent decades, but what is happening is not the death of the state, it is the way that the state is governing and exercising power has been changed (Pierre & Peters, 2006). In this connection, the modern governance literature highlights that while in modern societies the state alone is not a sufficient part of governance, it still has a crucial and irreplaceable role to play by creating platforms for fostering coordination, cooperation and collaboration between the state and different socio-economic actors (Cheung, 2009).

In their seminal work, *Governance, Politics and the State*, Jon Pierre and Guy B. Peters argued that modern governance is not simply the imposition of control and directive from above, and the state needs to play a central and irreplaceable role in the process of governance by bonding different state institutions and socio-economic constituents together. Thus, whether the state could strengthen its capacity to interact, coordinate and cooperate with different non-state actors is of paramount importance for maintaining effective governance (Pierre & Peters, 2000, pp. 45, 49). In his important publication *Governing as Governance* Jan Kooiman similarly pointed out that the state can no longer maintain effective governance on its own in modern, diversified, dynamic and complex societies. Therefore he argued that the governability of a society could be considered as a continuing process of interaction between the state and societal actors and the governing capacity of the state will depend very much on its power to facilitate the purposeful and directed forms of socio-political interactions from local and central to supra-national and global levels (Kooiman, 1993, 2003). All in all, for many modern governance theorists, the traditional model of governance where the state could make authoritative decisions on their own and implement such decisions with minimal direct participation of socio-economic actors is no longer applicable to our societies. The modern governance literature therefore argues that the state should govern and exercise its power by interacting, collaborating and bargaining with different socio-economic constituents in order to make sure its decisions resolve conflicts among sectors of society and command broad societal acceptance (Pierre & Peters, 2006).

The above theoretical review on the theories of governance all point to the importance and relevance of a state-centric perspective to the pursuit of collective objectives, while highlighting the importance of the interaction between the state and socio-economic actors in the modern governing process. From this perspective, the capacity of the state to interact and operate with major socio-economic constituents is an important independent variable that explains the state of governance in modern societies (Pierre & Peters, 2000, p. 26). Obviously the capacity of the states to govern varies considerably throughout different countries and regions. It is notable that well-developed and well-functioning states are more likely to cope with the various pressures from both the domestic and international fronts, while failing states such as those found in Africa and the Caucasus are present in form only but not in function and has been failing in maintaining effective governance (Pierre & Peters, 2006).

This will bring us to the following important questions: What are the reasons for these variations in governing capacity of different states? More precisely, what are the "enabling conditions" that facilitate the building up of an effective state with stronger capacity to govern, and what are the factors that result in the development of a failing state with weaker capacity to govern? Over the past few decades, political scientists in Western academia have produced an extensive literature to account for interactions between the state and socio-economic actors in the governing process. In the forthcoming sections we will revisit these major theoretical approaches to state capacity with a view to establishing our own *integrated conceptual framework*.

State capacity as political autonomy

> How can we account for the authoritative actions of the democratic state, its public policies broadly conceived? To what extent is the democratic state an autonomous entity, one that translates its own policy preferences into authoritative actions.... My answers are decidedly state centered: the preferences of the state are at least as important as those of civil society in accounting for what the democratic state does and does not do; the democratic state is not only frequently autonomous insofar as it regularly acts upon its preferences, but also markedly autonomous in doing so even when its preferences diverge from the demands of the most powerful groups in civil society.
>
> (Nordlinger, 1981, p. 1)

In the discussion of the role of the state in governing and public policy-making, the orthodox notion of "political autonomy" is commonly adopted by political scientists as the principal enabling condition for building up the capacity of the state to govern. To put it simply, political autonomy can be broadly defined as the ability of the state to resist pressures from powerful actors within its external environment. Such insulation from external pressure is considered by state theorists as the institutional prerequisite for the smooth execution of public policies and appropriate balancing of different interests within society. From this perspective, political autonomy is the important characteristic and trademark of a strong and effective state and the degree of autonomy of the state from external pressure will be a useful indicator for assessing the relative strength of state capacity (Pierre & Peters, 2000, p. 98).

In this connection, it is worth noting that the concept of political autonomy has a long history in political study and it can be traced back to the Marxist theories of "relative autonomy" of the modern capitalist states. Nevertheless, modern governance studies challenged this orthodox notion of political autonomy, and it was increasingly accepted by many political scientists that the capacity of the state to govern and make public policies not only hinges on its political autonomy from external pressure, but also on its ability to forge coalitions with different socio-economic actors. Such a theoretical concept has been gradually developed and expanded into more sophisticated theoretical approaches to state capacity, to be discussed in the later part of this chapter.

56 *Governance under hybrid regimes*

Marxist theories of relative autonomy of the state

Before discussing the Marxist theories of relative autonomy of the state, we first have to understand the nature and the role of the state in Marxism. In the eyes of Marxists, the capitalist mode of production determines the nature of the political system in modern industrialized societies, and therefore the state is an essential means of class domination and the repressive arm of the bourgeoisie (Carnoy, 1984, pp. 46–50).

In this connection, British political theorist Ralph Miliband (1969, p. 5), who followed the footsteps of Karl Marx in class analysis and developed a modern Marxist theory, highlighted that in capitalist societies the political power is exercised by the economic dominant class and the state is no more than a committee for managing the common affairs of the whole bourgeois. For Miliband, there are three reasons why the state should be considered as an instrument of the economic dominant class (Miliband, 1977, pp. 68–72). First and foremost, there is a common social background and origin between the bourgeois and the state elites (i.e. persons occupying commanding positions in the executive, legislative and judicial branches). This creates "a cluster of common ideological and political positions, common values and perspectives" and they constitute a narrow conservative spectrum in society. Second, the bourgeois functions as a major pressure group in capitalist societies and exerts strong influence over the governing process by virtue of its ownership and control over the economic and other resources. Third, the nature and requirements of capitalist means of production serves as "structural constraints" on the nature of state power and modern governments cannot ignore the interests of the bourgeois. For this reason, "bourgeois democracy" can be considered as a system in which the economic dominant class maintains their rule through democratic means, rather than by way of dictatorship (Miliband, 1969, p. 16).

While taking the view that in advanced capitalist countries public policies usually reflect the interests of the economic dominant class and the need to maintain the private enterprise system has been at the heart of the decision-making process of governments, Marxist theorists consider that capitalist states still enjoy a certain degree of autonomy and independence in the manner of their operation as a class state. This degree of freedom enjoyed by state institutions from the ruling economic class and from civil society at large is known as "relative autonomy" of the state (Miliband, 1977, p. 74).

How can the capitalist states enjoy a certain degree of political autonomy from the ruling bourgeois? Miliband (1977, pp. 83–89) observed that the modern state is not simply an "instrument" of the ruling class but an "agent" that is assigned by the bourgeoisie to manage the collective affairs of society. As a result, the state (in this context mainly referring to the executive power) as a political agent has enjoyed an "area of political manoeuvre" by which people in charge of state power can exercise a certain degree of autonomy in determining how best to serve the existing capitalist order and the interests of the ruling class. Miliband argued that such a relative autonomy of the state does not in any sense

Governance and the state 57

reduce its class character, because even when the state concedes or even goes against the immediate interests and demands of the economically and socially privileged class on certain occasions, the actions taken by the state are actually not contrary to the capitalist order but are usually designed to maintain the long-term sustainability of capitalism. In this connection, the theory of state autonomy highlighted that the state is far from an instrument of the bourgeoisie, but rather its actions are framed by the conditions of class struggle and the broader structure of a class society (Carnoy, 1984, p. 55).

The autonomy of democratic state in public policy making

The Marxist theories of relative autonomy of the state have subsequently been fashioned by some political scientists as an important theoretical approach to understanding the capacity of modern states in policy-making and implementation. One of the major contributors in this area is Eric A. Nordlinger.

In his book *On the Autonomy of the Democratic State*, Nordlinger pointed out that policy-making and implementation in modern democratic regimes should not be simply regarded as a response to the expectations and demands of those socio-economic actors, because the preferences of the state are also of great importance in accounting for what the democratic states does and does not do. Stressing a state-centred perspective rather than a society-centred perspective to understanding governance, Nordlinger elaborated two levels of political autonomy of democratic states: in the first is the ability of the states to translate its own policy preferences into authoritative actions; while the second level of autonomy is its ability to act upon its preferences when they are diverging from the demands and interests of the most powerful actors in society (Nordlinger, 1981, pp. 1–3). For Nordlinger, a strong state is conceived as an autonomous state by which the preferences of the state usually coincide with its actions, and also the state is able to overcome the demands and opposition of those influential socio-economic actors (Nordlinger, 1981, pp. 20–22).

Theda Skocpol, another important state theorist, also highlighted political autonomy as an indicator of the state's strength and similarly defined state capacity as the ability of the states to "implement official goals, especially over the actual or potential opposition of powerful social groups". Further, Skocpol observed that organizationally coherent collectivities of state officials, which are relatively insulated from ties with the external environment, are the foundation of autonomous state actions because they allow the state officials to pursue transformative strategies and projects even in the face of resistance from powerful socio-economic forces (Skocpol, 1985).

The notion of political autonomy is of great importance to the study of the role of the state in modern governance. Only when we could establish that the state may formulate and pursue goals that are not simply reflective of the demands and expectations of the economic and social groups in society, does the discussion of the role of the state in governance and policy-making become relevant and make sense (Skocpol, 1985). However, the concept of political

58 Governance under hybrid regimes

autonomy is not without its critics because it portrays the relationship between the state and society as a zero-sum game and assumes that either the state or society could only exercise its political influence at the expense of the other side. Such a perspective has clearly over-simplified the complexity of the contemporary policy-making process and ignored the fact that the state and society could also work in positive sum to increase each other's power in the development of public policies. In reality, it is almost impossible that state officials could, as described by Nordlinger and Skocpol, develop policies in complete isolation from powerful socio-economic actors and then impose the policies on society (Smith, 1993, pp. 54, 227). The remaining question is therefore how to achieve state autonomy, on the one hand, while promoting collaboration between the state and the socio-economic actors, on the other. This is also the major theme of Peter Evans' concept of "embedded autonomy".

State capacity as embedded autonomy

> A state that was only autonomous would lack both sources of intelligence and the ability to rely on decentralized private implementation. Dense connecting networks without a robust internal structure would leave the state incapable of resolving "collective action" problems, of transcending the individual interests of its private counterparts. Only when embeddedness and autonomy are joined together can a state be called developmental.
>
> (Evans, 1995, p. 12)

While political autonomy was considered by theorists like Nordlinger and Skocpol as the major sources of state capacity, Peter Evans went one step further by coining the notion of "embedded autonomy".

In his classical publication *Embedded Autonomy: States and Industrial Transformation*, Evans argued that embedded autonomy is the essential condition that endowed modern states with the capacity to translate their developmental goals into practice. In short, embedded autonomy referred to a set of institutions that simultaneously insulate the state from being captured by special interest groups and establish institutionalized linkages between the state and major socio-economic actors. In the eyes of Peter Evans, the effectiveness of modern developmental states depended very much on its ability to achieve two apparently contradictory missions: combined "Weberian bureaucratic insulation" (autonomy) with "intense connection to the surrounding social structure" (embeddedness) (Evans, 1995, p. 50). In the context of embedded autonomy, modern states must be sufficiently "autonomous" so that they can avoid capture by powerful interest groups, and insulated from external pressures in the formulation of collective objectives, but at the same they should also be sufficiently "embedded" in dense societal networks so as to foster institutionalized cooperation with the various stakeholders for effective implementation of development projects (Evans, 1995, p. 59).

In Peter Evans' view, embedded autonomy is the essential institutional prerequisite for sustaining constructive government–business relations in modern societies, and this was in fact the secret behind the economic success of East Asian newly industrializing countries (NICs) like Japan, Singapore, South Korea and Taiwan (Evans, 1998). Evans argued that these countries have put in place two important institutional infrastructures that allowed them to achieve the notion of embedded autonomy in pursuit of their economic development projects, namely a highly capable and coherent public bureaucracy and a close and dense policy network with the business sector. In terms of public bureaucracy, by establishing a system of meritocratic recruitment and a career structure that kept rewards in the public and private sectors broadly commensurate with each other, these East Asian NICs have all successfully maintained efficient and closely organized bureaucratic systems, which more closely approximate the ideal typical "Weberian bureaucracy", particularly when compared with developing countries in many other regions. Such a competent and coherent bureaucratic structure definitely gave the East Asian states a certain kind of political autonomy on the formulation of collective objectives and development projects. On the other hand, the East Asian NICs also immersed themselves in a close and dense policy network with the business sector by building up "pilot agencies" to coordinate government–business cooperation and negotiation over various economic development projects. These pilot agencies, such as the Ministry of International Trade and Industry (MITI) in Japan, the Council on Economic Planning and Development in Taiwan and the Economic Planning Boards in South Korea and Singapore, had put in place networks of efficient and effective "deliberation councils" for government officials and private entrepreneurs to coordinate, negotiate and exchange views on different policy initiatives. Through these institutionalized channels of negotiation, the East Asian NICs have successfully forged closer government–business collaboration over their economic development plans.

The concept of embedded autonomy was a major breakthrough in the study of state capacity and the role of the state in modern governance, because it highlighted that the power and efficacy of the state in making authoritative collective decisions is not only hinged on its ability to pursue and act upon its own preferences independent of external pressures (autonomy), as claimed by the orthodox theories of political autonomy, but also its ability to develop effective institutionalized connectedness with socio-economic actors in the society (embeddedness). This certainly opened up a new theoretical perspective to understanding the sources of state capacity and thereby paved the way for the development of more innovative concepts of "governed interdependence" and "state–society synergy".

State capacity as governed interdependence

Governed interdependence (GI) ... describes a system of central coordination based on the cooperation of government and industry.... Because of insulated policy-making, the government's transformative project does not lose out to clientelistic or sectional interests; because of institutional connectedness, business does not lose out to remote and bumbling bureaucrats.

(Weiss, 1998, p. 39)

60   Governance under hybrid regimes

The concept of "governed interdependence" was coined by Australian political scientist Linda Weiss in her comparative political studies *The Myth of the Powerless State: Governing the Economy in a Global Era*. Building upon Peter Evans' notion of embedded autonomy, Weiss came up with the concept of "governed interdependence" and put it in the context of globalized economic competition. Weiss' theory is firmly based on her challenges to the claims of state powerlessness that have been put forward by globalization theorists. Weiss argued that domestic states continue to play a vital role in national economic management, particularly in terms of industrial transformation, and thus state capacity has become an important comparative advantage in international competition in today's world economy. In this context Weiss narrowly defined state capacity as transformative capacity, namely the ability of the state to coordinate domestic economic adjustments in collaboration with organized economic groups (Weiss, 1998, pp. 5–8).

According to Linda Weiss, whether or not a domestic state can be equipped with such a transformative capacity depended on its ability to achieve the notion of "governed interdependence", which has been defined by her as a negotiated relationship through which both the state and the business sector maintained their autonomy, but worked in positive sum in pursuit of the economic development projects. For Linda Weiss, such collaboration between the government and the business sector is exercised through a robust organizational infrastructure nurtured and broadly set by the state agencies, in which the state takes a proactive role in drawing the business sector into an institutionalized negotiating relationship. Similar to the notion of embedded autonomy, governed interdependence began from the position of the institutional insulation of the state, which serves to ensure that government–business cooperation will not be degenerated into clientelism. Weiss observed that the existence of highly efficient bureaucracy and insulated "pilot agencies" (which are charged with the responsibility of coordinating economic change) are important conditions that contribute to the autonomy of the state (Weiss, 1998, p. 50). It will then be followed by embedding the autonomy of the state into "forums of negotiations" under which the state develops its economic transformative projects through regular and extensive consultation with the private sector. Weiss particularly pointed out that such institutionalized public–private cooperation will be facilitated by the existence of highly centralized and encompassing intermediaries (e.g. strong industry associations), under which they act as "interlocutors" facilitating cooperative coordination between the state and the business sector (Weiss, 1998, pp. 55–64). Linda Weiss argued that all these conditions will help develop systems of governed interdependence, so that the state could on the one hand achieve insulated policy-making and prevent a government's projects from losing out to clientelistic interests, while on the other hand stimulating institutional connectedness with the private sector so that the state received the information and cooperation it needs from the business sector to transform its economy and industries (Weiss, 1998, pp. 38–39).

Weiss substantiated her theory of governed interdependence by making reference to the development experiences of some East Asian and European countries. She pointed out that Japan and Taiwan have successfully used their insulation from special interest groups to develop encompassing policy networks with the business sector, and such capacities allowed the two countries to make coordinated responses to the changing international economy and to hold up well during the Asian Financial Crisis of 1997 (Weiss, 1998, p. 81). Germany, as argued by Weiss, provided another story of how state-sponsored public–private cooperation brought about governed interdependence and endowed the country with considerable transformative capacity. The German form of governed interdependence was achieved through the networks of deliberation committees and complex consultation processes by which senior civil servants extensively consulted the key economic groups like industry and trade associations at the drafting stage of the development projects, long before the proposals were submitted to Parliament. This enhanced the transformative capacity of the German state and boosted the promotion of new industries and technologies in the country in the past few decades (Weiss, 1998, pp. 144–150). On the contrary, Weiss observed that despite its strong business sector and a handful of highly successful international corporations, Sweden's lack of institutionalized public–private coordination and the under-embeddedness of its state machinery have slowed down the adaptive responses of its economy to the increasingly globalized environment, resulting in the weakening transformative capacity of the Swedish state and the decline of the country's economic growth rate in the 1970s and 1980s (Weiss, 1998, pp. 108–110). In view of the above, Linda Weiss argued that a convergence on neoliberalism and the American market-based ideals is not occurring as predicted by many globalization theorists, and indeed the experiences of countries like Japan, Taiwan, Singapore and Germany indicated that states are increasingly acting as catalysts seeking adaptation to various new challenges and external pressures by establishing stronger partnership with non-state actors. The emergence of "catalytic states", as argued by Weiss, suggested that building state capacity rather than discarding it has acquired new significance as we move into the twenty-first century (Weiss, 1998, pp. 188–212).

Weiss' theory of governed interdependence took one step further in the development of more sophisticated understanding of state capacity. The notion of governed interdependence not only expanded and enriched Evans' concept of embedded autonomy, it also shed new light on the role of modern states in economic transformation, particularly in the increasingly globalized environment. After all, Weiss' theory once again demonstrated that states continue to matter in steering policy changes, and the study of state capacity is necessary for us to understand the various economic and social changes in contemporary societies.

State capacity as state–society synergy

"State–society synergy" can be a catalyst for development. Norms of cooperation and networks of civic engagement among ordinary citizens can

62 *Governance under hybrid regimes*

be promoted by public agencies and used for developmental ends. Figuring out how such public–private cooperation might flourish more widely should be a priority for those interested in development.

(Evans, 1997b)

Theoretically speaking, although both Evans' concept of embedded autonomy and Weiss' theory of governed interdependence similarly pointed out that the building of state capacity has very much hinged on the productive interactions between the state and the major socio-economic constituents, their analysis primarily focused on exploring what sort of institutionalized arrangements would be essential to fostering public–private cooperation and collaboration over economic development projects. The interaction between the state and civil society at large, and its implication for state capacity, were basically left untouched in these two theoretical approaches. Such a theoretical gap was subsequently filled by political sociologist Peter Evans in another innovative work, *Government Action, Social Capital, and Development: Reviewing the Evidence on Synergy* (Evans, 1997b).

According to Evans there were two major intellectual movements concerning the conceptualization of human development in recent decades, including the theories of social capital and the revisionist perspectives on the role of state. The former approach defined social trust, social norms and community networks as "social capital" and considered all these conditions valuable assets for promoting human development, while the latter approach challenged the "market as magic bullet" model and reintroduced the state as a central actor in steering economic and social development. Evans observed that these two intellectual movements were not very well integrated, and indeed some theorists even portrayed "zero-sum relations" between these two theoretical approaches: state theorists usually had little discussion on the importance of social capital in furthering development projects, while many theorists of social capital considered that the expansion of state intervention would encroach the civil society and finally diminish social capital. In this connection, Evans tried to reconcile these two intellectual trends by coining the concept of "state–society synergy". For Evans, the idea of "state–society synergy" implied that civic engagement in the development process could strengthen state institutions and facilitate the formulation and implementation of various public projects, while effective state institutions could also create an environment that nurtures and promotes norms of social trust as well as networks of civic engagement (Evans, 1997a).

In the discussion of state–society synergy, Evans first clarified the meaning of "synergy" by distinguishing between the two concepts of "complementarity" and "embeddedness" (Evans, 1997b). For Evans, these two concepts implied different forms of synergy and theories of relations between public and private institutions. Synergy based on "complementarity" referred to the "conventional way of conceptualizing mutually supportive relations between public and private actors", which suggested a clear division of work between the state and non-state actors and a distinct public–private divide. The rationale behind the notion of

Governance and the state   63

"complementarity" was that on certain occasions the private sector was suited to complement the public sector by delivering certain kinds of public projects, but the civil society was easily threatened if government agencies become too intimately involved in community affairs. On the other hand, "embeddedness" suggested a new form of state–society networks that trespassed the boundary between the public and private sectors and effectively bound the state and civil society together in the development of public projects. From this perspective, state–society synergy is generated and based on concrete ties that effectively linked mobilized citizens to government agencies, thereby making it possible for the state to exploit various social capitals such as local knowledge and experience and community networks in the development of public projects (Evans, 1997b).

Evans cited a number of case studies to illustrate how synergy based on "embeddedness" represented a new form of collaboration between the state and civil society, and Taiwan's effective irrigation system was considered as one of the most typical examples (Evans, 1997b). In Taiwan, local officials and local farmers were closely connected in the development and management of irrigation facilities. On the one hand, local officials relied on the support of local farmers in allocating water to the fields, carrying out local operations and maintenance, providing voluntary labour and monetary "chip-in". On the other hand, local farmers depended on local officials who played an important role in integrating their local demands into the overall development plan for irrigation facilities. This network of trust and collaboration tightly connected the local government agencies and the local farmers so they could work closely to achieve a common objective.

In Evans' view, pre-existing endowments of social capital are valuable resources but not the precondition for state–society synergy. Rather, the key to achieve the notion of state–society synergy was to put in place a "competent and engaged set of public institutions" so as to "scale up" existing social capital for effective formulation and implementation of development projects. Evans argued that while endowments of social capital seemed to be "a resource that is at least latently available to most Third World communities", governments around the world varied dramatically in terms of their ability to create effective public organizations to engage civil society groups, and this was the fundamental factor that determined the potential for state–society synergy. From this perspective, state–society synergy was seen as "constructable" even in class-divided and disorganized societies, provided that the governments could devise an innovative organizational structure to foster connectedness between the state and the civil society (Evans, 1997b).

Evans' theory of state–society synergy represented another important contribution to the study of state capacity. It convincingly established that apart from the business sector and corporations, the civil society and organized social groups are also potential partners of the state in the modern governance processes. This implied that in the discussion of the capacity of modern states to steer policy-making and implementation, we should not only focus on state–business relations, but should also put equal emphasis on state–society relations.

State capacity as forging coalitions

> Governance implies, slightly paradoxically perhaps, softer and more subtle means of steering society, not least of all networks and coordinated mobilization of resources. States may maintain some of their former powers to impose their will, but supplement those with newer forms of governing. Institutional strength, in this view, is more a matter of entrepreneurial and networking skills than the exercise of regulatory or any other traditional governmental capability ... governance means forging coalitions with such actors.
>
> (Pierre & Peters, 2000, pp. 98–99)

The above theories of Peter Evans and Linda Weiss shared the common perspective that the capacity of modern states to steer public developmental projects depends on its collaboration and negotiation with those major socio-economic actors. Such a notion was further expanded by Jon Pierre and Guy B. Peters in their seminal work *Governance, Politics and the State*. Against the backdrop of contemporary governance literature, Pierre and Peters highlighted the importance of forging coalitions with external actors as a means of developing and mustering state capacity for governance (Pierre & Peters, 2000).

The concept of "coalition" and its implications for the exercise of governmental power are not something new in political studies. A coalition can be defined as the collection of groups and people which is constructed by ruling elites for the purpose of eliciting the necessary political support for its governance (Slater, 2010, p. 15). From this perspective, the strategic importance of coalition in the process of governance is that it is an important means of providing the state with a strong political support base for vanquishing its opponents and consolidating its rule. Some political scientists argued that coalition building is essential to the survival of all political leaders no matter whether they are in authoritarian regimes or democratic systems, because only by gaining the solid support from those who control "instruments of power" could political leaders remain in office and fend off their challengers. In authoritarian regimes the size of the coalition is usually smaller and limited to a few influential political elites (e.g. nobility in monarchical regimes and party officials in communist regimes), while under democratic systems the coalition is relatively larger in size and political leaders need to secure the support of the majority of the electorate through popular elections and party politics (Bueno de Mesquita, Smith, Siverson, & Morrow, 2003, pp. 49–55). While the notion of forging coalitions recognizes the profound influences of powerful societal actors in politics and governance, it does not mean that the autonomous role of the state will be overshadowed. In fact, many empirical studies indicate that it is always the state elites, not the external socio-economic constituents, who take the initiative in constructing coalitions by making deals and side-payments with those influential stakeholders (Waldner, 1999, pp. 4, 35).

In this connection Pierre and Peters conceptualized the notion of "forging coalition" (Pierre & Peters, 2000). Similar to Weiss and Evans, Pierre and Peters

Governance and the state 65

recognized that the capacity of modern states to steer developmental projects depends very much on its networking and coordination with external parties. By the same token, Pierre and Peters argued that the capacity of the modern state to govern and make public policies is not measured by its power to impose its will on the society as highlighted by the notion of political autonomy, but the strength of the state is more a matter of building coalitions across a wide range of interests: strong states in modern societies are defined as political entities which successfully forge coalitions with major socio-economic constituents in the external environment, because the development of a "corporatist model of policy-making" will help institutionalize the coalitions between the state and the influential external actors and thus "ensure broad societal acceptance for policies" (Pierre & Peters, 2000, pp. 98–99). Such a notion of governing coalition building is based upon the contention that in modern pluralistic and divided societies (where there are different and competing political institutions and organizations like legislature, political parties, interest groups, different government departments, central, local and regional governments), the state could only command broad acceptance for its policy initiatives by forming coalitions with the key societal actors (Peters, 1995).

Following the theories of Linda Weiss and Peter Evans, while Pierre and Peters emphasized that some forms of institutionalized negotiation and interest representation should be established to incorporate the major socio-economic constituents into the governance process, they also stressed that when building governing coalitions it is equally important for the state to maintain significant "power leverages" over those societal actors, so that where necessary it could exercise its regulatory and sanctioning powers to ensure societal compliance with its policies. In other word, the holding of power leverages and sanctioning powers by the state will make sure that building coalitions with powerful socio-economic actors will not impair its role in pursuing and defending collective interests (Pierre & Peters, 2000, p. 100). To sum up the arguments of Pierre and Peters, it is clear that the effective operation of governing coalitions in democratic contexts requires both the notions of "state autonomy" and "state embeddedness".

An integrated conceptual framework: state capacity as governing coalition building

The review of literature in the preceding paragraphs outlined the various major theoretical approaches to the study of governance and state capacity. These theoretical notions, including "political autonomy", "embedded autonomy", "governed interdependence", "state–society synergy" and "forging coalition", examined the nature of modern governance and state capacity from different perspectives and suggested different enabling conditions that endowed the state with the capacity to govern and steer public policy-making. The main arguments of these theoretical approaches are summarized in Table 2.1.

Although the above theoretical approaches represent different angles of emphasis in the discussion of state capacity, they follow and share similar lines

Table 2.1 Theoretical approaches to state capacity

Theoretical approach	Nature of state capacity	Enabling conditions for state capacity
Political autonomy	The capacity of the state rests on its ability to act upon its own preferences independent of external pressures.	• Insulation from external interest groups is the foundation of autonomous state actions. • It is implied that the state should make policies in complete isolation from powerful external actors.
Embedded autonomy	The capacity of the state depends on its ability to combine autonomy with embeddedness.	The capable and coherent bureaucracy facilitates insulated policy-making (autonomy), while the close and dense policy network promotes collaboration between the state and socio-economic actors (embeddedness).
Governed interdependence	The capacity of the state hinges on its ability to forge a negotiated relationship through which both the state and the business sector maintained their autonomy but worked in positive sum.	The "system of insulated policy-making" ensures that government–business cooperation will not degenerate into clientelism, while existence of "forums of negotiations" between the government and business sectors and "highly centralized and encompassing intermediaries" facilitate regular and extensive consultation with the private sector.
State–society synergy	The capacity of the state rests on its ability to facilitate civic engagement in the development process.	Whether the state could put in place an engaged set of institutions for scaling up existing social capital is the fundamental factor that determines the potential for state–society synergy in the development of public projects.
Forging coalitions	The capacity of the state is determined by its ability to forge coalitions with major socio-economic actors.	The development of a "corporatist model of policy-making" will help institutionalize the coalitions between the state and the influential external actors and ensure broad acceptance for its policies, while the maintenance of "power leverages" by the state will allow it to exercise its regulatory and sanctioning powers to maintain its autonomy in pursuing collective interests.

Governance and the state   67

of reasoning on several important aspects. First and foremost, all these theories (except for the theory of "political autonomy") stress that the power of the state in making and implementing authoritative decisions depends very much on the notion of "state embeddedness". Theories of "embedded autonomy", "governed interdependence" and "state–society synergy" all highlight that while the ability of the state to pursue and act upon its own preferences independent of external pressures is the precondition for state capacity, the efficacy of state actions also rests on its embeddedness and connectedness with the major socio-economic actors. For Evans and Weiss, building institutionalized channels of negotiations that encompass both the state and major socio-economic actors is the political foundation that allows the state to immerse itself in the wider society and to muster the capacity to steer policy changes. Weiss adds that the cooperative coordination between the state and the co-opted socio-economic actors is enhanced with the existence of highly centralized and "encompassing intermediaries" like strong industry associations to perform the role of interlocutors. Pierre and Peters further point out that the state can secure broad social acceptance for its policies by forging coalitions with major socio-economic actors.

Second, all these theoretical approaches attach great importance to the notion of "state autonomy" and consider it a precondition for the state to exercise its capacity to make and implement authoritative collective decisions. The significance of state autonomy lays in ensuring that the state can exercise a high degree of relative autonomy when determining how best to pursue collective interests for society. Without the foundation of state autonomy, public policies made by the state could easily be degenerated into clientelism, and would be dominated by the particular interests of the powerful external actors. Conversely, when the state successfully maintains a high degree of relative autonomy from its powerful coalition partners, it will be able to resist undue demands from those powerful interest groups and pursue public policies broader than interests of any particular group. Here, theorists like Skocpol and Evans consider the existence of a strong and organizationally coherent bureaucratic system as the enabling condition for state autonomy, while Pierre and Peters add that the maintenance of power leverages by the state is necessary to maintain its transcendence over different interests.

On the basis of the above theories of state capacity, this book has conceptualized an integrated theoretical framework for interpreting and examining the governing capacity of modern states. The essence of this *integrated conceptual framework* is that the different notions of "state embeddedness", "state autonomy" and "governing coalition building" are strategically linked and correlated when accounting for governance and state capacity: effective governing coalition building is the principal means of providing the state with a strong political support base for consolidating its governing capacity, while the notions of state autonomy and state embeddedness are the two necessary foundations that facilitate the state to elicit the cooperation from those major socio-economic constituents in the process of governing coalition building. Such an integrated theoretical approach to governance and state capacity, which can be described as "state

68 *Governance under hybrid regimes*

capacity as governing coalition building", can be summarized as the following theoretical propositions:

- *State embeddedness.* The existence of institutionalized negotiation mechanisms and encompassing intermediaries will enable the state to embed itself with the major socio-economic constituents in the decision-making process, thereby maintaining effective coordination of different interest groups and establishing a solid and extensive political support base for the policy initiatives of the state.
- *State autonomy.* The holding of significant power leverages by the state will enable it to maintain a high degree of relative autonomy vis-à-vis its powerful coalition partners in the decision-making process, thus strengthening the capacity of the state to resist the undue demands from the vested interests and reconcile different interests in the society.
- *Governing coalition building.* On the basis of state autonomy and state embeddedness, the state could engineer a cohesive and viable governing coalition for maintaining effective governance. On the foundation of state embeddedness, the state could embed itself with the major socio-economic constituents and mobilize the required societal support for delivering policy changes. On the foundation of state autonomy, the state could develop a considerable degree of relative autonomy to resist the undue demands from its coalition partners and formulate policies that serve the broader collective interest. Such a governing coalition will then function as an organizing machinery for the state to balance, negotiate and reconcile the different societal interests and provide it with a stable and solid political support base for maintaining governance.

In order to engineer a viable governing coalition for maintaining effective governance, it is therefore necessary for the modern state to simultaneously engage in institutionalized negotiation with major socio-economic actors (state embeddedness) while maintaining its relative autonomy from these co-opted interest groups (state autonomy). In this connection, it is worth noting that it is never easy to locate the optimal level of "state embeddedness" and "state autonomy", and in reality there is no such thing as a "fully embedded state" or "fully autonomous state". Nevertheless, the concepts of "state embeddedness" and "state autonomy" are still important and empirically testable, because through an in-depth and comprehensive analysis of the dynamics of governing coalition building, we could judge whether a state has embedded itself with major socioeconomic actors and whether it could maintain its relative autonomy vis-à-vis its coalition partners. In other words, while it is not easy to clearly state the optimal level of "state embeddedness" and "state autonomy", we could identify how and when they are not optimal through empirical research.

Conclusion

By reviewing the literature of governance and state, in this chapter we have defined state capacity as "the capacity of the state to govern", i.e. the capacity of the state to make authoritative collective decisions by managing its interactions with socio-economic actors. Drawing upon the various theories of state capacity – namely "political autonomy", "embedded autonomy", "governed interdependence", "state–society synergy" and "forging coalitions" – this research has come up with an integrated approach which can be termed as "state capacity as governing coalition building". On the basis of state embeddedness and state autonomy, the state should be able to elicit support from the major socio-economic actors and engineer a stable and broad-based governing coalition for maintaining effective governance.

The theoretical discussions in this chapter and the development of the above *integrated conceptual framework* on state capacity will provide a solid foundation for the further analysis in this book. By providing a nuanced analysis of governing coalition building in accounting for modern governance and public policy-making, this *integrated conceptual framework* will enable us to go beyond the opposition-centred explanation of the existing local literature on Hong Kong's governance crisis, which is mainly based on the notion of legitimacy deficit and theories of democratic transition. It will therefore provide a new direction for us to examine the changing governance in Hong Kong from colonial times to the post-1997 period and offer an important alternative theoretical perspective to interpreting the governance problems in the territory after 1997 in the forthcoming chapters.

Note

1 The origin of the term "governance" can be traced back to the Greek verb "Kubernan", which subsequently evolved to the medieval Latin "Gubernare", both meaning piloting, steering and rule-making. From this perspective, the notion of state in steering society is central to the theories of governance (Kjær, 2004).

References

Almond, G. A., & Powell, G. B. (1966). *Comparative politics: A developmental approach*. Boston, MA: Little, Brown.

Bueno de Mesquita, B., Smith, A., Siverson, R. M., & Morrow, J. D. (2003). *The logic of political survival*. Cambridge, MA: MIT Press.

Carnoy, M. (1984). *The state and political theory*. Princeton, NJ: Princeton University Press.

Cheung, A. (2009). A response to "building administrative capacity for the age of rapid globalization: A modest prescription for the twenty-first century. *Public Administration Review, 69*(6), 1034–1036.

Evans, P. B. (1995). *Embedded autonomy: States and industrial transformation*. Princeton, NJ: Princeton University Press.

Evans, P. B. (1997a). Introduction: Development strategies across the public–private divide. In P. Evans (Ed.), *State–society synergy: Government and social capital in development* (pp. 1–10). Berkeley, CA: University of California at Berkeley.

70 Governance under hybrid regimes

Evans, P. B. (1997b). Government action, social capital, and development: Reviewing the evidence on synergy. In P. Evans (Ed.), *State–society synergy: Government and social capital in development* (pp. 178–209). Berkeley, CA: University of California at Berkeley.

Evans, P. B. (1998). Transferable lessons? Re-examining the institutional prerequisites of East Asian economic policies. *Journal of Development Studies, 34*(6), 66–86.

Heywood, A. (2000). *Key concepts in politics.* New York: St. Martin's Press.

Kjær, A. M. (2004). *Governance.* Malden, MA: Polity Press.

Kooiman, J. (1993). Governance and governability: Using complexity, dynamics and diversity. In J. Kooiman (Ed.), *Modern governance: New government–society interactions* (pp. 35–48). London: Sage.

Kooiman, J. (2003). *Governing as governance.* London: Sage.

Mann, M. (1993). *The sources of social power: The rise of classes and nation-states, 1760–1914.* Cambridge: Cambridge University Press.

Miliband, R. (1969). *The state in capitalist society.* New York: Basic Books.

Miliband, R. (1977). *Marxism and politics.* Oxford: Oxford University Press.

Nordlinger, E. A. (1981). *On the autonomy of the democratic state.* Cambridge, MA: Harvard University Press.

Painter, M., & Pierre, J. (Eds.). (2005). *Challenges to state policy capacity: Global trends and comparative perspective.* New York: Palgrave Macmillan.

Peters, B. G. (1995). Introducing the topic. In B. G. Peters, & D. J. Savoie (Eds.), *Governance in a changing environment* (pp. 3–22). Buffalo: McGill-Queen's University Press.

Pierre, J., & Peters, G. (2000). *Governance, politics and the state.* New York: St. Martin's Press.

Pierre, J., & Peters, G. (2005). *Governing complex societies: Trajectories and scenarios.* New York: Palgrave Macmillan.

Pierre, J., & Peters, G. (2006). Governance, government and the state. In C. Hay, M. Lister, & D. Marsh (Eds.), *The state: Theories and issues* (pp. 209–222). Oxford: Oxford University Press.

Polidano, C. (2000). Measuring public sector capacity. *World Development, 28*(5), 805–822.

Skocpol, T. (1985). Bringing the state back in: Strategies of analysis in current research. In P. B. Evans, D. Rueschemeyer, & T. Skocpol (Eds.), *Bringing the state back in* (pp. 3–37). Cambridge: Cambridge University Press.

Slater, D (2010). *Ordering power: Contentious politics and authoritarian leviathans in Southeast Asia.* Cambridge: Cambridge University Press.

Smith, M. J. (1993). *Pressure, power and policy: State autonomy and policy networks in Britain and the United States.* New York: Harvester Wheatsheaf.

Sørensen, G. (2006). The transformation of the state. In C. Hay, M. Lister, & D. Marsh (Eds.), *The State: Theories and issues* (pp. 190–208). Oxford: Oxford University Press.

Stoker, G. (1998). Governance as theory: Five propositions. *International Social Science Journal, 50*(155), 17–28.

Waldner, D. (1999). *State building and late development.* Ithaca, NY: Cornell University Press.

Weber, M. (1947). *The theory of social and economic organization.* New York: Free Press.

Weiss, L. (1998). *The myth of the powerless state: Governing the economy in a global era.* Cambridge: Polity Press.

Part II

The legacy of state–business alliance

From the colonial time to the transitional period

3 Reinterpreting governance and state capacity in colonial time
The colonial state–business alliance

According to the integrated approach to state capacity we postulated in the preceding chapter, effective governing coalition building is the principal means of providing the state with a solid political support base for consolidating its governance capacity, while the notions of state autonomy and state embeddedness are the necessary enabling conditions for the effective operation of such a governing coalition. In this connection, local political science literature indicated that colonial Hong Kong was ruled by a governing coalition between the British colonial administration and the business sector, and the existence of such a state–business alliance was the foundation of effective governance during the colonial period.

Before we go on to discuss Hong Kong's governance crisis after 1997, in this chapter we first review the governance and state capacity in colonial Hong Kong. In the first place, we will briefly discuss the nature and major characteristics of the colonial state. Second, we will trace the emergence and development of Hong Kong's capitalist class in the British colonial days. Third, we will examine the dynamics of state–business relations in colonial times and also review the formation and evolution of the political alliance between the colonial state and the business sector. Last but not the least, we will review the various enabling conditions that contributed to the effective functioning of the colonial state–business alliance by drawing upon the *integrated conceptual framework* on state capacity. The discussions in this chapter will provide a good background analysis before we proceed to re-examine the governance and state capacity in post-1997 Hong Kong in the forthcoming chapters.

The nature of the colonial state: an administrative state dominated by bureaucrats

It is not easy to discover a simple formula by which Hong Kong can be described. Perhaps the best description is "administrative state".... The notion of the administrative state offers the clearest explanation of a thriving industrious community of about six million people who are "ruled" through expatriate elites and local bureaucrats. The ethos of Hong Kong is bureaucratic.

(Harris, 1988, p. 1)

74   *The legacy of state–business alliance*

Hong Kong, an overwhelmingly Chinese society and also an integral part of the Chinese territory since ancient times, became a British colony in the nineteenth century as a result of the British invasions of the Qing Empire. The Qing Empire's defeat in the Opium War in 1842 resulted in the cession of the Hong Kong Island to the British under the Treaty of Nanking. In 1860, the Kowloon Peninsula was ceded under the Convention of Peking, while the northern part of Kowloon and the surrounding island (i.e. the New Territories) were leased to Britain in 1898 for 99 years following the signing of the Convention on Extension of Hong Kong Territory.

Since becoming a colony of the British Empire, Hong Kong had been developed from a one-time fishing village into a business and trade centre. In the early twentieth century, Hong Kong had already developed into one of the most prosperous entrepots in the Far East. After the Second World War, the city-state underwent rapid industrialization and its real gross domestic product grew rapidly with an average annual rate of 8 per cent over the 30 years from 1948 to 1977 (Lau, 1982, p. 3). Under colonial rule, Hong Kong had become one of the most successful newly industrialized economies, and its economic miracle has attracted admiring glances from the rest of the world. Apart from economic success, another remarkable achievement of the British colonial administration was undoubtedly its ability to maintain political stability and effective governance throughout the colonial period. Except for the riots in 1956, 1966 and 1967, political stability had been largely maintained under colonial rule and the colonial administration's governing authority was singularly immune from serious challenges (Lau, 1982, pp. 1–23). How did the colonial state maintain effective governance during colonial times?

To get the answer, perhaps we should first re-examine the nature and major characteristics of the colonial state. In this connection, it was obvious that the most notable feature of the colonial Hong Kong state was that political power was invariably concentrated and exercised through a hierarchical bureaucratic system. In other words, the colonial state was by nature an administrative state dominated by expatriate and local bureaucrats.

Under the colonial power structure, political power was highly concentrated in the executive authority headed by the British Governor, who functioned like an absolute monarch (Miners, 1998, p. 69). In accordance with the two constitutional documents issued by the British government, namely the Letters Patent and the Royal Instructions, the Governor acted as both the head of the colonial government and the Command-in-Chief of the British military in Hong Kong. Undoubtedly, the British Governor was at the centre of the colonial power structure and had "personified the combination of executive and legislative, and civil and military powers" in Hong Kong. The Governor was the head of government, chairman of the Legislative Council and the Commander-in-Chief in Hong Kong; he also had power to appoint all of the members of the Executive Council and the Legislative Council (Cheung, 2007). Although the Letters Patent and the Royal Instructions gave the Governor almost autocratic constitutional powers, in practice the colonial civil service exercised the strongest influence over the

Reinterpreting governance and state capacity   75

whole policy-making process. The reason was that colonial Governors came and went on a regular basis and thus they depended very much on the support and advice of the civil service – a "permanent career institution" – to maintain effective governance (Cheung, 2007). As a matter of fact, colonial Governors could only put forth major initiatives and policy change with the "full co-operation and whole-hearted support of the civil service" (Miners, 1998, p. 70).

In his classical study *Hong Kong: A Study in Bureaucratic Politics*, Peter Harris described the colonial political system as an "administrative state" through which the expatriate and local bureaucrats ruled over the whole colony (Harris, 1988, p. 1). In another seminal study on colonial Hong Kong, *Society and Politics in Hong Kong*, Lau Sui-kai similarly described the colonial governmental system as a "bureaucratic polity" (Lau, 1982, p. 25). Anthony Cheung, another leading political scientist in Hong Kong, also argued that the senior administrators were not simply public servants but actually the masters of the colonial governmental system, who "governed as well as administered in the absence of accountable politics" (Cheung, 1998). After all, all these academic analyses pointed to the fact that the major political power resided in the bureaucracy and the administrative elites, mainly those senior administrative officers[1] who had established unchallenged authority in the governance of Hong Kong in the old colonial days. From the perspectives of these scholars, the operation of the colonial administrative state had two important characteristics. First of all, the bureaucrats were the dominant political players within the colonial administrative state and most of the policy decisions were made by the bureaucracy (Harris, 1988, pp. 72–73). In this connection, the administrative elites almost monopolized all functions in the polity – from policy formulation to policy implementation and from making of laws to enforcement of laws (Lau, 1982, p. 28). Second, there was neither division of power among various organs of government nor effective checks-and-balances mechanism that was capable of curbing the hegemony of the bureaucracy (Lau, 1982, p. 38). For much of the colonial period, there were neither strong political figures nor political organizations that were capable of checking the power of the bureaucracy (Harris, 1988, p. 75). Lau Sui-kai summarized the predominant position of administrative elites within the colonial state as follows:

> Formally at least, the political system of Hong Kong approximates an ideal-type version of a type of polity which is conceptualized as the "bureaucratic polity". The concept of bureaucratic polity is distinguishable from other forms of government by the degree to which national decision-making is insulated from social and political forces outside the highest elite echelons of the capital city.... Generally, the administrative bureaucracy in Hong Kong, consisting of officials directly or indirectly appointed by the British Crown, is the only significant political institution in the colony.
>
> (Lau, 1982, p. 25)

Clearly, colonial Hong Kong was ruled by a "vast and efficient Weberian type of bureaucracy" (King, 1991). From the perspective of state capacity theorists, the

76 The legacy of state–business alliance

strong and coherent bureaucracy was definitely an important foundation of the strong capacity of the colonial state, but it was far from an exhaustive answer to the existence of stable and effective governance under the British colonial rule. In accordance with the state capacity theories we discussed in the preceding chapter, it was of paramount importance to examine the relationship between the colonial state and those major socio-economic constituents in order to understand how and why the British colonial administration could successfully command respect and compliance from societal actors in the governing process. In the context of colonial Hong Kong, the British capitalists and the local Chinese capitalists were undoubtedly the two most powerful actors outside the realm of the colonial bureaucracy and they had exercised strong influences in socio-economic arenas since the founding of the colony. Tracing the evolution of the capitalist class is therefore crucial for us to understand the formation of the state–business alliance in colonial Hong Kong.

The making of the capitalist class: the emergence of British and Chinese merchants

> With the Hong Kong economy gradually developing during the nineteenth century, a capitalist class emerged.... British and European merchants were first attached to the colony by the security of the British flag.... On the Chinese side, the formation of the capitalist class initially behind its European counterpart.... By the turn of the century, the Chinese capitalists in Hong Kong had gained considerable economic power in the colony.
>
> (Chiu, 1994)

The emergence of the capitalist class in colonial Hong Kong was closely connected to its development into a major business and trade centre in the Far East during the nineteenth century. Because of its colonial background, Hong Kong's business sector comprised two different segments – the British capitalist class and the local Chinese capitalist class. Following the rapid development of Hong Kong's economy during the nineteenth century, both the British and Chinese merchants had developed and consolidated themselves into cohesive social classes (Chan, 1991).

The British capitalists: the princes of colonial Hong Kong

The British capitalist class could be considered as the first significant social class in colonial Hong Kong (Chan, 1991, p. 7). Although foreign merchants from different nationalities were all active in Hong Kong since the founding of the colony, the British businessmen were undoubtedly the dominant and most influential within the European merchant community, having regard to Hong Kong's status as a British colony. As a result, "British merchant" and "European merchant" were virtual synonyms in the colonial time (Chan, 1991, p. 9).

The business activities of British and European merchants in Hong Kong and the South China coast could be traced back to the early nineteenth century. The

Reinterpreting governance and state capacity 77

rapid industrialization of Britain in the nineteenth century had provided important driving forces for the rapid development of trade activities between the East and the West and many British merchants came to the Canton region of China to pursue their business adventures. Initially, all these British merchants conducted their trade activities in Canton under the licences of the East India Company, which monopolized Sino-British trade at that time (Chan, 1991, p. 20). Following the end of the monopoly of the East India Company in 1832, more and more "free" British and European traders came to Canton, and the number of foreign merchants rose significantly to over 213 (including 158 British merchants) in 1837 (Chan, 1991, p. 21). Many of these foreign merchants were of the view that the establishment of a colony in South China would provide a secure station for operating trade and commercial dealings in the Far East and therefore they campaigned strongly for the acquisition of the island of Hong Kong. For example, William Jardine and James Matheson, the two influential "Taipans" from the "princely hong" Jardine Matheson, were widely considered as playing an important role in the events leading up to the outbreak of the Opium War in 1842. As a consequence, the subsequent acquisition of Hong Kong by Britain after the Opium War was not only a victory for the British government, but also an important victory for British and European merchants in Canton (Chan, 1991, pp. 20–22; Crisswell, 1981, p. 4).

The establishment of the Hong Kong colony and the opening of five "treaty ports" after the Opium War had provided a secure base and important power leverages for the foreign merchants to consolidate their leading position in China coastal trade (Crisswell, 1981, p. 4). By the mid-nineteenth century there were altogether 12 major European "hongs" (merchant houses), including those famous companies like Jardine Matheson and Swire. These British and European hongs invested heavily in coastal trades by building warehouses and wharves, and later on extending their businesses into industries like shipbuilding, ship repairing, properties and lands and banking and finances (Chiu, 1994).

The growing economic power of expatriate merchants was accompanied by the development of extensive networks within the European business sector, through which the foreign merchants had cooperated with each together to promote and consolidate their interests. One of the important platforms was the establishment of the Hong Kong General Chamber of Commerce (HKGCC) in 1861. Formed by the major hongs, the HKGCC served to represent and protect the collective interests of the European business sector in Hong Kong, and Alexander Perceval from Jardine Matheson was elected as the Chamber's first chairman[2] (Chan, 1991, p. 31). In 1865, the major hongs founded the Hong Kong and Shanghai Bank (Hong Kong Bank). With more than 19 companies represented in its Board of Directors, the Hong Kong Bank not only effectively functioned as the largest commercial bank in the colony for financing business and trade-related activities, but it also became another important platform for the Taipans of various firms to get together (Chan, 1991, p. 32; Ngo, 2000). Apart from the HKGCC and the Hong Kong Bank, the formation of social clubs and associations exclusively for expatriates, such as the Hong Kong Club (established in

78 *The legacy of state–business alliance*

1846) and the Hong Kong Jockey Club (established in 1884), had further strengthened the social ties within the European business sector (Chan, 1991, pp. 35–43). Obviously, the development and existence of all these political, business and social networks had consolidated the British and European capitalists into a cohesive social class by the end of the nineteenth century (Chan, 1991, p. 17).

The local Chinese capitalists: the leaders of the Chinese community

Apart from the British and the European merchants, the local Chinese capitalists also started to emerge after the mid nineteenth century and increasingly exercised strong political and economic influence. These newly emerged local Chinese capitalists could be divided into three different types according to their origins: successful builders and contractors who were actively involved in the early development and infrastructural projects of the colony; merchants from South China who mainly engaged in coastal trade and later on moved to Hong Kong to engage in investments on real estate and lands; and finally compradors who served in the British and European hongs (Chiu, 1994). The rapid development of business and trade activities in Hong Kong after the occupation of the British imperialists had undoubtedly provided a historical opportunity for these Chinese businessmen to gradually accumulate considerable capital. By the end of the nineteenth century, the local Chinese capitalists had already caught up in terms of economic power with their British and European counterparts (Chiu, 1994).

Similar to their British and European counterparts, the Chinese merchants' expansion of economic power was accompanied by the development of different networks and platforms within the local Chinese community. The construction of the Man Mo Temple in 1847 represented the first attempt by the local Chinese capitalists to consolidate their influence and to establish themselves as leaders of the Chinese community. Since its establishment, the Man Mo Temple functioned as both a social and religious centre for the local community, where the Chinese merchants helped mediate social disputes through the management committee of the temple (Carroll, 2005, p. 60; Chan, 1991, pp. 75–76). In 1866 the Chinese merchants organized and financed the establishment of the District Watch Force, which acted as the unofficial police force for maintaining social order and managing various public affairs in the Chinese community under the supervision of the Registrar-General of the colonial state (Chan, 1991, p. 82). Another sign of the rising political and social influences of the local Chinese capitalists was the founding of the Nam Pak Hong[3] Association in 1868. The Association was not an ordinary chamber of commerce which only focused on promoting commercial interests, it was also engaged in performing various public and social functions like maintaining law and order in the neighbourhood and prevention of fires and other disasters (Chan, 1991, p. 78).

The leadership of local Chinese capitalists over the Chinese community was further strengthened when they established charitable organizations including

Reinterpreting governance and state capacity 79

the Tung Wah Hospital and the Po Leung Kuk to provide social welfare services to the Chinese population (Chan, 1991, p. 79). The opening of the Tung Wah Hospital in 1872 was particularly remarkable and symbolic because its management committee comprised the wealthiest and most influential Chinese businessmen at that time and could be claimed to present the voice of the whole Chinese community (Carroll, 2005, p. 62; Sinn, 2003, p. 4). By voluntarily providing social and charitable services to the general public through the Tung Wah Hospital and the Po Leung Kuk, the local Chinese capitalists had firmly established themselves as leaders of the Chinese community and also consolidated themselves into a formidable and cohesive social class (Chan, 1991, p. 194). The further consolidation of the Chinese capitalist class was also manifested in 1896 when the Chinese General Chamber of Commerce (CGCC) was formed to represent the collective commercial interests of the Chinese business sector (Carroll, 2005, p. 85; Chan, 1991, p. 105).

The above discussions demonstrate that the capitalist class in Hong Kong, which comprised both British and local Chinese merchants, had been firmly established in the territory by the end of the nineteenth century. Apart from controlling extensive economic resources, these two business communities[4] had also developed substantial power leverages and social influences by organizing and operating their own political, business and social platforms (such as the HKGCC and Hong Kong Bank for the British merchants, and the District Watch Force, Tung Wah Hospital and CGCC for the Chinese merchants). The emergence and consolidation of the British capitalist class and local Chinese capitalist class represented the coming of a new age of politics and governance in colonial Hong Kong.

State–business relations in colonial times: the formation and evolution of the state–business alliance

> It therefore appears that the strength of the Colonial Government rests on a tacit alliance between the British officials and the Chinese business sector. Its foundation is a very strong common self-interest in public order and the economic stability which goes with it.
>
> (Rear, 1971)

According to the state capacity theories we postulated in the preceding chapter, the existence of a viable governing coalition between the state and the major socio-economic actors in the community is the precondition for effective governance. The local capitalist class was firmly established and consolidated by the end of the nineteenth century; how to redefine and reconfigure its relationship with the rising and influential British and local Chinese capitalists had become an important governance challenge for the colonial state at the turn of the twentieth century.

It was important to note that for much of the nineteenth century the relationship between the colonial state and the capitalist class, particularly those British

80 *The legacy of state–business alliance*

and European merchants, was not really cordial and friendly, despite the fact that there was a long tradition of state–business cooperation since the founding of the colony[5] (Miners, 1996). In the eyes of the Taipans, the Hong Kong colony was primarily set up for the purposes of serving and promoting their business interests. Therefore, the expatriate merchants believed that rather than being merely subjects of the colonial state, they should have a stake in its governing and even have the responsibility of overseeing and sanctioning the colonial administration. This attitude was certainly the source of much conflict and tension between the colonial state and European business sector (Chan, 1991, pp. 25–26).

Throughout the nineteenth century, controversies surrounding the management of public finances, including taxation, government expenditure and size of the colonial bureaucracy, had been the major sources of conflicts between the colonial state and the business sector (Miners, 1996; Ngo, 2000). The reason was that those British and European merchants considered themselves as the "guardian of public purse" responsible for restraining the colonial state from "over-taxing" and "over-spending". They wanted to see a government that followed a low taxation policy and adopted stringent measures to control the growth of public expenditure, so that their tax burdens could be reduced (Chiu, 1994; Ngo, 2000). Against this backdrop, since the founding of the colony the capitalists had seriously challenged the colonial state whenever the latter tried to raise revenue to sustain its expenditure, such as waging a battle against the colonial government's attempt to introduce a poll tax on population and to levy rates on properties in 1845, opposing the introduction of stamp duty to cover British military expenditure in Hong Kong in 1864, resisting the London's imposition of charges for the military forces stationed in Hong Kong in 1890 and pressurizing the colonial state to abolish the Department of Registrar General and to reduce civil service salaries in 1892 (Chiu, 1994; Ngo, 2000; Scott, 1989).

Without doubt, when the capitalists had become more and more powerful economically by the end of the nineteenth century, they were increasingly vocal and aggressive in demanding from the colonial state a share in government power. Resolving its conflicts with the business sector and forging a more collaborative state–business alliance for maintaining effective governance had become a pressing task for the colonial state (Chiu, 1994; Scott, 1989, pp. 56–60). The most significant turning point that marked the reconfiguration of the colonial state–business relations was the political crisis that happened in 1894, in which the capitalist class seriously clashed with the colonial state over distribution of powers. In 1894 three unofficial Legislative Councillors from the business sector, including T. N. Whitehead, Paul Chater and Ho Kai, organized a petition widely signed by rate-payers to the Secretary of State requesting a constitutional reform. In their petition, the business sector claimed that the colony in Hong Kong was created by the merchants but they had only a minimal share of government power. The capitalists asked for the rights to "manage their local affairs and control the expenditure of the Colony", and they demanded that representatives of British nationality should be elected to the Legislative Council and these elected members should form the majority in the legislature (Endacott,

1964, p. 120). This petition was rejected by London because the Colonial Office considered that Hong Kong had prospered under the existing form of government, and that in the future the Crown Colony government and official majority in the Legislative Council should be maintained (Crisswell, 1981, p. 179). The Colonial Office also rejected the idea of representative government by referring to the population figures in Hong Kong: if only British nationals were eligible for election, then nine-tenths of the entire population would be excluded and an unrepresentative elected oligarchy would be created; but if a fully representative government was to be implemented, then it would bring about a Chinese majority in the Legislative Council and would effectively hand the colony over to the Chinese (Endacott, 1964, pp. 121–123).

However, both the London and Hong Kong governments recognized the need to address the political demands of the business sector and finally the colonial state chose to address this governance challenge by putting in place a more extensive consultative system for incorporating business interests into the state machinery (Scott, 1989, p. 59). This new consultative system included three major components and the essence of the whole system persisted in Hong Kong for the remaining days of colonial rule.

The first component of this consultative system was the appointment of unofficials to the Executive Council – the highest decision-making body of the colonial state. In response to the 1894 political crisis, two prominent businessmen were first appointed in 1896 and since then business representation in the Executive Council had become institutionalized and the vast majority of unofficials who sat in the Council were businessmen.[6]

Another component of the consultative system was the Legislative Council – the principal legislative body in the colony. Unofficial members in the legislature were introduced for the first time in 1850, and after the political crisis of 1894 two more businessmen (altogether six unofficial members) were appointed to the Legislative Council in 1896. Since then, business representation in the legislature had been gradually expanded, which allowed the business sector to continuously hold the majority of unofficial positions and to exercise substantial influence in the legislative process.[7]

The final component of the consultative system was the establishment of networks of advisory committees and statutory bodies, through which the business sector was widely and regularly consulted by the colonial administration on different policy areas. Starting from the late nineteenth century, more and more business representatives were appointed to the various advisory committees and government officials demonstrated greater willingness to listen to the opinions of the business sector on the formulation of public policies. All these reforms had effectively brought the British and Chinese merchants closer to the orbit of the colonial state, paving the way for the formation of a political alliance between the colonial state and the business sector (Chiu, 1994; Miners, 1996; Ngo, 2000; Scott, 1989, pp. 59–60).

To sum up, the 1894 political crisis was a major turning point of colonial Hong Kong's governance. The subsequent establishment of an institutionalized

82 *The legacy of state–business alliance*

consultative system for incorporating business interests into the state machinery had far-reaching political implications. Since the early twentieth century, the relationship between the British colonial state and the business sector had become increasingly stable, amicable and mutually supportive, contributing to the formation and smooth functioning of a more collaborative state–business alliance for the remaining days of colonial rule (Chiu, 1994).

Governing coalition building in colonial times: how did the state–business alliance contribute to the effective governance in colonial Hong Kong?

> Rule by small committees with interlocking memberships of bureaucrats and businessmen became an essential characteristic of government. Government's decisions were legitimized by the consensus reached by different elites within what had become a closed system. The bureaucracy's relative autonomy vis-à-vis economic interests remained, but those interests now had their representatives in the decision-making process.
>
> (Scott, 1989, p. 60)

Existing literature widely indicated that the effective governance under the colonial rule was contributed and underpinned by a collaborative state–business alliance (Chiu, 1994; Davies, 1989; Goodstadt, 2009; Lui & Chiu, 2007, 2009; Miners, 1996; Ngo, 2000; Rear 1971). However, what were the enabling conditions that contributed to the effective and smooth functioning of the state–business alliance in the old colonial days? How did the colonial state consolidate its governance by mobilizing the support of the business sector, on the one hand, while preserving its impartiality and transcendence over the business elites, on the other? More specifically, how did the smooth functioning of the state–business alliance contribute to the effective governance in colonial Hong Kong? All these are important questions that are related to the operation of the state–business alliance during the British colonial time, but they have not been systematically and thoroughly discussed by local political scientists in the existing literature.

The state capacity theories we discussed in the preceding chapter indicated that the three different notions of "state autonomy", "state embeddedness" and "governing coalition building" are strategically linked to the development of sufficient state capacity for maintaining effective governance: effective governing coalition building is the principal means of providing the state with a strong political support base for consolidating its governance, while the notions of state autonomy and state embeddedness are the two necessary enabling conditions that facilitate the state to elicit the cooperation from those major socio-economic constituents in the process of governing coalition building. Such a viable governing coalition will help the state to achieve two apparently contradictory political missions: it will enable the state to maintain a considerable degree of embeddedness for achieving widespread societal acceptance for its governance

Reinterpreting governance and state capacity   83

and public policies, on the one hand, while developing a considerable degree of relative autonomy to resist the undue pressures from its coalition partners on the other. In the forthcoming paragraphs, we will adopt this *integrated conceptual framework* on state capacity to re-examine the functioning of the state–business alliance in colonial Hong Kong and to discuss how this political alliance had furnished the colonial state with strong governing capacity.

The enabling conditions for state embeddedness: the existence of institutionalized negotiation mechanisms and the incorporation of encompassing intermediaries

State capacity theorists point out that the power and efficacy of modern states to govern depends on its embeddedness and connectedness with major socio-economic constituents: the existence of institutionalized negotiation mechanisms and encompassing intermediaries will effectively bind the state and societal actors together in the governance process, thereby facilitating information exchanges and development of a solid and extensive political support base for state policies (Evans, 1995, 1998; Weiss, 1998). In this regard, the British capitalists and the local Chinese capitalists were clearly the two major socio-economic forces in colonial Hong Kong. By embedding itself into dense policy networks with the British and local Chinese capitalists, the colonial state had established a stable political support base for its governance during much of the colonial period.

There were two enabling conditions that endowed the colonial state with a relatively high degree of state embeddedness. First, the advisory and consultative system functioned as the institutionalized negotiation mechanisms that bound the colonial state and British capitalists and local Chinese capitalists in the process of governing coalition building. Second, the British capitalists and the local Chinese capitalists functioned as the encompassing intermediaries that helped the colonial state to articulate and reconcile different socio-economic interests in colonial Hong Kong. These two enabling conditions facilitated the colonial state to embed itself with the major socio-economic constituents for much of the British colonial period, thereby establishing a solid societal support base for its governance and policies.

First and foremost, the advisory and consultative system, including the appointment of unofficial members in Executive Council and Legislative Council and the establishment of networks of advisory bodies, had effectively functioned as the "crucial institutional nexus" between the colonial state and the business sector (Chiu, 1994). By holding the majority of unofficial positions in the Executive Council, Legislative Council and other advisory bodies (see Table 3.1 for detailed figures), the business sector was allowed to participate in the different stages of policy process: when a new policy initiative was under consideration by the colonial administration, business elites could give their initial opinions at the relevant advisory committees; before a legislative bill was introduced into the Legislative Council, business elites could see and comment on the draft

84　*The legacy of state–business alliance*

Table 3.1 Unofficial members in the Executive Council and Legislative Council (1965–1986)

		Executive Council					Legislative Council				
		1965	1970	1975	1982	1986	1965	1970	1975	1982	1986
Business	No.	5.5	6.5	6	6	7	10	8.5	9	11	23
	%	68.8	81.3	75	66.7	87.5	76.9	65.4	60	40.7	50
Professionals	No.	2.5	1.5	2	3	1	2	2.5	4	7	10
	%	31.2	18.7	25	33.3	12.5	15.4	19.2	26.7	25.9	21.7
Caring	No.	0	0	0	0	0	0	1	2	6	11
professionals	%	0	0	0	0	0	0	7.7	13.3	22.2	23.9
Labour	No.	0	0	0	0	0	0	0	0	3	2
	%	0	0	0	0	0	0	0	0	11.1	4.3
Others	No.	0	0	0	0	0	1	1	0	0	0
	%	0	0	0	0	0	7.7	7.7	0	0	0
Total	No.	8	8	8	9	8	13	13	15	27	46
	%	100	100	100	100	100	100	100	100	100	100

Source: Adapted from Davies, 1989.

Note
In 1965 and 1970, the figures for "business" in Executive and Legislative Councils were recorded as "5.5", "6.5" and "8.5", respectively, so as to reflect those unofficial members who were both businessmen and professionals.

legislation at the Executive Council; after the bill was passed by the Legislative Council, business representatives in the advisory committees would also be involved in the drafting of subsidiary legislations for the detailed implementation of the public policies (Miners, 1996). Because business and professional elites were widely consulted in advance in the Executive Council and other advisory bodies, opposition was a rarity and government policies were usually rubber-stamped in the Legislative Council (Miners, 1996). Obviously, the dense network of advisory systems had functioned as the institutionalized negotiation mechanisms, as suggested by state capacity theorists, which effectively bound the colonial state and the business sector together in the process of governance. It had certainly helped the colonial state to secure the support and cooperation from the business elites on the formulation of public policies, therefore building a more extensive societal acceptance for its governance.

Second, the alliance between the colonial state and the business sector was not simply about incorporation of individual business elites into the advisory system, it actually featured the co-option of encompassing intermediaries, including major British business groups and prestigious local Chinese capitalists. The intermediary role played by the major British business groups enabled the formation and maintenance of a state–business alliance that mirrored the colonial economic power structure. Research indicated that for much of the colonial era (until the early 1980s), the business sector was relatively cohesive and was largely dominated by major British business groups. These major British hongs controlled a vast network of subsidiary corporations by means of interlocking directorships, i.e. a small group of directors commonly served on the management boards of different companies. By virtue of their dominant position in the economy, those major British hongs, particularly the Jardine Group and the Hong Kong Bank, functioned as organized groups performing the crucial role of intermediaries among clusters of business interests (Lui & Chiu, 2007, 2009; Wong, 1996). The existence of these centralized British business groups was essential for the colonial state to embed itself into the economic power structure in the colonial time, because they had effectively fulfilled the role of encompassing intermediaries that helped articulate the diverse interests of the business sector, making it easier for the colonial state to co-opt and consult (Ma, 2007, p. 78). The composition and functioning of the Executive Council best illustrated how the major British business groups made a great contribution to colonial governance by effectively binding the colonial state and the business sector together. Table 3.2 indicates that senior executives of the major British hongs like Jardine Group and Hong Kong Bank were routinely represented in the Executive Council. Because of the representation of major British hongs in the Executive Council, the opinions of the business sector were effectively incorporated into the policy-making process of the colonial administration and any conflict of interests (either among major business groups or between the colonial state and the business sector) would be largely handled in the Executive Council. This certainly allowed the colonial state to maintain its effective coordination of major business interests, making sure that the policy decisions made by the colonial state in the Executive Council would be broadly acceptable to the wider business sector. In other words, through the co-option of the senior executives of major British business groups, the Executive Council as the de facto cabinet of the Governor had effectively functioned as an institutionalized platform for mediating between major business interests and consolidating business support for government policies. At a time when the business sector was largely dominated by the British capitalists and electoral politics were absent in Hong Kong, such a system of business representation was proved to be effective in helping the colonial state to articulate major business interests and to consolidate its political support base in the business sector.

On the other hand, the intermediary role played by local Chinese capitalists facilitated the formation and maintenance of a state–business alliance that could command respect and acceptance of the Chinese community. For much of the colonial era, successful local Chinese merchants were well-respected and widely seen as the "natural leaders" of the Chinese community, and their leadership status was clearly built upon their active participation in different district organizations, dialect groups, trade associations or charity groups (Goodstadt, 2009, p. 99). The leadership of the local Chinese capitalists within the community enabled them to function as an effective link between the colonial state and the Chinese population, giving rise to a unique form of "collaborative colonialism" (Law, 2009, p. 22). Such an intermediary role of local Chinese capitalists was best illustrated by the role of the Tung Wah Hospital as a mediating platform

Table 3.2 List of unofficial members of the Executive Council (1896–1941)

Name	Tenure	Company/occupation
Catchick Paul Chater	1896–1926	Broker
James Jardine Bell-Irving	1896–1899, 1901–1902	Jardine, Matheson & Co.
James Johnstone Keswick	1899, 1900–1901	Jardine, Matheson & Co.
Charles Wedderburn Dickson	1902–1906	Jardine, Matheson & Co.
Thomas Henderson Whitehead	1902	Chartered Bank of India, Australia & China
Charles Stewart Sharp	1902	Gibb, Livingston & Co.
William Jardine Gresson	1904, 1905, 1908	Jardine, Matheson & Co.
Edbert Ansgar Hewett	1906–1915	P&O Steam Navigation Co.
Henry Keswick	1908, 1910	Jardine, Matheson & Co.
Henry Spencer Berkeley	1908	Barrister
Henry Ernest Pollock	1911, 1912, 1921–1941	Barrister
Ernest Hamilton Sharp	1916–1922	Barrister
David Landale	1916, 1918	Jardine, Matheson & Co.
N. J. Stabb	1919	Hong Kong and Shanghai Banking Corporation
Percy Hobson Holyoak	1920, 1921, 1923, 1924–1926	Reiss & Co.
Edward Victor David Parr	1920	Mackinnon, Mackenzie & Co.
Alexander Gordon Stephen	1922–1924	Jardine, Matheson & Co.
Charles Montague Ede	1924	Union Insurance Society of Canton
Archibald Orr Lang	1925, 1926–1927	Gibb, Livingston & Co.
Shouson Chow	1926–1936	Bank of East Asia
Dallas Gerald Mercer Bernard	1927	Jardine, Matheson & Co.
William Edward Leonard Shenton	1928–1936	Solicitor
Arthur Cecil Haynes	1928	Hong Kong and Shanghai Banking Corporation
John Owen Hughes	1930	Harry Wicking & Co.
Charles Gordon Stewart, Mackie	1930, 1931, 1933–1935	Gibb, Livingston & Co.
Robert Hormus Kotewall	1932, 1934, 1935–1941	Hong Kong Mercantile Co. Ltd.
John Johnstone Paterson	1936–1941	Jardine, Matheson & Co.
William Henry Bell	1936	Asiatic Petroleum Co. (South China) Ltd.
Stanley Hudson Dodwell	1936–1940	Dodwell & Co.

Source: Adapted from Endacott, 1964, p. 250.

between the colonial state and the Chinese population. Comprising the most prestigious local Chinese capitalists from major trades, directors of the Tung Wah Hospital Committee were widely recognized by both the public and the colonial state as representatives of the Chinese community (Sinn, 2003, pp. 83–84). Given their social standing and official recognition, the Tung Wah Hospital served as much more than a provider of welfare and medical services, but also as a "civic centre" where its directors mediated issues of public concern such as municipal services, law and order and local facilitates and could bring matters to the government's attention, thus effectively functioning as a nexus of interaction between the colonial state and the local Chinese community (Law, 2009, pp. 22–25; Sinn, 2003, pp. 89–91). In short, the high credibility and community networks of local Chinese capitalists had provided the colonial state with two valuable things in terms of mediating state–society relations. First, by co-opting these widely-accepted local Chinese capitalists into different advisory and consultative bodies, the colonial state improved its communication with the Chinese community and demonstrated a gesture of respect towards the local Chinese, therefore forging the necessary societal support base for the day-to-day government affairs and public policies (Goodstadt, 2009, p. 99; King, 1981). Second, by forming a collaborative partnership with the prestigious local Chinese capitalists, the colonial state could draw on their community networks and resources to defend the colonial regime and accommodate societal challenges in times of serious social unrest. For example, in the course of several important strikes and social disturbances, such as the Seamen's Strike in 1922,[8] the Canton–Hong Kong Strike-Boycott in 1925[9] and the 1967 Riots,[10] the local Chinese capitalists proved that they were reliable governing partners by joining hands with the colonial state in maintaining political stability and in overcoming the challenges of anti-colonial movements (Goodstadt, 2009, p. 100).

To conclude, the embeddedness of the colonial state was built upon the system of advisory committees and the role of major British business groups and local Chinese capitalists as encompassing intermediaries. By virtue of the operation of advisory machinery and the support of encompassing British business groups and local Chinese capitalists, the colonial state effectively embedded itself with the major socio-economic constituents and thus finally established a close linkage between the state, economy and society.

The enabling conditions for state autonomy: the transcendent position of the colonial Governor and his political autonomy from the sovereign state

According to the state capacity theories, the autonomy of the state vis-à-vis the powerful socio-economic actors is another important foundation of successful governing coalition building and strong governance capacity: the embeddedness and connectedness of modern states with major socio-economic actors will only be productive to the pursuit of collective interests when it is simultaneously combined with the notion of state autonomy; otherwise the state will be subject

88 *The legacy of state–business alliance*

to the danger of being captured by its powerful coalition partners. In this connection, state capacity theorists observe that it is crucial for the state to maintain a high degree of relative autonomy by holding significant power leverages vis-à-vis its coalition partners, so that it can resist the undue demands from those powerful vested interests and pursue public policies broader than the interests of any one particular group (Evans, 1995, 1998; Weiss, 1998).

In the context of colonial Hong Kong, many local political scientists had observed that the existence of the state–business alliance did not amount to the business capture and control of the government, because the colonial state had maintained a high degree of relative autonomy vis-à-vis its powerful business allies (Chiu, 1994; Scott, 1989, pp. 58–59). However, what were the factors that contributed to the colonial state's considerable degree of relative autonomy? Basically there were two enabling conditions that endowed the colonial state with a relatively high degree of state autonomy. First, the transcendent position of the colonial Governor vis-à-vis the business sector under the colonial political system enabled the colonial state to effectively command the respect and observance of the co-opted business elites. Second, the relationship between the capitalist class and the sovereign state in London was largely distant and remote and this allowed the colonial state to uphold is political authority as the ultimate power holder in the territory. These two enabling conditions facilitated the colonial state to maintain its relative autonomy over the powerful business sector and effectively perform its role as arbitrator of class interests as and when necessary.

First and foremost, the transcendent position of the colonial Governor vis-à-vis the business sector under the colonial political system enabled the colonial state to effectively command the respect and observance of the co-opted business elites. Under the colonial power structure, the Governor was undoubtedly the most powerful political actor and he generally stood above all the major socio-economic interests in colonial Hong Kong. The transcendent position enjoyed by the British Governor was built upon two important institutional foundations. First, the Governor, as the representative of the British Queen's sovereignty over the colonial Hong Kong, was directly selected and appointed by the Colonial Office in London. When there was a vacancy, the Secretary of State for the Colonies would normally select and appoint a new Governor on the basis of a list of potential candidates[11] (Miners, 1987, p. 44). Because all the major interest groups in Hong Kong including the British, and local Chinese capitalists had no direct influence over the selection and appointment of the colonial Governor as well as the formation of his government, it is obvious that the Governor's power flowed directly from London and was not accountable to any particular interest groups in Hong Kong. It is clear that this was an important institutional foundation that contributed to the relative autonomy of the colonial state, because when there was a major conflict of interest between the business sector and the colonial government, the transcendent position of the Governor would allow him and his administration to override the undue demands of the capitalist class (Chiu, 1994). Second, the colonial Governor held monopoly powers of political appointment and patronage. Until the final years of colonial

Reinterpreting governance and state capacity 89

rule, when functional constituencies and directly elected seats were subsequently introduced to the Legislative Council in 1984 and 1991, respectively, the single channel of access to power that was made available to the British and local Chinese businessmen was to secure the political blessings of the colonial Governor and his administration to join the advisory and consultative system. Under such circumstances, the colonial state had effectively monopolized political power and was the ultimate political patron in colonial Hong Kong (Lau, 1999a, 1999b). Because the colonial Governor and his officials controlled the ultimate power of political appointment, the business elites did not have their own political power bases and were dependent on the blessings of the colonial state for gaining access to the advisory and consultative system and obtaining the political status for influencing policy-making. It is clear that as a consequence of such an asymmetrical political relationship, business elites were politically dependent and subordinate to the colonial state and thus they were largely restrained from aggressively challenging the authority of the Governor and colonial officials (Lau, 1994). An equally important factor is that there was an official majority in the Legislative Council. By controlling the overriding official majority in the Legislative Council, the colonial state exercised considerable political leverage vis-à-vis those unofficial members over the legislative process (Scott, 1989, pp. 58–59; see Table 3.3 for the composition of the Legislative Council from 1843 to 1983). In view of the above, policy initiatives proposed by the colonial state were unlikely to encounter fierce opposition from the co-opted business elites and an "atmosphere of harmony and consensus" usually prevailed between the colonial officials and the business elites (Goodstadt, 2009, p. 108; Lau, 1982, p. 129). All in all, because the colonial Governor held the monopoly power of political patronage and his appointment process was largely immune to the influences of local interest groups, the colonial state developed important power leverages vis-à-vis its powerful business allies.

Second, the relationship between the business sector and the sovereign state in London was largely distant in the British colonial days and this allowed the colonial state to uphold its political authority as the ultimate power holder in the

Table 3.3 Composition of Legislative Council (1843–1983)

Year	Appointed official members	Appointed unofficial members	Elected members	Total
1843	4	0	0	4
1850	4	2	0	6
1896	8	6	0	14
1964	13	13	0	26
1966	13	13	0	26
1976	23	23	0	46
1977	25	25	0	50
1983	29	29	0	58

Source: Adapted from Buckley, 1997, p. 185 and Ma, 2007, p. 98.

90 *The legacy of state–business alliance*

territory. Constitutionally speaking, the Governor was answerable to the Secretary of State for the Colonies in London for the administration of Hong Kong. Because Hong Kong was not a sovereign state but a crown colony under the supervision of London, theoretically the Secretary of State had overriding authority over the Governor and it was possible that the business elites (in particular the British merchants) could take their cases directly to London if they were not satisfied with the policies of the Governor and his senior officials. From this perspective, the relationship between the business sector and the sovereign state and inclination of London to get involved in Hong Kong's matters would have strong implications for the relative autonomy of the colonial state vis-à-vis its business allies: for the colonial state, the existence of an arrogant capitalist class with direct access and close partnership with an interventionist London government would be a political nightmare, because under such circumstances the business sector could bypass the Governor and seriously undermine his governing authority by directly appealing to the Secretary of State.

In this connection, it was comprehensible that the relationship between the business elites and the sovereign state during the old colonial days was relatively distant for two major reasons. First, the business sector and the sovereign state did not share common political-economic agendas, leaving little room for the business elites to expand their influence by appealing for the support of London. Politically, it had been an established practice of the London government to prevent the business sector from controlling the political agenda in Hong Kong. The reason behind was that although the Hong Kong colony was established for facilitating British business and trade activities in the Far East, the London government could not afford to run the colony for the exclusive benefit of the business interests at the expense of the local Chinese population. Therefore, whenever the British capitalists sought to expand their power and influence by lobbying support in the United Kingdom, the London government usually chose not to entertain their requests and would join the Hong Kong government in resisting these political pressures (Goodstadt, 2009, p. 33).

Economically, although Hong Kong was once the business and trade centre of the United Kingdom in the Far East in the nineteenth and early twentieth centuries, the economic links between Hong Kong's business sector and the sovereign state had become less and less significant since the Second World War (see Table 3.4 for Hong Kong's total trade figures with the United Kingdom from 1972 to 1997). Furthermore, following the dissolution of the British Empire in the 1950s, the United Kingdom gradually developed closer economic ties with the European Economic Community and the economic linkages between Hong Kong and London weakened steadily (Goodstadt, 2009, pp. 53, 231). In addition, the business elites never gained institutionalized access to the London government, not only because they were discouraged from appealing to the Colonial Office rather than to the Governor in the event of policy conflicts with the colonial administration, but because the Governor remained the only official channel of communication between Hong Kong and London throughout the colonial period (Miners, 1987, pp. 38, 48). Although the business sector had on certain

Table 3.4 Hong Kong's total trade with United Kingdom (1972–1997)

Year	Amount (HK$ million)	Percentage of total trade with United Kingdom
1972	3,731	9.1
1973	4,620	8.4
1974	4,871	7.6
1975	4,606	7.3
1976	5,234	6.2
1977	5,344	5.7
1978	6,993	6.0
1979	10,699	6.6
1980	13,066	6.2
1981	14,901	5.7
1982	14,733	5.5
1983	16,865	5.0
1984	20,250	4.6
1985	18,812	4.0
1986	35,606	6.4
1987	28,888	3.8
1988	31,287	3.2
1989	30,844	2.7
1990	39,720	3.1
1991	44,923	2.9
1992	52,353	2.8
1993	56,745	2.7
1994	63,015	2.6
1995	73,646	2.6
1996	79,851	2.7
1997	86,074	2.8

Source: Figures obtained from the Census and Statistics Department.

occasions taken their complaints directly to the Secretary of State (such as the political crisis of 1894, as discussed in preceding paragraphs), these incidents happened only in the context of important political crises and were exceptional cases (Scott, 1989, p. 249).

Finally, the London government had not establish any local presence in Hong Kong and relied on the Governor to manage day-to-day affairs in the territory. A notable feature of British policy on managing its colonial empire was devolution of power to the local Governors in administering the colonies, by which London took no great interest in the day-to-day affairs of a colony unless there was a major crisis[12] (Goodstadat, 2009, p. 50; Lau, 1994). This governing principle was also applicable to colonial Hong Kong. For most of the time, the colonial administration had maintained a great deal of political autonomy in managing Hong Kong, although the Governor might seek advice and instruction from London from time to time (Miners, 1998, p. 214). Apart from its policy of devolution of power, the London government also lacked the necessary political machinery to direct the management of individual colonies. As the Governor

92 *The legacy of state–business alliance*

was the ultimate representative of the British Queen in colonial Hong Kong, London did not set up its own local agent or political institution in the territory and thus in making decisions on Hong Kong affairs the London officials had no choice but to rely on the advice and information provided by the Governor and his officials (Goodstadat, 2009, p. 50).

Following the dismantling of the British Empire in the 1950s, the capacity of London to control and direct Hong Kong affairs had been further diminished. The Colonial Office, which once played a pivotal role in overseeing different British colonies around the world, was subsequently disbanded and absorbed into the Commonwealth Office in 1966 and finally swallowed up by the Foreign Office in 1968. As a result, the expertise and resources available for the London government to oversee and direct Hong Kong declined sharply (Goodstadat, 2009, p. 51). To sum up, because of the lack of a common political and economic agenda, the absence of institutionalized communication channels and no strong local presence of the London government in Hong Kong, the relationship between the business sector and the sovereign state was relatively distant in the colonial days. It would be difficult for the business sector to voice their dissatisfactions to London by means of circumvention activities (Yep, 2009). All of the above factors helped sustain the political autonomy of the colonial state in administering Hong Kong and upheld the authority of the Governor as the ultimate power-holder in the territory.

To conclude, it was notable that there were two major enabling conditions that endowed the colonial state with a relatively high degree of state autonomy, including the transcendent position of the colonial Governor vis-à-vis the business sector under the colonial political system and the distant relationship between the business elites and the sovereign state in London. Thanks to these two enabling conditions, the colonial state effectively maintained its considerable degree of autonomy over the business sector. But it was worth noting that by highlighting the notion of state autonomy here we do not intend to picture the colonial state as completely above business interests. In fact, the high concentration of economic resources in the hands of business elites had effectively constituted a critical context that confined the colonial state on the formulation of public policies (Chiu, 1994). Nevertheless, within the general scopes of providing a business-friendly environment, keeping low government expenditure and maintaining a low taxation regime, the colonial state had a considerable degree of "relative autonomy" in making policy decisions, particularly in terms of resisting pressure from the business sector and performing its role as an arbitrator of different class interests (Scott, 1989, p. 59).

The role of the colonial state in resisting pressures from businesses and in arbitrating class interests was evident in two major aspects.

First, the colonial state had successfully enforced its non-intervention economic policy throughout the colonial period and resisted demands from the business sector to provide direct financial assistance to particular industries and business corporations (Goodstadt, 2009; Ngo, 2000). It was well-known that Hong Kong had a strong tradition of non-interventionist economic policy and such a traditional doctrine had been labelled as "positive non-interventionism" since the 1970s. According to this traditional doctrine of non-intervention, the colonial state would only adopt general pro-business policy measures to facilitate economic and commercial development (such as a low taxation regime, limited social welfare provisions, minimal regulations on labour protection and free flow of capital), but at the same time the government would be constrained from using public resources to provide direct financial assistance or protection to any particular business sectors or individual corporations. Such a policy of non-intervention had provided the colonial state with an important policy tool to settle conflicts between the colonial administration and the business sector over the deployment of public resources and to convince the general public that the state–business alliance would not be degenerated into clientelism and cronyism (Goodstadt, 2009; Ngo, 2000). The autonomy of the colonial state in enforcing the non-interventionist policy was most clearly evident from the business sector's repeated failures to press the colonial government to provide direct subsidies and assistance in the 1950s and 1960s. After the Second World War, the process of rapid industrialization had inspired widespread demands from both the British and local Chinese business communities that the colonial state should follow the example of other East Asian countries to promote industrial development by providing tax incentives, financial subsidies and protective tariffs. The expatriate merchants even formed a united front with the Chinese businessmen in demanding a change in the economic role of the colonial administration and lobbied hard for direct financial subsidies and assistance in the 1950s and 1960s. But all these demands and requests were rejected by the colonial state, including an unsuccessful joint campaign by the British and Chinese capitalists on the establishment of an industrial bank in 1959 (Goodstadt, 2009, pp. 164–167).

Second, the colonial state was capable of mitigating social imbalances by pursuing policy reforms that were not welcomed by the business sector. As part of its non-interventionist policy, the colonial state had all along been reluctant to expand social welfare provisions and labour protection because its business allies were always suspicious of extension of social services that would increase taxation and public expenditure (Wilding, 1996, pp. 18–20). While it was true to say that its political alliance with the business sector had contributed to its fiscal conservatism and prudence in social policy development (Tang, 1998, p. 81), it did not mean that the colonial state would always have its hands tied. Despite its nature as a capitalist state, the colonial state had demonstrated that it would have no hesitation in deviating from its usual non-interventionist policy and interfering in the economy and society if and when it saw the need (Scott, 1986). Throughout the British colonial period it was notable that when social imbalances were aggravating the colonial state, for the sake of preserving the stability and long-term interests of the overall colonial regime, the colonial state was prepared to pursue policy reforms that would jeopardize the immediate interests of the business sector. The introduction of a public housing programme after the Shek Kip Mei Fire in 1953 and the implementation of labour reforms in the aftermath of the 1966–1967 Riots are both illustrative examples. As early as the

94   *The legacy of state–business alliance*

late 1940s, Governor Alexander Grantham had thought of introducing subsidized public housing to accommodate the growing numbers of squatter populations, but his plans were strongly opposed by the business elites in both the Executive Council and the Legislative Council. On 25 December 1953 a major fire destroyed the Shek Kip Mei shantytown and left over 53,000 people homeless. In the face of such a huge social problem, Grantham overcame the opposition of the business elites and launched a massive resettlement programme by constructing multi-storey estates for sheltering homeless people (Faure, 2003, pp. 27–33). In the 1960s Hong Kong had undergone the process of rapid industrialization and there was growing pressure to carry out progressive labour reforms so as to provide better protection for factory workers. However, because of strong opposition from the business sector, the colonial administration was cautious in handling the issue and the progress of legislative reforms was slow (Clayton, 2007, 2009). However, the outbreak of the 1966–1967 Riots, which brought about a few nights of rioting in 1966 and a more prolonged period of demonstrations and violence in 1967, renewed the momentum for the introduction of comprehensive labour reforms (Cheung, 2009, pp. 132–142). Taking the view that the poor working conditions and disharmonious labour relations were part of the underlying causes of the 1966–1967 Riots, the colonial administration strongly believed that the implementation of progressive labour reforms was the key to future political stability in Hong Kong. Therefore although the business sector continued to resist many specific reforms, the colonial state managed to overcome their opposition and successfully introduced a series of significant legislative reforms to strengthen the labour protection regimes in Hong Kong, including the reduction of maximum working hours for women and young people in December 1967, the enactment of the Employment Ordinance in 1968 and the provision of maternity leave for women and rest days for all workers in 1969 (Scott, 1989, pp. 121–126).

The smooth functioning of the state–business alliance and its effectiveness in maintaining governance

The *integrated conceptual framework* on state capacity indicated that on the foundations of state autonomy and state embeddedness, the state could maintain productive cooperation with the major socio-economic constituents while resisting the undue pressures from the co-opted interest groups. On this basis, the state could engineer a viable governing coalition for maintaining effective governance.

In this connection, the overarching argument of this chapter is that the effective governance in colonial Hong Kong was built upon the formation and maintenance of a viable state–business alliance: the smooth functioning of the state–business alliance in colonial Hong Kong and its effectiveness in maintaining effective governance were enhanced by a number of enabling conditions, and such enabling conditions were closely connected to the political and socio-economic environments in the pre-1997 period.

First and foremost, because of the dominant position of British capital in the local economy and the leadership of local Chinese capitalists in the community before 1997, the British capitalists and the local Chinese capitalists represented the two major socio-economic forces in the colonial period. Therefore, by incorporating the representatives of major British hongs and prestigious local Chinese capitalists into the dense networks of advisory bodies and committees, the co-opted business elites had effectively performed the role of encompassing intermediaries: the major British hongs assumed an important bridging role between the colonial state and the business sector, while the prestigious local Chinese capitalists played the mediating role between the colonial state and the Chinese population. From this perspective, these unique enabling conditions endowed the colonial state with a considerable degree of state embeddedness so it could embed itself into the socio-economic power structures in the colonial time. On the foundation of state embeddedness, the colonial state had success-fully established a solid political support base for its governance in both the economic and social arenas and also thwarted important societal challenges in times of serious social unrest.

Second, in the colonial time the Governor had maintained a transcendent position vis-à-vis the business sector under the colonial political system (as a result of the independent selection process of Governors and his monopoly powers of political patronage) and the relationship between the capitalist class and the sovereign state in London was largely distant (as a result of the lack of a common political-economic agenda and absence of institutionalized communi-cation channels between the business sector and London, and also the absence of strong local presence of the London government in Hong Kong). All these unique enabling conditions endowed the colonial state with a considerable degree of state autonomy so that it could maintain significant power leverages vis-à-vis its powerful business allies. On the foundation of state autonomy the colonial state successfully resisted the pressures of the business sector and per-formed its role as arbitrator of different class interests if and when it saw the need.

All in all, the above unique enabling conditions for state embeddedness and state autonomy helped maintain a precious political balance that made the state–business alliance viable and effective for much of the colonial time. On the one hand, the encompassing British capitalists and local Chinese capitalists helped the colonial state to embed itself into the socio-economic structure and develop a solid political support base for maintaining its governance and steering policy changes; on the other hand, although the business elites could not obtain direct financial assistance from the colonial administration under its laissez-faire policy, its political alliance with the colonial state helped it secure the mainte-nance of a general pro-business policy environment (low taxation regime, limited welfare provision and minimal labour protection) and gained direct access to the colonial power structures.

Such a reciprocal relationship between the colonial state and the business sector, which was the consequences of the unique enabling conditions of state

96 *The legacy of state–business alliance*

embeddedness and state autonomy, as discussed in the preceding paragraphs, had served as the solid foundations for the smoothing functioning of the state–business alliance during the British colonial period. From the perspective of the colonial state, the existence of such a viable state–business alliance enabled it to consolidate its governance by mobilizing the support of the business sector while preventing the state–business partnership from degenerating into clientelism and cronyism. In other words, by virtue of its state embeddedness and state autonomy, the colonial state could, on the one hand, make successful use of the extensive economic and social networks of its business allies to consolidate its governance and steer policy-making, while on the other hand it also paid a limited price for its partnership with the business sector and minimized any possible fallout from the public for government–business collusion.

The relatively high levels of public satisfaction and public trust towards the colonial administration were clearly indicative of the contributions of such a viable state–business alliance to the effective governance in the colonial period as well as the Hong Kong people's general acceptance of the moral foundation of the colonial political order.

First of all, on the foundation of state embeddedness, the colonial state had embedded itself into the socio-economic structures and its connectedness with the major stakeholders significantly strengthened its policy-making and implementation capacity. As a consequence, the colonial state was able to produce sound policy outputs in response to the needs of the society and this undoubtedly helped sustain a relatively high level of public satisfaction toward its performance (Cheung, 2007). Public satisfaction towards the performance of the colonial state was clearly evident by the fact that even in the initial years of the transitional period of the mid 1980s (when the colonial administration had gradually been regarded as a lame-duck government due to the impending change of sovereignty), the vast majority of the Hong Kong people still held a very positive view of its overall performance (Table 3.5) (Lau, 1999b). The Hong Kong people's general satisfaction toward the performance of the colonial administration was also evident by the fact that for much of the colonial time there was no large-scale mass movement launched against the colonial administration (Lau, 1994).

Second, on the foundation of state autonomy, the colonial state had maintained a high degree of relative autonomy vis-à-vis the business sector, despite its political alliance with the big capitalists. The colonial state's relative autonomy over the vested business interests enabled it to perform its role as an

Table 3.5 Evaluation of performance of the colonial administration (%)

	Very poor	*Poor*	*Average*	*Good*	*Very good*
1986	0.6	9.5	49.9	40.0	0
1988	0.3	6.3	46.5	41.2	0.8

Source: Lau, 1996.

arbitrator of different class interests and prevented any possible fallout from the public for its collusion with the business sector: On the one hand the colonial state had successfully enforced its non-interventionist policy and restrained from providing direct financial assistance to the business sector; on the other hand it was capable of mitigating social contradictions by pursuing policy reforms that were not welcome by the business elites if and when it saw the need. As a result of its crucial role in arbitrating class interests, there was no strong public suspicion of "government–business collusion" in the colonial time. Despite its close political partnership with the business sector, the colonial state was seen by most of the public as conducting government affairs by and large fairly (Lau & Kuan, 1995) and people generally believed that the colonial officials had formulated policies in an impartial manner with the long-term interests of the community in mind (Lau, 1997, p. 32). For example, a territory-wide opinion survey conducted in 1992 indicated that 51.4 per cent and 23.5 per cent of people gave an average score or a high score to the colonial government, respectively, in terms of conducting government affairs fairly. Only 18.1 per cent of respondents said the colonial government had not acted in a fair manner (Lau & Kuan, 1995). Public confidence in the impartiality of the colonial state was also reflected in fact that the colonial state had successfully command a decent level of public trust even in the final years of its colonial rule (Table 3.6).

Conclusion

In this chapter we have adopted the *integrated conceptual framework* on state capacity to re-examine governance and politics in colonial Hong Kong. Our discussions demonstrated that on the foundations of state autonomy and state embeddedness, the colonial state had maintained a collaborative partnership with major British business groups and the local Chinese capitalists, the two major socio-economic constituents in the old colonial days, and thus successfully engineered a viable state–business alliance for maintaining effective governance.

It was notable that the smooth functioning of the state–business alliance in colonial Hong Kong and its effectiveness in maintaining effective governance were based upon a number of unique enabling conditions, including the incorporation of encompassing intermediaries (major British business groups and

Table 3.6 The level of public trust toward the Hong Kong government (1992–1997) (%)

	Trust	Half–half	Distrust
1992	56.9	14.7	23.8
1993	54.8	16.8	21.8
1994	46.6	22.8	24.0
1995	48.4	22.0	22.1
1996	60.6	22.2	12.7
1997	63.2	18.8	13.5

Source: University of Hong Kong's Public Opinion Programme (http://hkupop.hku.hk).

98 *The legacy of state–business alliance*

prestigious local Chinese capitalists) into the dense networks of advisory committees, the colonial Governor's transcendent position vis-à-vis the business sector under the colonial political system and the distant relationship between the capitalist class and the sovereign state in London. All these unique enabling conditions had endowed the colonial state with a considerable degree of state embeddedness and state autonomy, resulting in a precious political balance that made the state–business alliance viable for most of the colonial time. The colonial state could, on the one hand, make successful use of the extensive economic and social networks of its business allies to consolidate its governance and steer policy-making while, on the other hand, it minimized any possible fallout from the public for its collusion with the business sector. On the basis of the smooth functioning of such a viable state–business governing coalition, the colonial state could successfully command a decent level of public satisfaction and public trust for much of the colonial period, and the Hong Kong people generally accepted the whole colonial political order.

If smooth functioning of the state–business alliance had served as the cornerstone of effective governance in the British colonial era, the following questions arise: Why does the state–business alliance, which had been functioning effectively in the colonial past, fail to bring about effective governance after 1997? Is there any causal relationship between the failure of the state–business alliance and the post-1997 governance crisis? These are the questions we are going to address in the forthcoming chapters.

Notes

1 Administrative officers are political officers of the government who are groomed for top executive positions. They are the dominant force for policy making in Hong Kong and function like a ruling party (Cheung, 2004). For an account of the evolution of the administrative officers throughout the colonial period, see Tsang (2007).
2 From its establishment until the 1980s, the HKGCC was firmly under the control of the major British hongs and functioned as the bastion of business interests. During its first 100 years, for half of the period its chairmanship was in the hands of the big British hongs including Jardine Matheson (19 years), P&O Steam Navigation (12 years), Swire (ten years) and Turner & Co. (ten years) (Ngo, 2000).
3 The Nam Pak Hong merchants mainly engaged in the North–South trade and commercial activities between the China coast and Nanyang (Southeast Asia) (Sinn, 2003, p. 28).
4 It was worth noting that the British merchants and the Chinese merchants should be considered as two separate social classes because there was little mixing between the two business communities with regard to their different lifestyles and cultures (Chan, 1991).
5 Dating back to the 1840s, the colonial state had already worked very closely with the British and Chinese merchants in the early establishment and development of the Hong Kong colony. Historical research indicates that the founding and expansion of the infant colony during the 1840s were only made possible with the colonial state's success in securing the cooperation of the merchants, including British merchants and Chinese businessmen (Carroll, 1997). Both British and Chinese businessmen, such as landowners, contractors, compradors and merchants, had been actively involved in the various building and construction projects in the infant colony, from government and

commercial buildings to residential areas and basic infrastructure in the entire Hong Kong island. In cooperating with the colonial state, these businessmen were rewarded by the British administration with economic privileges like land grants and lucrative monopolies (Carroll, 1997).

6 According to statistics, a total of 29 unofficials were appointed to the Executive Council between 1896 and 1941 and about 24 of them were businessmen (Miners, 1996).

7 It was estimated that between 1850 and 1941 a total of 102 unofficials were appointed to the Legislative Council and about 74 of them were businessmen (Miners, 1996).

8 During the Seamen's Strike in 1922, the prestigious local Chinese capitalists such as Ho Tung, Liu Chu-po and leaders of the Tung Wah Hospital acted as intermediaries in the search for a settlement with the strikers. A settlement was at last worked out with the mediation of these local Chinese community leaders (Chan Lau, 1990, pp. 172–173).

9 Similar to their roles in combating the 1922 Seamen's Strike, the business elites such as Chou Shou-chen and R. H. Kotewall (a Eurasian businessman) played an important role in the handling of the Canton–Hong Kong Strike-Boycott in 1925. In the course of the strike the business elites advised the colonial administration on anti-strike strategies and measures, publicly supported the government, maintained stable food provision to the poor through the Tung Wah Hospital, recruited hundreds of volunteers to maintain the essential public transport services, assisted in the censorship of local Chinese newspapers, mobilized support of other businessmen and professionals and organized a counter-propaganda campaign (including the publication of the *Kung Sheung Yat Po* and distribution of leaflets to the Chinese communities) (Chan Lau, 1990, pp. 184–193; Goodstadt, 2009, pp. 100–101).

10 In the 1967 Riots the colonial administration once again relied on the co-opted local Chinese capitalists to resist the pressure from the Chinese communists. Business leaders in the Executive Council stood firmly behind Governor David Trench throughout the riot period. Hundreds of business groups, professional associations and community groups also pledged their support to the colonial administration during the early weeks of the riots and they also endorsed the police's combat actions against the rioters. Once again, the support of the business elites proved to be very effective in reinforcing the colonial rule in Hong Kong during the crisis period (Carroll, 2009; Yep, 2009).

11 Potential candidates for the governorship might come from sources like senior staff from the colonial service, diplomats transferred from the diplomatic service and retiring politicians (Miners, 1987, p. 48).

12 The indifference of the London government was evident by the fact that not until 1963 did the British Parliament hold its first debate after the Second World War on Hong Kong affairs (Goodstadt, 2009, p. 50).

References

Buckley, R. (1997). *Hong Kong: The road to 1997*. New York: Cambridge University Press.

Carroll, J. M. (1997). Colonialism and collaboration: Chinese subjects and the making of British Hong Kong. *China Information, 12*(1–2), 12–33.

Carroll, J. M. (2005). *Edge of empires: Chinese elites and British colonials in Hong Kong*. Cambridge, MA: Harvard University Press.

Carroll, J. M. (2009). A historical perspective: The 1967 riots and the strike–boycott of 1925–26. In R. Bickers & R. Yep (Eds.) *May days in Hong Kong: Riot and emergency in 1967* (pp. 69–85). Hong Kong: Hong Kong University Press.

100 *The legacy of state–business alliance*

Chan Lau, K. C. (1990). *China, Britain and Hong Kong, 1895–1945*. Hong Kong: Chinese University Press.

Chan, W. K. (1991). *The making of Hong Kong society: Three studies of class formation in early Hong Kong*. Oxford: Clarendon Press.

Cheung, A. (1998). The transition of bureaucratic authority: The political role of the senior civil service in the post-1997 governance of Hong Kong. In P. K. Li (Ed.), *Political order and power transition in Hong Kong* (pp. 79–108). Hong Kong: Chinese University Press.

Cheung, A. (2004). Strong executive, weak policy capacity: The changing environment of policy-making in Hong Kong. *Asian Journal of Political Science, 12*(1), 41–68.

Cheung, A. (2007). Executive-dominant governance or executive power "hollowed-out": the political quagmire of Hong Kong. *Asian Journal of Political Science, 15*(1), 17–38.

Cheung, G. K. W. (2009). *Hong Kong's watershed: The 1967 riots*. Hong Kong: Hong Kong University Press.

Chiu, S. W. K. (1994). *The politics of laissez-faire: Hong Kong's strategy of industrialization in historical perspective*. Hong Kong: Hong Kong Institute of Asia-Pacific Studies, Chinese University.

Clayton, D. (2007). From "free" to "fair" trade: The evolution of labour laws in colonial Hong Kong, 1958–62. *Journal of Imperial and Commonwealth History, 35*(2), 263–282.

Clayton, D. (2009). The riots and labour laws: The struggle for an eight-hour day for women factory workers, 1962–71. In R. Bickers, & R. Yep (Eds.), *May days in Hong Kong: Riot and emergency in 1967* (pp. 125–144). Hong Kong: Hong Kong University Press.

Crisswell, C. N. (1981). *The Taipans: Hong Kong's merchant princes*. New York: Oxford University Press.

Davies, S. N. G. (1989). The changing nature of representation in Hong Kong politics. In C. M. Kathleen, & M. Miron (Eds.), *Hong Kong: The challenge of transformation* (pp. 36–76). Hong Kong: Centre of Asian Studies, University of Hong Kong.

Endacott, G. B. (1964). *Government and people in Hong Kong, 1841–1962: A constitutional history*. Hong Kong: Hong Kong University Press.

Evans, P. B. (1995). *Embedded autonomy: States and industrial transformation*. Princeton, NJ: Princeton University Press.

Evans, P. B. (1998). Transferable lessons? Re-examining the institutional prerequisites of East Asian economic policies. *Journal of Development Studies, 34*(6), 66–86.

Faure, D. (2003). *Hong Kong: A reader in social history*. Hong Kong: Oxford University Press.

Goodstadt, L. F. (2009). *Uneasy partners: The conflict between public interest and private profit interest in Hong Kong*. Hong Kong: Hong Kong University Press.

Harris, P. (1988). *Hong Kong: A study in bureaucratic politics*. Hong Kong: Macmillan.

King, A. Y. C. (1981). Administrative absorption of politics in Hong Kong: Emphasis on the grass roots level. In A. Y. C. King, & R. P. L. Lee (Eds.), *Social life and development in Hong Kong* (pp. 127–146). Hong Kong: Chinese University Press.

Lau, C. K. (1997). *Hong Kong's colonial legacy*. Hong Kong: Chinese University Press.

Lau, S. K. (1982). *Society and politics in Hong Kong*. Hong Kong: Chinese University Press.

Lau, S. K. (1994). Hong Kong's "ungovernability" in the twilight of colonial rule. In Z. L. Lin, & T. W. Robinson (Eds.), *The Chinese and their future: Beijing, Taipei, and Hong Kong* (pp. 287–314). Washington, DC: AEI Press.

Lau, S. K. (1996). Democratization and decline of trust in public institutions in Hong Kong. *Democratization, 3*(2), 158–180.

Lau, S. K. (1999a). From elite unity to disunity: Political elite in post-1997 Hong Kong. In G. W. Wang, & J. Wong (Eds.), *Hong Kong in China: The challenges of transition* (pp. 47–74). Singapore: Times Academic Press.

Lau, S. K. (1999b). Political order and democratization in Hong Kong: The separation of elite and mass politics. In G. W. Wang, & S. L. Wong (Eds.), *Towards a new millennium: Building on Hong Kong's strengths* (pp. 62–79). Hong Kong: Centre of Asian Studies, University of Hong Kong.

Lau, S. K., & Kuan, H. C. (1995). Public attitudes toward political authorities and colonial legitimacy in Hong Kong. *Journal of Commonwealth & Comparative Politics, 33*(1), 79–102.

Law, W. S. (2009). *Collaborative colonial power: The making of the Hong Kong Chinese.* Hong Kong: Hong Kong University Press.

Lui, T. L., & Chiu, S. W. K. (2007). Governance crisis in post-1997 Hong Kong: A political economy perspective. *The China Review, 7*(2), 1–34.

Lui, T. L., & Chiu, S. W. K. (2009). *Hong Kong: Becoming a Chinese global city.* London: Routledge.

Ma, N. (2007). *Political development in Hong Kong: State, political society and civil society.* Hong Kong: Hong Kong University Press.

Miners, N. (1987). *Hong Kong under imperial rule, 1912–1941.* Hong Kong: Oxford University Press.

Miners, N. (1996). Consultation with business interests: The case of Hong Kong. *Asian Journal of Public Administration, 18*(2), 245–256.

Miners, N. (1998). *The government and politics of Hong Kong* (5th ed.). Hong Kong: Oxford University Press.

Ngo, T. W. (2000). Changing government–business relations and the governance of Hong Kong. In R. Ash, P. Ferdinand, B. Hook, & R. Porter (Eds.), *Hong Kong in transition: The handover years* (pp. 26–41). New York: St. Martin's Press.

Rear, J. (1971). One brand of politics. In K. Hopkins (Ed.), *Hong Kong: The industrial colony – a political, social and economic survey* (pp. 55–139). Hong Kong: Oxford University Press.

Scott, I. (1986). Policy-making in a turbulent environment: The case of Hong Kong. *International Review of Administration Science, 5*(2), 447–469.

Scott, I. (1989). *Political change and the crisis of legitimacy in Hong Kong.* Hong Kong: Oxford University Press.

Scott, I. (1989). *Political change and the crisis of legitimacy in Hong Kong.* Hong Kong: Oxford University Press.

Sinn, E. (2003). *Power and charity: A Chinese merchant elite in colonial Hong Kong.* Hong Kong: Hong Kong University Press.

Tang, K. L. (1998). *Colonial state and social policy: Social welfare development in Hong Kong.* Lanham, MD: University Press of America.

Tsang, S. (2007). *Governing Hong Kong: administrative officers from the nineteenth century to the handover to China, 1862–1997.* London: I.B. Tauris.

Weiss, L. (1998). *The myth of the powerless state: Governing the economy in a global era.* Cambridge: Polity Press.

Wilding, P. (1996). *Social policy and social development in Hong Kong.* Hong Kong: City University of Hong Kong.

Wong, G. (1996). Business groups in a dynamic environment: Hong Kong 1976–1986.

In G. G. Hamilton (Ed.), *Asian business networks* (pp. 87–114). New York: Walter de Gruyter.

Yep, R. (2009). Accommodating business interests in China and Hong Kong: Two systems, one way out. In K. H. Mok, & R. Forrest (Eds.), *Changing governance and public policy in East Asia* (pp. 185–205). New York: Routledge.

4 The crafting of the post-1997 state–business alliance

Beijing's governing strategy after 1997

The analyses and discussions in the preceding chapter indicated that the effective governance in colonial Hong Kong was built upon the colonial state's abilities in engineering a viable state–business alliance through which the colonial government had simultaneously combined the notions of state autonomy and state embeddedness. Such a viable state–business alliance had furnished the colonial Hong Kong state with strong capacity for maintaining effective governance and steering public policy-making throughout much of the British colonial period, at least until the 1980s.

The governance and politics in Hong Kong had entered a new phase of development in the early 1980s. The beginning of Sino-British negotiation over the future of Hong Kong in 1982 was an important and historical watershed for the territory's political development, which also marked a move towards a new turning point in the state–business relationship in Hong Kong. In this connection, the state–business governing coalition as engineered by the colonial state was considered and adopted by the new sovereign, the Chinese government, as a political formula that could help achieve its broad political and socio-economic objectives in Hong Kong, including maintaining Hong Kong's capitalist system and overall political and social stability, facilitating China's own economic modernization and fending off the challenges of the democrats. On the other hand, the capitalist class in Hong Kong also considered it necessary to forge a new political partnership with the incoming sovereign state so as to protect their vested political and economic interests in the territory. As a consequence of the convergence of the interests of the two parties, the formation of a new political partnership between Beijing and the local capitalists came smoothly in the 1980s. Against this background, the legacy of the state–business governing coalition has survived in Hong Kong, despite the transfer of sovereignty in 1997, and it has also been preserved as the foundation of the post-1997 political order.

In this chapter, we will first review the politics of transition and the making of the post-1997 governing coalition by the Chinese government. Then we will examine the various considerations and interest calculations that prompted the Beijing government and the business sector to join hands in the transitional period to engineer a new state–business alliance as the cornerstone of Hong Kong's post-1997 political order. Lastly, we will briefly discuss how the Beijing

104 *The legacy of state–business alliance*

government incorporated Hong Kong's capitalist class into its united front during the transitional period of the 1980s and 1990s. The historical review in this chapter will certainly help us understand the nature and evolution of the state–business alliance from the colonial period to the post-1997 period and pave the way for our re-examination of post-1997 Hong Kong's governance in the forthcoming chapters.

The politics of transition and the crafting of the post-1997 political order

> The handover of Hong Kong's sovereignty from Britain to China did not really shake the cornerstone of governance in Hong Kong: the state–business alliance ... the post-1997 political arrangement has in fact consolidated and institutionalized, rather than weakened, the political privileges of the business elite. The back door to power for business people remains secure and immune from popular pressure, despite growing vibrancy of civil society.
>
> (Yep, 2007)

The negotiation between the Beijing and London governments over the political future of Hong Kong had turned a new page in the history of the territory. The whole story formally began in September 1982 when Chinese leader Deng Xiaoping met British Prime Minister Margaret Thatcher in Beijing, kicking off the two countries' political negotiations over the future status of Hong Kong. After about two years of intensive negotiations and political bargaining, Beijing and London finally reached an agreement and signed the "Sino-British Joint Declaration on the Question of Hong Kong" on 19 December 1984.[1] In accordance with the Joint Declaration, the Chinese government would resume the exercise of its sovereignty over Hong Kong under the framework of "one country, two systems" with effect from 1 July 1997.

The signing of the Sino-British Joint Declaration in 1984 was a political watershed in Hong Kong, because the impending change of sovereignty had brought about reconfiguration and reconstitution of the political order in the territory (Cheung, 1998). For Beijing's leaders, once they had decided to take back Hong Kong from the British they needed to carefully plan the city-state's governance system and political order after 1997. In accordance with the principles of "one country, two systems" and "Hong Kong people ruling Hong Kong" as promised by the Chinese government under the Sino-British Joint Declaration, the HKSAR government after 1997 would be made up of the local people of Hong Kong and Mainland officials would not be deployed to govern the future HKSAR. In other words, the Beijing government would not have any official presence in the future HKSAR government and therefore they must groom reliable and capable local political agents to exercise the governing power in Hong Kong under their oversight and supervision after the handover of sovereignty in 1997 (Ma, 2007, p. 34). The key questions for Beijing's leaders were, therefore:

Crafting the post-1997 state–business alliance 105

Who would be trusted by the Chinese government to govern Hong Kong after 1997? Which groups of political elites were reliable and capable of implementing Beijing's post-1997 Hong Kong policy and safeguarding its interests in the territory? What political system should be put in place to facilitate the ruling elites chosen by the Chinese government to organize and maintain an effective government in post-1997 Hong Kong?

It was clear from the outset that it was the intention of the Chinese government to maintain institutional continuity and stability in Hong Kong during the process of political transition, and the British colonial system of governance, which was established and operated very effectively in the colonial period, should continue to be put in place in the territory after the handover of sovereignty (Cheung, 2010). From the perspectives of Beijing's leaders, the colonial governance system, including the executive-dominant tradition (the concentration of political powers in the hands of the British Governor and the executive branch), the collaborative alliance with the business sector, the extensive networks of advisory committees and the efficient civil service system, had all made significant contributions to maintaining effective governance, political stability and economic prosperity in colonial Hong Kong. Therefore in designing the political systems for the future HKSAR under the Basic Law, it was the Chinese government's intention to adopt and preserve the British colonial system of governance as far as possible. In fact, it has been argued that the political changes anticipated by the Chinese leaders after 1997 were no more than the replacement of the British flag with the Chinese flag, and also the replacement of the British colonial Governor with a Chinese Chief Executive as the head of the new HKSAR government (Xu, 1993, pp. 179–184).

In particular, it was the grand strategy of the Chinese government to leave the colonial state–business alliance largely intact after the handover of sovereignty in 1997, and they considered it necessary to maintain the pivotal position of the business sector in the future HKSAR governance system. Xu Jaitun, the Director of the Hong Kong Branch of the Xinhua News Agency (Xinhua Hong Kong) and Chinese official in charge of Hong Kong affairs in the 1980s has described the thoughts and intentions of the Chinese government as follows:

> The Central Authorities [Chinese government] decided that Hong Kong shall uphold its capitalist system for 50 years or a longer period of time. To put into practice the principle of "Hong Kong people ruling Hong Kong", the future HKSAR government shall be mainly made up of the local capitalist class with the participation of the working class. It shall be a cross-class political alliance, but the capitalist class should form the core of the whole alliance. [in Chinese].
>
> (Xu, 1993, pp. 141–142)

It was obvious that the Chinese government's definition of "Hong Kong people ruling Hong Kong" was indeed about building a political alliance between the future HKSAR government and the business sector. In the eyes of

106 *The legacy of state–business alliance*

Beijing's leaders, the state–business alliance after 1997 should retain two fundamental features of its colonial predecessor. First, the bureaucratic elites should continue to serve as the major pillar of the post-colonial state. Groomed by the British, the bureaucrats were widely praised for doing a good job in maintaining the efficient operation of government machinery under colonial rule, and Beijing's leaders hoped that senior civil servants would continue to play a similar role under Chinese sovereignty after 1997. Indeed, it was the intention of the Chinese government to take over the colonial bureaucracy and turn it into a loyal instrument of the future HKSAR government under its oversight (Cheung, 1998). Second, the business sector should continue to serve as the major coalition partner of the post-colonial state. In this regard, the dominant features of post-1997 political systems, namely the selection of the Chief Executive by an Election Committee and the election of half of the Legislative Council seats by functional constituencies,[2] were primarily designed to keep political power in the hands of the business elites under the HKSAR constitutional system (Cheung, 2010). In other words, the post-1997 governing coalition as crafted by the Chinese government was actually some form of co-rule between the bureaucrats and the capitalists, as in the colonial past (Cheung, 2007).

The making of the post-1997 state–business alliance: the convergence of interests between Beijing and the local capitalist class

> Central to the Chinese strategy for the management of Hong Kong is its alliance with the business sector.... The predilection for the capitalist class by a government which claims to be socialist arises out of what is perceived to be a significant convergence of the interests of the two parties in the maintenance of Hong Kong's previous economic system (with minimal provisions for welfare), preventing democratization, and in maintaining "stability".
>
> (Ghai, 1999, p. 289)

While it was not surprising that the Beijing leaders would choose to continue some forms of bureaucratic rule after 1997 given the strategic position of administrative elites in maintaining the efficient operation and functioning of the government machinery (Cheung, 1998), why did the Chinese government, which is by nature a communist and socialist regime, also choose the capitalist class as its coalition partner and even make business elites the majority of the new political establishment? A closer examination of the political and socio-economic contexts during the transition period will reveal that the convergence of the interests of the Chinese government and the Hong Kong capitalist class had paved the way for the replacement of the former "British-centred state–business alliance" by a new "China-centred state–business alliance".

First, securing the support of the business sector to the reunification plan was regarded by the Beijing leaders as essential to the sustainability of Hong Kong's capitalism and its overall economic and social stability, and therefore the

Crafting the post-1997 state–business alliance 107

continuation of the colonial state–business alliance to post-1997 period was unquestionable. In the eyes of Beijing's leaders, Hong Kong's capitalism is not just a system of competitive markets, but is actually a political and economic system dominated by a small group of business tycoons and Taipans who controlled the levers of powers in the territory (Goodstadt, 2000). In view of the dominant role of the business sector over Hong Kong's political economy, the Chinese government believed that the smooth functioning and stability of Hong Kong's capitalist system could not be maintained without the support and cooperation of the business sector, and therefore the big businessmen and capitalists in Hong Kong should be the natural coalition partner of the future HKSAR government (King, 1991; Ma, 2007, p. 70). The economic turbulence triggered by the Sino-British negotiation clearly showed to Beijing the strategic importance of the business sector in maintaining political and social stability in Hong Kong. In the 1980s, the Sino-British negotiation over the future of Hong Kong had resulted in unprecedented political uncertainties in the territories, and many people worried that their properties, wealth and way of life would be adversely affected if Hong Kong was returned to China after 1997. The political uncertainties triggered waves of emigration, capital outflow and economic slowdown, thereby seriously affecting the economic prosperity and social stability of Hong Kong. When Xu Jiatun was appointed to head the New China News Agency (NCNA) in 1983, he quickly found that maintaining the confidence of businessmen should be his chief political task. In reporting his work to the Beijing leaders, Xu Jiatun summarized his major tasks in Hong Kong as "delaying the outflow of British capital, stabilizing the local Chinese capital, solidifying Taiwan capital, attracting foreign capital and strengthening Mainland capital" (Xu, 1993, pp. 57–59). In this time of political uncertainty and economic turbulence, Beijing particularly found it necessary to co-opt and groom the local Chinese capitalists as its major coalition partners due to the subsequent exodus of British capital. In the colonial era, the business sector was dominated by the major British hongs and the British capitalists had exercised strong influence in both the political and economic arenas. However, in view of the "political risk" surrounding the impending change of sovereignty, since the mid-1980s the British capitalists had started to reduce their investments in Hong Kong and diversify their businesses to overseas countries. The Jardine Group and the Hong Kong Bank, the two most influential British hongs, took the lead in this trend of capital outflow by setting up new holding companies outside Hong Kong[3] and increasing their investments overseas.[4] Local Chinese capital filled the vacuum left by outflow of British capital by strengthening their investments in both Hong Kong and the Mainland (Feng, 1997, pp. 395–416). The economic turbulence surrounding the exodus of British capital and the rise of local Chinese capital in the transitional period not only strengthened the Chinese government's perception that maintaining the confidence of investors was the most important step in stabilizing Hong Kong's economy and society, but it also demonstrated that securing the support of the local Chinese capitalists was critical. As such, Beijing considered it necessary to co-opt and groom the local Chinese capitalists as the

108 *The legacy of state–business alliance*

majority of the political establishment of the future HKSAR (Goodstadt, 2000; Xu, 1993, pp. 127–128; Yep, 2009).

Second, maintaining the confidence of Hong Kong's business elites was also seen by Beijing's leaders as strategically important to China's own economic modernization. Since establishing its political regime in the Mainland in 1949, Beijing had all along adopted a rational and pragmatic policy towards Hong Kong and such a policy was formally described by the former Chinese premier Zhou Enlai as the principle of "formulating long-term plans, making maximum use of the place". In accordance with this policy, Beijing wanted to make full use of Hong Kong's special status to serve China's economic and social needs, including channelling much-needed foreign currencies to the Mainland, providing a valuable outlet for China's exports, obtaining foreign goods and supplies in the face of the United Nations' embargo amid the outbreak of the Korean War in 1950 (Lau, 2000). Since the implementation of economic reforms by Deng Xiaoping in 1978, Hong Kong's strategic role in supporting China's economic modernization had become particularly important. From the perspectives of Chinese leaders, Hong Kong's global business networks and economic linkages, its status as an international financial and trade centre and the cosmopolitan character and business knowledge of its entrepreneurs were all invaluable assets for China on its way towards a market economy (Yep, 2007). More importantly, Hong Kong's businessmen were the major investors in the Mainland since the 1978 reforms and had provided almost two-thirds of total foreign domestic investment to China's economy in the 1980s and 1990s. From this perspective, maintaining the confidence of Hong Kong's capitalists and securing their support for the resumption of Chinese sovereignty over Hong Kong was not only an important means to stabilize Hong Kong's economy and society, it was also of paramount importance to the Beijing government's own economic modernization. Losing the support of the Hong Kong capitalist class would be detrimental to Beijing's plan to recover Hong Kong and the financing of its modernization programmes would have been in jeopardy (Goodstadt, 2000). Against this background it was therefore not surprising that the Beijing leaders would consider the peaceful coexistence of Hong Kong's capitalism within China's socialism under the framework of one country–two systems as conducive to its national interests. Such a consideration was definitely another important reason behind the Chinese government's decision to engineer a new China-centred state–business alliance (Yep, 2007).

Third, the politically conservative business sector was also considered by the Chinese government as its most reliable coalition partner in fending off the pro-democrats' political challenges. Hong Kong's democratization was formally kicked off in the 1980s when the political controversies surrounding the impending change of sovereignty triggered the growth of the civil society and induced public participation in politics. With the rising political awareness of the Hong Kong people, many middle-class professionals who had been excluded from the power stratum of the colonial administration aggressively pursued their democratic and pro-welfare agendas. The middle-class professionals rapidly expanded

Crafting the post-1997 state–business alliance 109

their political influence by forming political parties and running for political offices in the District Boards, Municipal Council and Legislative Council elections (Ngo, 2000). For the Beijing leaders, they were afraid that the introduction of democratic reforms would gradually lead to the establishment of a highly autonomous, if not independent, government in Hong Kong that went beyond its political control and even allowed the British to continue their influences through elected pro-British and anti-Chinese politicians (Ngo, 2000; So, 1999). In particular, the active role played by the democrats in supporting and subsidizing the 1989 Tiananmen democratic movements had alarmed Beijing, who worried that rapid democratization in Hong Kong was also not conducive to its regime interests. As a result, the desire of Beijing was to postpone the implementation of universal suffrage in Hong Kong to a distant future date and the politically conservative business sector could be its reliable coalition partner in fighting against the challenges of the democrats (So, 1999; Yep, 2007, 2009).

Last, but not least, in the reconfiguration of the political order in Hong Kong the Chinese government did not have too many alternatives and the business elites were obviously its most convenient coalition partners. For Beijing's leaders, the local leftists, who maintained extensive organizational networks in the territory, should be its most loyal and reliable coalition partners. Nevertheless, there were several important factors that made it practically difficult for Beijing to rely on the local leftists and had to look elsewhere in the reconstitution of the post-1997 governing coalition (Ma, 2007, p. 35). First, the 1967 Riots had dealt a severe blow to the development of leftist organizations in Hong Kong, not only because the major leftist leaders who had participated in the riots were deported and imprisoned by the colonial administration, also the leftists had became extremely unpopular among the general public because of their violent actions in 1967. Second, throughout the British colonial period the local leftists were shunned within the colonial political establishment, and thus they had almost no knowledge or experience of government affairs. Having considered the low credibility and incompetency of the local leftists, the Beijing leaders had no choice but to look elsewhere in the making of the post-handover governing coalition. In this connection, the business elites became the most convenient coalition partners of the Chinese government, having regard to their extensive representation in the colonial political establishment and their weight in the Hong Kong economy (Ma, 2007, p. 36).

The above discussion points to the fact that there were strong political and economic incentives behind the Chinese government's strategy to construct its own state–business alliance as the cornerstone of the post-1997 political order. But one important question remains unanswered: why did the business elites, in particular the local Chinese capitalists, also take collective action to abandon their previous partnership with the British colonial administration and turn to the new political alliance engineered by the Chinese government? To better comprehend the nature and dynamics of the partnership between the Chinese government and the business sector since the transitional period, it would be useful for

110 *The legacy of state–business alliance*

us to move beyond the state-centric perspective and uncover a new path of inquiry by looking at the politics of transition from the angle of the business elites' response and calculations. In this connection, the latest political science literature on state building indicates that under authoritarian regimes political elites are more inclined to set aside their narrow factional interests in pursuit of broader class interests when they are facing common political challenges and, in particular, a "shared fear of enemies" in a time of "contentious politics" (Slater, 2010). From this perspective, the decision of the Hong Kong capitalist class to enter into a political partnership with the Chinese government was neither unintentional nor accidental – it was a calculated collective response made by the business elites for the purpose of coping with the common challenges and threats they faced during the critical moment of political transition in the 1980s and the 1990s.

The most important challenge that prompted the business elites to establish a political alliance with the Beijing government in the 1980s was undoubtedly the reconstitution of Hong Kong's political order as induced by the impending change of sovereignty. During the British colonial period, its collaborative alliance with the colonial state had allowed the local capitalists to enjoy the privileges of pro-business government policies, including low taxation, minimum welfare provision and little government intervention. The impending change of sovereignty and the coming of a new sovereign state pointed to the fact that the previous colonial political order in Hong Kong was going to be reconfigured and reconstituted, and this unavoidably induced a strong sense of uncertainty and insecurity among the business elites, in particular the Chinese capitalists, and they were required to explore a new approach to maintain their privileged positions in Hong Kong's political system after the change of sovereignty in 1997 (Ngo, 2000).

Worse still, the rising pressure for democratic reforms and the emergence of local democrats during the transitional period had added fuel to the business sector's sense of uncertainties and insecurity about their political position in Hong Kong. For the business elites, the democrats' demand for constitutional reform was an important and unprecedented challenge to their class interests, as the process of democratization was likely to affect their dominant position in the governance system of Hong Kong. The business sector was particularly worried that if their political voices and predominant influences over the governance process were eventually marginalized as a result of the democratic reforms, it would finally bring about stronger staff unions, higher taxes and more government regulations on business activities (Ngo, 2000; So, 1999). In fact, the business sector's worries were not without grounds. Since the 1980s politicians from the democratic camp had successfully mobilized strong popular support and won landslide victories in District Board, Municipal Council and Legislative Council elections by articulating pro-welfare and pro-grassroots electoral platforms (Ngo, 2000). As a result, both the foreign and local capitalists expressed strong opposition to radical democratic reforms in Hong Kong and thought they could rely on the Chinese government to resist the trend of democratic reforms (Loh, 2010,

Crafting the post-1997 state–business alliance   111

p. 163). Such considerations of the capitalist class were clearly revealed by Xu Jaitun in his memoir:

> Many people in the upper strata of Hong Kong's society were very worried about the trend of democratization ... the local Chinese capitalists hoped to preserve the pre-existing conditions and they were unready for the waves of democratic reforms and unprepared to participate in the games of democratic politics. They also feared that the participation of the middle and lower classes in politics will bring about "welfare fee lunch" and higher taxation, causing damage to Hong Kong's economic advantages. However they did not have any legitimate reason to oppose the trend of democratization, so they were in the state of depression and anxiety. In the process of drafting of the Basic Law, many of the local businessmen therefore made up their minds and took actions to collaborate with China in containing the democratic waves in Hong Kong. Like those local Chinese capitalists, the big capitalists from British enterprises held similar views.... They believed that Hong Kong's success was built upon on stability, and if democracy was implemented too quickly, they were afraid that it would only bring about instability and undermine the confidence of investors.
>
> (Xu, 1993, p. 186)

To use the words of Dan Slater, the shared fear of losing their political privileges surrounding the change of sovereignty and the growing pressures of democratic reforms had created some forms of "contentious politics" during the transitional period and induced a strong sense of uncertainty and insecurity within the business sector. In order to cope with these common challenges and threats, the business elites, in particular the local Chinese capitalists, believed it necessary to guarantee their vested political and economic interests by relying on the Beijing government and thus they took collective actions in the transitional period to seek political patronage from the incoming sovereign state. Clearly, the business sector's considerations and actions coincided with the political and economic calculations of the Chinese government, as discussed above. The two parties' common goal and interests in maintaining Hong Kong's capitalist system and social stability, in fending off the challenges of the democrats and in preserving the pro-business government policies finally resulted in the formation of a political alliance between the Beijing government and the Hong Kong capitalist class. The establishment of such an alliance would, on the one hand, allow the Chinese government to secure a reliable coalition partner in containing the waves of democratic movement and safeguarding the capitalist system and economic prosperity in Hong Kong, while on the other hand it provided the business sector with an important platform to extend their dominant influence over government affairs (Goodstadt, 2009, p. ix). It is therefore not surprising that Xu Jiatun once described the importance of forming a state–business governing coalition in Hong Kong as follows:

112 *The legacy of state–business alliance*

The principle of one country, two systems and the policy of keeping Hong Kong's capitalist system unchanged over a long period of time were made by top Chinese leaders including Deng Xiaoping. Such a policy was made for the purpose of making maximum use of Hong Kong and stabilizing the different social classes in the territory, particularly the capitalist class. In accordance with this policy direction, the capitalist class in Hong Kong is not our opponent, but is our close ally and also executor of our policies. The essence of "Hong Kong people ruling Hong Kong" is that Hong Kong should be managed by Hong Kong people of different classes but the capitalist class should play the pivotal role in the management of Hong Kong. [in Chinese]

(Xu, 1993, p. 128)

In view of the above, the continuation of the state–business alliance beyond 1997 was based upon the rational calculations by both the Chinese government and the local capitalist class. It is against this backdrop that the formula of establishing and maintaining a state–business alliance was adopted the foundation of the post-1997 political order.

The rise of a new China-centred state–business alliance: the co-option of the business sector by Beijing since the 1980s

Win over capitalists: In order to resume sovereignty in 1997, a massive fifth united front campaign had to be rolled out in Hong Kong to build alliances with all manners of groups, but in particular with the political and economic elites of the day so as to win their loyalties. The "landlord", "comprador' and "bourgeoisie" classes were all to be actively cultivated.... Those who were co-opted were invited to sit on important bodies to legitimise the transition process to Chinese rule.

(Loh, 2010, p. 29)

The convergence of the interests of the Beijing government and the local capitalist class had shaped the dynamics of politics during the transitional period, paving the way for the replacement of the former "British-centred state–business alliance" by a new "China-centred state–business alliance". In order to engineer and consolidate its political alliance with the local capitalist class, Beijing leaders started aggressively co-opting the business tycoons and elites into its united front following the signing of the Sino-British Joint Declaration in 1984.

In order to construct a united front in support of its Hong Kong policy and the future HKSAR government, the Chinese government actively cultivated and nurtured pro-Beijing local capitalists by incorporating them into two major types of political institutions during the transitional period (Cheung & Wong, 2004; Goodstadt, 2000). First, leading figures from the business sector were absorbed by the Chinese government into a number of special organizations and bodies responsible for administering the transition of sovereignty, including the Basic

Law Drafting Committee (BLDC), the Basic Law Consultative Committee (BLCC), the Hong Kong Affairs Advisers (HKAA), the Preliminary Working Committee (PWC) and the Hong Kong SAR Preparatory Committee (HKSARPC). Second, big businessmen were also extensively incorporated by the Beijing government into its own national political institutions as representatives of Hong Kong's compatriots, including the National People's Congress (NPC) and the National Committee of the Chinese People's Political Consultative Conference (CPPCC).[5]

Empirical research conducted by local political scientists indicated that the Chinese government's pattern of political co-option during the traditional period had shown a clear preference for incorporating the local capitalist class. Table 4.1 shows that during this period business elites were the major targets of political co-option by the Beijing government and they formed the single largest group in all the China-appointed political organizations in the 1990s, amounting to over 46 per cent of all these political appointments (Cheung & Wong, 2004). The over-representation of the business sector in the various China-appointed political bodies clearly reflected the Chinese government's strategy of making the local capitalist class the majority of its united front and its coalition partners in the governance of post-1997 Hong Kong.

Among the China-appointed political bodies, the composition of the BLDC was particularly illustrative and significant because this committee was responsible for designing the post-1997 political system and drawing up the Basic Law, the mini-constitution of the future HKSAR. The BLDC was chaired by Ji Pengfei, the Director of the Hong Kong and Macau Affairs Office (HKMAO) of the State Council, and there were also eight deputy directors (half of them Mainland deputy directors and another half Hong Kong deputy directors) and altogether 59 members (including 36 Mainland members and 23 Hong Kong members). In accordance with the Chinese government's policy of incorporating the local capitalist class as the majority of its united front and the new political establishment, there was a clear dominance of the business elites in the positions of Hong Kong deputy directors and Hong Kong members of the BLDC: three of the four Hong Kong deputy directors were well-known business tycoons including entrepreneur Ann Tse-kai, banker David Li Kwok-po and shipping tycoon Pao Yue-kong, while other big businessmen like Li Ka-shing, Cha Chi-min and Fok Ying-tung also occupied seats in the capacity of Hong Kong members. All these local business tycoons were political conservatives and were well-known for their opposition to democratic reforms; it was therefore not surprising that through their numerical dominance in the BLDC a constitutional system that clearly favoured the business sector was finally incorporated into the Basic Law and was imposed on the future HKSAR (Cheung, 2000; Lo, 2002).

Undoubtedly, the transitional period was a watershed moment for Hong Kong's political development, because it marked the replacement of the old "British-centred state–business political alliance" with the new "China-centred state–business governing coalition". The old state–business political alliance, engineered by the British colonial state, served the common interests of the

Table 4.1 Background analysis of members of China-appointed bodies in the 1990s

Background	NPC (1993)		CPPCC (1993)		BLDC (1985–1990)		BLCC (1985–1990)		HKAA (1992–1997)		PWC (1993–1995)		HKSARPC (1996–1997)		Total	
	No.	%	No.	%	No.	%	No.	%	No.	%	No.	%	No.	%	No.	%
Business	**10**	**38.4**	**47**	**56**	**9**	**39**	**71**	**39.8**	**91**	**49**	**18**	**47.4**	**45**	**49**	**291**	**46.3**
Professions	9	34.5	15	18	9	39	61	33.9	64	34.4	14	36.8	28	30.6	200	31.8
Labour	3	11.5	2	2.4	1	4.3	9	5	4	2.2	2	5.3	4	4.3	25	4
Culture and media	2	7.7	11	13.1	2	8.7	14	7.8	10	5.4	2	5.3	5	5.4	46	7.3
Others	2	7.7	9	10.8	2	8.7	24	13.4	17	9.1	2	5.3	10	10.9	66	10.5
Total	26	100	84	100	23	100	179	100	186	100	38	100	92	100	628	100

Source: Adapted from Cheung & Wong, 2004.

London government, the British merchants and the local Chinese businessmen in maintaining political stability and economic prosperity in Hong Kong and had ruled the territory for over a century. The transitional period of the 1980s and 1990s marked the replacement of the old political alliance between the colonial state and Hong Kong's capitalist class with a new "China-centred state–business alliance". As Alvin So has put it:

> London ... ruled Hong Kong through an expatriate alliance with pro-British businesspeople.... This institutional alliance was highly stable for over a century. However it began to crack during the negotiation process in the early 1980s.... In the late 1980s, a new unholy alliance between Beijing and Hong Kong Chinese businesspeople gradually replaced the traditional expatriate alliance of London and pro-British businesspeople.... This alliance was institutionalized through the appointment of big businesspeople to the Basic Law committees in the late 1980s and to the Preliminary Working Committees, the Preparatory Committee, and the Provisional Legislative Council in the 1990s, thus again guaranteeing business's continued dominance in the government of the SAR.
>
> (So, 1999, p. 259)

In view of the above, it was clearly the grand strategy of the Chinese government to nurture and incorporate the local capitalists as the majority of the post-1997 governing elites, and the Beijing leaders had carefully crafted the Basic Law with the explicit intention of making the state–business alliance the foundation of the future HKSAR governance system. Perhaps the only significant political change expected by the Beijing leaders was that the Chinese government should take over from the British Governor as the centre of this state–business alliance after the handover of sovereignty in July 1997.

Conclusion

Maintaining its governance in Hong Kong through a viable state–business alliance was considered as the cornerstone of the political order engineered by the British colonial state. In this connection, the discussions in this chapter clearly demonstrate that the Chinese government intended to retain this key feature of the colonial governance system with a view to achieving its wide political and economic objectives, including maintaining Hong Kong's capitalist system and social stability, facilitating China's own economic modernization and resisting the political pressure for rapid democratization by the local democrats. On the other hand, the shared fear of losing their political influence also prompted the business sector in Hong Kong to think they could rely on Beijing to fend off the political challenges of democrats and to safeguard their political and economic interests after 1997. The convergence of interests between the Chinese government and the business sector finally drove the two parties to join hands in making the state–business alliance the cornerstone of the future HKSAR political order. Against

116 *The legacy of state–business alliance*

this background, local business elites were extensively co-opted by the Beijing government into its various China-appointed political institutions, including the BLDC, BLCC, HKAA, PWC, HKSARPC, NPC and CPPCC. As a result, the local capitalist class not only formed the majority of the new political establishment and was considered as the single largest group of the post-1997 governing elites, but a political system that clearly favoured the business sector was also imposed on the future HKSAR through the drafting process of the Basic Law.

Obviously, the desire of the Chinese government was that the state–business alliance, which operated smoothly and effectively during the British colonial period, would continue to function well after the handover, and furnish the future HKSAR government with strong governing capacity. However, things did not turn out as Beijing's leaders anticipated after 1997. The post-1997 political developments showed that despite the careful political engineering by Beijing, the HKSAR government encountered many difficulties in maintaining effective governance, and the state–business alliance also failed to perform its original function in furnishing the post-colonial state with strong governance capacity. What were the structural and contextual factors that resulted in the failure of the state–business alliance after the handover? How did the failure of the state–business alliance undermine the governing capacity of the post-colonial state and bring about the governance crisis in the post-1997 period? Our analysis in the forthcoming chapters will demonstrate that the failure of the state–business alliance after 1997 was actually the result of a number of political and socio-economic changes since the handover. These political and socio-economic changes, including the disarticulation of encompassing agents of business interests, the growing disconnection of co-opted business elites, the institutionalization of business power in the post-1997 political system and the business sector's increased access to the sovereign state, have all contributed to the failure of the state–business governing coalition after 1997 and have severely undermined the governing capacity of the post-colonial Hong Kong state.

Notes

1 For an account of the Sino-British negotiation, see Tsang (1997, pp. 81–110).
2 Details of the Chief Executive Election Committee and the functional constituencies of the Legislative Council will be discussed in Chapter 7.
3 For example, in March 1984 when the Sino-British negotiation over the future of Hong Kong had not yet been settled, the Jardine Group surprisingly announced the formation of Jardine Matheson Holdings Limited, a company incorporated in Bermuda, as the group's new holding company. Similarly, the Hong Kong Bank also set up a new company called the HSBC Holdings in the United Kingdom and made it the bank's new holding company in 1990 (Feng, 1996, pp. 289–311).
4 Since the mid 1980s the Jardine Group planned to reduce the "risk of 1997" by strengthening their investment outside Hong Kong and China. Its major subsidiaries, including Dairy Farm, Mandarin Oriental and Jardine Pacific, made a number of acquisitions around the world during the transitional period. Similarly, the Hong Kong Bank also developed itself into an international bank in the 1990s by expanding its business in Asia, North America and Europe (Feng, 1996, pp. 312–339).

Crafting the post-1997 state–business alliance   117

5 Before the 1980s most of the Hong Kong NPC and CPPCC delegates were leading leftist figures from the labour, education, culture and patriotic business sectors and the local Chinese capitalists were not the Chinese government's targets of political co-option. The situation changed significantly following the signing of the Sino-British Joint Declaration in 1984. In order to cultivate its supporters in the Hong Kong business sector and to engineer a new united front for implementing its Hong Kong policy, the Chinese government started to make use of the Hong Kong NPC and CPPCC as the platforms for incorporating local capitalists, and appointments to these two political institutions begun to shift to those business elites who were never part of the traditional leftist camp (Loh, 2010, p. 192).

References

Cheung, A. (1998). The transition of bureaucratic authority: The political role of the senior civil service in the post-1997 governance of Hong Kong. In P. K. Li (Ed.), *Political order and power transition in Hong Kong* (pp. 79–108). Hong Kong: Chinese University Press.

Cheung, A. (2000). Social conflicts: 1975–1986. In S. K. Lau (Ed.), *Social development and political change in Hong Kong* (pp. 63–114). Hong Kong: Chinese University Press.

Cheung, A. (2007). Executive-dominant governance or executive power "hollowed-out": The political quagmire of Hong Kong. *Asian Journal of Political Science, 15*(1), 17–38.

Cheung, A. (2010). Restoring governability in Hong Kong: Managing plurality and joining up governance. In J. Tao, A. B. L. Cheung, M. Painter, & C. Y. Li (Eds.), *Governance for harmony in Asia and beyond* (pp. 158–185). New York: Routledge.

Cheung, A., & Wong, P. C. W. (2004). Who advised the Hong Kong government? The politics of absorption before and after 1997. *Asian Survey, 44*(6), 874–894.

Feng, B. Y. (1996). *Xianggang ying zi cai tuan: 1841–1996 (Hong Kong's British consortiums, 1841–1996)*. Hong Kong: Joint Publishing (H.K.) Co. Ltd (in Chinese).

Feng, B. Y. (1997). *Xianggang hua zi cai tuan: 1841–1997 (Hong Kong's local Chinese consortiums, 1841–1997)*. Hong Kong: Joint Publishing (H.K.) Co. Ltd (in Chinese).

Ghai, Y. (1999) *Hong Kong's new constitutional order: The resumption of Chinese sovereignty and the Basic Law* (2nd ed.). Hong Kong: Hong Kong University Press.

Goodstadt, L. F. (2000). China and the selection of Hong Kong's post-colonial political elite. *China Quarterly, 163*, 721–741.

Goodstadt, L. F. (2009). *Uneasy partners: The conflict between public interest and private profit interest in Hong Kong*. Hong Kong: Hong Kong University Press.

King, A. Y. C. (1991). *The Hong Kong talks and Hong Kong politics*. Hong Kong: Hong Kong Institute of Asia-Pacific Studies.

Lau, S. K. (2002). Tung Chee-hwa's governing strategy: The shortfall in politics. In S. K. Lau (Ed.), *The first Tung Chee-hwa administration* (pp. 1–39). Hong Kong: Chinese University Press.

Lo, S. H. (2002). The Chief Executive and the business: A Marxist class perspective. In S. K. Lau (Ed.), *The first Tung Chee-hwa administration* (pp. 289–328). Hong Kong: Chinese University Press.

Loh, C. (2010). *Underground front: The Chinese Communist Party in Hong Kong*. Hong Kong: Hong Kong University Press.

Ma, N. (2007). *Political development in Hong Kong: State, political society and civil society*. Hong Kong: Hong Kong University Press.

118 *The legacy of state–business alliance*

Ngo, T. W. (2000). Changing government–business relations and the governance of Hong Kong. In R. Ash, P. Ferdinand, B. Hook, & R. Porter (Eds.), *Hong Kong in transition: The handover years* (pp. 26–41). New York: St. Martin's Press.

Slater, D. (2010). *Ordering power: Contentious politics and authoritarian leviathans in Southeast Asia.* Cambridge: Cambridge University Press.

So, A. Y. (1999). *Hong Kong's embattled democracy: A societal analysis.* Baltimore, MD: Johns Hopkins University Press.

Tsang, S. (1997). *Hong Kong: Appointment with China.* New York: I.B. Tauris.

Xu, J. T. (1993). *Xu Jiatun Xianggang Huiyilu* (Xu Jiatun's memoir on Hong Kong). Taipei: Lianhebao (in Chinese).

Yep, R. (2007). Links with the Mainland. In W. M. Lam, P. L. T. Lui, W. Wong, & I. Holiday (Eds.), *Contemporary Hong Kong politics: Governance in the post-1997 era* (pp. 245–264). Hong Kong: Hong Kong University Press.

Yep, R. (2009). The 1967 riots in Hong Kong: The domestic and diplomatic fronts of the Governor. In R. Bickers, & R. Yep (Eds.), *May days in Hong Kong: Riot and emergency in 1967* (pp. 21–36). Hong Kong: Hong Kong University Press.

Part III

Missing link between state, business and society

The growing erosion of the intermediary
role of business elites after 1997

5 The missing link between state and business

The fragmentation of agents of business interests

The formation of a state–business alliance in the post-1997 period is based on the assumption that by co-opting business elites as the majority of the HKSAR political establishment, the business sector could provide strong and stable political support to the post-colonial state in maintaining effective governance and steering policy-making as in the colonial past. While the business elites have been extensively incorporated in the HKSAR political establishment as originally planned, the post-1997 political developments demonstrated that the business representation system does not function smoothly when compared with the British colonial period and the post-colonial state is encountering increasing difficulties in articulating the interests of the business sector and consolidating business support for its policy initiatives. In the process of policy-making, the post-colonial state has been directly confronting different agents of business interests and even been dragged into the conflicts among competing business groups.

Why does the extensive co-option of business elites into the HKSAR political establishment, which is apparently more or less the same as in the colonial era, fail to consolidate business support to the post-colonial state? In his memoir, Xu Jiatun revealed that it was the original plan of Beijing to re-engineer the business sector in Hong Kong into an organized bloc, just like the "Keidanren" in Japan, with a view to maintaining effective coordination of major business interests and providing a more stable political support base to the post-colonial state after 1997 (Xu, 1993, pp. 189–190). However, until today the idea of developing such an encompassing political organization or political party for representing business interests in Hong Kong has remained empty talk. What are the structural factors resulting in the underdevelopment of business-oriented political parties in post-1997 Hong Kong? How does the fragmentation of agents of business interest after the handover bring about growing challenges for the post-colonial state to articulate and reconcile major business interests? Is there any causal relationship between the fragmentation of business agents and the increasing difficulties faced by the post-colonial state in consolidating business support for its policies?

This chapter argues that the traditional business representation system in colonial Hong Kong was not simply about co-option of individual business elites, but it was actually featured by the incorporation of senior executives of

122 *Missing link between state, business and society*

British business groups. But since the 1980s, such a business representation system has already broken down, because the changing configurations of economic and political structures in Hong Kong have put an end to the vital role of "encompassing intermediaries" previously performed by the British hongs. Nevertheless, because of the underdevelopment of business-oriented political parties after 1997, such a vital missing link between the post-colonial state and the business sector has not been effectively filled up and the co-opted business elites could no longer fulfil the role of "encompassing intermediaries" as in the British colonial past. As a consequence of the fragmentation of agents of business interests in the post-1997 period, the post-colonial state is facing growing difficulties in mediating between major business interests and consolidating business support for its policy initiatives. On certain controversial public policies, the post-colonial state is required to directly confront different agents of business interests, resulting in intense conflicts and open clashes within the state–business alliance.

The end of the traditional business representation system: the changing configuration of the economic and political structures since the 1980s

> [T]he power of the British hongs has steadily declined since the 1970s.... The high concentration of business power was gone. There was no longer a large tightly knit group that encompassed a large number of companies and that linked up the Chinese and non-Chinese business groups.
>
> (Wong, 1994)

The traditional business representation system in colonial Hong Kong was not simply about co-option of individual business elites, but it feature the incorporation of encompassing British business groups. By virtue of their dense networks of subsidiary companies and dominant position in Hong Kong's economy, major British hongs effectively performed the role of "encompassing intermediaries", helping the colonial state articulate the interests of the business sector and consolidating their political support. Such a business representation system ensured that when the business elites were co-opted into the state machinery, they did not act individually but would function as an organized group. The existence of encompassing British business groups was therefore an important enabling condition that linked the colonial state and the business sector, thereby contributing to the smooth functioning of the state–business alliance during the colonial era (see Chapter 3).

Nevertheless, this important pillar of the state–business alliance has been gradually broken in recent years, as a result of the changing configuration of the economic and political structures in Hong Kong since the 1980s. The downfall of the major British business groups during the transitional period, together with the rise of local Chinese and Mainland capital, has resulted in the growing diversity of Hong Kong's business sector and has finally put an end to the vital role of

Missing link between state and business 123

"encompassing intermediaries" previously performed by the major British hongs. Coupled with the implementation of democratic reforms to the Legislative Council, the political-economic foundations of the traditional business representation system have been shaken during the transitional period of the 1980s and 1990s. Such a new political economy has called for the development of a new agent of business interests for articulating and reconciling the interests of the business sector.

The end of the era of "princely hongs": the transition from a British-dominated economy into a more diversified business sector since the 1980s

Since the founding of the colony in the nineteenth century, Hong Kong had been dominated by the British business groups. In this connection, Jardine Matheson, Swire, Hutchison-Whampoa and Wheelock were widely considered as the four most influential British business groups and the Jardine Group had even been described as the "princely hong" (Wong, 1996). Until the late 1970s, these four major British hongs, together with their subsidiaries and associated companies, had accounted for over 70 per cent of all listed companies in Hong Kong (Lau, 1997, p. 87).

Nevertheless, the strategic and commanding position of British capital in Hong Kong had finally come to an end in the early 1980s as a result of the rise of local Chinese capital. In this regard, the rapid growth of manufacturing industries in the 1960s and, in particular, the booming development of the property sector in the 1970s were the two major driving factors that accounted for the emergence of local Chinese capital. The prosperous growth of the manufacturing industries and the property development sector in the 1960s and 1970s had opened up two new avenues in Hong Kong's economy, and the local Chinese entrepreneurs had made good use of these new business opportunities to accumulate a tremendous amount of wealth and build up their business empires outside the traditional sphere of influence of the established British hongs (Wong, 1996). The fall of the British Taipans and the rise of the local Chinese tycoons were marked by several dramatic acquisitions that happened in the late 1970s and the early 1980s, where ownership of a number of major British companies had fallen into the hands of local Chinese business groups (Lau, 1997, pp. 87–88). These historical ownership changes included: Li Ka-shing's acquisitions of Green Island Cement, Hutchison-Whampoa and Hong Kong Electric in 1978, 1979 and 1985, respectively; Pao Yue-kong's takeover of Kowloon Wharf and the Wheelock Group in 1980 and 1985, respectively; Lee Siu-kei's acquisitions of Hong Kong & China Gas and Hong Kong & Yaumati Ferry in 1980 and 1981, respectively[1] (Feng, 1996, 1997; Wong, 1996).

Starting from the 1990s, the configuration of Hong Kong's economic structures has undergone another important change as a consequence of the growing presence of Mainland capital in the territory. The process of Mainland–Hong Kong economic integration, together with the impending change of sovereignty,

124 *Missing link between state, business and society*

had greatly strengthened the presence of Mainland capital in Hong Kong's economy during the transitional period of the 1980s and 1990s, under which the Mainland enterprises substantially increased and diversified their investments in the different economic sectors of Hong Kong, such as banking and finance, aviation, infrastructure, property development, building and construction, telecommunications, import and export trade[2] (Huang, 1997; Sung, 1997).

The changing configuration of Hong Kong's economic structures in the past few decades is illustrated in Figure 5.1. According to the empirical findings on the total market capitalization of all Hang Seng Index constituents from 1978 to 2003, British capital had maintained a predominant position in Hong Kong's economy in the late 1970s, with the major British business groups accounting for over 84.69 per cent and 76.94 per cent of the total market capitalization of the Hang Seng Index in 1978 and 1979, respectively. However, the commanding position of British capital in Hong Kong gradually diminished, starting from the early 1980s as a consequence of the growing economic power of the local Chinese entrepreneurs. Between the periods from the early 1980s to the late 1990s there was a clear shift in the balance of economic power in Hong Kong, because local Chinese capital had already caught up with British capital in terms of market power and influence. Starting from the 1990s, local Chinese capital

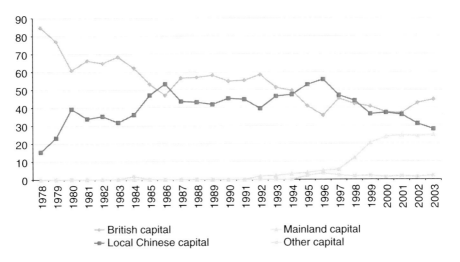

Figure 5.1 Percentage of equity of British capital, local Chinese capital, Mainland capital and other capital in the total market capitalization of the Hang Seng Index (1978–2003) (source: author's own research based on the historical figures available in the *Hong Kong Economic Journal* monthlies from 1978 to 2003).

Note
* The companies are classified according to the national background of their major shareholders in the respective years, while the market capitalization of the Hang Seng Index constituents was measured in terms of their year-end closing prices of respective years. This analysis only covers the period from 1978 to 2003 because starting from 2003 more heavyweight Mainland companies with no real businesses in Hong Kong have been listed, and thus the figures of total capitalization thereafter may not be indicative of Hong Kong's economic power structure.

Missing link between state and business 125

and British capital were at the same level as measured by their market capitalization in the Hang Seng Index, and the longstanding predominant position of the major British business groups in Hong Kong had finally came to an end. The empirical findings of this book also demonstrate that during the same period of the 1990s Mainland capital had been rapidly expanding its economic influences in Hong Kong, with the total market capitalization of Mainland enterprises in the Hang Seng Index increasing substantially from only 1.83 per cent in 1992 to 25 per cent in 2003.

The above discussions point to the fact that the high concentration of economic powers in the hands of a few major British business groups, which was an important foundation of the colonial political order and the traditional business representation system, had already gone by the 1980s and as a consequence Hong Kong's business sector became increasingly diversified and fragmented. Existing research on interlocking directorate analysis provided further empirical evidence that because of the decline of British capital and the emergence of local Chinese capital and Mainland capital in Hong Kong, the business sector had become increasingly differentiated and fragmented in the past few decades. Taking the company as a unit of analysis, the number of listed companies with interlocks with 20 or more companies was 72 in 1980, while the figure had decreased significantly to 32 in 1997 and 27 in 2004. Taking the individual director as a unit of analysis, 81 directors held four or more positions in 1982, but the number decreased sharply to 27 in 1997 and 19 in 2004 (Tables 5.1–5.2). All of the above statistics illustrate that, as measured by interlocked directorships, there was a significant drop in the cohesiveness of the business sector and the density of business networks in the past few decades (Lui & Chiu, 2007, 2009).

Apart from the decreasing density of business networks as indicated by the existing research on interlocking directorate analysis, the uncohesive nature of the business sector in Hong Kong today could also be illustrated by comparing the market capitalizations of major British business groups and local Chinese

Table 5.1 Number of interlocks per company (1982–2004)

Number of interlocks per company	Number of companies		
	1982	*1997*	*2004*
50 or more	**8**	**0**	**1**
40–49	**17**	**1**	**4**
30–39	**20**	**9**	**4**
20–29	**27**	**22**	**18**
15–19	27	16	30
10–14	29	42	31
5–9	31	62	49
3–4	27	35	42
1–2	29	32	31

Source: Lui & Chiu, 2007, 2009.

126 *Missing link between state, business and society*

Table 5.2 Multiple directorships held by individual directors (1982–2004)

Number of multiple directorships	*Number of individuals*		
	1982	*1997*	*2004*
Seven or more positions	22	3	2
Six or more positions	30	5	4
Five or more positions	48	9	10
Four or more positions	**81**	**27**	**19**

Source: Lui & Chiu, 2007, 2009.

business groups before and after 1997. In the colonial time, the commanding position of the major British business groups in Hong Kong's economy was clearly evident by the fact that the market capitalization of their companies and subsidiaries had accounted for a predominant proportion of the local stock market. Figure 5.2 indicates that the five major British business groups in colonial Hong Kong – Jardine, Hutchison, Swire, Wheelock and the Hong Kong Bank – had accounted for more than 51.39 per cent of the total market capitalization of all listed companies in 1979. In this connection, the Jardine Group and the Hong Kong Bank Group, which were major coalition partners of the colonial state and enjoyed stable representation in the Executive Council for much of the colonial period, were the two most influential business groups. All these empirical findings demonstrate that the state–business alliance as engineered by the British colonial administration had largely mirrored the economic power structure in colonial Hong Kong.

Nevertheless, Figure 5.3 offers a completely different picture about the economic power structure in post-1997 Hong Kong. Unlike the classical colonial period by which the local economy was clearly dominated by a few major British business groups, the five major local Chinese business groups in Hong Kong today, namely Cheung Kong-Hutchison Group, Sun Hung Kai Group, New World Group, Henderson Group and Hang Lung Group, altogether only accounted for 16.83 per cent of the total market capitalization of all listed companies in 2003. The Cheung Kong-Hutchison Group is undoubtedly the most powerful local Chinese business group in the post-1997 period, but its overall weight and importance in Hong Kong's economy are clearly not on a par with the predominant position of the Jardine Group and Hong Kong Bank Group during the British colonial time. All of the above statistics illustrate that when compared with its colonial predecessor, the post-colonial state is facing a more fragmented and differentiated business sector.

Both the interlocking directorship analysis and the market capitalization analysis point to the conclusion that the business sector in Hong Kong has become more diversified and fragmented in the past few decades. Such a changing configuration of Hong Kong's economic power structure since the 1980s has brought about far-reaching implications on the dynamics of the state–business relationship in the territory. As discussed in the preceding paragraphs, the

Missing link between state and business 127

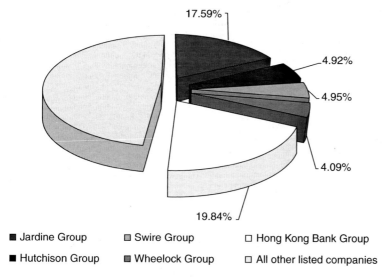

Figure 5.2 Market capitalization of major British business groups in the Hong Kong stock market in 1979 (source: author's own research based on the figures available in Feng, 1996: 208).

Notes
1 The Jardine Group included the following listed companies: Jardine Matheson, Hong Kong Wharf, Hong Kong Land, Jardine Securities, Harbour Centre Development and Zung Fu.
2 The Hutchison Group included the following listed companies: Hutchison Whampoa, Hutchison Property, Anderson Asia, Watsons, Wealthmark and Habour Works.
3 The Swire Group included the following listed companies: Swire Pacific, Swire Properties and Hong Kong Aircraft Engineering.
4 The Wheelock Group included the following listed companies: Wheelock Marden, Wheelock Maritime, Cross Harbour Tunnel, Realty Development, Realty & Trust, Lane Crawford, Allied Inv., Harriman Development and Beauforte Development.
5 The Hong Kong Bank Group included the following listed companies: Hong Kong Bank and Hang Seng Bank.

traditional business representation system in colonial Hong Kong was not simply about the incorporation of individual business elites, but it was characterized by the co-option of senior executives of those highly centralized and encompassing British business groups (in particular on the level of the Executive Council). By virtue of their predominant position in the colonial economic power structure and their extensive influence over a large number of subsidiary companies through interlocking directorships, the co-opted business elites from those major British hongs were capable of functioning as the "encompassing intermediaries" when they were appointed to the various advisory committees. On the one hand these "Taipans" performed the crucial role as effective agents of business interests, and on the other they also functioned as an effective link between the colonial state and the wider business sector. The existence of such a relatively cohesive business sector, with the major British hongs such as the Jardine Group and the Hong Kong Bank as the power centre, was therefore an important

128 *Missing link between state, business and society*

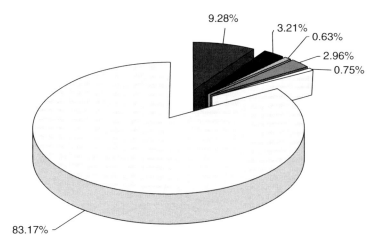

■ Cheung Kong-Hutchison Group □ New World Group □ Hang Lung Group
■ Sun Hung Kai Group ■ Henderson Group □ All other listed companies

Figure 5.3 Market capitalization of major local Chinese business groups in Hong Kong stock market (both main board and growth enterprise market) in 2003 (source: author's own research based on the figures available in the *Hong Kong Economic Journal* monthlies).

Notes
1 The Cheung Kong-Hutchison Group includes the following listed companies in Hong Kong: Cheung Kong Holdings, Hutchison Whampoa, Hong Kong Electric, Cheung Kong Infrastructure Holdings, CK Life Sciences International, Hutchison Harbour Ring and TOM Group.
2 The Sun Hung Kai Group includes the following listed companies in Hong Kong: Sun Hung Kai Properties, SUNeVision, SmarTone Telecommunications, Kowloon Bus Holdings and RoadShow Holdings.
3 The New World Group includes the following listed companies in Hong Kong: New World Development, New World China Land, NWS Holdings, Wai Kee Holdings and Road King Infrastructure.
4 The Henderson Group includes the following listed companies in Hong Kong: Henderson Land Development, Hong Kong Ferry, Henderson, Hong Kong & China Gas, Miramar Hotel and Investment and Panva Gas Holdings.
5 The Hang Lung Group includes the following listed companies in Hong Kong: Hang Lung Group and Hang Lung Properties.
6 The year 2003 was chosen as the benchmark for comparison because starting from 2003 more and more heavyweight Mainland companies with very limited real businesses in Hong Kong have been listed, and thus the figures of total market capitalization thereafter may not be indicative of the weight of major local Chinese business groups in Hong Kong's economy.

enabling condition for the smooth functioning of the state–business alliance in colonial Hong Kong. Because it helped make sure that the political co-option of senior executives of those major British hongs would largely mirror the economic power structures in the territory and thus the consensus of these co-opted business elites on major government policies would also be more acceptable to the wider business sector. It was on this basis the colonial state could effectively mediate between major business interests and consolidate business support for its policy initiatives (Lui & Chiu, 2007, 2009).

However, the increasing fragmentation of the business sector since the 1980s has removed the economic foundation of such a traditional business representation system, making it practically difficult for the post-colonial state to follow the colonial practice of consolidating business support through co-opting representatives of major business groups (Lui & Chiu, 2007, 2009). While the economic power structures before the 1980s were characterized by the concentration of economic powers in the hands of a few major British business groups such as the Jardine Group and the Hong Kong Bank, and provided the necessary foundation for these British hongs to function as agents of business interests, the economic power structures that have emerged since the 1980s have brought about a more fragmented and decentralized business sector. As a consequence of a more differentiated business sector, after the 1980s the co-opted businessmen and corporate elites are no longer capable of fulfilling the vital role of encompassing intermediaries previously performed by the representatives of major British business groups during the classical British colonial period, because they are not economically powerful enough to represent, articulate and reconcile the divergent interests of the fragmented business sector in post-1997 Hong Kong.

Electoral politics comes of age: the gradual introduction of elected seats into the Legislative Council since the 1980s

Apart from the fragmentation and decentralization of the economic power structures since the 1980s, the gradual development of electoral politics, which took place almost concurrently with the above process of economic transformation, has further shaken the political foundation of the traditional business representation system. The dominant feature of the traditional business representation system was that individual business elites would be directly appointed into the advisory system set up by the colonial state. But the smooth functioning of such a system was not only built upon the high concentration of economic powers in the hands of major British business groups, it was also facilitated by the closed political system during the British colonial time. Because of the absence of electoral politics for much of the colonial period, the senior executives of the princely hongs would be guaranteed their seats in the Legislative Council and Executive Council through the system of appointment and therefore there was no need for them to compete for political offices by means of contesting in elections and organizing political parties (Kuan, 1995).

Nevertheless, such a political formula was no longer workable after the gradual democratization of the Legislative Council since the 1980s. As part of its overall strategy to ensure an "honourable retreat" from Hong Kong, the British colonial administration introduced various reforms to democratize the political system in the territory in the final years of its colonial rule (Sing, 2003). The first wave of the reform was the incorporation of 12 functional constituency seats and 12 electoral college seats (the electoral college was formed by district

130   *Missing link between state, business and society*

board, urban council and regional council members) in the Legislative Council in 1985. Shortly after that, the colonial administration formally kicked off the democratization of the Legislative Council in 1991 by returned 18 out of the 60 seats to direct election in the geographical constituencies. In 1995 the last British Governor, Chris Patten, implemented further democratic reforms to the Legislative Council: the number of directly elected seats in geographical constituencies was increased to 20, nine new functional constituency seats were created which extended the electoral base to individual voters[3] and the ten election committee seats were indirectly selected by the directly elected District Board members (Miners, 1998, p. 128a).

The gradual introduction of elected seats into the Legislative Council has brought about revolutionary changes to the political landscape in Hong Kong (Table 5.3). While the implementation of democratic reforms since the 1980s has yet to turn the Legislative Council into a full democratic legislative chamber, the process of democratization has opened up a new avenue for the development of electoral and party politics[4] and resulted in fundamental changes to the relationship between the state and the business sector. Following the abolition of the appointment system, the senior executives of the major business conglomerates could no longer be assured of a seat in the Legislative Council as in the classical colonial era and the business elites have to be more assertive in competing for legislative seats through direct elections or functional constituency elections (Lau, 1997, p. 97; Wong, 1994).

The making of a new political economy in Hong Kong

The above discussions have pointed to the conclusion that the changing configurations of the economic and political structures since the 1980s have led to the breakdown of the traditional business representation system. The traditional business representation system as engineered by the colonial state was

Table 5.3 Composition of Legislative Council (from 1984–2008)

Year	Appointed members		Elected members			Total
	Official	*Unofficial*	*Election committee*	*Functional constituency*	*Direct election*	
1984	29	32	0	0	0	61
1985	11	22	12	12	0	57
1988	11	22	12	14	0	59
1991	3	17	0	21	18	59
1995	0	0	10	30	20	60
1998	0	0	10	30	20	60
2000	0	0	6	30	24	60
2004	0	0	0	30	30	60
2008	0	0	0	30	30	60

Source: Adapted from Ma, 2007a.

characterized by the direct appointment of senior executives from the highly centralized British business groups into its advisory system, particularly the Executive Council and the Legislative Council. The smooth functioning of such a business representation system was, however, built upon Hong Kong's unique colonial history and political-economic order. Economically, the high concentration of power in the hands of the British business groups gave rise to a few central players such as the Jardine Group and the Hong Kong Bank. By virtue of their dominant position in the economy and extensive business networks, the major British hongs effectively fulfilled the role of encompassing intermediaries between the colonial state and the business sector and therefore the extensive incorporation of their senior executives could help the colonial state effectively mediate its relationship with major business interests and consolidate its political support base within the business sector. Politically, the closed nature of the colonial political system and the absence of electoral politics also facilitated the smooth functioning of such a business representation system. Through the system of appointment, the senior executives of the major British business groups would be guaranteed their representations in the Legislative Council and Executive Council and therefore they were not required to organize political parties nor rely on any political agents to exert their political influences in the governing process.

However, since the 1980s the process of decolonization, which brought about increasing fragmentation of the business sector and the implementation of democratic reforms, has fundamentally changed Hong Kong's political-economic system. Following the downfall of the major British business groups and the emergence of electoral politics in the 1980s, the traditional business representation system had already been broken down and there is a general lack of effective agents of business interests to assume the role of encompassing intermediaries previously fulfilled by the princely hongs. Such a new political economy has therefore called for the development of a new encompassing agent of business interests to fill in the missing link between the post-colonial state and the business sector.

Who can represent the business sector in the post-1997 political-economic order? The underdevelopment of business-oriented political parties

> The Election Committee's composition guarantees business influence on chief executive selection, the functional constituencies guarantee Legislative Council representation for business interests, and the voting-by-group rule gives them the veto power over members' proposals. The protection is so good that the business groups in Hong Kong had little incentive to form, donate to, sponsor or even lobby political parties.
>
> (Ma, 2007a, p. 144)

The traditional business representation system was based upon Hong Kong's unique colonial history and political-economic order, where the dominant

132 *Missing link between state, business and society*

position of the British capital in the local economy and the closed political system provided the foundation for the senior executives of major British business groups to fulfil the role of encompassing intermediaries between the colonial state and the business sector. However, when the process of decolonization put an end to the dominance of the princely hongs and opened up Hong Kong's political system in the 1980s, where was the new encompassing agent of business interests? Who can represent the business sector in the post-1997 political-economic order?

Business representation under modern capitalist economies: overseas experiences

It is worth noting that the traditional business representation system in Hong Kong, which was characterized by the extensive incorporation of representatives from individual business conglomerates into state machinery, was an extraordinary pattern of state–business relationship and was exceptional among modern capitalist economies. For most of the Western capitalist economies, the role of individual business corporations in shaping the state–business relationship is usually not significant and when seeking advice and cooperation from the business sector state officials often focus on organized business groups "that represent the collective interests of groups of businesses" (Wilson, 2003, p. 9).

While the patterns of organizing business interests may vary from one country to another, in most of the modern capitalist economies the collective interests of the business sector are usually organized and represented in two major ways. The first major way of organizing business interests is the formation of various business associations. Generally speaking, business associations in Western democratic countries may either operate in the form of "trade associations" which represent the collective interests of individual business corporations within the same industry (e.g. the American Bankers' Association), or "peak organizations" which represent the collective interests of the business sector as a whole (the US Chamber of Commerce) (Wilson, 2003, p. 8).

Apart from forming business associations, another more significant way of organizing business interests in modern capitalist economies is the establishment and sponsorship of business-oriented political parties. For example, in the United States the Republican Party is commonly considered as the traditional business-oriented political party representing the interests of a variety of industries from the financial and manufacturing sectors to small- and medium-sized enterprises. It is estimated that more than half of the members of the Republican Party are self-employed business owners and business executives from different business corporations (Fried, 2008, pp. 104–105). Apart from directly participating in the organization of business-oriented political parties, the business sector in Western democracies will usually exert their influences over politics through making campaign contributions to pro-business parties and politicians. For example, in the United States business corporations could either make contributions to politicians and congressmen through the Political Action Committees or make "soft money" contributions directly to the political party as a whole in the name of party building and other activities not directly related to the election of specific candidates (Wilson, 2003, pp. 41–42). Similarly, the Conservative Party of the United Kingdom, which is the "natural party of business" in the country, has absorbed the vast majority of campaign contributions from the business sector and in return the Tories have on most occasions pursued pro-business policies in the areas of taxation and labour laws (Wilson, 2003, p. 72).

From the experience of most Western democracies, business-oriented political parties usually play a more important role than business associations in organizing and representing business interests. This is not only because the business-oriented political parties could exert more extensive and direct influence over the policy-making process and normally function as the most powerful spokesperson for business interests in the political arena, but also because the business associations in Anglo-American democracies are usually more fragmented and proliferated. Trade associations and peak associations in many capitalist economies such as the United States and the United Kingdom are highly fragmented because there is neither a moral nor legal requirement for individual companies to belong to their trade associations and peak associations, and thus there are usually keen competitions between several rival business associations claiming to be the most representative business organization. For instance, in the United States the US Chamber of Commerce, the National Association of Manufacturers, the Business Roundtable and the National Federation of Independent Business compete with each other as the most representative peak association of business interests (Wilson, 2003, pp. 8, 40). However, some continental European countries like Germany are exceptions to this rule. The peak associations and trade associations in continental European countries are generally better organized and more powerful than their counterparts in Anglo-American democracies because individual companies are legally obliged to join the trade associations in their respective industries (which are responsible for negotiating wage agreements with labour unions under the statutory collective bargaining system) and the peak associations are formed on the basis of these encompassing and influential trade associations (Wilson, 2003, p. 70).

The experiences of Western capitalist economies in organizing business interests have been illuminating for Hong Kong. Because of the closed political system in colonial Hong Kong, business-oriented political parties, which is the most important way of organizing business interests in Western countries, had been absent for much of the British colonial period. On the other hand, while trade associations and peak associations had a long history of development in Hong Kong, they are generally fragmented and proliferated both before and after 1997.[5] The most notable of these is the existence of four major peak associations in the territory since the colonial period, namely the Hong Kong General Chamber of Commerce, the Chinese General Chamber of Commerce, the Chinese Manufacturers' Association of Hong Kong and the Federation of Hong Kong Industries. Although business-oriented political parties and business associations (the two most common ways of organizing business interests in the

134 *Missing link between state, business and society*

Western capitalist economies) were either absent or underdeveloped during the colonial time, such a missing link between the colonial state and the business sector was competently filled in by the senior executives of the major British business groups who effectively fulfilled the role of encompassing intermediaries among clusters of business interests.

However, as discussed in the preceding paragraphs, such a unique system of business representation had already come to an end in the 1980s as a result of the changing configurations of the economic and political power structures. As a consequence of the growing diversity of Hong Kong's business sector and the rise of electoral politics since the 1980s, the co-opted business elites could no longer fulfil the crucial role of encompassing intermediaries previously performed by the senior executive of major British hongs. On the other hand, the peak associations in Hong Kong remain fragmented and proliferated in the post-1997 period and their role in articulating and organizing business interests is limited. Given the breakdown of the traditional business representation system and the continual disarticulation of business associations in Hong Kong, the development of an overcharging business-oriented political party should be the most desirable way forward for organizing business interests under the post-1997 political-economic order. The formation of an encompassing business-oriented political party should play an important role in articulating the diversified interests of the business sector, contesting for political offices in elections and representing business interests in the policy-making process. From this perspective, Xu Jiatun should have asked the right question in the 1980s by calling for the development of an overarching business-oriented political party to organize and represent the collective interests of the capitalist class in Hong Kong. However, the idea of developing an encompassing business-oriented political party has remained empty talk for many decades. How and why do business-oriented political parties in Hong Kong remain underdeveloped?

The rise and fall of business-oriented political parties in post-1997 Hong Kong: a historical review

Before we examine the different structural factors that obstruct the formation of a viable business-oriented political party in Hong Kong, it would be useful for us to first review the development history of various pro-business parties in the past two decades.

The development of business-oriented political parties in Hong Kong could be dated back to the early 1990s. The first major pro-business political group was the Liberal Democratic Federation, which was established in 1990 by a group of pro-Beijing businessmen and professionals like Hu Fa-kuang, Maria Tam Wai-chu, David Chu Yu-lin and Wong Siu-yee. Claiming to represent business interests, the Liberal Democratic Federation was formed by the pro-Beijing camp for the purpose of balancing the pro-democratic United Democrats of Hong Kong. However, the Liberal Democratic Federation failed to achieve this task and its five candidates were all defeated in the 1991 Legislative Council

Missing link between state and business 135

direct elections (Miners, 1998, pp. 200–202a; Yu, 2005). Another political group claiming to represent business interests was the Cooperative Resource Centre. It was formed by a group of pro-business Legislative Councillors in 1992 and its core members included Allen Lee Peng-fei, James Tien Pei-chun and Selina Chow Liang Shuk-yee. Largely formed in reaction to the landslide victory of the United Democrats of Hong Kong in the 1991 Legislative Council election, the Cooperative Resource Centre was organized by the pro-business Legislative Councillors in an attempt to counter the growing influence of the democrats in the local political scene. In 1994 the Cooperative Resource Centre was reorganized into the Liberal Party, which today remains the chief business-oriented political party in Hong Kong (Ma, 2007b; Yu, 2005). In the same year, another group of pro-Beijing businessmen including Lau Hon-chuen, Wan Ka-shuen and Yeung Suen-sai joined together to establish the Hong Kong Progressive Alliance. Once it was established, the Hong Kong Progressive Alliance quickly absorbed the Liberal Democratic Federation and became the second major business-oriented political party in Hong Kong (Lo, 2010, p. 180; Ma, 2007a, p. 140).

In the post-1997 era, the Hong Kong Progressive Alliance and the Liberal Party are the two major business-oriented political parties, but both of them have been caught in a series of political mistakes and internal splits. For the Hong Kong Progressive Alliance, although after the handover it had managed to secure several seats in the Legislative Council through functional constituencies and the election committee, it had never established a meaningful party organization or extensive community networks in society (Ma, 2007a, p. 141). Following the abolition of the election committee in the 2004 Legislative Council, the Hong Kong Progressive Alliance lost all its seats in the legislature and found it difficult to survive. Finally, it was "merged" with the Democratic Alliance for the Betterment of Hong Kong in 2005 to prolong its political longevity (Lo, 2010, pp. 170–180).

On the other hand, although after 1997 the Liberal Party had successfully maintained a more stable representation in the Legislative Council through functional constituencies, it has all along been dragged into internal rivalries between two party factions. One faction insisted that the Liberal Party should focus on consolidating its support base in the business sector by strengthening its influence in the functional constituencies instead of geographical constituencies, while the other faction argued that the Liberal Party should strengthen its commitment to direct elections and reach out to the wider public. The victories of its party leaders, James Tien and Selina Chow, in the 2004 Legislative Council geographical constituency elections did not help resolve these internal contradictions, and a major internal split within the Liberal Party was finally broken out after the 2008 Legislative Council election. In 2008 both James Tien and Selina Chow were defeated in the geographical constituency elections and after the electoral defeat both of them resigned as party leaders. The subsequent intense power struggles for party leadership finally led four of its seven legislators, namely Lau Wong-fat, Jeffery Lam Kin-fung, Andrew Leung Kwan-yuen and

136 *Missing link between state, business and society*

Sophie Leung Lau Yau-fun, to quit the Liberal Party and establish another political group called Economic Synergy (Lam, 2010). The internal split not only once again sparked debates within the Liberal Party over their commitment to future geographical constituency elections, it also dealt a further blow to its ambition to develop into an encompassing business-oriented political party.

The underdevelopment of business-oriented political parties is clearly evident by their weak party organizations and fragile financial positions. Contrary to the popular view that pro-business parties should possess rich financial resources, Table 5.4 demonstrates that both the Liberal Party and the Hong Kong Progressive Alliance experienced financial difficulties since their establishment in the 1990s. The Liberal Party faced nine years of budget deficits out of its past 17 financial years, and the Hong Kong Progressive Alliance also encountered consecutive years of financial deficits. As the flagship business-oriented political party in Hong Kong, the Liberal Party only maintained a relatively small annual budget of around 14 million on average, and it is comprehensible that its party leaders experienced great difficulties in soliciting donations from the business sector.[6] Obviously, the limited financial capabilities of pro-business parties have made it difficult for them to expand their political influence by investing resources in maintaining meaningful party machineries, running internal research units or building community networks.

The structural constraints on the underdevelopment of business-oriented political parties in Hong Kong

The business sector in Hong Kong has no shortage of financial resources and talents, so why do the business-oriented political parties remain disarticulated and fragmented and fail to develop themselves into an encompassing agent of business interests? Obviously, there are both structural political and economic factors behind the underdevelopment of business-oriented political parties in post-1997 Hong Kong.

First and foremost, the functional constituency system and the divided nature of the Legislative Council have hindered the development of an encompassing and cohesive business-oriented political party in Hong Kong. Although the functional constituency system was originally designed for guaranteeing the representation of business interests in the Legislative Council and it did return a substantial number of pro-business legislators after 1997 (see Chapter 7), its operational logic is contradictory to the development of a viable business-oriented political party for two reasons. First, for any business-oriented political parties there are inherent contradictions between participating in both functional constituency elections and direct elections: running for direct elections requires the business-oriented political party to represent an aggregate of societal interests, which is usually in conflict with the political interests of functional constituency legislators as they are supposed to act as the representatives of more specified and narrow functional interests (Lam, 2010). Thus, business-oriented political parties have usually been dragged into internal rivalries if they try to

Missing link between state and business 137

run for both functional constituency elections and geographical constituency elections. The internal split of the Liberal Party in recent years is highly illustrative of this problem. Second, functional constituencies are characterized by narrow electorate bases, thus pro-business politicians running for these offices usually do not need party help for mobilizing voters and they could count on their own personal networks or the support of relevant business associations to win the elections. In fact, party affiliation can even be a liability for functional constituency legislators because the party platform (which usually represents an aggregate of societal interests) may run counter to the narrow sectoral interests they need to represent. Therefore, for functional constituency candidates, maintaining their political status as a pro-business independent legislator is usually a better choice than joining business-oriented political parties like the Liberal Party (Ma, 2007a, p. 142). All of the above problems generated by the functional constituency electoral system not only give rise to the existence of a large number of pro-business independent legislators in the post-1997 Legislative Councils, they also bring about factional rivalries within business-oriented political parties and prevent them from being developed into a more encompassing agent of business interests.

In addition, the reluctance of many business elites to sponsor and participate in party politics has also discouraged the development of business-oriented political parties in Hong Kong. It is well understood that despite the growing importance of electoral and party politics in recent decades, business elites are generally reluctant to get involved in popular elections and their attitude towards organizing and sponsoring political parties has so far remained very negative (Wong, 1996). Ironically, the passive attitude of the business sector towards party politics is the consequence of the design of the post-1997 political system, under which business elites have already enjoyed extensive political influence and therefore they do not see any need to participate in organizing political parties to represent and defend their interests (Lo, 2010, pp. 178–179). After the handover, the business sector has maintained many privileged channels to gain access to political power, not only in terms of establishing their influence in the local political arena (by virtue of their predominant control over majority seats in the Chief Executive Election Committee and guaranteed seats in the Legislative Council through functional constituencies) but also in terms of having access to the sovereign state (by virtue of their dominant representation in Hong Kong's delegations to the National People's Congress and the National Committee of the Chinese People's Political Consultative Conference). Given all this privileged access to political powers, for the business sector organizing and sponsoring parties has become a too indirect and ineffective way to influence public policy.[7] Therefore many business leaders so far only provide half-hearted support for the development of business-oriented political parties and prefer to spend their time and money to directly lobby government officials behind the scenes (Lo, 2010, pp. 196–198; Ma, 2007a, p. 143).

Third, the diffusion and diversity of Hong Kong's capital is not conducive to the formation of an encompassing business-oriented political party. As a former

Table 5.4 Income and expenditure accounts of the Liberal Party and Hong Kong Progressive Alliance

	1994	1995	1996	1997	1998	1999	2000	2001	2002
Liberal Party									
Donations	21,391,900	12,286,855	9,014,342	8,495,479	11,501,000	12,508,250	15,314,277	9,789,736	9,797,908
Other income	639,094	288,691	544,925	363,918	154,014	59,987	69,914	137,721	148,167
Total income	22,030,994	12,575,546	9,559,267	8,859,397	11,655,014	12,568,237	15,384,191	9,927,457	9,946,075
Salaries and allowances	8,224,876	6,194,924	4,375,171	4,245,923	4,480,096	5,161,519	7,440,075	6,743,144	6,504,393
Other expenses	14,442,943	8,342,910	4,336,381	4,573,666	7,590,747	5,592,842	7,626,622	4,039,677	3,459,310
Total expenses	22,667,819	14,537,834	8,711,552	8,819,589	12,070,843	10,754,361	15,066,697	10,782,821	9,963,703
Surplus/deficit	−636,825	−1,962,288	847,715	39,808	−415,829	1,813,876	317,494	−855,364	−17,628

	2003	2004	2005	2006	2007	2008	2009	2010	Average
Donations	9,686,197	21,985,907	11,458,180	13,264,952	19,875,400	27,491,809	13,698,197	9,613,924	13,951,430
Other income	947,372	770,340	2,688,788	1,143,737	1,070,681	2,861,259	1,103,952	1,168,725	833,017
Total income	10,633,569	22,756,247	14,146,968	14,408,689	20,946,081	30,353,068	14,802,149	10,782,649	14,784,447
Salaries and allowances	5,539,770	7,902,950	7,412,689	7,295,218	7,370,377	8,126,572	7,769,533	7,715,116	6,617,785
Other expenses	5,526,345	13,731,808	7,552,071	6,675,703	9,350,284	24,030,046	6,981,583	4,328,817	8,128,339
Total expenses	11,066,115	21,634,758	14,964,760	13,970,921	16,720,661	32,156,618	14,751,116	12,043,933	14,746,124
Surplus/deficit	−432,546	1,121,489	−817,792	437,768	4,225,420	−1,803,550	51,033	−1,261,284	38,323

	1994	1995	1996	1997	1998	1999	2000	2001	2002
Hong Kong Progressive Alliance									
Donations	–	4,511,511	1,600,000	3,438,500	3,905,000	0	5,649,434	8,900,000	5,800,000
Other income	–	414,841	88,462	63,279	203,027	4,347	86,347	74,072	66,206
Total income	–	4,926,352	1,688,462	3,501,779	4,108,027	4,347	5,735,781	8,974,072	5,866,206
Salaries and allowances	–	1,527,318	1,367,935	1,412,251	1,627,615	1,056,499	2,332,068	2,081,756	1,908,946
Other expenses	–	3,082,836	1,914,032	2,257,205	2,415,701	1,818,312	3,445,486	6,933,257	4,009,395
Total expenses	–	4,610,154	3,281,967	3,669,456	4,043,316	2,874,811	5,777,554	9,015,013	5,918,341
Surplus/deficit	–	316,198	−1,593,505	−167,677	64,711	−2,870,464	−41,773	−40,941	−52,135

	2003	2004	2005	2006	2007	2008	2009	2010	*Average*
Donations	5,850,000	14,422,406	7,557,071	–	–	–	–	–	5,603,084
Other income	27,500	67,875	5,000	–	–	–	–	–	100,087
Total income	5,877,500	14,490,281	7,562,071	–	–	–	–	–	5,703,171
Salaries and allowances	1,870,263	1,971,147	2,604,319	–	–	–	–	–	1,796,374
Other expenses	4,027,454	8,155,026	4,957,134	–	–	–	–	–	3,910,531
Total expenses	5,897,717	10,126,173	7,561,453	–	–	–	–	–	5,706,905
Surplus/deficit	−20,217	4,364,108	618	–	–	–	–	–	−3,734

Source: Author's own research based on the annual financial statements of Liberal Party and Hong Kong Progressive Alliance (available at Companies Registry's Cyber Search Centre: www.icris.cr.gov.hk).

Note
All the figures are denoted in Hong Kong dollars.

140 *Missing link between state, business and society*

British colony, Hong Kong's economy was dominated by British capital, particularly before the 1980s. Nevertheless, when Hong Kong moved towards a business and professional services centre, starting from the 1980s, its economy was increasingly differentiated into various clusters of capital, including local Chinese capital, British capital, Mainland Chinese capital, foreign capital and numerous small and medium enterprises (Wong, 1994, 1995). The diffusion and diversity of Hong Kong's capital could be best illustrated through statistical figures. Figures 5.4 and 5.5 indicate the number of regional headquarters and regional offices in Hong Kong by country, and the figures clearly show the diversity of commercial corporations located in Hong Kong in terms of their country backgrounds, as well as the proliferation of non-local capital (i.e. the Mainland Chinese capital and other foreign capital) in Hong Kong's economy.

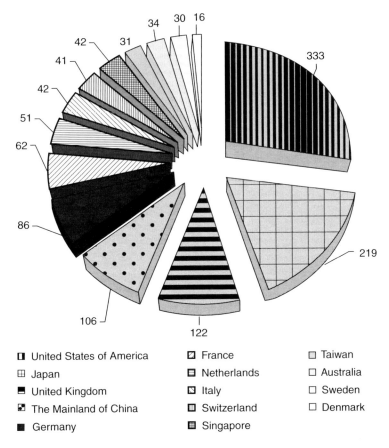

Figure 5.4 Number of regional headquarters in Hong Kong by country (2012) (source: adapted from the statistical tables available at the Census and Statistics Department's website at www.censtatd.gov.hk).

Note
The regional headquarters are classified in accordance with the location of the parent companies.

Missing link between state and business 141

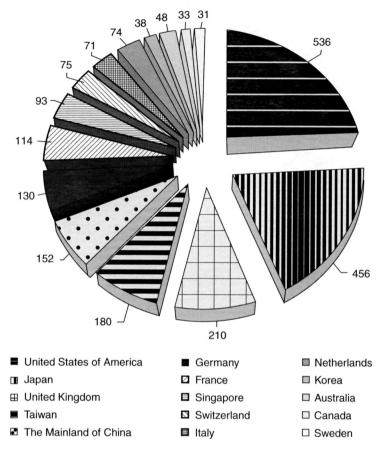

- United States of America
- Japan
- United Kingdom
- Taiwan
- The Mainland of China
- Germany
- France
- Singapore
- Switzerland
- Italy
- Netherlands
- Korea
- Australia
- Canada
- Sweden

Figure 5.5 Number of regional offices in Hong Kong by country (2012) (source: adapted from the statistical tables available at the Census and Statistics Department's website at www.censtatd.gov.hk).

Note
The regional offices are classified in accord with the location of the parent companies.

Table 5.5 demonstrates that there are about 300,000 small and medium enterprises in Hong Kong, accounting for over 98 per cent of the total business units and providing 48 per cent of total employment opportunities. The proliferation of non-local capital and existence of multitudinous small and medium enterprises in today's Hong Kong are clearly not conducive to the political unity and cohesion of the business sector. It is comprehensible that business-oriented political parties such as the Liberal Party have encountered many difficulties in reconciling the different interests of big businesses, while small and medium enterprises and companies from different country backgrounds are usually of the view that the Liberal Party cannot represent their interests.[8] The diversity of

142 *Missing link between state, business and society*

Table 5.5 Distribution of small and medium enterprises (as of June 2011)

Sector	No. SMEs	No. individuals
Manufacturing	11,358	68,134
Mining and quarrying; electricity and gas supply; waste management; and construction	1,090	11,625
Import/export trade and wholesale	113,841	449,941
Retail	45,454	144,971
Transportation, storage, postal and courier services	8,369	45,382
Accommodation and food services	11,806	121,743
Information and communications	10,066	40,131
Financing and insurance	17,515	60,685
Real estate	11,677	36,023
Professional and business services	36,103	130,893
Social and personal services	33,194	140,182
Total	300,473	1,249,710

Source: Trade and Industry Department's website available at www.success.tid.gov.hk.

Note
Manufacturing enterprises with fewer than 100 employees and non-manufacturing enterprises with fewer than 50 employees are regarded as small and medium enterprises in Hong Kong.

Hong Kong's economic structure has definitely hindered the rise of an overarching political organization that could represent the differentiated interests of different clusters of capital. Instead, it has encouraged the formation of a string of business associations which are set up to represent companies of different country backgrounds or small and medium enterprises (Table 5.6).

Implications of the fragmentation of agents of business interests: the paradox of "strong business representation, weak political support"

> [C]oalition between the colonial government and major business groups was made possible by a cohesive business sector composed of a dense network of major corporations. The consensus of the business sector (or at least among its dominant segments) on major policy issues, positive non-interventionism prominent among them, was the pillar of the colonial governance. This made it easier for the colonial government to forge social support for its policies. Since the 1990s, however, cohesion within the business sector has declined.... While the colonial state could appear to be an impartial arbiter of conflicts of interest between big businesses, the SAR government does not have this luxury but has been dragged into rivalries among the business groups.
>
> (Lui & Chiu, 2009)

The underdevelopment of business-oriented political parties in the post-handover era has profound implications for the dynamics of the state–business relationship.

Missing link between state and business   143

Table 5.6 Business associations in Hong Kong

Business associations representing companies from different country backgrounds
The American Chamber of Commerce in Hong Kong
Danish Chamber of Commerce
Finnish Business Council Hong Kong
German Chamber of Commerce, Hong Kong
Hong Kong New Zealand Business Association
Norwegian Chamber of Commerce, Hong Kong
South African Business Forum
Spanish Chamber of Commerce, Hong Kong
Swedish Chamber of Commerce in Hong Kong
Taiwan Business Association (HK) Ltd
The Arab Chamber of Commerce & Industry (Hong Kong)
The Australian Chamber of Commerce in Hong Kong
The British Chamber of Commerce in Hong Kong
The Canadian Chamber of Commerce in Hong Kong
The Hong Kong Chinese Enterprises Association
The Dutch Business Association
The French Chamber of Commerce and Industry in Hong Kong
The Hong Kong Japanese Chamber of Commerce & Industry
The Indian Chamber of Commerce Hong Kong
The Korean Chamber of Commerce in Hong Kong
The Singapore Chamber of Commerce (Hong Kong)

Business associations representing small and medium enterprises
Hong Kong Association for Promotion & Development of SMEs
Hong Kong Small and Medium Enterprises Association
Hong Kong Small & Medium Enterprises Development Association
Hong Kong Small and Medium Enterprises General Association
Hong Kong (SME) Economic and Trade Promotional Association Ltd
The Hong Kong Association of International Co-operation of Small and Medium
    Enterprises
The Hong Kong Chamber of Small and Medium Business Ltd
Major peak associations of business
Hong Kong General Chamber of Commerce
Chinese General Chamber of Commerce
Chinese Manufacturers Association
Federation of Hong Kong Industries

Source: Hong Kong Trade and Development Council's list of "Trade Associations" available at:
www.hktdc.com.

The effective functioning of the state–business alliance requires not only the
incorporation of business elites into the advisory system, but also the co-option
of encompassing intermediaries which could effectively organize and represent
major business interests. Such a business representation system would enable the
post-colonial state to better articulate and reconcile the diverse interests of the
wider business sector and consolidate the business sector's support for its policies. During the colonial time, such an important role of encompassing intermediaries was effectively performed by the major British business groups and their
representation in the advisory committees, particularly in the Executive Council,

144 *Missing link between state, business and society*

had made it easier for the colonial state to consult and co-opt the major business interests in the process of governance (Lui & Chiu, 2007, 2009; Ma, 2007a, p. 78). However, such a traditional business representation system was no longer workable now as a result of the changing configurations of economic and political structures since the 1980s. Having regard to the growing diversity of Hong Kong's business sector and the emergence of electoral politics since the 1980s, the post-colonial state could no longer rely on the co-option of senior executives of individual corporations to maintain its embeddedness and connectedness with the business sector.

Ideally, such an important missing link between the post-colonial state and the business sector should best be filled by business-oriented political parties as similar to other Western democracies, provided that co-opted business elites in post-1997 Hong Kong could organize themselves into an overarching political party for articulating and representing business interests. Nevertheless, the discussions in the preceding sections have fully illustrated that despite more than 20 years of development, business-oriented political parties are still underdeveloped in Hong Kong. As a consequence, instead of having an overarching political organization to function as the encompassing intermediary between the post-colonial state and the business sector, there exists a high degree of fragmentation among different agents of business interests in the political arena under which business-oriented political parties, business associations, non affiliated pro-business legislators and individual corporations all claim to represent business interests and get involved in the political process.

The disjointed nature of pro-business political forces in the legislature and the remote relationship between the business-oriented political parties and major business associations are highly indicative of the fragmentation of business agents in the political arena. Table 5.7 indicates that pro-business parties such as the Liberal Party and Economic Synergy are not quite capable of organizing business interests into a more coherent force in the legislature, as non-affiliated legislators occupied an average of 39.4 per cent of the total number of pro-business legislators in the post-1997 Legislative Councils (let alone the fact that the majority of professional legislators with similar pro-business orientations also keep their status as independents). Even at its apex in the 2004–2008 Legislative Council, the Liberal Party could not claim itself as the chief spokesperson for the business sector in the legislature. Following the internal split of the Liberal Party in 2008, the pro-business political forces in the Legislative Council have become much more disjointed and divided. On the other hand, Table 5.8 demonstrates that from 1997 to 2010 over 90.4 per cent of the Liberal Party's executive committee directors had no formal connection with the four major business associations. Only 9.4 per cent of the Liberal Party's executive committee directors had concurrently held directorships in the executive committees of any of the four major business associations.[9] All these empirical findings show that despite its efforts to position itself as the chief spokesperson of the business sector in the political arena, the Liberal Party fails to establish close partnerships with the major business associations and it is comprehensible that there has been

Table 5.7 Background analysis of pro-business Legislative Councillors (1998–2012)

Political affiliation	1998 to 2000		2000–2004		2004–2008		2008–2012		Total	
	No.	%	No.	%	No.	%	No.	%	No.	%
Non-affiliated pro-business legislators	**7**	**31.8**	**7**	**38.9**	**6**	**37.5**	**8**	**53.3**	**28**	**39.4**
Pro-business legislators with political party affiliation	15	68.2	11	61.1	10	62.5	7	46.7	43	60.6
Liberal Party	10	45.5	8	44.4	10	62.5	3	20	31	43.7
Economic Synergy	–	–	–	–	–	–	4	26.7	4	5.6
Hong Kong Progressive Alliance	5	22.7	3	16.7	–	–	–	–	8	11.3
Total	22	100	18	100	16	100	15	100	71	100

Source: Author's own research based on the biographies of Legislative Councillors (available at www.legco.gov.hk).

Notes
1 "Pro-business member" basically refer to Legislative Councillors who were returned by the 15 functional constituencies that represent the various business sectors, plus those Legislative Councillors who were returned by geographical constituencies or election committee but claimed to represent business interests.
2 "Non-affiliated pro-business member" refer to pro-business Legislative Councillors who are not affiliated with any pro-business political parties/political groups.
3 "Pro-business members with political party affiliation" refers to pro-business Legislative Councillors who are affiliated with any pro-business political parties/political groups, including the Liberal Party, Economic Synergy and Hong Kong Progressive Alliance.

Table 5.8 Interlocking directorships of the Liberal Party and four major business associations (1997–2010)

	1997	1998	1999	2000	2001	2002	2003	2004	2005	2006	2007	2008	2009	2010	Total
Number of the Liberal Party's executive committee directors concurrently holding directorships in the executive committees of any of the four major business associations*	1	1	1	1	1	1	3	2	2	2	4	4	2	2	27
Total number of the Liberal Party's executive committee directors	15	13	13	17	18	18	19	20	20	19	29	26	27	27	281
Percentage of interlocking directorships	**6.7**	**7.7**	**7.7**	**5.9**	**5.6**	**5.6**	**15.8**	**10.0**	**10.0**	**10.5**	**13.8**	**15.4**	**7.4**	**7.4**	**9.6**
Percentage of Liberal Party executive committee directors with no connection with any of the four major business associations	**93.3**	**92.3**	**92.3**	**94.1**	**94.4**	**94.4**	**84.2**	**90.0**	**90.0**	**89.5**	**86.2**	**84.6**	**92.6**	**92.6**	**90.4**

Source: Author's own research based on the annual returns of the Liberal Party (available at Companies Registry's Cyber Search Centre: www.icris.cr.gov.hk) and the annual reports of the four major business associations.

Note
* The four major business associations denote the Hong Kong General Chamber of Commerce, Chinese General Chamber of Commerce, Chinese Manufacturers Association and Federation of Hong Kong Industries.

Missing link between state and business 147

little coordination between the two sides in articulating business interests in the policy process.[10] As a consequence of its remote relationship with major business associations, it would be practically difficult for the Liberal Party to articulate a common position for the business sector on major policy issues and there is even a growing tendency for the major business associations to directly participate in the policy debates. The recent controversies on the enactment of the competition law are very indicative of this phenomenon. Instead of relying on those business-oriented political parties like the Liberal Party and Economic Synergy to represent their interests and opinions in the legislative process, the four major business associations voiced their concerns and opinions on the competition law directly to the post-colonial state and actively organized their own campaigns to oppose the legislation.[11]

The fragmentation of agents of business interests has brought about far-reaching impacts on the functioning of the state–business alliance after 1997. Because of the fragmentation of business agents, there exists no overarching political organization to represent business interests in the political arena and different business agents, including business-oriented political parties, major business associations, non-affiliated pro-business legislators and individual corporations, all get involved in the policy process. Under such circumstances, the post-colonial state is facing growing difficulties in consulting and mediating the diverse interests of the business sector, and the extensive incorporation of business elites into its advisory system, unlike the British colonial era, could no longer effectively serve the purpose of binding the post-colonial state and the business sector together in the governing process. The reason is that unlike the senior executives of the major British hongs in the colonial time, co-opted business elites in the post-handover period, no matter whether they are from business-oriented political parties, major business associations or individual corporations, are not encompassing agents of business interests and thus they are not quite capable of organizing, representing and reconciling the diverse interests of the business sector. As a consequence, instead of relying on these co-opted business elites to mediate and articulate the major business interests in the advisory system, the post-colonial state is required to engage in particularistic bargaining with different agents of business interests (i.e. business-oriented parties, non-affiliated pro-business legislators, major business associations and individual corporations) in the policy process and is struggling to consolidate business support for its policy initiatives. In other words, the post-colonial state has been increasingly trapped in a political paradox of "strong business representation, weak political support". Although the business elites are extensively co-opted and well represented in the HKSAR political establishment, the business sector's political support to the post-colonial state remains fragile and vulnerable.

The deterioration of the post-1997 Executive Council's function as an institutionalized platform for articulating and mediating between major business interests best illustrates such a paradox of "strong business representation, weak political support" facing the post-colonial state. During the British colonial era,

148 *Missing link between state, business and society*

the interests of the business sector were effectively incorporated into the policy-making process of the colonial administration through the co-option of senior executives of encompassing British hongs into the Executive Council. As a consequence, the colonial Executive Council had effectively functioned as an institutionalized platform for mediating between major business interests and consolidating business support for government policies, and it was rare to see either open clashes between the colonial state and the business sector over policy issues or conflicts of interests among major business groups (Chapter 3).

However, the fragmentation of agents of business interests in the post-handover era has made it practically difficult for the Executive Council to function as an institutionalized negotiation mechanism between the post-colonial state and the business sector, as in the colonial past. Table 5.9 shows that although the business elites continue to constitute the single largest group among unofficial Executive Councillors in the post-1997 period, the representation of business interests in this de facto cabinet of the post-colonial state was fragmented and the vast majority of the co-opted business elites were not drawn from any organized business group. Statistics show that most of the co-opted business elites sitting on the post-colonial Executive Council were individual businessmen or corporate elites and they were not affiliated to any business-oriented political parties. In addition, the four major business associations –the Hong Kong General Chamber of Commerce, the Chinese General Chamber of Commerce, the Chinese Manufacturers Association and the Federation of Hong Kong Industries – were basically unrepresented in the post-1997 Executive Council. The Liberal Party was the only organized business group that kept a stable seat in the post-1997 Executive Councils, but as discussed earlier it had all along failed to establish itself as an encompassing force representing business interests and even lost its seat after its electoral defeat in 2008. From this perspective, unlike the British colonial era, the Executive Council no longer functioned as a platform for mediating business interests after 1997.

Because of the fragmentation of agents of business interests and the deterioration of the Executive Council's function as an institutionalized negotiation mechanism for mediating business interests, the post-colonial state could no longer effectively consolidate business support for its policy initiatives and reconcile major business interests by means of extensive incorporation of business elites into its advisory system. Although after 1997 the post-colonial state continues to follow the British colonial practice of consulting and clearing with the Executive Council before introducing any bill and subsidiary legislation into the Legislative Council, there will be no more guarantee that a policy decision endorsed by the co-opted business elites in the Executive Council would be broadly acceptable to the wider business sector. In fact, on many occasions when the policy initiative is subsequently passed to the Legislative Council for consideration the post-colonial state may still encounter stronger than expected resistance from different agents of business interests, resulting in the open clashes between the post-colonial state and the business sector over the legislative process. On certain highly controversial public policies, the failure of the

Missing link between state and business 149

Executive Council to function as an institutionalized platform for mediating major business interests may even plunge the post-colonial state into a political quagmire of intense rivalries among the competing business groups. The cases of the Nutrition Labelling Scheme and the West Kowloon Cultural District (WKCD) are both highly indicative of these governance problems.

The case of the Nutrition Labelling Scheme

The political controversies surrounding the introduction of a statutory Nutrition Labelling Scheme in 2008 are an illustrating example. The open confrontation between the post-colonial state and the business sector over the Nutrition Labelling Scheme fully demonstrated that the fragmentation of agents of business interests has already made it difficult for the post-colonial state to consolidate the support of the business sector for its policy initiatives through the co-opted business elites.

The proposal of introducing a Nutrition Labelling Scheme had been out for public consultation since 2003. According to the public consultation document published by the post-colonial state in 2003, a mandatory Nutrition Labelling Scheme should be implemented with a view to protecting public health and ensuring food safety (Health, Welfare and Food Bureau, 2003). The proposal of introducing a Nutrition Labelling Scheme was well-received by the public and most of the political parties. The business sector also supported the policy in principle, despite the fact that many food suppliers and retailers expressed concerns about the possible increase in business operating and compliance costs. In response to the concerns of the business sector, particularly the food suppliers and retailers, the proposal finally put forward by the Food and Health Bureau in December 2007 contained two major business-friendly measures, including the imposition of a two-year grace period and a small-volume exemption for food items that sold 30,000 units or fewer per year and did not carry nutritional claims. According to the legislative plan of the Food and Health Bureau, the proposed Nutrition Labelling Scheme would be legislated by means of subsidiary legislation in early 2008 (Food and Health Bureau, 2007).

When the Food and Health Bureau outlined its proposal in December 2007, it did not encounter strong opposition from the business sector and the Liberal Party legislators, including Tommy Cheung Yu-yan and Vincent Fang Kang, also pledged their support to the government plan in the Legislative Council panel meeting (Legislative Council Secretariat, 2007). In accordance with the normal practice, the proposed Nutrition Labelling Scheme was cleared with the Executive Council and was subsequently introduced to the Legislative Council for scrutiny in April 2008. Meanwhile, the voice of opposition from the business sector on the proposal was getting louder and louder, creating new hurdles for the Food and Health Bureau's legislative plan. Major business associations, including the Hong Kong General Chamber of Commerce, the Chinese Manufacturers Association, the Federation of Hong Kong Industries, the Hong Kong Chinese Importers' & Exporters' Association, the American Chamber of

Table 5.9 Representation of business interests in the Executive Council (1998–2010)

Background of unofficial members	1998		1999		2000		2001		2002		2003		2004		2005		2006		2007		2008		2009		2010		Total	
	No.	%	No.	%	No.	%	No.	%	No.	%	No.	%	No.	%	No.	%	No.	%	No.	%	No.	%	No.	%	No.	%	No.	%
Representative of pro-business parties	0.5	4.5	0.5	4.5	0.5	4.5	1	10.0	1	11.1	0.5	10.0	1	20.0	1	14.3	1	6.7	1	6.7	1	6.3	0	0.0	1	7.1	10	7.0
Liberal Party	0.5	4.5	0.5	4.5	0.5	4.5	1	10.0	1	11.1	0.5	10.0	1	20.0	1	14.3	1	6.7	1	6.7	1	6.3	0	0.0	0	0.0	9	6.3
Economic Synergy	0	0.0	0	0.0	0	0.0	0	0.0	0	0.0	0	0.0	0	0.0	0	0.0	0	0.0	0	0.0	0	0.0	0	0.0	1	7.1	1	0.7
Hong Kong Progressive Alliance	0	0.0	0	0.0	0	0.0	0	0.0	0	0.0	0	0.0	0	0.0	0	0.0	0	0.0	0	0.0	0	0.0	0	0.0	0	0.0	0	0.0
Representative of business associations	0.5	4.5	0.5	4.5	0.5	4.5	0	0.0	0	0.0	0.5	10.0	0	0.0	0	0.0	0	0.0	0	0.0	0	0.0	0	0.0	0	0.0	2	1.4
Hong Kong General Chamber of Commerce	0	0.0	0	0.0	0	0.0	0	0.0	0	0.0	0.5	10.0	0	0.0	0	0.0	0	0.0	0	0.0	0	0.0	0	0.0	0	0.0	0.5	0.3
Chinese General Chamber of Commerce	0	0.0	0	0.0	0	0.0	0	0.0	0	0.0	0	0.0	0	0.0	0	0.0	0	0.0	0	0.0	0	0.0	0	0.0	0	0.0	0	0.0
Chinese Manufacturers Association	0	0.0	0	0.0	0	0.0	0	0.0	0	0.0	0	0.0	0	0.0	0	0.0	0	0.0	0	0.0	0	0.0	0	0.0	0	0.0	0	0.0
Federation of Hong Kong Industries	0.5	4.5	0.5	4.5	0.5	4.5	0	0.0	0	0.0	0	0.0	0	0.0	0	0.0	0	0.0	0	0.0	0	0.0	0	0.0	0	0.0	1.5	1.0

Individual businessmen	5	45.5	5	45.5	5	45.5	4	40.0	3	33.3	1	20.0	1	20.0	2	28.6	5	33.3	5	33.3	5	31.3	5	35.7	4	28.6	50	35.0
Other unofficial members	5	45.5	5	45.5	5	45.5	5	50.0	5	55.6	3	60.0	3	60.0	4	57.1	9	60.0	9	60.0	10	62.5	9	64.3	9	64.3	81	56.6
Total	11	100	11	100	11	100	10	100	9	100	5	100	5	100	7	100	15	100	15	100	16	100	14	100	14	100	143	100

Source: Author's own research based on the list of unofficial members provided by the Executive Council Secretariat.

Notes

1 Pro-business political parties will be counted as having representation in the Executive Council if the Legislative Councillors from these parties were appointed as unofficial members.

2 Major business associations will be counted as having representation in the Executive Council if its Chairman, Vice-Chairman or Executive Committee Members were appointed as unofficial members.

3 Henry Tang Ying-yen concurrently held the offices of Liberal Party Legislative Councillor and Chairman of the Federation of Hong Kong Industries from 1998 to 2000. Thus, his representation in the Executive Council from 1998 to 2001 was divided between the Liberal Party and the Federation of Hong Kong Industries. Henry Tang stepped down from the Chairmanship of the Federation of Hong Kong Industries after July 2001 and therefore he was counted as representing the Liberal Party in the Executive Council in 2001 and 2002.

4 James Tien Pei-chun concurrently held the offices of Liberal Party Legislative Councillor and Legislative Council Representative of the Hong Kong General Chamber of Commerce from 2003. Thus, his representation in the Executive Council from 2003 was divided between the Liberal Party and the Hong Kong General Chamber of Commerce.

152 *Missing link between state, business and society*

Commerce and the British Chamber of Commerce all raised opposition to the proposed Nutrition Labelling Scheme.[12] The Hong Kong Retail Management Association and the Hong Kong Suppliers Association, which represented the interests of the food retailers and suppliers, even advertised in several local newspapers claiming that up to 15,000 low-sales-volume food products with nutritional claims might disappear if the proposed food labelling regime came into force (*South China Morning Post*, 2008, 26 April). Meanwhile, the Liberal Party also changed its position and vowed not to support the government proposal. In collaboration with other major business associations and the food trade, the Liberal Party requested the Food and Health Bureau to further exempt all small-volume food products including those making nutritional claims and also to extend the grace period of the legislation from two years to three years (*Hong Kong Economic Times*, 2008a, 3 April).

The stronger than expected resistance from the business sector was obviously unexpected by the post-colonial state, given the fact that a two-year grace period and a small-volume exemption arrangement in its original subsidiary legislation proposal were all designed to address the concerns of the food trade, and the Liberal Party, which held a seat in the Executive Council, did not raise strong opposition to the government plan initially (*Hong Kong Economic Times*, 2008b, 3 May). Despite its previous consultation with the co-opted business elites, the whole issue had been gradually evolved into an open confrontation between the post-colonial state and the business sector: the different business agents, including the Liberal Party, the major business chambers and the trade associations all pressed for further exemptions, while the Food and Health Bureau took the view that further exemptions would only defeat its original policy objective of providing better protection for public health and tried to resist business demands by mobilizing support from the medical sector and consumer organizations (*Ming Pao*, 2008, 6 May). Nevertheless, in view of the stronger and stronger voice of opposition from the business sector, the post-colonial state finally made a compromise in May 2008 by agreeing to extend the food labelling exemption to all kinds of food products with sale volumes of fewer than 30,000 units per year, even if they made nutritional claims.[13]

The case of the Nutrition Labelling Scheme fully illustrates the growing difficulties facing the post-colonial state in consulting and co-opting the business sector in the policy process. Because of the fragmentation of agents of business interests, the business sector initially failed to come up with a common and informed policy position on the Food and Health Bureau's legislative proposal.[14] The Liberal Party, the so-called flagship business-oriented political party representing business interests in the Executive Council, even pledged its support for the government plan in the first instance. Nevertheless, after the details of the subsidiary legislation proposal were more clearly made known to the food trade, the business sector's feelings on the government proposal rapidly turned sour. When the voice of opposition from the business sector became loud enough, the major business chambers and trade associations were all mobilized to raise their concerns and the Liberal Party also stepped up its opposition against the government's legislative plan. As a consequence, the officials from the Food and Health Bureau suddenly found that their previous consultations with the Liberal Party and other co-opted business elites were far from effective in consolidating the support of the business sector for the proposed Nutrition Labelling Scheme, and they were required to directly confront the opposition campaigns organized by different agents of business interests. Also, despite the representation of the Liberal Party and many corporate executives in the Executive Council, these co-opted business elites failed to function as encompassing intermediaries bridging the gap between the post-colonial state and the business sector. Throughout the whole legislative process, the Executive Council was unable to function as an institutionalized negotiation mechanism mediating business interests, and the legislative plan endorsed by the Executive Council still faced strong resistance from the major business chambers and the food trade when it was formally introduced into the Legislative Council. To conclude, the case of the Nutrition Labelling Scheme best illustrated that as a consequence of the fragmentation of agents of business interests in the post-1997 period, the post-colonial state finds it practically difficult in organizing and articulating business interests through the co-opted business elites and its political support base in the business sector has therefore become increasingly fragile and vulnerable.

The case of West Kowloon Cultural District

The case of WKCD is another good example to illustrate the growing difficulties faced by the post-colonial state in reconciling major business interests over controversial public policies. Instead of eliciting strong political support from the business sector for this important policy initiative, the post-colonial state has been dragged into the intense rivalries and conflicts among the competing business groups in the development process of the WKCD.

The WKCD project was first outlined by the Chief Executive Tung Chee-hwa in his 1999 Policy Address, by which the government planned to build a world-class arts and cultural performance centre in the West Kowloon waterfront. To reduce the possible financial burden of this cultural project, the Tung Administration announced in 2003 that a single development approach would be adopted in the development of the WKCD, by which a 50-year land grant would be awarded to a single business consortium for financing, constructing, managing and maintaining all the cultural, commercial and residential facilities in the entire 40-hectare site. However, the government plan not only aroused the concerns of arts groups and cultural activists fearing that the WKCD would become just another property development project, it also stirred up discontent within the business sector (Ng, 2005). Many property developers complained that the single development approach was not a fair arrangement and would only benefit the biggest developers, because such an arrangement would make it very difficult for small and medium developers to participate. In January 2005, Stanley Ho Hung-san, in his capacity as Chairman of the Real Estate Developers Association of Hong Kong, openly criticized the single development approach and

154   *Missing link between state, business and society*

stated that the lot should be broken into small pieces of land for tendering (*Hong Kong Economic Journal*, 2005, 8 January). After several years of controversies, the new Donald Tsang Administration finally announced in February 2006 that it would abandon the single development approach and put on hold the whole WKCD project pending a new round of public consultation (*Hong Kong Economic Journal*, 2006, 22 February). In 2008 the Tsang Administration decided to set up a new statutory body called the WKCD Authority to take forward the project and completely abandoned its original plan to develop the WKCD by means of a public–private partnership.

The case of the WKCD project has fully illustrated the growing difficulties facing the post-colonial state in mediating business interests and in consolidating business support for major government initiatives. In the midst of controversies, business-oriented political parties including the Liberal Party played no role in mediating clusters of business interests and as a result the post-colonial state has been directly dragged into the conflicts among the competing business conglomerates. In the face of the fragmented and differentiated business interests, the post-colonial state struggled to come up with a development approach that is broadly acceptable to most property developers and this resulted in the sluggish implementation of the WKCD project. Moreover, the WKCD project also indicated that the Executive Council failed to function as an institutionalized negotiation mechanism to mediate business interests. Despite the fact that the majority of unofficial Executive Councillors were businessmen and the idea of developing the WKCD through the single development approach had been discussed and approved by the Chief Executive in Council,[15] all these political arrangements proved to be ineffective in consolidating the business sector's support for the project and the government proposals remained subject to challenges by rival business conglomerates. While the criticisms from the democratic opposition and civil society should have created pressures for government officials to put on hold its development plan as argued by theorists of legitimacy deficit (e.g. Scott, 2007), the sluggish implementation of the WKCD project had to a greater extent reflected the difficulties faced by the post-colonial state in reconciling business interests (Wong & Zheng, 2006). This showed that rather than the challenges from the democratic opposition and civil society, how to articulate and consolidate the support of its business allies in the policy process is a more imperative governance challenge facing the post-colonial state.

Conclusion

This chapter discusses the business representation system before and after 1997. The traditional business representation system in the colonial era was not simply about extensive incorporation of individual business elites, but it was actually featured by the co-option of major British hongs which effectively functioned as the encompassing intermediaries bridging the colonial state and the business sector. The effective operation of such a business representation system was, however, built upon Hong Kong's unique colonial history and political-economic order, where the high concentration of economic powers in the hands of major British hongs and the closed political system both gave rise to a few central players like the Jardine Group and the Hong Kong Bank acting as the encompassing intermediaries between the colonial state and the business sector.

Following the changing configuration of economic and political structures in Hong Kong since the 1980s, such a traditional business representation system has already been broken down. Unfortunately, due to the underdevelopment of business-oriented political parties after 1997, the vital missing link between the post-colonial state and the business sector has not been competently filled in and there is a general lack of an effective business agent to play the role of encompassing intermediaries previously fulfilled by the major British business groups. The fragmentation of agents of business interests in the post-1997 period pointed to the fact that there exists no overarching political organization to represent business interests in the political arena and therefore there are many different business agents in the policy process, including business-oriented political parties, major business associations, non-affiliated pro-business legislators and individual corporations. All these have made it difficult for the post-colonial state to come up with a coherent policy agenda that is broadly acceptable to the business sector and also undermined the function of the Executive Council as an institutionalized negotiation mechanism between the post-colonial state and the business sector. As a consequence, the post-colonial state finds it increasingly difficult to rely on the co-opted business elites to consult and mediate business interests and is required to engage in particularistic bargaining with different agents of business interests in the process of policy-making.

The latest comparative studies on hybrid regimes and authoritarian systems indicate that a well-organized governing party or governing coalition is crucial in encouraging cooperation among governing elites, managing intra-elite conflicts and preventing elite defection (e.g. Brownlee, 2007; Levitsky & Way, 2010, pp. 61–62). From this perspective, the growing challenges facing the post-colonial Hong Kong state in articulating and reconciling business interests are not accidental. Because of the underdevelopment of business-oriented political parties after 1997, the post-colonial state does not have any effective political machinery to articulate the interests of its business allies and to mediate the possible intra-elite conflicts within the governing coalition. As a consequence of this important structural defect of the state–business alliance, the post-colonial state is facing increasing difficulties in consolidating the support of the business sector for maintaining effective governance despite the extensive co-option of business elites into the HKSAR political establishment and the government's general pro-business policy agenda. The resultant paradox of "strong business representation, weak political support" has certainly made the political alliance between the post-colonial state and the business sector increasingly fragile and vulnerable.

Notes

1 For an account of the fall of British capital and the rise of local Chinese capital, see Feng (1996, 1997).
2 For an account of the rise of Mainland capital in Hong Kong, see Guo (2009).
3 For the nine new functional constituencies created by Chris Patten's constitutional reform proposals, the electorate of these functional constituencies were all from individual workers in relevant sectors, including primary production, power and construction, textile and garments, manufacturing, import and export, wholesale and retail, hotels and catering, transport and communication, financing, insurance, real estate and business services and community, social and personal services.
4 For an account of the development of party politics in Hong Kong, see Ma (2007a, 2007b).
5 It is comprehensible that there are socio-economic and political reasons behind the fragmentation of business associations in Hong Kong. First, similar to the experiences of the United States and the United Kingdom, Hong Kong does not have any mandatory requirement for individual companies to join trade associations and peak associations. There is no statutory collective bargaining system in Hong Kong (Ng, 2010, p. 267). Labour-management issues are resolved at the level of the individual company and thus business corporations are not legally obliged to join trade associations of their industries. Second, because of its colonial history traditionally the four major business associations in Hong Kong are considered as having different constituencies in the business sector. The Hong Kong General Chamber of Commerce, which was formed by the major British and European hongs in 1861, is the main organization representing the interests of the British and European business sector. Established in 1896 by prominent Chinese merchants, the Chinese General Chamber of Commerce has all along functioned as the umbrella organizations for local Chinese enterprises and claimed to represent the collective interests of the local Chinese business sector. On the other hand, the Chinese Manufacturers' Association was established in 1934 as a result of the rapid industrial development in Hong Kong and it was the major business association claimed to represent the interests of industrialists rather than commercial interests of merchant houses as represented by the Hong Kong General Chamber of Commerce and the Chinese General Chamber of Commerce. Finally, the Federation of Hong Kong Industries was established by statute in 1960, and aims at providing a variety of industrial back-up and technical support to its members (Clayton, 2000; Zanko, 2002, pp. 238–240). It is therefore likely that all these factors have contributed to the proliferation and fragmentation of business associations in Hong Kong, both before and after 1997, making them unable to take up the role of encompassing agents of business interests.
6 Anonymous interviewee.
7 Anonymous interviewee.
8 Anonymous interviewee.
9 The major exception was James Tien Puk-chun, who held executive committee directorships in the Hong Kong General Chamber of Commerce and the Federation of Hong Kong Industries regularly.
10 Anonymous interviewee.
11 Anthony Wu Ting-yuk, Chairman of the Hong Kong General Chamber of Commerce, mentioned in a newspaper interview that as one of the major business associations in Hong Kong, the Chamber should be more active in voicing and representing the views of the business sector with a view to influencing the policy-making of the Hong Kong government (*Apple Daily*, 2011, 30 June). The views of Anthony Wu have illustrated the growing tendency of the major business associations to directly participate in local politics instead of relying on pro-business parties to represent their interests.

Missing link between state and business 157

12 For more details, read the submissions made by the major business associations to the Legislative Council, available at: www.legco.gov.hk/yr07-08/english/hc/sub_leg/sc53/papers/sc53_d.htm.

13 However, this amendment proposal put forward by the Food and Health Bureau was surprisingly voted down by the Legislative Council by a narrow margin of one vote at its meeting on 28 May 2008. Therefore the Food and Health Bureau's original proposal was finally enacted and came into implementation (*Hong Kong Economic Times*, 2008c, 29 May).

14 Anonymous interviewee.

15 According to official records, the HKSAR government has consulted the Executive Council in the various development stages of the WKCD project. It is recorded that at a meeting of the Executive Council on 16 November 1999, the Chief Executive in Council ordered that the use of the southern portion of the West Kowloon Reclamation should be reviewed to facilitate the development of a world-class cultural district (Legislative Council Secretariat, 2004). In September 2003 the Chief Executive in Council approved Invitation for Proposals arrangements for the development of the WKCD (including the single development approach) and invited private developers to submit proposals. At the meeting of the Executive Council held on 9 November 2004 the Chief Executive in Council approved the screening result of the first stage of assessment and decided that three out of the five proponents have complied with the requirements (Housing, Planning and Lands Bureau, 2004).

References

Apple Daily. (2011, 30 July). Two faces of Wu Ting-Yuk. B06 (in Chinese).

Brownlee, J. (2007). *Authoritarianism in an age of democratization.* New York: Cambridge University Press.

Clayton, D. (2000). Industrialization and institutional change in Hong Kong 1842–1960. In A. J. H. Latham, & H. Kawakatsu (Eds.), *Asia-Pacific Dynamism, 1550–2000* (pp. 149–169). London: Routledge.

Feng, B. Y. (1996). *Xianggang ying zi cai tuan: 1841–1996 (Hong Kong's British consortiums, 1841–1996).* Hong Kong: Joint Publishing (H.K.) Co. Ltd (in Chinese).

Feng, B. Y. (1997). *Xianggang hua zi cai tuan: 1841–1997 (Hong Kong's local Chinese consortiums, 1841–1997).* Hong Kong: Joint Publishing (H.K.) Co. Ltd (in Chinese).

Food and Health Bureau. (2007). *Proposed nutrition labelling scheme on nutrition for prepackaged food: Discussion Paper for the Legislative Council Panel on Food Safety and Environmental Hygiene on 11 December 2007.* Retrieved 1 January 2013 from www.legco.gov.hk/yr07-08/english/panels/fseh/papers/fe1211cb2-516-3-e.pdf.

Fried, J. (2008). *Democrats and republicans – rhetoric and reality: Comparing the voters in statistics and anecdotes.* New York: Algora Publishing.

Guo, G. C. (2009). *Xianggang zhong zi cai tuan (Hong Kong's Mainland consortiums).* Hong Kong: Joint Publishing (H.K.) Co. Ltd (in Chinese).

Health, Welfare and Food Bureau. (2003). *Public consultation on proposed labelling scheme on nutrition information: Discussion Paper for the Legislative Council Panel on Food Safety and Environmental Hygiene on 25 November 2003.* Retrieved 1 January 2013 from www.legco.gov.hk/yr03-04/english/panels/fseh/papers/fe1125cb2-407-03-e.pdf.

Hong Kong Economic Journal. (2005, 8 January). Ho Hung-san criticizes the single development approach of the West Kowloon Project. P04 (in Chinese).

Hong Kong Economic Journal. (2006, 22 February). The West Kowloon Project will be put on hold pending further consultation. P02 (in Chinese).

158 *Missing link between state, business and society*

Hong Kong Economic Times. (2008a, 3 April). Estimated that 70% food products will disappear from the market because of nutrition labeling. A20 (in Chinese).

Hong Kong Economic Times. (2008b, 6 May). Business sector criticized nutrition labelling as "surpassing Britain and catching up with the United States". A26 (in Chinese).

Hong Kong Economic Times. (2008c, 29 May). Amendments to the nutrition labelling scheme have been voted down, the original proposal prevails. A22 (in Chinese).

Housing, Planning and Lands Bureau. (2004). *Legislative Council brief on the development of the West Kowloon Cultural District: Screening results of proposals.* Retrieved 1 January 2013 from www.legco.gov.hk/yr04-05/english/panels/plw/papers/plw_eng.pdf.

Huang, Y. S. (1997). The economic and political integration of Hong Kong: Implications for government–business relations. In W. I. Cohen, & L. Zhao (Eds.), *Hong Kong under Chinese rule: The economic and political implications of reversion* (pp. 96–113). Cambridge: Cambridge University Press.

Kuan, H. C. (1995). Xianggang zhengzhi liliang de chongzu (Political realignment in Hong Kong). In Y. H. Zhu (Ed.), *Yi jiu jiu qi qian xide xianggang zheng jing xing shi yu tai gang guan x (Hong Kong's political and economic landscape and Hong Kong–Taiwan relations on the eve of 1997)* (pp. 71–90). Taibei Shi: Ye Qiang Chu Ban She (Taibei: Ye Qiang Press) (in Chinese).

Lam, Jermain T. M. (2010). Party institutionalization in Hong Kong. *Asian Perspective, 34*(2), 43–83.

Lau, C. K. (1997). *Hong Kong's colonial legacy.* Hong Kong: Chinese University Press.

Legislative Council Secretariat. (2004). *Updated background brief on West Kowloon Cultural District: Paper for the Panel on Planning, Lands and Works.* Retrieved 1 January 2013 from www.legco.gov.hk/yr03-04/english/panels/plw/papers/plw0714cb1-2364-3e.pdf.

Legislative Council Secretariat. (2007). *Minutes of meeting of the Legislative Council Panel on Food Safety and Environmental Hygiene on 11 December 2007.* Retrieved 1 January 2013 from www.legco.gov.hk/yr07-08/english/panels/fseh/minutes/fe071211.pdf.

Levitsky, S., & Way, L. A. (2010). *Competitive authoritarianism: Hybrid regimes after the Cold War.* New York: Cambridge University Press.

Lo, S. H. (2010). *Competing Chinese political visions: Hong Kong vs. Beijing on democracy.* Santa Barbara, CA: Praeger Security International.

Lui, T. L., & Chiu, S. W. K. (2007). Governance crisis in post-1997 Hong Kong: A political economy perspective. *The China Review, 7*(2), 1–34.

Lui, T. L., & Chiu, S. W. K. (2009). *Hong Kong: Becoming a Chinese global city.* London: Routledge.

Ma, N. (2007a). *Political development in Hong Kong: State, political society and civil society.* Hong Kong: Hong Kong University Press.

Ma, N. (2007b). Political parties and elections. In W. M. Lam, P. L. T. Lui, W. Wong, & I. Holiday (Eds.), *Contemporary Hong Kong politics: Governance in the post-1997 era* (pp. 117–134). Hong Kong: Hong Kong University Press.

Miners, N. (1998). *The government and politics of Hong Kong* (5th ed.). Hong Kong: Oxford University Press.

Ming Pao. (2008, 6 May). The legislative struggle over nutritional labelling legislation. A10 (in Chinese).

Ng, M. K. (2005). Governance beyond government: Political crisis and sustainable world city building. In J. Y. S. Cheng (Ed.), *The July 1 protest rally: Interpreting a historic event* (pp. 469–499). Hong Kong: City University of Hong Kong Press.

Missing link between state and business 159

Ng, S. H. (2010). *Labour law in Hong Kong.* Alphen aan den Rijn: Kluwer Law International.

Scott, I. (2007). Legitimacy, governance and public policy in post-1997 Hong Kong. *Asia Pacific Journal of Public Administration, 29*(1), 29–49.

Sing, M. (2003). Legislative–executive interface in Hong Kong. In C. Loh, & Civic Exchange (Eds.), *Building democracy: Creating good government for Hong Kong* (pp. 27–34). Hong Kong: Hong Kong University Press.

South China Morning Post. (2008, 26 April). Food retailers appeal to public in bid for labelling law exemption. CITY1.

Sung, Y. W. (1997). Hong Kong and the economic integration of the China circle. In B. Naughton (Ed.), *The China circle: Economics and electronics in the PRC, Taiwan, and Hong Kong* (pp. 419–480). Washington, DC: Brookings Institution Press.

Wilson, G. K. (2003). *Business and politics: A comparative introduction.* Basingstoke: Palgrave Macmillan.

Wong, G. (1996). Business groups in a dynamic environment: Hong Kong 1976–1986. In G. G. Hamilton (Ed.), *Asian business networks* (pp. 87–114). New York: Walter de Gruyter.

Wong, S. L. (1994). Business and politics in Hong Kong during the transition. In B. K. P. Leung, & T. Y. C. Wong (Eds.), *25 Years of social and economic development in Hong Kong* (pp. 217–235). Hong Kong: University of Hong Kong.

Wong, S. L. (1995). Yi jiu jiu qi guo Du yu xianggang zheng shang guan xi de yan bian (The evolution of government–business relations in Hong Kong). In Y. H. Zhu (Ed.), *Yi jiu jiuqQi qian xi de xianggang zheng jing sing shi yu tai gang guan xi (Hong Kong's political and economic landscape and Hong Kong–Taiwan relations on the eve of 1997)* (pp. 91–120). Taibei Shi: Ye Qiang Chu Ban She (Taibei: Ye Qiang Press) (in Chinese).

Wong, S. L., & Zheng, H. T. (2006). *Guan Shang Gou Jie: Xianggang Shi Min Yan Zhong De Zheng Shang Guan Xi (Government–business collusion: Public perception of government–business relations in Hong Kong).* Hong Kong culture and society programme occasional paper series no. 3. Hong Kong: The University of Hong Kong.

Yu, W. Y. (2005). Dynamics of party–mass relations: The organizational failure of Hong Kong's political parties. In J. Y. S. Cheng (Ed.), *The July 1 protest rally: Interpreting a historic event* (pp. 249–276). Hong Kong: City University of Hong Kong Press.

Zanko, M. (2002). *The handbook of human resource management policies and practices in Asia-Pacific economies.* Northampton, MA: Edward Elgar.

6 The widening gap between state and society

The growing disconnection of the business sector from the local community[1]

Similar to the British colonial period, business elites have been extensively incorporated by the post-colonial state into its advisory bodies and committees. Such a political formula is based upon the assumption that as in the British colonial past, the post-colonial state should be able to mobilize sufficient societal support for its governance and policy initiatives and accommodating societal challenges by relying on the support of co-opted business elites. However, the post-1997 political developments indicated that it is just wishful thinking to hope that the post-colonial state could still count on the co-opted business elites to mediate its relationship with the local community after 1997, in the light of the fact that the business sector is generally too vulnerable and powerless to accommodate the political challenges of the civil society. The increasing public challenges to the state–business alliance has become the last straw for the political support base of the post-colonial state and pushes it into serious crises of governance.

In this chapter we are going to trace the development of civil society and examine how the rise of civil society activism in the post-1997 era has posed important challenges to the state–business alliance. The central argument of this chapter is that the old practice of co-opting business elites into the state machinery, as inherited from the colonial era, is no longer effective in furnishing the post-colonial state with sufficient capacity to accommodate the waves of "growing citizen participation" in the policy process after 1997. In the face of the increasing challenges from the civil society, the post-colonial state struggles to establish broad societal support for its policy initiatives and to mediate state–society relations by relying on its business allies. As a result, the governing capacity of the post-colonial state is seriously undermined by the growing level of state–society conflicts and the political support base of the state–business alliance has become increasingly fragile and vulnerable.

The dominant representation of business elites in the advisory bodies after 1997: old wine in a new bottle

The general pattern of political absorption by the colonial government showed a clear preference for people from the trade, business, finance, and

The widening gap between state and society 161

industry sectors.... The SAR government ... has largely extended the previous colonial pattern of advisory appointments.

(Cheung & Wong, 2004)

In the colonial era, the most notable feature of the state–business alliance was the extensive incorporation of business elites into the advisory system. Business elites, in particular prestigious local Chinese capitalists, were appointed by the colonial state as unofficial Executive Councillors and Legislative Councillors and they also held the majority of unofficial seats in these two most powerful political institutions. Apart from this, business elites were absorbed into the vast networks of advisory bodies, through which the business sector was consulted by the colonial state on different policies. Because the local Chinese capitalists were widely seen as the "natural leaders" of the local Chinese community and could effectively claim to represent the local opinion, they could make great contributions to the colonial governance by mediating between the colonial state and the local community and establishing the necessary social support base for its governance (see Chapter 3).

This political formula of eliciting the support of the co-opted business elites to consolidate its governance was subsequently adopted and followed by the incoming sovereign state, the Chinese government, as the foundation of the post-handover political order. As part of its overall strategy to engineer and consolidate a state–business alliance after 1997, the post-colonial state has maintained a dense network of advisory bodies and committees and extensively incorporated business elites into its advisory system. As a consequence, business elites were strongly represented in different advisory bodies and committees set up by the post-colonial state in the post-1997 period (Cheung & Wong, 2004). Similar to the governing strategy adopted by the British colonial state, the extensive incorporation of business elites into the advisory system after 1997 is based upon the contention that the co-opted business elites could play the intermediary role between the government and society, as in the British colonial past, and therefore by relying on its coalition partners in the business sector the post-colonial state could mobilize sufficient societal support for its governance and policy initiatives and accommodate any possible societal challenges.

Empirical research on the post-1997 membership of the three central-level advisory committees of the post-colonial state, namely the Executive Council, the Commission on Strategic Development and the Central Policy Unit, provided strong evidence on the intentions of the post-colonial state to establish societal support for its governance by means of maintaining and consolidating the traditional state–business alliance. Tables 6.1–6.3 indicate that since the handover of sovereignty in 1997, representatives from the business sector have always held the majority seats in the Executive Council,[2] the Commission on Strategic Development[3] and the Central Policy Unit.[4] Because these three institutions are generally considered as the most important advisory bodies in the government secretariat they are regularly consulted by the post-colonial state on the formulation and implementation of an extensive range of public policies. From this

162   *Missing link between state, business and society*

perspective, the over-representation of the business elites in these major advisory bodies has largely illustrated the post-colonial state's attempt to follow the footsteps of its colonial predecessor in eliciting the political support of the business sector for consolidating its governance and mediating state–society relations.

This brings us to an important research question which is crucial to the understanding of Hong Kong's governance after 1997: if the British colonial practice of co-opting business elites was largely followed and maintained after the handover, why does the post-colonial state, unlike its colonial predecessor, fail to mediate its relationship with the local community by relying on its coalition partners in the business sector?

The central argument of this chapter is that such different political outcomes could be explained by the erosion of the intermediary role of business elites amid the emergence of civil society activism after 1997. For much of the colonial era, successful local Chinese businessmen were well-respected and widely seen as the "natural leaders" of the Chinese community, and their leadership status was clearly built upon their active participation in district organizations, dialect groups, trade associations or charity groups (Goodstadt, 2009, p. 99). The leadership of the business elites within the community enabled them to function as an effective link between the colonial state and the Chinese population (Chapter 3). However, the rise of civil society activism has effectively put an end to the business elite's previous intermediary role between the state and society. As such, the business elite have become increasingly disconnected from the local community and now they are no longer capable of mobilizing sufficient societal support for the post-colonial state.

New challenges for the state–business alliance: the rise of civil society activism

> Civil society in Hong Kong has gone through an important period of maturity in the ten years since the handover, with 2003 being a watershed. Around 2003, civil society assumed a separate identity, and from that point on it has been active in various aspects on the policy-making scene.
>
> (Chan & Chan, 2007)

To better illustrate how the rise of civil society activism in recent years has posed unprecedented political challenges to the state–business alliance in the post-1997 period, we have to first review the development trajectory of civil society in Hong Kong.

The development of civil society activism: from an apolitical community to a vibrant civil society

As a matter of fact, Hong Kong's civil society was weak and underdeveloped for much of the colonial period. The underdevelopment of the civil society was mostly related to the "refugee mentality" of the local population and the colonial

Table 6.1 Background analysis of unofficial members in the Executive Council (1998–2011)

Occupational background	1998		1999		2000		2001		2002		2003		2004		2005		2006		2007		2008		2009		2010		2011		Total	
	No.	%	No.	%	No.	%	No.	%	No.	%	No.	%	No.	%	No.	%	No.	%	No.	%	No.	%	No.	%	No.	%	No.	%	No.	%
Politician	0	0.0	0	0.0	0	0.0	0	0.0	0	0.0	1	20.0	2	40.0	2	28.6	2	13.3	2	13.3	2	12.5	1	7.1	1	7.1	1	7.1	14	8.9
Business	**6**	**54.5**	**6**	**54.5**	**6**	**54.5**	**5**	**50.0**	**4**	**44.4**	**2**	**40.0**	**1**	**20.0**	**3**	**42.9**	**6**	**40.0**	**6**	**40.0**	**6**	**37.5**	**5**	**35.7**	**6**	**42.9**	**6**	**42.9**	**68**	**43.3**
Profession	2	18.2	2	18.2	2	18.2	2	20.0	2	22.2	1	20.0	1	20.0	1	14.3	4	26.7	4	26.7	4	25.0	4	28.6	4	28.6	4	28.6	37	23.6
Social services	1	9.1	1	9.1	1	9.1	1	10.0	1	11.1	0	0.0	0	0.0	0	0.0	1	6.7	1	6.7	1	6.3	1	7.1	1	7.1	1	7.1	11	7.0
Labour	1	9.1	1	9.1	1	9.1	1	10.0	1	11.1	1	20.0	1	20.0	1	14.3	1	6.7	1	6.7	1	6.3	1	7.1	1	7.1	1	7.1	14	8.9
Others	1	9.1	1	9.1	1	9.1	1	10.0	1	11.1	0	0.0	0	0.0	0	0.0	1	6.7	1	6.7	2	12.5	2	14.3	1	7.1	1	7.1	13	8.3
Total	11	100.0	11	100.0	11	100.0	10	100.0	9	100.0	5	100.0	5	100.0	7	100.0	15	100.0	15	100.0	16	100.0	14	100.0	14	100.0	14	100.0	157	100.0

Source: Author's own research based on the list of unofficial members provided by the Executive Council Secretariat.

Notes
1 "Politician" refers to full-time Legislative Councillors and District Councillors.
2 "Business" refers to chairmen, directors, executives and managers from commercial corporations.
3 "Profession" refers to professionals from legal, accounting, architecture, surveying, planning, engineering, medical and health sectors.
4 "Social services" refers to practitioners from education, community and social services and religious sectors.
5 "Labour" refers to trade unionists.

164 *Missing link between state, business and society*

Table 6.2 Background analysis of unofficial members in the commission on strategic development (2005–2009)

Occupational background	2005		2007		2009		Total	
	No.	%	No.	%	No.	%	No.	%
Politician	9	5.9	4	6.1	4	5.8	17	5.9
Business	**64**	**42.1**	**29**	**43.9**	**31**	**44.9**	**124**	**43.2**
Profession	26	17.1	9	13.6	10	14.5	45	15.7
Social services	41	27.0	18	27.3	16	23.2	75	26.1
Labour	3	2.0	3	4.5	3	4.3	9	3.1
Culture and media	7	4.6	2	3.0	2	2.9	11	3.8
Others	2	1.3	1	1.5	3	4.3	6	2.1
Total	152	100.0	66	100.0	69	100.0	287	100.0

Source: Author's own research based on the list of unofficial members provided by the Central Policy Unit.

Notes
1 "Politician" refers to full-time Legislative Councillors and District Councillors.
2 "Business" refers to chairmen, directors, executives and managers from commercial corporations.
3 "Profession" refers to professionals from legal, accounting, architecture, surveying, planning, engineering, medical and health sectors.
4 "Social services" refers to practitioners from education, community and social services and religious sectors.
5 "Labour" refers to trade unionists.
6 "Culture and media" refers to practitioners from arts, culture, media and publishing sectors.

administration's successful practice of administrative absorption of politics, which resulted in a low level of political mobilizations and people's low expectations towards the government (Cheung, 2007a). The only major and active civil society organizations during this period were the charitable groups formed by Chinese businessmen like the Po Leung Kuk, the Tung Wah Group of Hospitals and Lok Sin Tong, which voluntarily undertook various relief and social services to those refugees from Mainland China (Ip, 1998). Apart from these local groups, religious organizations have also been central welfare providers since founding of the colony. Foreign missionaries have been involved in setting up schools and offering medical services to the underprivileged in society (Civil Society Index Team, 2006). Nevertheless, the civil society at this stage was small, underdeveloped and largely non-political, which did not pose any threat to the colonial administration.

The dynamics of the state–society relationship began to change in the 1970s with the rise of a wide range of social movements like the Protection of the Diaoyu Islands Movement and the promotion of Chinese as an official language in the early 1970s, anti-corruption and anti-Godber movement in 1973–1974 and requests for the provision of adequate housing, etc. (Lo, 1998). The gradual emergence of the local civil society during the 1970s was aided by a number of factors (Ip, 1998; Ma, 2009). Politically, the colonial administration's greater emphasis on "consultative democracy" led to a higher level of tolerance of social protests and petitions, creating a window of opportunity that encouraged political

Table 6.3 Background analysis of part-time members in the Central Policy Unit (2003–2011)

Occupational background	2003		2004		2005		2006		2007		2008		2009		2010		2011		Total	
	No.	*%*	*No.*	*%*	*No.*	*%*	*No.*	*%*	*No.*	*%*	*No.*	*%*	*No.*	*%*	*No.*	*%*	*No.*	*%*	*No.*	*%*
Politician	1	2.7	1	2.6	0	0.0	0	0.0	1	2.0	4	9.8	3	7.1	2	4.8	3	7.0	15	4.0
Business	**9**	**24.3**	**11**	**28.2**	**15**	**38.5**	**18**	**43.9**	**22**	**43.1**	**19**	**46.3**	**22**	**52.4**	**20**	**47.6**	**23**	**53.5**	**159**	**42.4**
Profession	7	18.9	8	20.5	9	23.1	7	17.1	11	21.6	5	12.2	7	16.7	8	19.0	3	7.0	65	17.3
Social services	17	45.9	16	41.0	11	28.2	15	36.6	15	29.4	12	29.3	9	21.4	12	28.6	14	32.6	121	32.3
Labour	2	5.4	2	5.1	2	5.1	1	2.4	1	2.0	1	2.4	0	0.0	0	0.0	0	0.0	9	2.4
Culture and media	1	2.7	1	2.6	2	5.1	0	0.0	1	2.0	0	0.0	0	0.0	0	0.0	0	0.0	5	1.3
Others	0	0.0	0	0.0	0	0.0	0	0.0	0	0.0	0	0.0	1	2.4	0	0.0	0	0.0	1	0.3
Total	37	100.0	39	100.0	39	100.0	41	100.0	51	100.0	41	100.0	42	100.0	42	100.0	43	100.0	375	100.0

Source: Author's own research based on the list of unofficial members provided by the Central Policy Unit.

Notes
1 "Politician" refers to full-time Legislative Councillors and District Councillors.
2 "Business" refers to chairmen, directors, executives and senior managers from commercial corporations.
3 "Profession" refers to professionals from legal, accounting, architecture, surveying, planning, engineering, medical and health sectors.
4 "Social services" refers to practitioners from education, community and social services and religious sectors.
5 "Labour" refers to trade unionists.
6 "Culture and media" refers to practitioners from arts, culture, media and publishing sectors.

166 *Missing link between state, business and society*

participation and the development of social pluralism during the 1970s. Economically, Hong Kong was becoming a wealthy society in the 1970s, which helped to create a more rights-conscious and vocal middle class with rising social and political expectations. Socially, the social reforms implemented by the colonial administration in the 1970s raised people's expectations towards the government and encouraged more demands for social improvement. Demographically, the 1970s marked the replacement of a largely refugee society by a new generation of educated youth who were born or brought up in the territory and showed a strong sense of belonging to Hong Kong. Culturally, a Hong Kong identity was beginning to emerge and the 1970s was a period in which the Hong Kong people collectively thought about their identity and the future of the whole society. Since the 1970s, civil society activists have become more eager to exert pressure on the government by mobilizing public opinion support and organizing street-level protests, bringing about the rise of a social movement industry (Ma, 2009).

The real turning points that marked the rapid expansion of civil society activism were the Sino-British negotiations over the future of Hong Kong in 1982–1984 and the June 4 Incident of 1989 (Lo, 1998). Political controversies had triggered the development of the civil society and political activism in the 1980s and induced public participation in politics. With the rising political awareness of the Hong Kong people, the whole society became rapidly politicized and an active civil society started to emerge. The higher degree of political activism was reflected in the growing number of social conflicts in the 1980s and 1990s. Research indicated that starting from the 1980s, the Hong Kong people have become more active in pressing the government for improvements in quality of life and for political and civic rights, resulting in a much higher rate of incidence of social conflicts (Cheung & Louie, 2000; Lau & Wan, 2000).

Hong Kong's civil society has "gone through an important period of maturity in the ten years since the handover" (Chan & Chan, 2007). After 1997 the political slogan of "Hong Kong's people ruling Hong Kong" has, by intention or default, inspired public demand and aspiration towards the post-colonial state. Unfortunately, the increasing public expectations towards the Tung Chee-hwa Administration coincided with prolonged economic malaise as well as a series of policy blunders. The interaction of these forces finally resulted in rising public dissatisfaction with the Tung Administration and provoked waves of political activism and opposition against the post-colonial state (Fong, 2008). The development of civil society activism hit another important milestone in 2003 and 2004 as a result of the two 1 July protest rallies.[5] Following the two rallies, the Hong Kong people generally felt "empowered and confident" and civil society became more active in organizing various policy advocacy activities (Chan & Chan, 2007).

The growing waves of civil society activism

The rise of civil society activism in recent years could be illustrated through four major areas:

1 *Expansion of the number of civil society organizations.* Statistics showed that between the period 1997–2012, the number of civil society organizations (registered societies) in Hong Kong have increased by 251.1 per cent from 8,695 to 30,531 (Figure 6.1).
2 *Expansion of the forms of citizen participation.* The channels of citizen participation have been expanded from traditional methods like demonstrations and voting to new platforms including think-tanks, internet mobilization (e.g. internet radio, YouTube, Facebook) and religious groups[6] (Lam, 2007).
3 *Expansion of the extent of citizen participation.* Nowadays citizen participation in local politics is no longer limited to the traditional professional sectors (e.g. lawyers, accountants, doctors, social workers and teachers), but also ordinary citizens and people from different social backgrounds have been mobilized (e.g. truck drivers, poultry workers, residents of urban communities and young people)[7] (Lam & Tong, 2007).
4 *Expansion of the civil society policy agenda.* Apart from traditional social policy areas like housing, healthcare and social welfare, civil society organizations have increasingly paid attention to other new policy areas including environmental protection, culture, heritage protection, town planning and urban renewal[8] (Chan & Chan, 2007).

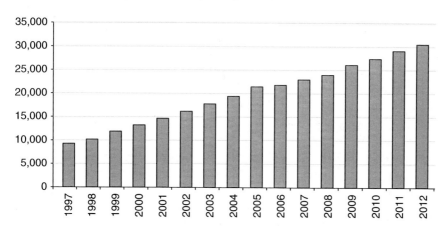

Figure 6.1 Number of civil society organizations (1997–2012) (source: data obtained from the Hong Kong Police Force).

Note
Most of the civil society groups in Hong Kong are registered in Society Ordinance (as societies). While some civil society groups may be registered under Companies Ordinance, relevant figures have not been maintained by the Companies Registry and therefore such organizations have not been included in this figure.

Implications of the growing disconnection of the business sector: the widening gap between the post-colonial state and the society

> [A]fter the end of colonialism, the public had become less tolerant of the alliance between the government and business interests. The partnership had been created originally by the British because the rulers were alien and needed "respectable" intermediaries to represent the Chinese community. Beyond 1997, the government could claim no such justification for giving the business and professional class's pride of place in the power structure.
>
> (Goodstadt, 2009, p. 138)

The rise of civil society activism has posed unprecedented challenges to the state–business alliance after 1997. Many local political scientists have already pointed out that nowadays the civil society has become more active in challenging the governance of the post-colonial state, making it increasingly difficult to establish broad societal acceptance for government policies (Chan & Chan, 2007; Cheung, 2007a).

Existing literature indicates that the apolitical society of the colonial time had provided a sufficient condition for the survival of the political alliance between the colonial state and the business sector (Cheung, 2007a; King, 1981). Scholars generally argue that in the colonial era it would not be difficult for the colonial state to mobilize a satisfactory level of societal support for its governance by means of co-opting business elites into the advisory system, but the smooth functioning of such a political formula was clearly built upon the underdevelopment of civil society in colonial Hong Kong, which made the business sector the dominant societal force and the state–business alliance immune to challenges by the civil society. However, many scholars who analysed the situation found that it fundamentally changed once the civil society in Hong Kong became more active and vibrant in recent years (Chan & Chan, 2007). After 1997, although the business elites continue to hold the majority of seats in the advisory system, they could no longer help the post-colonial state to control the public as in the colonial past. Because nowadays even if the post-colonial state's policies have been endorsed by those co-opted business allies, it does not mean that the initiatives can be implemented smoothly as those civil society activists who have been marginalized under the HKSAR political establishment are always ready to challenge the policy decisions made by the state–business alliance. In other words, unlike the British colonial era, state–business partnership after 1997 cannot in any way guarantee that the post-colonial state could establish the necessary societal support to steer policy-making, and government policies could always be blocked by explosive political events and social movements (Chan & Chan, 2007; Cheung, 2007a).[9]

While the increasing challenges from the civil society have undoubtedly created new governance problems for the post-colonial state, as pointed out by the existing literature, one important question remains unanswered: why does the post-colonial state fail to accommodate the challenges of the civil society? In spite of its rapid expansion in recent years, it is fair to say that the civil society in Hong Kong is still far from developed into a full-fledged political society and its mobilization power is still constrained by many factors such as inadequate financial and manpower resources, internal division and the depoliticized values of the Hong Kong people (Lam & Tong, 2007). To use the words of Levitsky and Way, why does the authoritarian house of the post-colonial state fail to mediate the political challenges of the civil society, which is not really vigorous by nature?

If we move beyond the existing opposition-centred explanation of the existing literature by re-examining the relationship between the post-colonial state–business alliance and the civil society, the answer to the above question is certainly related to the failure of governing coalition building in the HKSAR era. Because the business sector has become increasingly disconnected from the local community after the handover, the co-opted business elites fail to fulfil the role of intermediaries bridging the gap between the post-colonial state and the local community, as in the pre-handover era. As a consequence, the post-colonial state could no longer rely on its traditional political alliance with the business sector to maintain governance and to accommodate the challenges of the civil society. In other words, the rising level of state–society conflicts in post-colonial Hong Kong is not only the result of growing activism in the civil society as pointed out by the existing literature, but is also a demonstration of the powerlessness of the post-colonial state and its business allies in accommodating societal challenges.

There are three major reasons behind the growing disconnection of the business sector from the local community, which have eventually eroded the role of co-opted business elites in mediating the challenges of the civil society.

First, the co-opted business elites have limited community networks and few connections with newly emerged civil society groups and thus, unlike the British colonial era, they are not considered by the public as leaders of the community. During the colonial time, particularly before the 1970s, local Chinese capitalists were widely seen as the "natural leaders" of the Chinese community owing to the high credibility, prestige and community networks they had developed through their personal service in the different district and welfare organizations (Goodstadt, 2009, p. 99). Nevertheless, such a political foundation of the business elites has become increasing obsolete since the 1970s as a result of the gradual expansion of the government role in the provision of social services and its subvention on the traditional charity groups. As such, the co-opted business elites have become increasing remote from district and welfare organizations (Goodstadt, 2009, p. 105). Unfortunately, most of the business elites so far have not realized the negative consequences of their increasing disconnection from the community and have done nothing to re-establish its connectedness with the general population by participating in mass politics. The underdevelopment of business-oriented political parties and their limited community networks have been most illustrating. Despite over 20 years of development, the pro-business parties remain very much elite parties with limited community networks and

170 *Missing link between state, business and society*

lacking sufficient power of mass mobilization (Ma, 2007, p. 141). Table 6.4 indicates that when compared with other major political parties, the community networks of business-oriented political parties, including the Liberal Party and the Economic Synergy, are particularly weak in terms of their limited number of district offices and District Councillors. In the face of the rise of civil society activism in recent years, most of the business elites remain ignorant of the values and policy agenda of social activists and they are generally out of touch with those newly emerged civil society groups.[10] As a result of their limited community networks and connections with the civil society, unlike the British colonial era the co-opted business elites are no longer considered as leaders of the community and in fact they rarely possess recognizable political identities. It is therefore not surprising that in times of large-scale social movements, the co-opted business elites are powerless in mobilizing public opinion support and defending the policy decisions of the post-colonial state.[11]

Second, growing public suspicions of "government–business collusion" in recent years have created negative images of the business sector, eroding the credibility of co-opted business elites in the public's eyes. After 1997 there have been increasing public allegations that the government has provided preferential treatment for big businesses on several controversial issues (e.g. construction of Cyberport, the development of West Kowloon Cultural District and the sale of Hunghom Peninsula) and the credibility of government officials and the business sector has been severely challenged due to these incidents[12] (Wong & Zheng, 2006; Zheng & Wan, 2011a, 2011b). In recent years the growing public suspicions of government–business collusion have even sparked off an anti-business and anti-rich sentiment within the society, resulting in a new public discourse

Table 6.4 Community networks of major political parties

Political parties	Number of district offices	Number of elected district councillors	Number of appointed district councillors
Pro-democracy political parties			
Democratic Party	78	50	0
Civic Party	19	12	0
Hong Kong Association for Democracy and People's Livelihood	20	16	0
League of Social Democrats	8	4	0
Pro-Beijing leftist political parties			
Democratic Alliance for the Betterment and Progress of Hong Kong	178	119	14
Hong Kong Federation of Trade Unions	41	19	3
Business-oriented political parties			
Liberal Party	**22**	**7**	**8**
Economic Synergy	**2**	**1**	**2**

Source: Figures obtained from various political parties in June 2011.

against the business sector (Figure 6.2). As a result of the proliferation of such a public discourse, there is a growing number of people holding negative impressions of business leaders, seeing them as distrustful, profit-oriented, politically conservative and not respectful[13] (Table 6.5). Therefore, unlike the British colonial period when the co-opted business elites were widely seen as "respectable intermediaries" representing the Chinese community and helping the colonial state to carry local opinion (Goodstadt, 2009, p. 138), the public image of business leaders has become extremely negative after 1997. As a result, instead of

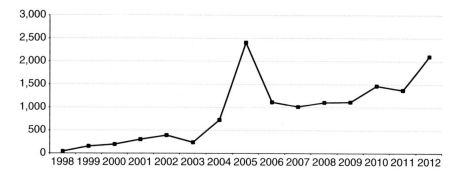

Figure 6.2 The development of a public discourse against the business sector in the post-1997 period (source: author's own research based on the information obtained from the WiseNews electronic platform. The research counted the number of newspaper reports which mentioned the above between 1998 to 2012. The local newspapers covered in this research are *Apple Daily, Hong Kong Commercial Daily, Hong Kong Daily News, Hong Kong Economic Journal, Hong Kong Economic Times, Ming Pao Daily News, Oriental Daily News, Sing Pao, Sing Tao Daily, Ta Kung Pao, The Sun* and *Wen Wei Po*).

Table 6.5 Public perceptions of business leaders

Question	Percentage of respondents	
	2006 survey	*2011 survey*
(1) Public trust in business leaders		
Distrust	**25.3**	**38.8**
Half–half	54.8	48.0
Trust	19.9	13.2
(2) Public opinion on whether business leaders are profit-oriented and anti-democracy		
Strongly agree or agree	**46.6**	**54.5**
Moderate	27.0	27.0
Disagree or strongly disagree	26.4	18.5
(3) Public opinion on whether business leaders have any respectable character		
No	**43.2**	**52.2**
Yes	56.8	47.8

Source: Zheng & Wan, 2013.

172 *Missing link between state, business and society*

mobilizing societal support for the post-colonial state, the co-opted business elite struggles to earn the respect of the Hong Kong people, and the endorsement by the co-opted business elite of a government initiative has even brought about counter-productive results and become the target of public criticism.

Finally, the business sector's longstanding ideological weapon of "economism" has become increasingly out of touch with the public and thus the co-opted business elite struggles to defend the pro-business policy agenda in the public sphere. In the colonial era, the discourse of economism, which emphasized the importance of economic growth and its contribution to improvement of people's livelihood, perpetrated the domination of the state–business alliance. By reinforcing the idea that the general public would be better-off under the free market and everyone could move upward on the social ladder through hard work, the ideology of economism sustained public acceptance for pro-business policies and neutralized social inequalities (Henders, 2008). However, in recent years Hong Kong economic growth has been coupled with the trend of growing income disparity. Since its transformation into an international financial and business services centre in the 1990s, Hong Kong has been characterized by dual social structures where incomes of high-skilled managers/professionals and low-skilled blue-collar workers have been polarized (Lui & Chiu, 2009, pp. 81–102). As income inequality becomes a structural rather than a cyclical phenomenon in Hong Kong, more and more people begin to doubt the idea that pro-business policies and free market capitalism are really good for the whole society (Table 6.6). As such, the political narrative of economism is becoming less appealing to the public and less effective in countering the civil society's growing demands for social justice (Henders, 2008). The gradual erosion of the discourse of economism has effectively undermined the credibility of co-opted business elites and deprived them of an important ideological weapon to defend and justify the pro-business policies of the post-colonial state.

To sum up, because of the erosion of the intermediary role of the business elites, even though the post-colonial state could still press through its policies by

Table 6.6 Public perceptions on the political discourse of economism (%)

	2006 survey	2011 survey
Public opinion on the statement "Do you think the HKSAR government should avoid intervening in the operation of the market?"		
Strongly agree or agree	57.5	47.3
Moderate	23.5	25.7
Disagree or strongly disagree	**19.0**	**27.0**
Public opinion on the statement "Do you think allowing business leaders to maximize profits is good for everyone?"		
Strongly agree or agree	30.7	20.9
Moderate	29.7	22.9
Disagree or strongly disagree	**39.6**	**56.2**

Source: Zheng & Wan, 2013.

The widening gap between state and society 173

resorting to the pro-government majority in the Legislative Council (i.e. the support of business/professional legislators from the functional constituencies and pro-Beijing leftist legislators), it cannot rely on the support of co-opted business elites to manage the rising challenges of civil society activism and mobilize sufficient social support for its governance.[14] In times of growing state–society conflicts, the co-opted business elites are generally powerless in bridging the widening gap between the post-colonial state and the civil society.

The case of Express Rail Link

The controversies surrounding the construction of the Hong Kong section of the Guangzhou–Shenzhen–Hong Kong Express Rail Link (Express Rail Link) is a good example to illustrate how the growing disconnection of the business sector has undermined the capacity of the post-colonial state in managing the challenges of civil society. Connecting Hong Kong with the national high-speed rail network, the construction of the Express Rail Link is supposed to bring about enormous benefits to Hong Kong's long-term economic and social development and foster Mainland–Hong Kong integration[15] (Transport and Housing Bureau, 2008). Nevertheless, the construction of the Express Rail Link has attracted strong opposition from some villagers from the Tsoi Yuen Tsuen at Shek Kong (an area affected by the relevant land resumption works) who refused to move out of their homes. These villagers, together with a group of heritage activists and civil society organizers, launched a series of social movements and protests in 2009 to voice their opposition to the construction project and requested revision of the alignment of the whole Express Rail Link. The social movements organized by the Choi Yuen villagers and the heritage activists successfully increased public attention to the Express Rail Link project and significantly changed the course of development. The alternative rail route proposal[16] put forth by the Professional Commons, a think-tank formed by professionals like lawyers, engineers, accountants and academics, added further doubt to the cost-effectiveness of the Tsang Administration's proposal. By the end of 2009 there had been an important change in public opinion and opinion polls demonstrated that more and more people expressed reservations about the whole construction project.[17]

In the face of widespread public concerns about the Express Rail Link project, the Tsang Administration tried to counter the opposition waves by mobilizing the support of its coalition partners in the business sector. The Executive Council approved the Express Rail Link project on 20 October 2009 and those unofficial Executive Councillors with business backgrounds were mobilized to give high-profile support to the Express Rail Link project by highlighting its economic benefits to Hong Kong.[18] The Mass Transit Railway Corporation, an alliance of 67 business chambers and the major business associations also placed full-page newspaper advertisements calling on the public to support the Express Rail Link project (*South China Morning Post*, 2010a, 14 January). With the support votes of business and professional legislators returned by functional constituencies, the

174 *Missing link between state, business and society*

Tsang Administration finally secured the endorsement of the Legislative Council Finance Committee to approve the relevant funding proposals on 16 January 2010.

While the support of the business elites in both the Executive Council and the Legislative Council had allowed the Tsang Administration to successfully press through the Express Rail Link proposal, it did not help establish broad societal support for the project within the wider community. It was comprehensible that the co-opted business elites, due to their limited community networks and disconnection from the civil society organizations, were generally powerless in bridging the political gap between the post-colonial state and the anti-Express Rail Link activists.[19] During the deliberation of the funding proposals in the Legislative Council, the support of business legislators from the functional constituencies proved to produce counterproductive effects and brought about public suspicions of "transfer of interests", because several business legislators like Raymond Ho and Abraham Shen were found to hold directorships in construction companies that would benefit from the Express Rail Link project (*Apple Daily*, 2009, 3 December).

In the midst of the controversies, the state–business alliance also found that its political discourse of economism had become less useful to shape public opinion. While the government officials and their business allies had been trying very hard to highlight the economic value of the Express Rail Link, they had been severely criticized by the public as promoting "central values" which paid too much attention to economic competitiveness but generally ignored the growing public concerns on post-materialistic values such as environment, heritage and neighbourhood (*Hong Kong Economic Journal*, 2010, 9 January). As a consequence of the vulnerability of the state–business alliance in accommodating the challenges of civil society organizations, following the passage of the funding proposals the Tsang Administration paid heavy political prices in terms of its credibility and public image for pressing ahead with the project with the support of the business sector.[20] Briefly, the case of the Express Rail Link clearly demonstrated that in the midst of serious state–society conflicts the state–business alliance is no longer an effective governing machine that the post-colonial state can rely on to thwart civil society challenges and to establish broad societal support for its policies.

Conclusion

This chapter examines the post-1997 governance crisis facing the post-colonial state by focusing on the dynamics between the state–business alliance and the civil society. With the rise of civil society activism after 1997, the alienated civil society activists are now ready to challenge the state–business alliance by means of social movements and demonstrations. However, in the face of rising challenges from the civil society, the post-colonial Hong Kong state is handicapped by its narrow-based and loose governing coalition with the business sector. Unlike their colonial predecessors, business elites after 1997 could no longer

The widening gap between state and society   175

fulfil the role of encompassing intermediaries in the social arena as in the British colonial past and they generally lack the necessary community networks, public reputation and ideological weapons to mediate state–society relations.

As highlighted by Levitsky and Way in their latest research on hybrid regimes, a well-organized governing party with mass organizations and activist bases could help the authoritarian incumbents to resist and overcome opposition challenges (Levitsky & Way, 2010, pp. 62–64). Unfortunately, the post-colonial Hong Kong state does not have this luxury. Hong Kong has been moving towards a hybrid regime featuring limited electoral franchise but strong civil society activism over the past few decades; the post-colonial state and its business allies have been slow to re-engineer their governing coalition into a cohesive governing party so as to accommodate themselves to the changing political environment. Their failure to organize the ruling elites into a cohesive governing party, establish connectedness with those newly emerged civil society groups, develop community networks and sharpen their political discourse have made the state–business alliance too vulnerable in the face of the challenges of the civil society after 1997. Because of this structural defect of the state–business alliance, the post-colonial state could no longer rely on its political alliance with the business sector to establish widespread societal acceptance for its governance and improve its communication with the society. The political divide between the state–business alliance and the civil society has increasingly become a huge political gap that the post-colonial state struggles to stride across and this has unavoidably added fuel to the serious governance crisis in the post-1997 period.

Notes

1 © 2013 by The Regents of the University of California. Originally published in a slightly different form, reprinted from *Asian Survey*, Vol. 53, No. 5, September/October 2013, pp. 854–882, by permission of The Regents.

2 Under Article 56 of the Basic Law, the Chief Executive shall consult the Executive Council before making important policy decisions, introducing bills to the Legislative Council, making subordinate legislation or dissolving the Legislative Council. Therefore, all major policy decisions are in principle made by the Chief Executive in Council, and the Executive Council, just like its colonial predecessor, should function as the de facto cabinet of the Chief Executive (Li, 2007).

3 The Commission on Strategic Development was first established by Chief Executive Tung Chee-hwa in 1998 to discuss Hong Kong's long-term development strategies. In October 2005 the incumbent Chief Executive Donald Tsang announced in his maiden Policy Address that the Commission would be re-organized as the most important advisory body. Personally chaired by the Chief Executive, the Commission on Strategic Development has served as the platform under which the government will gauge the views of unofficial members at the early stage of policy formulation (Commission on Strategic Development's website: www.cpu.gov.hk/tc/2009_csd.htm).

4 The Central Policy Unit's principal function is to provide policy advice and research support to the Chief Executive, Chief Secretary and Financial Secretary. While full-time researchers and supporting personnel are employed to fulfil the above functions, the Central Policy Unit also operates as an advisory body by appointing part-time members drawn from different sectors. These part-time members will meet regularly

176 *Missing link between state, business and society*

on a bi-weekly basis to tender policy advice to the government on a wide range of policy issues (Central Policy Unit's website: www.cpu.gov.hk/tc/index.htm).

5 On 1 July 2003 over half a million people took part in the mass procession to express their dissatisfaction with the controversial Basic Law Article 23 legislation and the HKSAR government's repeated policy failures in the post-1997 period. In 2004 another large-scale rally happened when hundreds of thousands of people marched on the streets again to fight for universal suffrage.

6 In recent years many think-tanks have been formed to conduct policy advocacy activities, such as SynergyNet, Civic Exchange, Professional Commons, Roundtable and Savantas. On the other hand, the rapid development of the internet has also facilitated the growth of internet-based advocacy organizations in recent years, such as the Inmedia, Left 21 and Post-80's Youth against Unrightful Authority. These internet-based advocacy organizations have made use of the internet platform to mobilize and line-up supporters in their opposition against the post-colonial state's policies. Finally, religious groups such as Catholic Commission for Justice and Peace and Hong Kong Women Christian Council are also active in promoting human rights, labour and women's rights issues.

7 Two notable examples were the organization of the campaign for protecting Victoria Harbour and setting up of the H15 Concern Group. In the campaign for protecting Victoria Harbour, a group of private citizens joined hands to protest against the further reclamation of Victoria Harbour. In the setting up of the H15 Concern Group, a group of homemakers and ordinary residents with little political experience joined together to establish the Concern Group demanding participation in the Wanchai urban renewal project (Lam & Tong, 2007).

8 The broadening of the civil society agenda have been illustrated in a number of incidents such as protection of the Victoria Harbour and Hunghom Peninsula incident (environmental protection), opposition to the construction of the West Kowloon Cultural District (culture), demolition of the Star Ferry Pier and the Queen's Pier (heritage protection) and redevelopment of the Lei Tung Street in Wanchai (town planning and urban renewal).

9 The Star Ferry Pier episode in 2006 was an example commonly used by local academics to illustrate the rising challenges of civil society on the advisory system. As part of the Central Reclamation Phase III Project, the Star Ferry clock tower would be demolished. The government had followed the due process of public consultation by consulting the Legislative Council, the District Council and Antiquities Advisory Board and the plan did not meet with strong opposition. However, the demolition works were still blocked in December 2006 when a group of protestors stormed the construction site. This incident, which inspired widespread political controversy, has forced the government to review its built heritage conversation policy. Following this incident, the HKSAR government launched a public consultation exercise and committed to expanding the current built heritage assessment criteria by incorporating the element of "collective memory" (Cheung, 2007b).

10 Anonymous interviewee.

11 Anonymous interviewee.

12 For opinion polls on the public perceptions of government–business collusion and the growing anti-business sentiment, see Tables 1.5–1.7.

13 The changing public perceptions of Hong Kong's richest tycoon, Li Ka-shing, are indicative of the growing negative image of business leaders after the handover. In the pre-1997 period, Li Ka-shing was generally seen by the public as the epitome of success and a role model for the Hong Kong people. Opinion polls conducted in 1985 showed that over 71.8 per cent of respondents agreed or strong agreed that successful businessmen such as Li Ka-shing, who succeeded under conditions of intense competition, should be the model for young people to admire and learn from (Lau & Kuan, 1988, p. 64). In the post-1997 period, public perception of Li Ka-shing changed

The widening gap between state and society 177

significantly and on many occasions the general public criticized Li and his business kingdom as monopolizing Hong Kong's economy. To express their dissatisfaction towards the "real estate hegemony", civil society activists even increasingly turned to stage protests in the Cheung Kong Centre and ParknShop owned by Li Ka-shing (*South China Morning Post*, 2011b, 7 March).

14 Apart from the erosion of the intermediary role of business elites, one important idea that we should qualify in establishing the growing disconnection of the state–business alliance from local society after 1997 is the limited role of pro-Beijing leftists. As shown in Table 6.4, while the community networks of business-oriented political parties are obviously weak, pro-Beijing political parties – namely the Democratic Alliance for the Betterment and Progress of Hong Kong and the Hong Kong Federation of Trade Unions – have maintained extensive local networks. Unfortunately, for two important reasons pro-Beijing leftists also fail to play a bridging function between the post-colonial state and the civil society, despite extensive local networks. First, the pro-Beijing leftists were only marginal actors in the post-colonial governing coalition. Tracing back to the mid-1980s, the Beijing leaders had already decided to engineer a governing coalition with business elites forming the core of the whole alliance and the leftists only playing a marginal role (Ma, 2007, p. 80). Such a governing strategy had been largely followed by the first two HKSAR Chief Executives, Tung Chee-hwa (1997–2005) and Donald Tsang Yam-kuen (2005–2012) (Lau, 2012, pp. 69–191). With no real executive power in terms of cabinet positions and no actual influence in the policy-making process, the pro-Beijing leftists are incapable of aggregating and channelling social interests (Ma, 2007 p. 153). Second, the community network as forged by the pro-Beijing leftists has its own limitation. While the pro-Beijing leftists have established an extensive network of united front organizations covering trade unions, neighbourhood bodies, youth and women groups, and such a united front machinery has occasionally been rolled out to support the post-colonial state in times of major political controversy after 1997 (Lau, 2012, pp. 194–195), the grassroots orientation and politically conservative outlook of the leftist organizations have made them basically disconnected from the middle class and particularly the newly emerged civil society organizations. Therefore, the pro-Beijing leftists are ineffective in mobilizing mainstream public opinion support for the post-colonial state (Loh, 2010, pp. 207–208).

15 The proposed Express Rail Link runs wholly in a 26-km long underground tunnel from the West Kowloon terminus to join the Mainland section at the boundary at Huanggang. It will be connected with the proposed Beijing–Guangzhou Passenger Line at Shibi, the Hangzhou–Fuzhou–Shenzhen Passenger Line at Longhua and the Rapid Transit System of the Pearl River Delta area. Upon completion of the project there will be shuttle services between Hong Kong and Guangzhou, Dongguan and Shenzhen, and express long-haul services to major Mainland cities such as Beijing, Shanghai and Chongqing. The post-colonial state estimated that improved rail connectivity will bring an additional 1.2 million Mainland visitors to Hong Kong by 2016, giving a boost to Hong Kong's tourism and business sectors. The government also estimated that the Express Rail Link project will create about 5,500 jobs during the construction process and an additional 10,000 jobs after the Express Railway Link has been put into operation (Transport and Housing Bureau, 2008).

16 The Professional Commons challenged the government's plan to locate the Hong Kong terminus for the Express Rail Link at West Kowloon. Experts from Professional Commons argued that it was more cost-effective to locate the terminus at Kam Sheung Road so as to integrate the Express Rail Link with the existing West Rail Link and Airport Railway (Professional Commons, 2009).

17 According to an opinion poll conducted by the University of Hong Kong in January 2010, 47 per cent of respondents supported the post-colonial state's funding proposals for the Express Rail Link. However, 23 per cent of respondents opposed the funding

178 *Missing link between state, business and society*

proposals and another 22 per cent of respondents wanted to put the funding proposals on hold. The opinion polls showed that public opinion was divided over the project (Public Opinion Programme, University of Hong Kong, 2010a).

18 For example, unofficial Executive Councillors Leung Chun-ying and Ronald Arculli both argued that the construction of the Express Rail Link is crucial to Hong Kong–Mainland integration and will boost economic development in the territory (*Hong Kong Commercial Daily*, 2010, 13 January).

19 Anonymous interviewee.

20 According to a poll conducted by the University of Hong Kong in January 2010, the support rate and approval rate of the Chief Executive Donald Tsang have dropped significantly by 2.8 marks and 4 per cent following the passage of Express Rail Link proposals (Public Opinion Programme, University of Hong Kong, 2010b).

References

Apple Daily. (2009, 3 December). Raymond Ho and Abraham Shen were forced to withdraw from Legco meeting on Express Rail Link amid accusations of conflict of interests. A06 (in Chinese).

Chan, E., & Chan, J. (2007). The first ten years of the HKSAR: Civil society comes of age. *Asia Pacific Journal of Public Administration, 29*(1), 77–99.

Cheung, A. (2007a). Executive-dominant governance or executive power "hollowed-out": The political quagmire of Hong Kong. *Asian Journal of Political Science, 15*(1), 17–38.

Cheung, A. (2007b). Policy capacity in post-1997 Hong Kong: Constrained institutions facing a crowding and differentiated polity. *Asia Pacific Journal of Public Administration, 29*(1), 51–75.

Cheung, A. and Louie, K. S. (2000). Social conflicts: 1975–1986. In S. K. Lau (Ed.), *Social development and political change in Hong Kong* (pp. 63–114). Hong Kong: Chinese University Press.

Cheung, A. & Wong, P. C. W. (2004). Who advised the Hong Kong government? The politics of absorption before and after 1997. *Asian Survey, 44*(6), 874–894.

Civil Society Index Team. (2006). *The CIVICUS civil society index report for the Hong Kong Special Administrative Region.* Hong Kong: The Hong Kong Council of Social Service.

Fong, B. (2008). An analysis of the 2003 "Zero-Three-Three" civil service pay reduction settlement in Hong Kong: A neopluralist perspective. *Asian Profile, 36*(6), 559–580.

Goodstadt, L. F. (2009). *Uneasy partners: The conflict between public interest and private profit interest in Hong Kong.* Hong Kong: Hong Kong University Press.

Henders, S. J. (2008). The Hong Kong Special Administrative Region: Implications for world order. In A. Laliberté, & M. Lanteigne (Eds.), *The Chinese party-state in the 21st century: Adaptation and the reinvention of legitimacy* (pp. 106–129). New York: Routledge.

Hong Kong Commercial Daily. (2010, 13 January). Executive councillors support the early construction of Express Rail Link. A13 (in Chinese).

Hong Kong Economic Journal. (2010, 9 January). The delay of the funding proposal of the Express Rail Link exposed social contradictions. P02 (in Chinese).

Ip, P. K. (1998). Development of civil society in Hong Kong: Constraints, problems and risks. In P. K. Li (Ed.), *Political order and power transition in Hong Kong* (pp. 159–186). Hong Kong: Chinese University Press.

King, A. Y. C. (1981). Administrative absorption of politics in Hong Kong: Emphasis on the grass roots level. In A. Y. C. King, & R. P. L. Lee (Eds.), *Social life and development in Hong Kong* (pp. 127–146). Hong Kong: Chinese University Press.

Lam, W. M. (2007). Political context. In W. M. Lam, P. L. T. Lui, W. Wong, & I. Holiday (Eds.), *Contemporary Hong Kong politics: Governance in the post-1997 era* (pp. 1–17). Hong Kong: Hong Kong University Press.

Lam, W. M., & Tong, I. L. K. (2007). Civil society and NGOs. In W. M. Lam, P. L. T. Lui, W. Wong, & I. Holiday (Eds.), *Contemporary Hong Kong politics: Governance in the post-1997 era* (pp. 135–154). Hong Kong: Hong Kong University Press.

Lau, S. K. (2012). *Hui hui shi wu nian yi lai xianggang te qu guan zhi ji xin zhrng quan jian (HKSAR governance and regime building 15 years since the handover)*. Xianggang: Shang Wu Yin Shu Guan (Hong Kong: Hong Kong Commercial Press) (in Chinese).

Lau, S. K., & Kuan, H. C. (1988). *The ethos of the Hong Kong Chinese*. Hong Kong: Chinese University Press.

Lau, S. K., & Wan, P. S. (2000). Social conflicts: 1987–1995. In S. K. Lau (Ed.), *Social development and political change in Hong Kong* (pp. 115–170). Hong Kong: Chinese University Press.

Levitsky, S., & Way, L. A. (2010). *Competitive authoritarianism: Hybrid regimes after the Cold War*. New York: Cambridge University Press.

Li, P. K. (2007). The executive. In W. M. Lam, P. L. T. Lui, W. Wong, & I. Holiday (Eds.), *Contemporary Hong Kong politics: Governance in the post-1997 era* (pp. 23–37). Hong Kong: Hong Kong University Press.

Lo, S. H. (1998). Political opposition, co-option and democratization: The case of Hong Kong. In P. K. Li (Ed.), *Political order and power transition in Hong Kong* (pp. 127–157). Hong Kong: Chinese University Press.

Loh, C. (2010). *Underground front: The Chinese Communist Party in Hong Kong*. Hong Kong: Hong Kong University Press.

Lui, T. L., & Chiu, S. W. K. (2009). *Hong Kong: Becoming a Chinese global city*. London: Routledge.

Ma, N. (2007). *Political development in Hong Kong: State, political society and civil society*. Hong Kong: Hong Kong University Press.

Ma, N. (2009). Reinventing the Hong Kong state or rediscovering it? From low intervention to eclectic corporatism. *Economy and Society, 38*(3), 492–519.

Professional Commons (2009). *Hong Kong Interchange option: A cheaper, faster and better Express Rail Link*. Retrieved 1 January 2013 from: www.procommons.org.hk/hong-kong-interchange-option-a-cheaper-faster-and-better-express-rail-link?lang=en

Public Opinion Programme, University of Hong Kong. (2010a). *HKU POP SITE releases second survey on Express Rail Link*. Retrieved 1 January 2013 from http://hkupop.hku.hk/chinese/release/release729.html.

Public Opinion Programme, University of Hong Kong. (2010b). *HKU POP SITE releases the latest popularity figures of CE Donald Tsang*. Retrieved 1 January 2013 from http://hkupop.hku.hk/chinese/release/release733.html.

South China Morning Post. (2010a, 14 January). Battle waged in newspaper advertisements. EDT2.

South China Morning Post. (2011b, 7 March). Unhappy campers take on "superman". CITY1.

Transport and Housing Bureau. (2008). *Hong Kong section of Guangzhou–Shenzhen–Hong Kong Express Rail Link: Legislative Council brief for the Subcommittee on Matters Relating to Railways of the Legislative Council Panel on Transport*. Retrieved

180 *Missing link between state, business and society*

1 January 2013 from www.legco.gov.hk/yr07-08/english/panels/tp/tp_rdp/papers/tp_rdp-thbtcr11658199-e.pdf.

Wong, S. L., & Zheng, H. T. (2006). *Guan Shang Gou Jie: Xianggang Shi Min Yan Zhong De Zheng Shang Guan Xi (Government–business collusion: Public perception of government–business relations in Hong Kong)*. Hong Kong culture and society programme occasional paper series no. 3. Hong Kong: The University of Hong Kong.

Zheng, H. T., & Wan, P. S. (2011a, 8 August). Public perception of government–business relations in Hong Kong. *Hong Kong Economic Journal.* P15 (in Chinese).

Zheng, H. T., & Wan, P. S. (2011b, 14 September). Public perception of the changing business environment in Hong Kong. *Ming Pao.* A24 (in Chinese).

Zheng, H. T., & Wan, P. S. (2013). Zeng yinquan ren nei zheng shang guan xi di bianhua (The evolution of government–business relations under Donald Tsang administration). In J. Y. Luo, & Y. S. Zheng (Eds.), *Liu gei Liang Zhenying de qi ju: Tong xi Zeng Yinquan shi dai (On the chessboard: Donald Tsang's legacy for CY Leung)* (pp. 49–74). Xianggang: Xianggang Cheng Shi Da Xue Chu Ban She (Hong Kong: City University of Hong Kong Press) (in Chinese).

Part IV

Uneasy partnership between state and business

The rising power leverage of the business sector in post-1997 Hong Kong

7 Institutionalization of business power under the HKSAR political system

Chief Executive Election Committee and functional constituencies

The dynamics of state–business relations in Hong Kong have undergone fundamental changes in the post-1997 period. Unlike the British colonial period, when the relationship between the colonial state and the business sector was largely amicable and mutually supportive (Chiu, 1994), since the handover of sovereignty it is not uncommon for the business sector to openly challenge and oppose the policy agenda of the HKSAR Chief Executive. Nowadays the business elites have dared to show their political muscle in order to exert their influences and control over the decision-making process of the post-colonial state. The partnership between the post-colonial state and its business allies has become increasingly uneasy, if not confrontational, after 1997. What are the structural factors that have contributed to such a drastic change in the dynamics of state–business relations after 1997? The institutionalization of business power under the HKSAR political systems, including the Chief Executive Election Committees and functional constituency seats in the Legislative Council, should be one of the important answers to this question.

In this chapter we will first trace the constitutional design of the HKSAR political system and examine how the state–business alliance has been institutionalized under the Basic Law. Then we will go on to examine how business power has been effectively consolidated and institutionalized in the executive branch and legislative process through the Chief Executive Election Committees and the functional constituency electoral system of the Legislative Council, respectively. Finally, we will put forward an argument that the HKSAR political system has equipped the business sector with unprecedented power leverages vis-à-vis the post-colonial state after 1997, bringing about new tensions and cleavages to the state–business alliance in the post-1997 period.

The constitutional design of the post-1997 political system: the making of the state–business alliance

> The political structure is designed to ensure the dominance of the business and professional classes, the principal devices being the system for appointment of Chief Executive, functional constituencies, and the systems of

184 *Uneasy partnership between state and business*

voting in the legislature which seeks to give the business sector a veto over initiatives of more democratically elected members.... The drafters of the Basic Law assumed an alliance between the Chief Executive and the business sector.

(Ghai, 1999, p. 289)

The political systems of the HKSAR have been clearly specified by the territory's "mini-constitution" – the Basic Law. Officially speaking, the fundamental objectives of the Basic Law were to provide the constitutional foundation for the establishment of the HKSAR on 1 July 1997 and set out in legal form the basic policies of the Chinese government regarding Hong Kong as enshrined in the Sino-British Joint Declaration of 1984.[1] The drafting process of the Basic Law was formally started in 1985, when the Basic Law Drafting Committee (BLDC) and the Basic Law Consultative Committee (BLCC) were set up by the Chinese government as the two principal institutions responsible for drafting the Basic Law. The whole drafting process involved what was called the "two ups and two downs" process, that is, the first draft prepared by the BLDC was handed down to the BLCC for consultation and public discussion in April 1988, while the second draft was released for public consultation again in February 1989. The draft of the Basic Law was finally submitted to the Standing Committee of the National People's Congress (NPC) for decision and was formally promulgated by the Chinese government in April 1990 (Chan, 1991).

The drafting of the Basic Law was undoubtedly the most formidable and complex political project during the critical juncture of transition of sovereignty. In this connection, what kind of political structure should be adopted for the future HKSAR, in particular the electoral system of the Chief Executive and the methods for the election of Legislative Councillors was the most contentious issue that drew considerable public debate and political controversy (Chan, 1991; Ghai, 1999, p. 63). For the Chinese government, careful thought must be given to the design of the post-handover political systems because how the political powers would be distributed in the HKSAR would have far-reaching implications for the maintenance of its overall political and economic interests in the territory after 1997. To use the words of a renowned academic from the pro-Beijing camp, the design of the post-1997 political systems should be "to the advantage of implementing the policy of one country, two systems" in Hong Kong after the handover of sovereignty (Xiao, 2001, p. 230). In this connection, one of the principal objectives[2] that the Beijing leaders intended to achieve in the design of the post-1997 constitutional systems was undoubtedly to engineer and consolidate the state–business alliance. For the Chinese government, the maintenance of the state–business alliance after 1997 is central to its governing strategy in Hong Kong (see Chapter 4) and thus in the drafting process of the Basic Law it was of paramount importance that the business sector would form the majority of the new HKSAR political establishment. To consolidate the state–business alliance after 1997, the Chief Executive Election Committees and the functional constituencies in the Legislative Council were adopted by the

Chinese authorities as the principal constitutional devices for guaranteeing the dominance and representation of the business elites in the post-handover political systems (Ghai, 1999, p. 289).

Under the Basic Law, the Chief Executive shall be selected by the Chief Executive Election Committee and be appointed by the Chinese government, and in this connection designated seats have been assigned to the business sector in the Election Committee so that the business sector could have a say over the selection of the head of the HKSAR government. On the other hand, half of the members of the Legislative Council shall be returned by functional constituencies and such an electoral system has effectively guaranteed the representation of various business and industrial sectors in the legislature. The discussions in the forthcoming sections will reveal that such a constitutional system, by which the methods for selecting the head of the government and forming the Legislative Council are significantly different from that of the British colonial period, has fundamentally changed the dynamics of state–business relations in post-1997 Hong Kong and brought about far-reaching implications on the overall governance of the HKSAR.

Chief Executive Election Committees: institutionalization of business power in the executive branch

[T]he Election Committee that elects the chief executive ... has one fourth of the members assigned to business sectors. It should also be noted a lot of the EC members who were selected from other sectors were businessmen by profession, including the NPC and CPPCC delegates ... those sectors representing the district council members, the rural interests, and even in sectors such as sports. The system more or less guaranteed that the CE candidate has to be acceptable to the business sector at large, although Beijing's preference remained paramount.

(Ma, 2007, pp. 70–71)

Under the HKSAR political system, the Chief Executive is the most powerful political office in the HKSAR. According to the Basic Law, the Chief Executive performs the dual leadership roles of both the "Head of the HKSAR" (Article 43) and "Head of the HKSAR Government" (Article 48). Representing the whole HKSAR and being the highest-ranking public official in the executive branch, the Chief Executive should have a superior constitutional status when compared with public officials in any other branch of the government, including the President of the Legislative Council and the Chief Justice of the Court of Final Appeal (Lau, 2000a). Apart from his superior constitutional status, the Chief Executive also enjoys and exercises an extensive range of political powers, including implementing the Basic Law and other laws in Hong Kong, signing bills passed by the Legislative Council and promulgating laws, signing budgets passed by the Legislative Council, deciding on government policies and issuing executive orders, nominating principal officials for appointment by the Chinese

186 *Uneasy partnership between state and business*

government, appointing or removing judges of the courts at all levels, appointing or removing holders of public offices in the executive branch (including civil servants of different ranks and members of various advisory and statutory bodies), conducting external affairs on behalf of the HKSAR government, pardoning persons convicted of criminal offences or commuting their penalties, and handling petitions and complaints (Article 48). The above provisions of the Basic Law were all tactfully designed to give the Chief Executive superior constitutional status, substantive powers of policy-making and implementation and extensive powers of political appointment and patronage, so that the holder of the office could effectively play a pivotal role over the political affairs of the HKSAR (Cheung, 2007; Lau, 2000a).

Given the paramount importance of the office of the Chief Executive under the HKSAR political system, what kind of institution will be adopted for selecting and appointing the Chief Executive will have strong implications for distribution of political power in the HKSAR after 1997. In this connection, the methods for selecting and appointing the Chief Executive under the Basic Law could be considered as a very special kind of political arrangement which has to a significant extent reflected the Chinese government's governing strategy in the post-1997 period. In accordance with the Basic Law, the "Chief Executive of the Hong Kong Special Administrative Region shall be selected by election or through consultations held locally and be appointed by the Central People's Government" and the "specific method for selecting the Chief Executive is prescribed in Annex I" (Article 45). In other words, under the present system the HKSAR Chief Executive will first be elected by an Election Committee in the locality, and then the Chief Executive-elect will be appointed by the Central Authorities. From this perspective, the Election Committee operates as a system of electoral college and provides a method of indirect election for selecting the Chief Executive (Young & Cullen, 2010, p. 13).

Annex I of the Basic Law gives an overall framework for the composition of the Chief Executive Election Committee. It should be an 1,200-member electoral college composed of four sectors of 300 members, including "industrial, commercial and financial sectors", "professions", "labour, social services, religious and other sectors" and the "political sector" (Table 7.1). Nevertheless, Annex I has not provided details about how the members of these four sectors are selected and the details are to be specified by a local legislation in the HKSAR. According to the *Chief Executive Election Ordinance* passed by the Legislative Council after 1997, each of these four sectors is further divided into 38 subsectors that return a fixed number of members either by means of election (1,044 members are elected from 35 subsectors), by nomination (60 members are nominated by the religious subsector) or by ex-officio status (96 ex-officio members, including Hong Kong deputies to the NPC and Legislative Councillors). For the 35 subsectors that return members by means of election, the size of franchise varied (Table 7.2). Elected members from the various professional subsectors (i.e. subsectors in the second sector) are mainly returned by individual electors with a relatively larger size of electorate basis, but these members only account

Institutionalization of business power 187

Table 7.1 Composition of the Chief Executive Election Committee

Sector	Number of members
First sector: industrial, commercial and financial sectors	300
Second sector: professions	300
Third sector: labour, social services, religious and other sectors	300
Fourth sector: political sector	300
Total	1,200

Note
The 2000 and 2006 Election Committees comprised 800 members. Following the passage of the 2012 constitutional reform package in 2010, Annex I of the Basic Law was amended and the 2011 Election Committee comprised 1,200 members.

for one-quarter of the whole Election Committee. On the other hand, elected members in the various business, agricultural, labour and cultural subsectors (i.e. subsectors in the first and third sectors) are basically returned by corporate electors with a very limited electorate basis (generally a few hundred corporate electors in each subsector), but these members occupy almost half of the seats in the Election Committee. Under such an electoral system, it is quite obvious that the Chief Executive is in effect selected by a small group of political elites.

Apart from the first Chief Executive of the HKSAR who was elected by a 400-member Selection Committee in 1996,[3] the term of office of each Chief Executive Election Committee, including the two 800-member Election Committees formed in 2000 and 2006 and the 1,200-member Election Committee[4] formed in 2011, shall normally be five years under Annex I of the Basic Law.

The dominant position of the business sector in the Chief Executive Election Committee

In accordance with Beijing's strategy of making the business sector the majority of the HKSAR political establishment, the above electoral system for selecting the Chief Executive, including the division of the Election Committee into four major sectors and the election of the majority of its members by corporate electors, were basically designed to make the Chief Executive Election Committee an institutional platform for incorporating the interests of the business sector. First of all, by dividing the Election Committee into four major sectors, the business sector could effectively control at least one-quarter of the seats by virtue of their memberships in the various business subsectors in the first sector. In addition, a lot of Election Committee members from many other non-business subsectors are in fact businessmen by occupation (e.g. sports and culture subsectors and Hong Kong deputies to the NPC), thereby allowing the capitalist class to extend its influences from the first sector to the other three sectors of the Election Committee. Finally, the "small-circle nature" (narrow electorate basis) of many subsectors also facilitates the business elites to secure their seats in the Election Committee through their own personal networks and the support of the Central Liaison Office.[5]

Table 7.2 Register of electors for Chief Executive Election Committee subsectors: an illustration of the 2011 Chief Executive Election Committee

Subsector	Number of electors registered			Number of members
	Corporate electors (i)	Individual electors (ii)	Total (i + ii)	
First sector (industrial, commercial and financial sectors)				
1 Catering	728	7,206	7,934	17
2 Commercial (first)	860	–	860	18
3 Commercial (second)	662	1,121	1,783	18
4 Employers' Federation of Hong Kong	122	–	122	16
5 Finance	125	–	125	18
6 Financial Services	568	–	568	18
7 Hong Kong Chinese Enterprises Association	306	15	321	16
8 Hotel	101	–	101	17
9 Import and export	806	628	1,434	18
10 Industrial (first)	610	0	610	18
11 Industrial (second)	695	–	695	18
12 Insurance	135	–	135	18
13 Real estate and construction	482	272	754	18
14 Textiles and garment	3,055	133	3,188	18
15 Tourism	1,118	–	1,118	18
16 Transport	201	–	201	18
17 Wholesale and retail	1,795	5,084	6,879	18
Sub-total	*12,369*	*14,459*	*26,828*	*300*
Second sector (professions)				
1 Accountancy	–	24,630	24,630	30
2 Architectural, surveying and planning	–	6,778	6,778	30
3 Chinese medicine	–	5,864	5,864	30
4 Education	–	86,618	86,618	30
5 Engineering	–	9,052	9,052	30

6 Health services	–	39,128	39,128	30
7 Higher education	–	9,106	9,106	30
8 Information technology	347	5,175	5,522	30
9 Legal	–	6,583	6,583	30
10 Medical	–	11,118	11,118	30
Sub-total	*347*	*204,052*	*204,399*	*300*
Third sector (labour, social services, religious and other sectors)				
1 Agriculture and fisheries	159	–	159	60
2 Labour	626	–	626	60
3 Social welfare	277	14,152	14,429	60
4 Sports, performing arts, culture and publication	2,149	209	2,358	60
5 Religious*	–	–	–	60
Sub-total	*3,211*	*14,361*	*17,572*	*300*
Fourth sector (political sector)				
1 Chinese People's Political Consultative Conference	–	141	141	55
2 Heung Yee Kuk	–	147	147	28
3 Hong Kong and Kowloon District Councils	–	200	200	59
4 New Territories District Councils	–	212	212	62
5 National People's Congress#	–	–	–	36
6 Legislative Council#	–	–	–	60
Sub-total	*–*	*700*	*700*	*300*
Total	*15,927*	*233,572*	*249,499*	*1,200*

Source: Data obtained from Registration and Electoral Office.

Note
* Members nominated by designated religious bodies.
# Ex-officio members of the Chief Executive Election Committee.

190　*Uneasy partnership between state and business*

Research on the occupational backgrounds of all the members of the 1996 Selection Committee and the 2000, 2006 and 2011 Election Committees confirmed that the business sector held predominant position under the existing electoral system for electing the Chief Executive (see Tables 7.3–7.6). The quantitative analysis showed that the business elites constituted the single largest group in both the 1996 Selection Committee and the three post-1997 Election Committees, amounting to over 40 per cent of the total number of seats in all these political institutions. The predominance of the business sector over the Election Committees was actually caused by the fact that the business sector not only controlled almost all the seats in the industrial, commercial and financial sectors (first sector), but they also occupied a large number of positions in the other three sectors, in particular the political sector.

The above analysis demonstrated that through the platforms of the Chief Executive Election Committees, the power of the business sector has been effectively institutionalized and strengthened in the HKSAR political system. For any politician who is ambitious to become Chief Executive, seeking the political blessing of Beijing's leaders is undoubtedly the most crucial step, but securing the support of the local business sector is no less important. In view of the business sector's predominant control over the majority of seats in the Election Committees, all possible Chief Executive candidates are required to solicit the support of the business sector with a view to obtaining the highest possible number of nominations and votes in the Election Committees.[6] From this perspective, such an electoral system has in effect provided an important institutional channel for the business elites to bargain with the Chief Executive candidate over policy directions and the distribution of political offices in his new administration.

The case of the 2007 Chief Executive Election

The interactions between Donald Tsang and James Tien Pei-chun of the Liberal Party in the 2007 Chief Executive Election was a prominent example to illustrate how the Election Committees provided the business sector with the power leverages to influence the policy-making of the HKSAR government.

In December 2006, when Donald Tsang was about to announce his re-election campaign, James Tien openly claimed that the Liberal Party and its business allies, which altogether controlled over 110 seats in the Chief Executive Election Committee, would support the re-election bid of Donald Tsang. However, James Tien said the business sector had strong reservation about the three major policy initiatives proposed by Donald Tsang – the statutory minimum wage, the fair competition law and the race discrimination legislation – and he requested the Tsang administration to handle these policy issues carefully (*Singtao Daily*, 2006, 14 December). James Tien also reckoned that Donald Tsang should form a "ruling coalition" with the Liberal Party after re-election. He said under the existing system, the representative of the Liberal Party in the Executive Council was not consulted before government decided a new policy. Tien said the Liberal

Table 7.3 Background analysis of members of the 1996 Chief Executive Selection Committee

Occupational background	First sector		Second sector		Third sector		Fourth sector		Total	
	No.	*%*	*No.*	*%*	*No.*	*%*	*No.*	*%*	*No.*	*%*
Politician	0	0.0	0	0.0	14	14.0	10	10.0	24	6.0
Business	**99**	**99.0**	**17**	**17.0**	**22**	**22.0**	**49**	**49.0**	**187**	**46.8**
Profession	1	1.0	45	45.0	9	9.0	12	12.0	67	16.8
Social services	0	0.0	21	21.0	25	25.0	9	9.0	55	13.8
Labour	0	0.0	0	0.0	10	10.0	5	5.0	15	3.8
Culture and media	0	0.0	11	11.0	1	1.0	4	4.0	16	4.0
Agriculture	0	0.0	0	0.0	1	1.0	0	0.0	1	0.3
Others	0	0.0	6	6.0	18	18.0	11	11.0	35	8.8
Total	100	100.0	100	100.0	100	100.0	100	100.0	400	100.0

Source: Author's own research based on the membership list of the 1996 Chief Executive Selection Committee available in Young & Cullen, 2010.

Notes
1 "Politician" refers to full-time Legislative Councillors and District Councillors.
2 "Business" refers to chairmen, directors, executives and managers from commercial corporations.
3 "Profession" refers to professionals from legal, accounting, architecture, surveying, planning, engineering, medical and health sectors.
4 "Social services" refers to practitioners from education, community and social services and religious sectors.
5 "Labour" refers to trade unionists.
6 "Culture and media" refers to practitioners from arts, culture, media and publishing sectors.
7 "Agriculture" refers to practitioners from agriculture, fishery and poultry sectors.

Table 7.4 Background analysis of members of the 2000 Chief Executive Election Committee

Occupational background	First sector		Second sector		Third sector		Fourth sector		Total	
	No.	*%*	*No.*	*%*	*No.*	*%*	*No.*	*%*	*No.*	*%*
Politician	0	0.0	0	0.0	1	0.5	29	14.8	30	3.8
Business	**180**	**90.0**	**32**	**16.0**	**32**	**16.1**	**94**	**48.0**	**338**	**42.5**
Profession	7	3.5	101	50.5	4	2.0	24	12.2	136	17.1
Social services	3	1.5	55	27.5	67	33.7	24	12.2	149	18.7
Labour	0	0.0	0	0.0	16	8.0	10	5.1	26	3.3
Culture and media	0	0.0	1	0.5	13	6.5	5	2.6	19	2.4
Agriculture	0	0.0	0	0.0	29	14.8	1	0.5	30	3.8
Others	10	5.0	11	5.5	37	18.6	9	4.6	67	8.4
Total	200	100.0	200	100.0	199	100.0	196	100.0	795	100.0

Source: Author's own research based on the membership list of the 2000 Chief Executive Selection Committee available at the official website of the Electoral Affairs Commission (www.eac.gov.hk).

Notes
1 "Politician" refers to full-time Legislative Councillors and District Councillors.
2 "Business" refers to chairmen, directors, executives and managers from commercial corporations.
3 "Profession" refers to professionals from legal, accounting, architecture, surveying, planning, engineering, medical and health sectors.
4 "Social services" refers to practitioners from education, community and social services and religious sectors.
5 "Labour" refers to trade unionists.
6 "Culture and media" refers to practitioners from arts, culture, media and publishing sectors.
7 "Agriculture" refers to practitioners from agriculture, fishery and poultry sectors.

Table 7.5 Background analysis of members of the 2006 Chief Executive Election Committee

Occupational background	First sector		Second sector		Third sector		Fourth sector		Total	
	No.	%	No.	%	No.	%	No.	%	No.	%
Politician	0	0.0	0	0.0	2	1.0	35	17.9	37	4.6
Business	**195**	**97.5**	**28**	**14.0**	**44**	**22.0**	**100**	**51.0**	**366**	**46.0**
Profession	3	1.5	150	75.0	14	7.0	29	14.8	198	24.9
Social services	0	0.0	22	11.0	54	27.0	17	8.7	93	11.7
Labour	0	0.0	0	0.0	18	9.0	9	4.6	27	3.4
Culture and media	1	0.5	0	0.0	21	10.5	2	1.0	17	2.1
Agriculture	0	0.0	0	0.0	28	14.0	1	0.5	30	3.8
Others	1	0.5	0	0.0	19	9.5	3	1.5	21	2.6
Total	200	100.0	200	100.0	200	100.0	196	100.0	796	100.0

Source: Author's own research based on the membership list of 2006 Chief Executive Selection Committee available at the official website of the Electoral Affairs Commission (www.eac.gov.hk).

Notes
1 "Politician" refers to full-time Legislative Councillors and District Councillors.
2 "Business" refers to chairmen, directors, executives and managers from commercial corporations.
3 "Profession" refers to professionals from legal, accounting, architecture, surveying, planning, engineering, medical and health sectors.
4 "Social services" refers to practitioners from education, community and social services, and religious sectors.
5 "Labour" refers to trade unionists.
6 "Culture and media" refers to practitioners from arts, culture, media and publishing sectors.
7 "Agriculture" refers to practitioners from agriculture, fishery and poultry sectors.

Table 7.6 Background analysis of members of the 2011 Chief Executive Election Committee

Occupational background	First sector		Second sector		Third sector		Fourth sector		Total	
	No.	*%*	*No.*	*%*	*No.*	*%*	*No.*	*%*	*No.*	*%*
Politician	0	0.0	0	0.0	4	1.3	88	29.8	92	7.7
Business	**293**	**97.7**	**33**	**11.0**	**64**	**21.4**	**118**	**40.0**	**508**	**42.5**
Profession	5	1.7	190	63.3	13	4.3	43	14.6	251	21.0
Social services	2	0.7	71	23.7	92	30.8	27	9.2	192	16.1
Labour	0	0.0	1	0.3	27	9.0	9	3.1	37	3.1
Culture and media	0	0.0	0	0.0	26	8.7	1	0.3	29	2.4
Agriculture	0	0.0	0	0.0	42	14.0	1	0.3	43	3.6
Others	0	0.0	5	1.7	31	10.4	8	2.7	44	3.7
Total	300	100.0	300	100.0	299	100.0	295	100.0	1196	100.0

Source: Author's own research based on the membership list of the 2011 Chief Executive Selection Committee available at the official website of the Electoral Affairs Commission (www.eac.gov.hk).

Notes
1 "Politician" refers to full-time Legislative Councillors and District Councillors.
2 "Business" refers to chairmen, directors, executives and managers from commercial corporations.
3 "Profession" refers to professionals from legal, accounting, architecture, surveying, planning, engineering, medical and health sectors.
4 "Social services" refers to practitioners from education, community and social services and religious sectors.
5 "Labour" refers to trade unionists.
6 "Culture and media" refers to practitioners from arts, culture, media and publishing sectors.
7 "Agriculture" refers to practitioners from agriculture, fishery and poultry sectors.

Institutionalization of business power   195

Party should be allowed to perform a more proactive role in the formulation of government policies, otherwise its party would turn down any seat in the Executive Council (*South China Morning Post*, 2007b, 8 February). Shortly, James Tien further remarked that although the Liberal Party and its business allies in the Election Committee were prepared to nominate Donald Tsang as Chief Executive candidate, they might not vote for him in the election because the business sector was not satisfied with some of the policies proposed by the Tsang Administration, such as the minimum wage law, competition law and goods and services tax. Tien warned that Donald Tsang was likely to face more than 50 "protesting blank votes" from the business sector in the Chief Executive Election and this would certainly cause embarrassment to both Tsang and Beijing's leaders (*South China Morning Post*, 2007a, 30 January). These open remarks made by James Tien were widely regarded by the political community as putting pressure on Donald Tsang and also setting "conditions" that the Liberal Party requested Tsang fulfil in exchange for their nominations and votes in the coming Chief Executive Election Committee.

Donald Tsang had obviously taken heed of the open demands made by James Tien. In his visit to the Liberal Party's headquarters in February 2007, Tsang pledged that if he was re-elected, he would forge a closer partnership with the Liberal Party and would seek its input before putting forward any policy initiatives (*Hong Kong Economic Journal*, 2007, 7 February). Tsang also admitted that the role of the Executive Council as a bridge between the HKSAR government and the Legislative Council was not satisfactory, and he would consider ways to enhance his cooperation with pro-government parties in the light of the Liberal Party's opinions (*Ming Pao*, 2007, 12 February). On 27 March 2007, James Tien was appointed by the HKSAR government as the new Chairman of the Tourism Board, an important statutory body responsible for promoting Hong Kong's tourism industry. The appointment of James Tien was announced just two days after Donald Tsang was re-elected with the support of the Liberal Party and other pro-Beijing figures in the Chief Executive Election Committee and thus the appointment had been widely reported by the local media as a political deal made between Donald Tsang and the Liberal Party (*South China Morning Post*, 2007c, 28 March). In June 2007 the Tsang Administration announced the reorganization of the Executive Council and Selina Chow Liang Shuk-yee, Liberal Party Vice-chairperson, was re-appointed as a non-official member. There were prominent reports that as the representative of the Liberal Party, Selina Chow was given the "right" by the Chief Executive to consult her party members on government proposals and report their feedback before the Executive Council made a final decision. Such "relaxation" to the Executive Council's longstanding "rule of confidentiality" was considered in political circles as concessions made by Donald Tsang in exchange for the Liberal Party's support on the Executive Council (*South China Morning Post*, 2007d, 25 June).

It is comprehensible that the above incident could only represent the tip of the iceberg, and there might be more "horse-trading" or "political deals" that made behind closed doors that could not be easily identified by the public.[7] In any

196 Uneasy partnership between state and business

case, the predominant position of the business sector in the Chief Executive Election Committee points to the fact that the business elites now possess considerable power in bargaining with the Chief Executive, and under such an electoral system the HKSAR government is under pressure to adopt public policies that are in favour of business interests.

Functional constituency electoral system and voting-by-group system of the Legislative Council: institutionalization of business power in the legislative process

> The business sector is guaranteed Legislative Council representation by the functional constituency system. The Basic Law stipulates that from 1997 to 2007 half of the Legislative Council would be elected by functional constituencies that represent the most influential business and professional groups in the territory.... The voting-by-group arrangement in the Basic Law also gives veto power to the groups represented in the functional constituencies.... This means 15 members from the functional constituencies can veto any private proposals in the legislature.
>
> (Ma, 2007, p. 70)

Analysis in the preceding section clearly demonstrated how the Chief Executive Election Committees provided an institutional platform for the business sector to exercise strong influence over the governance and policy-making of the HKSAR government. The system of Chief Executive Election Committees has in effect institutionalized the interests of the business sector in the decision-making process of the executive branch and the post-colonial state is institutionally bound to make and implement public policies that are in favour of business interests. Apart from the Chief Executive electoral system, the post-1997 constitutional system under the Basic Law also institutionalizes the predominant position of the business sector throughout the legislative process. Such a privileged position of the business sector in the Legislative Council is achieved through the functional constituency electoral system and the voting-by-group system as specified by the Annex II of the Basic Law.

The institutional design of functional constituencies and voting-by-group system

Under the post-1997 political system, the HKSAR Legislative Council performs three core political functions, including enacting laws (enacting, amending or repealing legislation), controlling public expenditure (examining and approving annual budgets introduced by the government, and approving taxation and public expenditure proposals) and monitoring government's performance (debating the Policy Addresses of the Chief Executive, raising questions on the work of the HKSAR government and debating issues of public concerns) (Lui, 2007). While the distribution of power under the Basic Law was obviously in favour of the

Institutionalization of business power 197

Chief Executive rather than the Legislative Council, with a view to strengthening and consolidating the so-called "executive-dominant governance system" after the handover (Cheung, 2007; Lau, 2000b, 2002c; Li, 2001), the Legislative Council is still a very important and influential institution in the HKSAR, and its composition and membership will certainly have a direct bearing on the governance and politics in post-1997 Hong Kong.

From this perspective, although it was of paramount importance for Beijing's leaders to carefully design the selection methods for the HKSAR Chief Executive with a view to maintaining its political control over the territory, the crafting of the electoral system of the Legislative Council was equally important to the implementation of the Chinese government's governing strategy in post-1997 Hong Kong. From the viewpoint of Beijing's leaders, it was necessary to restrict the pro-democratic and anti-Communist legislators to a minority position in the Legislative Council so as to constrict the political space of the democratic activists and prevent them from exercising their negative power to veto legislative bills and budgetary proposals initiated by the Chief Executive and his administration. In this connection, the functional constituencies, which serve to institutionalize business and professional interests and guarantee their representation in the legislature, were considered by the Chinese government as an effective political arrangement for installing a stable pro-government majority in the post-1997 Legislative Council (Lau, 1999).

The functional constituency electoral system[8] was first introduced by the colonial administration in 1985 as the first phase of reforms to democratize the Legislative Council. Before 1985 all the Legislative Councillors, including official members and unofficial members, were appointed by the colonial Governor and business and professional elites were extensively incorporated through this system of appointment. Functional constituencies were primarily designed by the British colonial administration for replacing this appointment system, on the one hand, while on the other hand guaranteeing the continual dominance and representation of business and professional elites in the Legislative Council after the implementation of democratic reforms (Goodstadt, 2006; Lau, 1999; Leung, 1990).

The political formula of returning business and professional elites to the Legislative Council through functional constituencies was followed by the Chinese government when the Beijing leaders designed the electoral system of the HKSAR legislature during the transitional period. The final version of the Basic Law made the functional constituencies an integral part of the post-1997 electoral system. According to *Annex II of the Basic Law*, the HKSAR Legislative Council from 1998 to 2007 would comprised 60 members, and half of the seats would be returned by functional constituencies[9] (Annex II). Such a composition method was to kill two birds with one stone – making sure that a substantial number of pro-Beijing business and professional legislators will be returned by functional constituencies for providing stable political support to the Chief Executive, and also limiting the potential political influences of those pro-democracy legislators returned by direct elections in the geographical constituencies (Lau, 2002a).

198 Uneasy partnership between state and business

Among those 30 Legislative Council members returned by functional constituencies, at least 15 could be said to represent the various industrial and business sectors in Hong Kong (Table 7.7). All these functional constituencies are based on corporate voting with a very limited electoral basis ranging from a few hundred electors to a few thousands electors. Therefore, the legislators returned by these functional constituencies are commonly considered as elected by very narrow groups of business organizations and are said to have close connections with local business tycoons and large commercial corporations (Loh, 2006a,

Table 7.7 Distribution of registered electors by functional constituencies in 2011

Functional constituency	Number of seats	Number of registered electors
Heung Yee Kuk*	1	157
Agriculture and fisheries[#]	1	159
Insurance[#]	**1**	**137**
Transport[#]	**1**	**201**
Education*	1	95,787
Legal*	1	6,596
Accountancy*	1	24,641
Medical*	1	11,121
Health services*	1	39,161
Engineering*	1	9,055
Architectural, surveying and planning*	1	6,780
Labour[#]	3	626
Social welfare*	1	14,172
Real estate and construction[#]	**1**	**767**
Tourism[#]	**1**	**1,227**
Commercial (first)[#]	**1**	**904**
Commercial (second)[#]	**1**	**1,823**
Industrial (first)[#]	**1**	**617**
Industrial (second)[#]	**1**	**702**
Finance[#]	**1**	**128**
Financial services	**1**	**568**
Sports, performing arts, culture and publication[#]	1	2,367
Import and export[#]	**1**	**1,459**
Textiles and garment[#]	**1**	**3,190**
Wholesale and retail[#]	**1**	**6,903**
Information technology	**1**	**5,532**
Catering[#]	**1**	**7,946**
District Council*	1	416
Total	30	243,142

Source: www.voterregistration.gov.hk.

Notes
1 Those marked in bold are functional constituencies that represent the various business sectors.
2 Those marked with an asterisk (*) are functional constituencies based on individual voting, while those marked with a hash ([#]) are functional constituencies based on corporate voting. The "financial services" and "information technology" sectors partly use individual voting and partly use corporate voting.

Institutionalization of business power 199

2006b). Similar to the arrangements adopted for the Chief Executive Election Committee, the "small-circle nature" (narrow electorate basis) of these functional constituencies also facilitated the business elites to secure their seats in the Legislative Council through their own personal networks and the coordination of the Central Liaison Office. Such an electoral arrangement therefore served to make sure the business sector could effectively control at least one-quarter of the seats in the Legislative Council.

The privileged position of the business sector over the legislative process as guaranteed by the functional constituencies must be discussed together with the so-called "voting-by-group system". According to Annex II of the Basic Law, all the bills and amendments introduced by the HKSAR government need only a simple majority vote to pass the Legislative Council, while all the bills, amendments and motions proposed by legislators have to be approved simultaneously by separate majority vote among both groups of members returned by functional constituencies and those returned by geographical constituencies (Annex II). This voting-by-group system effectively gives the power of veto to those business and professional legislators who are returned by functional constituencies. Under such a voting arrangement the opposition of only 15 functional constituency legislators is powerful enough to veto any non-government legislative proposals, even though the proposals may be supported by an overall simple majority of the Legislative Council members. As a consequence, the voting-by-group system has effectively provided an institutional protection for business interests, as the business sector could make use of their guaranteed seats in the legislature (i.e. the 15 functional constituencies representing various business sectors) to veto any legislative proposals that are not consistent with their vested interests (Ma, 2007, p. 143).

The privileged position of the business sector in the legislative process

The political developments after 1997 demonstrated that the functional constituency electoral system and the voting-by-group system have effectively performed their functions in institutionalizing the dominant position of the business sector in the Legislative Council and provided the business elites with unprecedented power leverages to exercise their political influence.

The empirical research on the occupational backgrounds of all the HKSAR Legislative Councillors returned by functional constituencies after 1997 confirmed that such an electoral system has effectively institutionalized business representation in the legislature (Table 7.8). Since the handover business elites constituted the single largest group among legislators returned by functional constituencies, amounting to over 50 per cent of the total number of functional constituency legislators in the HKSAR Legislative Councils on average (or one-quarter of the total number of seats in the Legislative Council). These business legislators, together with those professional legislators who are returned by accountancy, engineering and architectural, surveying and planning functional constituencies and have similar pro-business orientations (Huang, 2007, p. 4),

Table 7.8 Background analysis of legislative councillors returned by functional constituencies

Occupational background	1998 to 2000		2000–2004		2004–2008		2008–2012		Total	
	No.	%	No.	%	No.	%	No.	%	No.	%
Politician	3	10.0	2	6.7	0	0.0	2	6.7	7	5.8
Business	**15**	**50.0**	**15**	**50.0**	**17**	**56.7**	**13**	**43.3**	**60**	**50.0**
Profession	8	26.7	6	20.0	6	20.0	10	33.3	30	25.0
Social services	2	6.7	3	10.0	3	10.0	2	6.7	10	8.3
Labour	1	3.3	3	10.0	3	10.0	2	6.7	9	7.5
Culture and media	0	0.0	0	0.0	0	0.0	0	0.0	0	0.0
Others	1	3.3	1	3.3	1	3.3	1	3.3	4	3.3
Total	30	100.0	30	100.0	30	100.0	30	100.0	120	100.0

Source: Author's own research based on the membership lists of Legislative Council from available aty the official website of the Legislative Council (www.legco. gov.hk).

Notes
1 "Politician" refers to full-time Legislative Councillors and District Councillors.
2 "Business" refers to chairmen, directors, executives and managers from commercial corporations.
3 "Profession" refers to professionals from legal, accounting, architecture, surveying, planning, engineering, medical and health sectors.
4 "Social services" refers to practitioners from education, community and social services and religious sectors.
5 "Labour" refers to trade unionists.
6 "Culture and media" refers to practitioners from arts, culture, media and publishing sectors.

Institutionalization of business power 201

occupied around one-third of seats in each post-1997 Legislative Council, and all of them act as strong defenders of various industrial and business interests.

By controlling half of the seats in functional constituencies, the business sector could also exercise its constitutional privilege under the voting-by-group system to veto those private proposals it considered as challenges to its class interests. Tables 7.9–7.10 summarize those private member motions that were rejected by functional constituencies under the voting-by-group system from 2004 to 2010. Most of these motions were proposed by directly elected and grassroots legislators to advance social equality and they had been supported by a clear majority of Legislative Councillors, but all these proposals were finally vetoed by pro-business functional constituency members because they went against the interests of the business sector. The most obvious example was the repeated rejection of the motions on introducing the system of minimum wage and maximum working hours from 2004 to 2007.

Implications of the institutionalization of business power under the HKSAR political system: the unprecedented power bases for the business sector

> The Basic Law instituted a corporatist design by which business representation was well guaranteed.... The business was thus granted the power of both king-making (i.e. electing the Chief Executive) and the privilege of exclusive representation in the legislature.
>
> (Yep, 2009)

Hong Kong has always been ruled by a state–business alliance from the colonial time to the post-1997 period. However, although the business elites had been extensively incorporated as the majority of the political establishment both

Table 7.9 Number of motions rejected by functional constituencies under the voting-by-group system

Legislative year	Number of motions	Number of motions rejected under the voting-by-group system*	Percentage
2004/2005	59	5	8.47
2005/2006	58	9	15.52
2006/2007	56	5	8.93
2007/2008	56	2	3.57
2008/2009	59	3	5.08
2009/2010	58	1	1.72
Total	346	25	7.23

Source: SynergyNet, 2010.

Note

"Motions rejected under the voting-by-group system" are defined as motions which were supported by the majority of the Legislative Councillors (i.e. over half of the Legislative Councillors present) but were finally vetoed by functional constituency legislators despite their minority position.

Table 7.10 List of motions rejected by functional constituencies under the voting-by-group system

Motion	Support votes (geographical constituency)	Support votes (functional constituency)	Total number of support votes	Opposition vote in functional constituency (oppose + abstain)	Total number present
2004/2005					
1 Minimum wage, maximum working hours	27	11	38	16 + 1	57
2 Enacting a fair competition law	23	10	33	13 + 0	48
3 Public inquiry on irregularities in the 2004 Legislative Council Election	16	8	24	9 + 6	47
4 Conserving the Central Police Station Compound and formulating a comprehensive policy on antiquities and monuments	19	11	30	14 + 0	46
5 Enhancing the safety of railway and road traffic	19	6	25	6 + 12	45
2005/2006					
1 Minimum wage, standard working hours	25	11	36	15 + 0	53
2 Fair competition law	17	11	28	14 + 1	50
3 Comprehensive review of labour legislation	24	7	31	13 + 0	46
4 Implementing the recommendations of the United Nations Human Rights Committee	18	8	26	16 + 0	51
5 Universal retirement protection	23	10	33	1 + 9	45
6 Maintaining the competitive edge of Hong Kong	15	10	25	13 + 1	46
7 Review on Urban Renewal Strategy	14	9	23	4 + 10	43
8 Regulating the transactions of new private residential properties	20	11	31	12 + 0	44
9 Women in poverty	21	11	32	0 + 11	45

2006/2007

1 Minimum wage, standard working hours	20	11	31	15 + 0	50
2 Urging the Housing Authority to grant rent remission to public rental housing tenants and expeditiously reduce the rent	21	9	30	16 + 0	47
3 Creating job opportunities and improving the income of elementary workers	17	11	28	0 + 12	41
4 The 4 June incident	17	7	24	5 + 10	47
5 Transforming Radio Television Hong Kong to become the Hong Kong Public Broadcasting Corporation	17	9	26	2 + 10	44

2007/2008

1 Franchised bus fares	22	9	31	1 + 13	46
2 Setting up a fund to meet the needs of the ageing population and help the poor	17	11	28	0 + 15	50

2008/2009

1 Buying back the shares of The Link	18	9	27	13 + 0	44
2 Assisting grassroots workers in counteracting economic adversities	17	7	24	12 + 6	47
3 Reviewing the Interception of Communications and Surveillance Ordinance	19	5	24	10 + 2	42

2009/2010

1 Reviewing occupational safety and health and employees' compensation system	24	9	33	1+12	47

Source: SynergyNet, 2010.

204 *Uneasy partnership between state and business*

before and after 1997, the dynamics of the state–business relationship are fundamentally different. In the past, the British colonial administration had always been cautious not to grant any institutionalized privileges for the business sector in order to prevent the business elites from establishing the power leverages to challenge its governing authority.[10] Under the colonial political system, political co-option was therefore largely operated on an ad hoc and individual basis, and in advancing the interests of the capitalist class the co-opted business elites were still required to be responsible to the colonial state, which held the formal power of appointment and selection (Cheung & Wong, 2004; Leung, 1990). Because the business elites under the colonial political system did not have their own power bases and were heavily dependent on the support of the colonial administration for gaining access to the decision-making process, they were largely restrained from challenging the governing authority and policies of the colonial state publicly (Lau, 1997, p. 24). As a result, state–business relations during the colonial period tended to be more mutually supportive and cooperative (see Chapter 3).

On the face of it, the HKSAR Chief Executive should be able to exercise the same extensive power of political appointment and patronage under Article 48 of the Basic Law. Except for the appointment of the Court of Final Appeal's judges and the Chief Justice of the High Court which needs the consent of the Legislative Council, the Chief Executive could appoint civil servants of all ranks in the HKSAR government, most of the judges, members of and chairmen of advisory committees and statutory organizations without the approval of the legislature and could also nominate principal officials for appointment by the Chinese government. On the surface, the HKSAR Chief Executive has largely inherited the previous colonial Governor's power of political appointment and patronage, which should allow him to subjugate the business elites and to forge a state–business alliance centred on him through political co-option as in the British colonial past (Cheung, 2007; Ma, 2007, p. 75).

However, things had turned quite the other way. When compared with the colonial Governor's transcendent position and absolute power of political patronage, the balance of power has shifted in favour of the business sector against the HKSAR Chief Executive after 1997, because the business elites have been given exclusive representation in the legislature and unprecedented "king-making power" under the Basic Law – these are the two new but influential power leverages that the business sector has established over the post-colonial state after 1997. Through the functional constituencies, the representation of the business sector in the Legislative Council has been effectively institutionalized. Thus, unlike the British colonial period, when the business elites had to rely on the appointment of the colonial Governor to secure their representation in the legislature, business elites no longer need to seek the blessing and support of the post-colonial state to gain access to the Legislative Council after 1997. Also, thanks to the functional constituency system, the business elites could now exercise extensive influences in the legislative process by making use of their constitutional privilege under the voting-by-group system. More importantly, unlike the British colonial period when the power of selecting and appointing the colonial Governor was monopolized by the London government and the business elites were completely excluded from the relevant processes, the business sector has established "king-making power" by virtue of their extensive representation in the Chief Executive Election Committees in the post-1997 period.

The above structural changes under the Basic Law have given "the business and professional class's direct and formal leverage over the political system in a way that the colonial administration had always avoided" (Goodstadt, 2009, p. 132), thus resulting in a fundamental shift in the balance of power between the post-colonial state and the business sector. As a result of the installation of the Chief Executive Election Committees and functional constituency electoral system after 1997, the business sector has been equipped with its own institutionalized power base and has been empowered to develop significant power leverages vis-à-vis the post-colonial state. When compared with its colonial predecessor, the HKSAR Chief Executive's powers of political patronage (e.g. the appointment of members of advisory bodies and the nomination of principal officials) are no longer sufficient to sanction and subdue the business sector, in view of the fact that business elites have developed their own more influential and institutionalized power bases through the functional constituencies seats in the Legislative Council. By virtue of their representation in the Chief Executive Election Committee, the business sector has even gained unprecedented power to influence the selection of the HKSAR Chief Executive.

Given their increasing power leverages vis-à-vis the post-colonial state under the HKSAR political system, the business elites have become more aggressive in advancing their own interests and bargaining for policy concessions (Cheung & Wong, 2004). Instead of supporting the governance and policy agenda of the post-colonial state, nowadays the business sector is more eager to make use of their own institutionalized privileges to challenge the governing authority of the post-colonial state and as a result the state–business relations after 1997 have tended to be characterized by "various business and industrial interests seeking to capture the government for their gains" (Cheung, 2008). As a consequence of the business sector's considerable power leverages vis-à-vis the post-colonial state, the Chief Executive is now facing growing difficulties in commanding the business elites and is always mindful of not infringing on the vested business interests.[11] As the business sector has increasingly become an uneasy and uncooperative coalition partner, the smooth functioning of the state–business governing coalition has increasingly been put at risk in the post-1997 era.

Conclusion

The HKSAR political system as specified under the Basic Law has been widely considered as "a pact between the Chinese government and the business and industrial elites in Hong Kong" (Kuan, 1991). In the eyes of the Beijing leaders, the restricted democracy under the Basic Law will facilitate the selection of pro-Beijing business elites as Chief Executives and therefore enable the Chinese

206 *Uneasy partnership between state and business*

government "to rule Hong Kong through surrogates and collaborators from the big businesses" (So, 1997). In accordance with this governing strategy of the Chinese government, the political power of the business sector has been effectively institutionalized through the Chief Executive Election Committees and the functional constituencies (together with the voting-by-group system).

While the institutionalization of business power in the HKSAR political system was deliberately designed by Beijing's leaders in the 1980s for consolidating the support of the business sector to the post-colonial state and perpetuating the state–business alliance, the political developments after the handover showed that such political arrangements have produced entirely counter-productive outcomes. Instead of supporting the governance of the post-colonial state through its institutionalized privileges in the Chief Executive Election Committees and the functional constituencies, the business sector tends to make use of these power leverages to challenge the governing authority of the Chief Executive and to bargain for policy concessions. As such, the installation of the Chief Executive Election Committee and functional constituency system has by intention or default shifted the balance of power in favour of the business sector as against the post-colonial state and has therefore fundamentally changed the dynamics of the state–business relationship. As the business sector has increasingly become an uneasy coalition partner, the post-colonial state struggles to maintain its leadership within the state–business alliance. Ironically, a political system that was deliberately designed by the Chinese government to consolidate the state–business alliance has finally brought about completely counter-productive effects.

Notes

1 The legal foundation of the Basic Law comes from Article 31 of the PRC constitution, which states that "The state may establish special administrative regions when necessary. The systems to be instituted in special administrative regions shall be prescribed by law enacted by the National People's Congress in the light of the specific conditions" (Ghai, 1999, p. 56).

2 Apart from consolidating the dominance of the business sector, constitutional experts argue that in the design of the post-1997 political systems the Chinese government also wanted to ensure its ultimate control over the HKSAR and to contain the powers of the Legislative Council (Ghai, 1999, pp. 288–302). According to Yash Ghai, the Chinese leaders intended to maintain their control over politics in Hong Kong by holding the formal power to appoint the Chief Executive (Article 45 of the Basic Law) and principal officials (Article 48 of the Basic Law), as well as the power to disregard the motion of impeachment passed by the Legislative Council against the Chief Executive (Article 73 of the Basic Law). Ghai also points out that by making half of the Legislative Councillors returned by the functional constituencies, the Basic Law discourages the development of party politics in Hong Kong and makes it difficult for the rise of large political parties with strong popular support. Article 74 (which prohibits legislators from introducing private member bills that are related to public expenditure or political structure or the operation of the government) and Annex II (which specifies that all non-government bills and motions require the double majority of both functional constituency members and directly elected members under the voting-by-group system) of the Basic Law both aimed at marginalizing the political influence of the democrats in the Legislative Council.

Institutionalization of business power   207

3 The first Chief Executive was elected by a Selection Committee rather than an Election Committee as specified by Annex I of the Basic Law. The reason was that the election of the first Chief Executive should be made before the handover of sovereignty on 1 July 1997, but before then Hong Kong was still under British rule and thus no election could be held in accordance with the Basic Law (Xiao, 2001, p. 274). Thus, the Selection Committee was set up by the Preparatory Committee in 1996 for selecting the Chief Executive. This 400-member Selection Committee elected Tung Chee-hwa as the first Chief Executive in December 1996 (Young & Cullen, 2010, pp. 16–17).

4 According to the 2012 constitutional reform package passed by the two-thirds majority of Legislative Council in June 2010, the Chief Executive Election Committee will be expanded from 800 members to 1,200 members.

5 The Central Liaison Office was set up in 2002 and it functions as the Chinese government's official agency in Hong Kong after 1997. It is well understood that one of the core functions of the Central Liaison Office is to mobilize pro-Beijing forces to win various levels of elections (Loh, 2010, p. 209).

6 For the Chief Executive candidates, it is necessary to get the highest possible number of nominations and votes, otherwise it will bring about embarrassment to him and impair the political credibility of his new administration. For example, in the 2002 election Tung Chee-hwa mobilized all the pro-Beijing supporters in the Election Committee with a view to obtaining 714 nominations, while in the 2005 by-election Donald Tsang expended a lot of effort on getting 674 nominations, despite the fact that both elections were uncontested (Li, 2007).

7 "Horse-trading" or "political deals" made between Chief Executive candidates and business elites in the Election Committee, if any, must be done in secrecy and difficult to trace. Nevertheless, recent research showed that companies with major shareholders or directors holding a seat on the Chief Executive Election Committee generally have better business performance in terms of equity, market-to-book ratio and earnings per share (Wong, 2010).

8 When it was first introduced to the Legislative Council in 1985, the voting basis of functional constituencies was defined by the colonial administration either as corporate voting or individual voting. Functional constituencies based on corporate voting were returned by major organizations recognized by law, under which these corporate members will nominate a representative to vote on their behalf. On the other hand, functional constituencies based on individual voting were returned by professionals with well-established qualifications, by which the electoral roll will be based on the membership lists of various professional bodies (Lau, 1999). Such a system for specifying functional constituencies has been followed by the HKSAR government after the handover.

9 The other 30 members of the Legislative Council shall be returned by geographical constituencies and the Election Committee. Annex II of the Basic Law states that in the 1998 Legislative Council election geographical constituencies will elect 20 members and the Election Committee will return ten members; in the 2000 Legislative Council election geographical constituencies will elect 24 members and the Election Committee will return six members; in the 2004 Legislative Council election the geographical constituencies will elect 30 members and the Election Committee will be phased out.

10 During the colonial era there were several important disruptions (e.g. the open petitions of 1894, 1916 and 1919) by which the expatriate merchant class campaigned aggressively for institutionalizing their representation in the political establishment. In these incidents the British and European businessmen demanded an unofficial majority in the Legislative Council, and they even requested that the unofficial members should no longer be nominated by the colonial Governor on his own discretion but should be exclusively elected by the British and European business sector. However, all these

208 *Uneasy partnership between state and business*

attempts were rejected by the London and Hong Kong governments on the grounds that if exclusive representation was granted to the expatriate merchant class it would only create a small oligarchy of businessmen who would rule over the Chinese majority and seize control of the colonial state (Miners, 1987, pp. 126–145).

11 Anonymous interviewee.

References

Chan, M. K. (1991). Democracy derailed: Realpolitik in the making of the Hong Kong Basic Law, 1985–90. In M. K. Chan, & D. J. Clark (Eds.), *The Hong Kong Basic Law: Blueprint for "stability and prosperity" under Chinese sovereignty?* (pp. 3–35). Hong Kong: Hong Kong University Press.

Cheung, A. (2007). Executive-dominant governance or executive power "hollowed-out": the political quagmire of Hong Kong. *Asian Journal of Political Science, 15*(1), 17–38.

Cheung, A. (2008). The story of two administrative states: State capacity in Hong Kong and Singapore. *The Pacific Review, 21*(2), 121–145.

Cheung, A. & Wong, P. C. W. (2004). Who advised the Hong Kong government? The politics of absorption before and after 1997. *Asian Survey, 44*(6), 874–894.

Chiu, S. W. K. (1994). *The politics of laissez-faire: Hong Kong's strategy of industrialization in historical perspective.* Hong Kong: Hong Kong Institute of Asia-Pacific Studies, Chinese University.

Ghai, Y. (1999) *Hong Kong's new constitutional order: The resumption of Chinese sovereignty and the Basic Law* (2nd ed.). Hong Kong: Hong Kong University Press.

Goodstadt, L. F. (2006). Business friendly and politically convenient: The historical role of functional constituencies. In C. Loh & Civic Exchange (Eds.), *Functional constituencies: A unique feature of the Hong Kong Legislative Council* (pp. 41–58). Hong Kong: Hong Kong University Press.

Goodstadt, L. F. (2009). *Uneasy partners: The conflict between public interest and private profit interest in Hong Kong.* Hong Kong: Hong Kong University Press.

Hong Kong Economic Journal. (2007, 7 February). Donald Tsang pledges to enhance his cooperation with the Liberal Party. A07 (in Chinese).

Huang, Z. Z. (2007). *Lun Gang Ao Zheng Shang Guan Xi* (On Hong Kong and Macau's government–business relations). Aomen: Aomen Xue Zhe Tong Meng (in Chinese).

Kuan, H. C. (1991). Power dependence and democratic transition: The case of Hong Kong. *The China Quarterly, 128*(1991), 774–793.

Lau, C. K. (1997). *Hong Kong's colonial legacy.* Hong Kong: Chinese University Press.

Lau, S. K. (1999). The making of the electoral system. In H. C. Kuan, S. K. Lau, T. K. Y. Wong, & K. S. Louie (Eds.), *Power transfer and electoral politics: The first legislative election in the Hong Kong Special Administrative Region* (pp. 3–35). Hong Kong: Chinese University Press.

Lau, S. K. (2000a). The executive-dominant system of governance: Theory and practice. In S. K. Lau (Ed.), *Blueprint for the 21st century Hong Kong* (pp. 1–36). Hong Kong: Chinese University Press (in Chinese).

Lau, S. K. (2002b). Hong Kong's partial democracy under stress. In Y. M. Yeung (Ed.), *New challenges for development and modernization: Hong Kong and the Asia-Pacific region in the new millennium* (pp. 181–205). Hong Kong: Chinese University Press.

Lau, S. K. (2002c). Tung Chee-hwa's governing strategy: The shortfall in politics. In S. K. Lau (Ed.), *The first Tung Chee-hwa administration* (pp. 1–39). Hong Kong: Chinese University Press.

Leung, B. K. P. (1990). Power and politics: A critical analysis. In B. K. P. Leung (Ed.), *Social issues in Hong Kong* (pp. 13–26). Hong Kong: Oxford University Press.

Li, P. K. (2001). The executive–legislature relationship in Hong Kong: Evolution and development. In J. Y. S. Cheng (Ed.), *Political development in the HKSAR* (pp. 85–100). Hong Kong: City University of Hong Kong.

Li, P. K. (2007). The executive. In W. M. Lam, P. L. T. Lui, W. Wong, & I. Holiday (Eds.), *Contemporary Hong Kong politics: Governance in the post-1997 era* (pp. 23–37). Hong Kong: Hong Kong University Press.

Loh, C. (2006a). Introduction. In C. Loh, & Civic Exchange (Eds.), *Functional constituencies: A unique feature of the Hong Kong Legislative Council* (pp. 1–17). Hong Kong: Hong Kong University Press.

Loh, C. (2006b). Government and business alliance: Hong Kong functional constituencies. In C. Loh, & Civic Exchange (Eds.), *Functional constituencies: A unique feature of the Hong Kong Legislative Council* (pp. 19–40). Hong Kong: Hong Kong University Press.

Loh, C. (2010). *Underground front: The Chinese Communist Party in Hong Kong*. Hong Kong: Hong Kong University Press.

Lui, P. L. T. (2007). The legislature. In W. M. Lam, P. L. T. Lui, W. Wong, & I. Holiday (Eds.), *Contemporary Hong Kong politics: Governance in the post-1997 era* (pp. 39–58). Hong Kong: Hong Kong University Press.

Ma, N. (2007). *Political development in Hong Kong: State, political society and civil society*. Hong Kong: Hong Kong University Press.

Miners, N. (1987). *Hong Kong under imperial rule, 1912–1941*. Hong Kong: Oxford University Press.

Ming Pao. (2007, 12 February). Chief Executive: it's normal to make deals with political parties. A12 (in Chinese).

Singtao Daily. (2006, 14 December). The Liberal Party proposes "Three-Noes" policy. A17 (in Chinese).

So, A. Y. (1997). The Tiananmen Incident, Patten's electoral reforms, and the roots of contested democracy in Hong Kong. In M. K. Chan (Ed.), *The challenge of Hong Kong's reintegration with China* (pp. 49–84). Hong Kong: Hong Kong University Press.

South China Morning Post. (2007a, 30 January). Liberals plan Tsang poll protest. EDT2.

South China Morning Post. (2007b, 8 February). Liberals will shun Exco without greater role, says Tien. EDT2.

South China Morning Post. (2007c, 28 March). Liberal denies deal for tourism post. EDT3.

South China Morning Post. (2007d, 25 June). Tsang offering liberals Exco seal, says Source. EDT2.

SynergyNet. (2010). *Review of the HKSAR Legislative Council 2010*. Hong Kong: SynergyNet.

Wong, H. W. (2010). Political connections and firm performance: The case of Hong Kong. *Journal of East Asian Studies, 10*(2), 275–313.

Xiao, W. Y. (2001). *One Country, two systems: An account of the drafting of the Hong Kong Basic Law*. Beijing: Peking University Press.

Yep, R. (2009). Accommodating business interests in China and Hong Kong: Two systems, one way out. In K. H. Mok, & R. Forrest (Eds.), *Changing governance and public policy in East Asia* (pp. 185–205). New York: Routledge.

Young, S. N. M., & Cullen, R. (2010). *Electing Hong Kong's chief executive*. Hong Kong: Hong Kong University Press.

8 The business sector's direct access to the sovereign state

The close partnership between Beijing and the local capitalists[1]

When attending the celebration ceremony for the thirtieth anniversary of the founding of the Shenzhen Special Economic Zone in September 2010, Hong Kong's richest tycoon, Li Ka-shing, was given a high-profile reception by Chinese President Hu Jintao and the two persons shook hands in front of television cameras. During their one-to-one meeting, Hu Jintao highly praised Li Ka-shing as an outstanding entrepreneur who had made enormous contributions to the country's economic reform and the preservation of Hong Kong's stability and prosperity (*South China Morning Post*, 2010a, 7 September). The high-profile meeting was widely regarded by the local media as another illustration of the high level of cordiality and friendship between the Beijing leaders and the Hong Kong business sector (*South China Morning Post*, 2010b, 7 September). This kind of high-profile private meeting is, however, not an isolated incident, because since the handover the local capitalists have been warmly received by Chinese leaders regularly either in Beijing or during their visits to Hong Kong, and those big names include former Chinese President Jiang Zemin, former Vice-President Zeng Qinghong and the incumbent President Xi Jinping.

The dynamics of state–business relations in Hong Kong have undergone fundamental changes since 1997 and without doubt the closer partnership between the business sector and the new sovereign state (Chinese government) is one of the significant contributing factors for this change. Unlike the colonial period, when the relationship between the business sector and the London government was relatively distant, the business sector nowadays enjoys direct access to the Chinese authorities. There are several structural factors that contributed to the development of a closer partnership between the business sector and the Chinese government, including the extensive incorporation of business elites into the Hong Kong delegations to the National People's Congress (NPC) and the National Committee of the Chinese People's Political Consultative Conference (CPPCC), the united-front work of the Central Liaison Office and also the business sector's increased economic links with the Mainland authorities. By establishing direct access to the sovereign state, the business sector has established another important power leverage vis-à-vis the post-colonial Hong Kong state after 1997, and this has brought about unprecedented challenges to the smooth functioning of the state–business alliance.

The business sector's institutionalized access to the sovereign state: the National People's Congress and the National Committee of Chinese People's Political Consultative Conference

> Major business leaders or their associates are mostly "elected" to the People's Congress at national or provincial levels, or appointed to the leading advisory body to the Party, the People's Political Consultative Conference. Business tycoons are thus guaranteed direct access to top leaders.
>
> (Yep, 2009)

In line with its post-1997 governing strategy, since the signing of the 1984 Sino-British Joint Declaration the Chinese government has actively incorporated the local capitalists into its united front with a view to engineering a new China-centred state–business alliance in Hong Kong. In this regard, business elites have been extensively co-opted by the Chinese government since the 1980s and the NPC and the CPPCC are the principal platforms for incorporating business elites (see Chapter 4). This trend has been continued uninterrupted in the post-1997 period.

Under China's constitutional system, the NPC and the CPPCC are two political organs under the leadership and control of the Chinese Communist Party (CCP). Pursuant to Article 57 of the Chinese constitution, the NPC is described as the "highest organ of state power" and its approximately 3,000 representatives are elected by the provinces, autonomous regions and the largest cities for a term of five years. The functions of the NPC include enacting legislation on key domestic and foreign policy areas, electing important government officials (e.g. State President, State Premier, Chairman of Military Affairs Commission, Head of the Supreme People's Court and the Procuratorate) and supervising the work of the State Council (Dillon, 2009, p. 139). On the other hand, the CPPCC is a consultative body composed of delegates from different social strata, including ethnic minority groups, religious organizations and democratic political parties officially recognized by the CCP. The principal function of the CPPCC is to maintain a united front for the CCP with a view to forging broad-based social support for its public policies (Dillon, 2009, p. 140).

Since the handover of sovereignty in 1997, the Hong Kong Deputies to the NPC are elected locally through an election conference,[2] while the Hong Kong Members to the CPPCC are "invited" by Beijing authorities by way of nomination. In practice, the Hong Kong delegates to the NPC and the CPPCC are essentially handpicked by the Chinese government because the Central Liaison Office in Hong Kong will coordinate behind the scenes in order to ensure that only those candidates who are favoured by Beijing's leaders will be selected. From this perspective, the membership distribution of the Hong Kong NPC and the CPPCC largely reflects the united-front building strategy of the Chinese government and unsurprisingly the business sector continues to be the principal target of Beijing's political co-option in the post-1997 period (Cheung & Wong, 2004).

212   Uneasy partnership between state and business

Empirical research on the occupational backgrounds of all Hong Kong NPC and CPPCC delegates after 1997 showed that the business sector was consistently the dominant player within Beijing's united front (Tables 8.1–8.2). Within Hong Kong the NPC delegation's businessmen occupied an average of 43.7 per cent of the total number of seats, while the representation of the business sector within the CPPCC delegation was more overwhelming, occupying 70.8 per cent of seats. Business elites on the lists included famous tycoons such as Chan Yau-hing and Tsang Hin-chi (NPC delegation) and Victor Li Tzar-kuoi, Cheng Kar-shun, Kwok Ping-sheung, Spencer Lee Ka-kit, Woo Kwong-ching, Lo Hong-sui, Victor Fung Kwok-king, Cha Mou-sing, Wu Ying-sheung, Larry Yung Chi-kan, Robert Ng Chee-siong and Charles Ho Tsu-kwok (CPPCC delegation), covering almost all the big business families in Hong Kong today.[3]

The dominance of the business sector within the Hong Kong NPC and CPPCC delegations not only gives local capitalists political prestige, but also provides them with an unprecedented institutionalized channel to gain direct access to top Beijing leaders. In the first quarter of every year, the annual full sessions of the NPC and the CPPCC will meet in Beijing and all Hong Kong

Table 8.1 Background analysis of Hong Kong Deputies to the National People's Congress (1998–2012)

Occupational background	9th NPC (1998 to 2002)		10th NPC (2003 to 2007)		11th NPC (2008 to 2012)		Total	
	No.	%	No.	%	No.	%	No.	%
Politician	1	3.00	1	2.90	0	0.00	2	1.90
Business	**14**	**42.40**	**15**	**42.90**	**16**	**45.70**	**45**	**43.70**
Profession	3	9.10	3	8.60	8	22.90	14	13.60
Social services	10	30.30	10	28.60	8	22.90	28	27.20
Labour	2	6.10	3	8.60	1	2.90	6	5.80
Culture and media	1	3.00	1	2.90	0	0.00	2	1.90
Others	2	6.10	2	5.70	2	5.70	6	5.80
Total*	33	100.00	35	100.00	35	100.00	103	100.00

Source: Author's own research based on the information available at the official website of the NPC and CPPCC Sessions (http://2011lianghui.people.com.cn).

Notes
* In each NPC delegation there were a few "Chinese members" who are Mainland officials stationed in the HKSAR including officials from the Central Liaison Office, Chinese People's Liberation Army Forces and the Office of the Commissioner of the Ministry of Foreign Affairs. These Chinese members have been excluded in this table.
1 "Politician" refers to full-time Legislative Councillors and District Councillors.
2 "Business" refers to chairmen, directors, executives and managers from commercial corporations.
3 "Profession" refers to professionals from legal, accounting, architecture, surveying, planning, engineering, medical and health sectors.
4 "Social services" refers to practitioners from education, community and social services and religious sectors.
5 "Labour" refers to trade unionists.
6 "Culture and media" refers to practitioners from arts, culture, media and publishing sectors.

Table 8.2 Background analysis of Hong Kong members of the National Committee of the Chinese People's Political Consultative Conference (1998–2012)

Occupational background	9th CPPCC (1998 to 2002)		10th CPPCC (2003 to 2007)		11th CPPCC (2008 to 2012)		Total	
	No.	%	No.	%	No.	%	No.	%
Politician	1	0.90	1	0.80	1	0.80	3	0.80
Business	**79**	**69.90**	**80**	**67.80**	**91**	**74.60**	**250**	**70.80**
Profession	7	6.20	11	9.30	7	5.70	25	7.10
Social services	11	9.70	12	10.20	8	6.60	31	8.80
Labour	3	2.70	2	1.70	2	1.60	7	2.00
Culture and media	10	8.80	7	5.90	5	4.10	22	6.20
Others	2	1.80	5	4.20	8	6.60	15	4.20
Total*	113	100.00	118	100.00	122	100.00	353	100.00

Source: Author's own research based on the information available at the official website of the NPC and CPPCC Sessions (http://2011lianghui.people.com.cn).

Notes
* In each CPPCC delegation there were a few "Chinese members" who are Mainland officials stationed in the HKSAR including officials from the Central Liaison Office, Chinese People's Liberation Army Forces and the Office of the Commissioner of the Ministry of Foreign Affairs. These Chinese members have been excluded in this table.
1 "Politician" refers to full-time Legislative Councillors and District Councillors.
2 "Business" refers to chairmen, directors, executives and managers from commercial corporations.
3 "Profession" refers to professionals from legal, accounting, architecture, surveying, planning, engineering, medical and health sectors.
4 "Social services" refers to practitioners from education, community and social services and religious sectors.
5 "Labour" refers to trade unionists.
6 "Culture and media" refers to practitioners from arts, culture, media and publishing sectors.

delegates will stay for around two weeks to deliberate national-level affairs (known as "Lianghui" in Chinese). The "Lianghui" held every year thus provides a regular communication channel for the business elites to directly air their views on Hong Kong affairs to the Mainland officials through making formal submissions or informal exchanges. On most occasions the NPC and CPPCC delegations will also be given the opportunity to meet top Beijing leaders responsible for making Hong Kong and Macau policy.[4]

Political co-option of the business elites by the local agent of the sovereign state: the united front work of the Central Liaison Office

Since Xu Jiatun's time, CCP Hong Kong had already begun to institutionalise the co-option mechanism by first focusing on the capitalist class to bring them onside in the belief that the business elites were the most crucial in maintaining prosperity.

(Loh, 2010, p. 183)

214 *Uneasy partnership between state and business*

The closer relationship between Beijing and the business sector is not only reflected in the dominant representation of business elites in the Hong Kong NPC and CPPCC delegations, but is also strikingly evident in the extensive united-front work conducted by the local agent of the sovereign state – the Liaison Office of the Central People's Government in the HKSAR (Central Liaison Office).

Unlike the British colonial period under which the London government did not attempt to govern Hong Kong directly and the Colonial Office in London generally left it to the Governor to prescribe in detail what should be done (Miner, 1987, p. 38), the Chinese government does maintain a "local machinery" in the HKSAR despite the political rhetoric of "High Degree of Autonomy" and "Hong Kong People Ruling Hong Kong" (Yep, 2010). Under the hierarchical structure of the Chinese government and the CCP, the Central Leading Group on Hong Kong–Macao Affairs is the top-level task force responsible for overseeing Hong Kong affairs. Headed by a Politburo Standing Committee Member, this high-level Central Leading Group comprises officials from relevant departments, including the Ministry of Foreign Affairs, Ministry of Commerce, United Front Work Department, Propaganda Department and other units with portfolios related to Hong Kong and Macau affairs (Yep, 2010). In performing its functions, the Central Leading Group is supported by four major work units which provide it with the necessary intelligence, information, local networks and feedbacks for decision-making, including the State Council Hong Kong and Macau Affairs Office (which functions as major communication channel between the HKSAR government and the various executive departments of the Central People's Government), the Central Liaison Office (which serves as the representative organization of the Central People's Government in the HKSAR), the Office of the Commissioner of the Ministry of Foreign Affairs (which coordinates diplomatic affairs concerning Hong Kong) and the People's Liberation Army Hong Kong Garrison (the 4,000-strong military force stationed in Hong Kong) (Loh, 2010, pp. 201–206; Yep, 2010).

In this connection, the role of the Central Liaison Office, as the local agent of the Chinese government in the HKSAR after the handover, is of particular importance. The Central Liaison Office, which was known as the Xinhua News Agency Hong Kong Branch (Xinhua Hong Kong) before January 2000, is the official representative organization of the Chinese government in the territory and it is also where the Hong Kong and Macau Work Committee (HKMWC) of the CCP is located.[5] As the local agent of the sovereign state after the handover, the Central Liaison Office commands an extensive network of "leftist organizations" in Hong Kong, including commercial organizations (e.g. banks, commercial corporations, department stores and tourist agencies), educational and cultural organizations (e.g. schools, newspapers and bookstores) and mass organizations (e.g. labour unions, district-based organizations, elderly, youth and women organizations). Given its strong presence in the territory, the Central Liaison Office is undoubtedly a well-organized and resourceful political institution which exercises considerable day-to-day influence in the affairs of Hong Kong (Loh, 2010, p. 13).

The business sector's direct access 215

No matter whether it was operated under the name of Xinhua Hong Kong or the Liaison Office, the principal function of the HKMWC is to conduct united-front work in Hong Kong with a view to building up broad-based social support for the CCP's Hong Kong policy (Loh, 2010). From the perspective of the Chinese government, the implementation of the "one country, two systems" in Hong Kong is an unprecedented political experiment and how to make it work is an unusual governance challenge to Beijing's leaders. It is therefore imperative for the Chinese government to maintain an extensive united front in post-1997 Hong Kong by grooming and incorporating a large pool of "patriotic" political elites so that such a united-front machinery could be mobilized to publicly defend the policies of the Central Authorities and the HKSAR government as and when necessary and to canvass votes for pro-Beijing political parties and candidates in various levels of elections (Loh, 2010, p. 207).

In the construction of the united front, the business sector is always the Central Liaison Office's principal target of co-option. Since Xu Jiatun had headed the Xinua Hong Kong in the 1980s, the HKMWC has already put in place a political co-option mechanism that focuses on bringing the business sector to the side of the Chinese government (Loh, 2010, p. 183) and such a political strategy has continued to direct its united-front work after 1997. The extensiveness of the united-front work on the business sector is evident in the membership lists of the "Presidium of the Preparatory Committee of Hong Kong Compatriots in Celebration of the Founding Anniversary of the People's Republic of China" (Preparation Committees for National Day Celebration). These Preparatory Committees were organized annually by the Central Liaison Office for coordinating national-day celebration activities. Empirical research on the occupational backgrounds of the members showed that the business sector consistently constituted the single largest group in the Central Liaison Office's united front, occupying an average of 58.1 per cent of seats from 1998 to 2011 (Table 8.3). A closer examination on the membership lists revealed that local business tycoons are regular members. Taking the 2011 Preparation Committee for National Day Celebration as an example, the membership list includes almost all big business tycoons in Hong Kong, such as Li Ka-shing, Lee Shau-kee, Kwok Ping-sheung, Cheng Yu-tung, Ronnie Chan Chi-chung, Chen Din-hwa, William Fung Kwok-lung, Tung Chee-chen, David Li Kwok-po, Shaw Run-run, Cha Mou-sing, Robert Ng Chee-siong, Charles Ho Tsu-kwok, Stanley Ho Hung-sun and Lui Che-woo. Apart from these billionaires, leaders of the four major business associations in the territory were also co-opted as regular members of the Preparation Committees, including Anthony Wu Ting-yuk (Chairman of the Hong Kong General Chamber of Commerce), Jonathan Choi Koon-shum (Chairman of the Chinese General Chamber of Commerce), David Wong Yau-ka (President of the Chinese Manufacturers' Association of Hong Kong) and Zhong Zhi-ping (Chairman of the Federation of Hong Kong Industries). While it would be difficult to trace the behind-the-scenes united-front work done by the Central Liaison Office, these empirical findings have provided insightful evidence about the close relationship between the business sector and the local agents of sovereign state after 1997.

Table 8.3 Background analysis of members of the Presidium of Preparatory Committee of Hong Kong Compatriots in celebration of the founding anniversary of the People's Republic of China (1998–2011)

Occupational background	1998		1999		2000		2001		2002		2003		2004		2005	
	No.	%	No.	%	No.	%	No.	%	No.	%	No.	%	No.	%	No.	%
Government	13	9.90	12	8.20	15	10.10	16	10.70	15	10.00	15	9.90	15	9.90	17	11.30
Politician	3	2.30	3	2.00	3	2.00	3	2.00	3	2.00	3	2.00	3	2.00	3	2.00
Business	79	60.30	87	59.20	82	55.40	85	56.70	84	56.00	89	58.90	90	59.60	90	59.60
Profession	5	3.80	6	4.10	7	4.70	8	5.30	8	5.30	8	5.30	8	5.30	8	5.30
Social services	15	11.50	16	10.90	16	10.80	17	11.30	16	10.70	14	9.30	15	9.90	15	9.90
Labour	4	3.10	5	3.40	6	4.10	5	3.30	6	4.00	6	4.00	6	4.00	6	4.00
Culture and media	10	7.60	16	10.90	16	10.80	15	10.00	16	10.70	13	8.60	13	8.60	11	7.30
Others	2	1.50	2	1.40	3	2.00	1	0.70	2	1.30	3	2.00	1	0.70	1	0.70
Total*	131	100	147	100	148	100	150	100	150	100	151	100	151	100	151	100

Occupational background	2006		2007		2008		2009		2010		2011		Total	
	No.	%	No.	%	No.	%	No.	%	No.	%	No.	%	No.	%
Government	16	10.10	13	8.60	10	6.50	11	7.10	10	6.30	13	8.30	191	9.00
Politician	3	1.90	3	2.00	3	1.90	3	1.90	2	1.30	3	1.90	41	1.90
Business	92	58.20	90	59.60	90	58.10	91	58.30	93	58.10	86	55.10	1,228	58.10
Profession	9	5.70	7	4.60	6	3.90	6	3.80	7	4.40	8	5.10	101	4.80
Social services	20	12.70	21	13.90	24	15.50	25	16.00	26	16.30	25	16.00	265	12.50
Labour	6	3.80	5	3.30	5	3.20	5	3.20	5	3.10	5	3.20	75	3.50
Culture and media	11	7.00	11	7.30	11	7.10	11	7.10	11	6.90	14	9.00	179	8.50
Others	1	0.60	1	0.70	6	3.90	4	2.60	6	3.80	2	1.30	35	1.70
Total*	158	100	151	100	155	100	156	100	160	100	156	100	2,115	100

Source: Author's own research based on the membership lists of the Presidium of Preparatory Committee for National Day Celebration available in Ta Kung Po and Wen Wei Po.

Notes

* There were a few "Chinese members" (i.e. Mainland officials from Central People's Government offices in the HKSAR including the Liaison Office, Chinese People's Liberation Army Forces Hong Kong and the Office of the Commissioner of the Ministry of Foreign Affairs in Hong Kong) in each Preparatory Committees and we have excluded these Chinese members in the above table.

1 "Government" refers to political officials or civil servants of the HKSAR government.
2 "Politician" refers to full-time Legislative Councillors and District Councillors.
3 "Business" refers to chairmen, directors, executives and managers from commercial corporations.
4 "Profession" refers to professionals from legal, accounting, architecture, surveying, planning, engineering, medical and health sectors.
5 "Social services" refers to practitioners from education, community and social services and religious sectors.
6 "Labour" refers to trade unionists.
7 "Culture and media" refers to practitioners from arts, culture, media and publishing sectors.

218 *Uneasy partnership between state and business*

Business sector's increased economic links with the Mainland authorities: Mainland–Hong Kong economic integration and its political implications

> Growing integration with the Chinese economy, the rising Chinese economic presence in Hong Kong, and Chinese sovereignty over Hong Kong will determine the shape of future government–business relations in Hong Kong.
>
> (Huang, 1997)

The closer relationship between the business sector and the sovereign state after the handover is not only contributed by political factors, as discussed in the preceding section, but it is also the result of macro-economic changes across the Mainland–Hong Kong boundaries. In a word, the growing Mainland–Hong Kong economic integration since the 1980s has further consolidated the privileged access of business interests to the policy process (Yep, 2009).

Hong Kong was traditionally an entrepot between China and the rest of the world. Since the 1980s, when the Chinese government began its economic reforms and adopted an open-door policy for attracting foreign investments, hundreds of thousands of Hong Kong manufacturers moved their factories to the Mainland and Hong Kong's economy has become increasingly integrated with China's (Huang, 1997). The business model of "front shop and back factory" (those advanced management functions like product design and marketing are stationed in Hong Kong, while the labour-intensive production units are located in the Mainland) has been widely adopted by Hong Kong businessmen since the 1980s to reduce their business operating costs. Such a business model greatly boosted the demand for Hong Kong's service industries such as trade, insurance and financial services, and it successfully transformed Hong Kong from a one-time manufacturing centre into a service-based economy (Sung, 1997). Mainland–Hong Kong economic integration marked an important stage in the 1990s when Hong Kong and Chinese enterprises have substantially increased their investments across the border. Starting from the 1990s, Hong Kong's major conglomerates have started to diversify their investments in the Mainland from labour-intensive manufacturing industries into other sectors such as real estate, basic infrastructure, retail and technology (Huang, 1997). During the same period, Chinese firms also strengthened and diversified their investments in Hong Kong, covering all sectors of the territory's economy such as banking, aviation, property, trade and shipping (Sung, 1997). The signing of the Closer Economic Partnership Agreement (CEPA) in 2003 provided further impetus to Mainland–Hong Kong economic integration (Wang & Liang, 2004). The CEPA, on the one hand, provided Hong Kong's businesses and professionals more growth opportunities by giving them greater access to China's markets and, on the other hand, it also facilitated Mainland enterprises to internationalize their businesses by making better use of Hong Kong's financial and business services (Qu, 2007). Now Hong Kong has already been developed into a major service centre for China's economy, providing a wide variety of value-added business and financial services to Mainland enterprises such as issue of shares and bonds, coordination of project financing and provision of syndicated loans (Yep, 2007, 2009).

The breadth and depth of Mainland–Hong Kong economic integration in recent decades is illustrated in Figures 8.1–8.4. Figure 8.1 shows that Hong Kong's total trade with the Mainland has been increased from 13.43 per cent in 1980 to 50.35 per cent in 2012 and the annual trade volumes between the two economies have reached HK$3,698,621 million. Figure 8.2 shows that Mainland

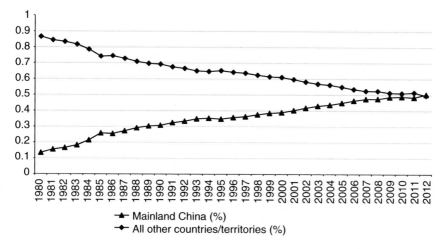

Figure 8.1 Hong Kong's total trade with Mainland China (1981–2012) (source: adapted from the statistical tables available at the Census and Statistics Department's website at www.censtatd.gov.hk).

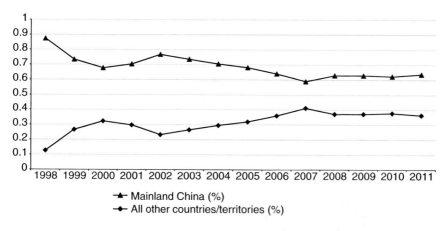

Figure 8.2 Inward direct investment in Hong Kong by major countries at market value (1998 to 2011) (source: adapted from the statistical tables available at the Census and Statistics Department's website at www.censtatd.gov.hk).

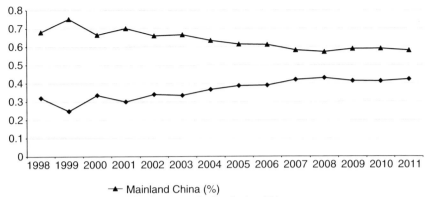

Figure 8.3 Outward direct investment of Hong Kong by major recipient country at market value (1998–2011) (source: adapted from the statistical tables available at the Census and Statistics Department's website at www.censtatd.gov.hk).

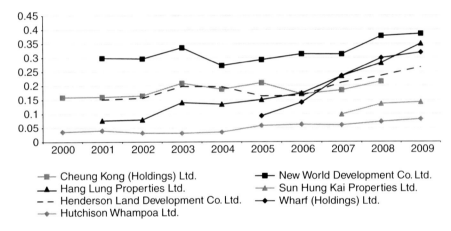

Figure 8.4 Percentage of assets hold by Hong Kong conglomerates in the Mainland (source: author's own research based on the annual financial reports of the chosen companies).

Note
According to the "Hong Kong Financial Reporting Standard 8 – Operating Segments", listed companies are required to disclose and report segment information about the different types of products and services it produces and the different geographical areas in which it operates. Such a standard arises from the International Accounting Standards Board's consideration of the Financial Accounting Standards Board in the United States Statement No. 131 Disclosures about Segments of an Enterprise and Related Information issued in 1997 (Hong Kong Institute of Certified Public Accountants, 2009). In this connection, most of the major conglomerates in Hong Kong have started reporting such geographical information since 2000, but on certain occasions some companies will choose not to disclose their geographical information if the amount of its assets, revenues and profits outside Hong Kong is not material or significant enough. Therefore this figure aimed at collecting the geographical information of those chosen major conglomerates in Hong Kong so long as such information and data are available in their annual financial reports.

The business sector's direct access   221

China has already become the biggest investor in Hong Kong and investments made by Chinese enterprises in 2011 accounted for 36.32 per cent of the total inward direct investment of Hong Kong. Figure 8.3 also illustrates that the Mainland is the principal investment location of Hong Kong companies and it absorbed over HK$3,346.4 billion from Hong Kong businessmen in 2011, representing 42.11 per cent of Hong Kong's total outward direct investment. Figure 8.4 shows that major Hong Kong conglomerates had substantially increased their investments in the Mainland over the past decade. All of the above statistics point to the conclusion that after about 30 years of economic integration, Hong Kong and the Mainland's economies have been intimately tied together and it is no exaggeration to say that the Chinese government and the local capitalists share common economic interests and agenda.

Mainland–Hong Kong economic integration has further consolidated the business sector's privileged access to the Mainland authorities. While the economic reforms implemented by the Chinese government over the past few decades have developed a robust private sector, the CCP has still retained its control over many strategic economic sectors such as telecommunications and finance through the state-owned enterprises, and various levels of governments in the Mainland have also directly engaged in the economy by setting up their own enterprises and subsidiaries (Dillon, 2009, pp. 43–45). Provincial and municipal governments also have the power to approve investment projects initiated by "foreign capital" (including Hong Kong capital).[6] Therefore, when Hong Kong's conglomerates expand their investments in China, they often work closely with central and provincial governments and their subsidiary companies or actively obtain the patronage from senior CCP leaders so as to overcome the various bureaucratic blocks to approving investment projects.[7] On the other hand, those subsidiaries owned by central and local governments will also cooperate with Hong Kong capitalists when they start their businesses in the HKSAR, and provincial and municipal officials are also eager to attract investment from Hong Kong capitalists.[8] Cross-border economic activities have allowed the local capitalists to develop intricate business networks and close personal ties with Mainland officials (Ngo, 2000a, 2000b).

Implications of the business sector's direct access to the sovereign state: the circumvention activities by the business elites

> [L]ocal business leaders had never enjoyed the same level of cordiality with the sovereign state before 1997 as they do now ... business leaders now all enjoy some form of direct access to top Chinese leaders, and they always bypass the SAR government in making claims or even complaints directly to Beijing. Reference to private conversation with senior Chinese officials is a common tactic to undermine the Chief Executive's authority when business leaders see their interests affected by policies of the SAR government.

222　*Uneasy partnership between state and business*

Business leaders are, in short, emboldened by their access to sympathetic ears at the very top level in Beijing and have become more assertive in the public policy process.

(Yep, 2009)

When Beijing's leaders decided to make the state–business alliance the cornerstone of the HKSAR political order, they envisaged that the business sector would, as in the colonial past, continue to be the major coalition partner providing strong support to the post-colonial state. On the surface, Hong Kong was governed by a similar political alliance between the government and the business sector both before and after 1997, but the different roles played by the sovereign states implied that the internal dynamics of the governing coalition were fundamentally different. Before 1997 London had largely taken a back seat and the colonial state headed by the Governor was the ultimate power holder within the state–business alliance. After 1997, although the post-colonial state headed by the Chief Executive has continued to absorb business elites into the political establishment as in the colonial past, the new sovereign state – Beijing – has stepped in by co-opting the business sector on its own through the appointment of NPC and CPPCC delegates and the united-front work of the Central Liaison Office.

In the colonial time, the relationship between the business sector and the sovereign state (London) was relatively distant. From time to time the colonial Governor remained the only official channel of communication between Hong Kong and London and the business sector was generally discouraged from bypassing the colonial state to take their complaints directly to the London government. Moreover, the business sector and London did not share much common political and economic agenda, leaving little room for the business elites to expand their influence by engaging in circumvention. Finally, the London government had not established any local presence in Hong Kong and relied on the Governor to manage the day-to-day affairs in the territory. The remote relationship between the business sector and the sovereign state in the pre-1997 period had made it practically difficult for the business sector to exert political influence by means of circumvention activities. All of the above factors helped sustain the relative autonomy of the colonial state in administering Hong Kong and upheld the authority of the Governor as the ultimate power holder in the territory (see Chapter 3).

However, the dynamic of the state–business relations changed fundamentally after 1997 because the business sector gained direct access to the sovereign state. Unlike London, which relied on the Governor to maintain Hong Kong's governance and chose to keep its distance from the business sector, Beijing considers itself as having a direct stake in the governance of the HKSAR and treats the business sector as its major coalition partner (see Chapter 4). As such, the Chinese government has directly engaged in the making of the post-1997 state–business alliance and has seen the business sector as its principal target of co-option. While these rules of engagement were deliberately designed by Beijing

The business sector's direct access   223

to perpetuate the state–business alliance after 1997, they have effectively allowed the business sector to establish direct access to the sovereign state and significantly changed the rules of political games in the HKSAR era.

Because of the business sector's direct access to Beijing, the nature and functioning of the state–business alliance is essentially different before and after 1997. In the colonial era, due to the business sector's restricted access to the sovereign state, governing coalition building was basically a two-player game between the colonial Hong Kong state and the business sector, and the Governor was the final arbitrator within the state–business alliance. It was difficult for business elites to challenge the authority of the Governor by making claims to London, enabling the colonial state to maintain a higher degree of relative autonomy vis-à-vis the business sector. But after 1997, because of the close partnership between business elites and the sovereign state, governing coalition building has been evolved into a three-player game among the sovereign state, post-colonial Hong Kong state and business sector. Beijing's leaders, rather than the Chief Executive, have become the real power centre of the state–business alliance. When Beijing's leaders, rather than the Chief Executive, became the de facto power centre of the state–business alliance after 1997, business elites could always resort to sympathetic ears either in Beijing or the Central Liaison Office and bring pressure on the post-colonial state if they saw their interests affected by government policies.[9] The direct political consequence of these circumvention activities is that the balance of power between the post-colonial state and the business sector has been effectively changed and the post-colonial state is encountering growing challenges from the business sector.

The growing tendency of the business sector to influence local politics by directly lobbying the Mainland officials was reflected by the large number of business delegations organized to visit Beijing. Table 8.4 summarizes the number of Hong Kong delegations to Beijing from 1998 to 2011 and empirical findings indicate that the business sector has been most active in organizing such delegations, amounting to nearly 40 per cent of the total number of delegations. Table 8.5 illustrates that during their visits the local capitalists were received by senior Beijing officials, including state leaders, NPC and CPPCC officials and other senior ministers. While we are unable to trace the behind-the-scenes discussions between the business elites and Beijing officials and those visits that were not publicly organized have not been covered by our research, all these statistics have showed how commonly local businessmen resort to direct lobbying of Beijing officials by means of circumvention activities. Table 8.6 provides concrete examples to illustrate how the governing authority and relative autonomy of the post-colonial state are being challenged by the circumvention activities of the business sector after 1997, including the 85,000 housing targets, the single development approach for the West Kowloon Cultural Development Project and the extension of the "black out period" for listed company directors. This table is far from exhaustive as it only includes those high-profile circumvention activities extensively reported by the media. However, this provided us with useful insights as to how the Hong Kong capitalists establish unprecedented

Table 8.4 Number of Hong Kong delegations to Beijing (1998–2011)

Number of delegations by background	1998	1999	2000	2001	2002	2003	2004	2005	2006	2007	2008	2009	2010	2011	Total
Business organizations	9	4	10	9	4	9	6	6	5	5	4	9	3	13	96
Charity bodies	3	2	4	2	3	4	3	6	3	1	2	3	2	2	40
Professional bodies	2	2	2	7	2	2	1	2	1	0	0	2	3	3	29
Townsmen associations	0	1	0	2	2	0	4	4	1	0	0	1	2	3	20
Political parties/political groups	0	0	2	0	0	4	2	0	3	2	3	0	0	2	18
District bodies	0	1	2	1	0	2	1	1	0	0	1	0	2	1	12
Women associations	1	0	0	1	2	2	0	0	0	1	0	2	0	0	9
Cultural bodies	3	0	0	1	0	2	0	0	1	0	0	0	0	0	7
Youth associations	2	0	0	0	0	0	0	0	0	0	0	0	0	5	7
Religious bodies	2	1	0	0	0	0	0	0	0	1	0	0	0	0	4
Others	0	3	3	1	0	2	1	0	0	0	0	0	0	3	13
Total	22	14	23	24	13	27	18	19	14	10	10	17	12	32	255

Source: Author's own research based on the content analysis of newspaper reports of four local newspapers: *Ming Pao*, *Hong Kong Economic Journal*, *Ta Kung Po* and *Wen Wei Po*. The essence of the content analysis was to search all the newspaper reports with the keyword "*Fang Jing Tuan*" through the WiseNews electronic platform.

The business sector's direct access   225

Table 8.5 State officials visited by business delegations (1997–2011)

Staff officials	No.*	%
State leaders (President, Vice-President, Premier and Vice-Premier)	30	10.70
Officials of the National People's Congress	1	0.40
Officials of the National Committee of Chinese People's Political Consultative Committee	15	5.40
Officials of the Hong Kong and Macao Affairs Office of the State Council	44	15.70
Officials of other State Council ministries and commissions	146	52.10
United Front Work Department	43	15.40
Others	1	0.40
Total	280	100

Note
* This refers to the number of Hong Kong delegations received by state officials. Because a delegation may be received by more than one state officials, the total number here is not the same as the total of number of business delegations in Table 8.4.

power leverages vis-à-vis the post-colonial state through their political and economic access to the Mainland authorities. Since the business sector's circumvention activities have become a normal part of post-1997 political life, the post-colonial state has struggled to maintain its effective governance and uphold its authority as the ultimate power holder in the territory.

Conclusion

Hong Kong has always been a dependent polity subject to the ultimate control of a more powerful sovereign state – London before 1997 and Beijing after 1997 (Kuan, 1991). Given its political status as a local polity, the relationship between the business sector and the sovereign state will have strong implications for the relative autonomy of the Hong Kong state: a relatively distant relationship between the business sector and the sovereign state will help the Hong Kong state to uphold its governing authority in the territory, while a close partnership between the business sector and the sovereign state will undermine the authority of the Hong Kong state as the final arbitrator in the territory.

Unfortunately, the post-colonial state has been trapped in the latter situation. Unlike the colonial era, the business sector has become the major coalition partner of the sovereign state after 1997 and the local capitalists have gained privileged access to Beijing by virtue of their over-representation in the NPC and CPPCC delegations, close relationship with the Central Liaison Office and intricate business networks with Mainland authorities. Although these rules of engagement were deliberately designed by Beijing to perpetuate the state–business alliance after 1997, the ultimate irony is that they have allowed the business sector to establish direct access to the sovereign state and equipped it with unprecedented power leverages vis-à-vis the post-colonial state. As a consequence of the close partnership between the Chinese government and the

Table 8.6 Selected circumvention activities by the business sector after 1997

Policy initiative	Year	Dissatisfaction of business sector	Circumvention activities by business sector	Results
85,000 housing targets	2000	Property prices dropped by over 50 per cent after the implementation of 85,000 annual housing targets by the Tung Chee-hwa Administration in 1997. Jeopardized by the collapse in property values, the property tycoons wanted the HKSAR government to change its public housing programme, which they considered as seriously affecting their interests.	Property tycoons made use of their political connections to take their complaints to Beijing's leaders (Goodstadt, 2009: 136). It was reported that some tycoons had expressed their concerns about Hong Kong's property market to state leaders during their visit to Beijing in June 2000 (*Hong Kong Economic Times*, 2000; *Singtao Daily*, 2000).	Shortly after the property tycoons' visit to Beijing, the Chief Executive Tung Chee-hwa stated that the targets of constructing 85,000 housing flats had no longer existed.
Single development approach for West Kowloon Cultural Development Project	2004	The HKSAR government proposed to adopt a single development approach under which a single tender would be awarded to develop the entire 40-hectare West Kowloon site. Many property developers complained that such an approach would only benefit the biggest developers and made it difficult for small and medium developers to participate.	It was reported that many property developers complained to the Mainland authorities that the single development approach was not a fair arrangement and requested that the lot should be broken into small pieces of land for public tender so that small and medium developers could participate in the West Kowloon project (*Ming Pao*, 2004).	In February 2006 the new Donald Tsang Administration announced abandonment of the single development approach and conducted a new round of public consultation for the whole project.
Extension of the "black-out" period for listed company directors	2009	The business sector strongly opposed the Hong Kong Stock Exchange's proposal to extend the "black-out" period for listed company directors from currently one month to seven months.	It was reported that some business leaders had taken their complaints directly to the Mainland authorities. Ronnie Chan, Chairman of Hang Lung Properties Ltd, publicly confirmed the existence of such circumvention activities (*Ming Pao*, 2009)	In February 2009 the Hong Kong Stock Exchange modified its proposal by which the "black-out" period will only be extended from one month to three months.

The business sector's direct access   227

business sector, business elites have usually resorted to the sympathetic ears of the Mainland authorities when they see their interests affected by the post-colonial state. This kind of circumvention activity has already become a part of post-1997 politics, undermining the relative autonomy of the post-colonial state and resulting in growing cleavages within the state–business alliance in the first 15 years of HKSAR era.

Notes

1 Originally published in a slightly different form, reprinted from *China Quarterly*, Vol. 217, March 2014, pp. 854–882, by permission of Cambridge University Press.
2 Since the Fourth NPC (1975–1978) there has been a number of Hong Kong delegates to the NPC, but they did not represent British Hong Kong and were considered as Chinese Hong Kong residents forming a distinct bloc within the Guangdong Province NPC delegation. These Hong Kong NPC delegates were selected by the New China News Agency and deemed elected by the Guangdong Provincial People's Congress. This arrangement was adopted for the subsequent NPC sessions until the final days of colonial rule in Hong Kong. By the time of the Ninth NPC (1998–2003), Hong Kong deputies for the first time participated as a separate Hong Kong delegation and a total of 36 seats were allocated to the HKSAR (Young & Cullen, 2010, pp. 45–47). Since then, the Hong Kong Deputies to the NPC have been elected locally by an election conference and such a conference normally comprises all members of the Chief Executive Election Committee and Hong Kong members of CPPCC who are not Election Committee members (Cheung & Wong, 2004).
3 Apart from the national NPC and CPPCC, less influential Hong Kong businessmen were also being appointed by the Chinese government to provincial and municipal people's congresses and CPPCCs (Loh, 2010, pp. 30–31). Because it is difficult to keep track of all the backgrounds of appointees in provincial and municipal levels, the empirical research only covers the national NPC and CPPCC.
4 Normally the Hong Kong delegations will arrange to meet the Director and Deputy Directors of the Hong Kong and Macau Affairs Office and also other state leaders. For example, in the 2011 Lianghui the Hong Kong delegations arranged to have private meetings with Vice-President Xi Jinping and Director of Hong Kong and Macau Affairs Office Wang Guangya, the principal Chinese officials responsible for Hong Kong affairs (*South China Morning Post*, 2011, 5 March; 2012, 26 March).
5 The CCP has a long history in Hong Kong since the early 1920s in which Hong Kong had been an important operational base for CCP activities. After the CCP took power in Mainland China it began to build an elaborate structure of political organizations in Hong Kong and set up the Hong Kong Work Committee to handle party organization in the territory. In 1955 this committee was restructured to become the Hong Kong and Macau Work Committee (HKMWC) to oversee party work in both Hong Kong and Macau. Because the Chinese government did not recognise British sovereignty over Hong Kong, an official representative organization could not be set up. As a result, the HKMWC was based inside the headquarters of the Xinhua Hong Kong as the de facto diplomatic mission of China in the territory and its director also served as the CCP party secretary in Hong Kong. After the handover, the Central Liaison Office was setup on 18 January 2000 to function as Beijing's official agency in Hong Kong. After the setting up of the Central Liaison Office, the Xinhua Hong Kong Branch became a true press office (Ma, 2007).
6 For example, Li Ka-shing had developed intricate business connections with Deng Xiaoping's family by assisting the Shougang Group to become one of the largest "red chip companies" in Hong Kong's stock market in the 1990s. In return, the blessing of

228   *Uneasy partnership between state and business*

Deng's family facilitated Li Ka-shing in expanding his business empire in the Mainland and also realizing the controversial Oriental Plaza project in the prime areas of Beijing (see Ngo, 2000b).

7 It is common for local party officials to lead business delegations (*Zhao Shang Tuan*) to Hong Kong so as to attract investment from local capitalists. For example, Xi Jinping, who served as Party Chief of Zhejiang Province from 2002 to 2007, led a large-scale business delegation to Hong Kong in 2005 and held private meetings with local tycoons and leaders of major business associations (see *Wen Wei Po*, 2005, 17 January).

8 For example, Zhang Gaoli, who was promoted to Politburo Standing Committee in the 18th Party Congress in 2012, developed close ties with Li Ka-shing throughout his career. Zhang developed his friendship with Li during his tenure as the Party Chief of Shenzhen and Li even visited Shenzhen to personally bid farewell to Zhang before he moved to Shandong in 2002. When Zhang Gaoli led a business delegation to Hong Kong in 2002 in his capacity as Governor of Shandong Province, he was warmly welcomed by Li Ka-shing, who openly pledged to increase his investment in Shandong. Since Zhang had served as the Party Chief of Tianjin Province in 2007, Li's companies have also stepped up their investments in Tianjin (see *Hong Kong Economic Times*, 2008, 18 September; *Ta Kung Po*, 2001, 13 December; *Wen Wei Po*, 2002, 9 May).

9 Anonymous interviewee.

References

Cheung, A., & Wong, P. C. W. (2004). Who advised the Hong Kong government? The politics of absorption before and after 1997. *Asian Survey*, *44*(6), 874–894.

Dillon, M. (2009). *Contemporary China: An introduction*. New York: Routledge.

Goodstadt, L. F. (2009). *Uneasy partners: The conflict between public interest and private profit interest in Hong Kong*. Hong Kong: Hong Kong University Press.

Hong Kong Economic Times. (2000, 23 June). Business tycoons to visit Beijing: Ng Chee-siong plans to express concerns on property market. A6 (in Chinese).

Hong Kong Economic Times. (2008, 18 September). Zhang Gaoli advocated Hong Kong-Tianjin cooperation. A38 (in Chinese).

Hong Kong Institute of Certified Public Accountants (2009). *Hong Kong financial reporting standard 8: Operating segments*. Retrieved 1 January 2013 from: http://app1. hkicpa.org.hk/ebook/HKSA_Members_Handbook_Master/volumeII/hkfrs8.pdf.

Huang, Y. S. (1997). The economic and political integration of Hong Kong: Implications for government–business relations. In W. I. Cohen, & L. Zhao (Eds.), *Hong Kong under Chinese rule: The economic and political implications of reversion* (pp. 96–113). Cambridge: Cambridge University Press.

Kuan, K. C. (1991). Power dependence and democratic transition: The case of Hong Kong. *The China Quarterly, 128*, 774–793.

Loh, C. (2010). *Underground front: The Chinese Communist Party in Hong Kong*. Hong Kong: Hong Kong University Press.

Ma, N. (2007). *Political development in Hong Kong: State, political society and civil society*. Hong Kong: Hong Kong University Press.

Miners, N. (1987). *Hong Kong under imperial rule, 1912–1941*. Hong Kong: Oxford University Press.

Ming Pao. (2004, 27 November). The business sector complained to Beijing that the single development approach was unfair. A3 (in Chinese).

Ming Pao. (2009, 11 February). Ronnie Chan said some people protested the extension of black out period to Beijing. B01 (in Chinese).

The business sector's direct access 229

Ngo, T. W. (2000a). Changing government–business relations and the governance of Hong Kong. In R. Ash, P. Ferdinand, B. Hook, & R. Porter (Eds.), *Hong Kong in transition: The handover years* (pp. 26–41). New York: St. Martin's Press.

Ngo, T. W. (2000b). Business strategy, state intervention, and regionalization in East Asia. In M. Vellinga (Ed.), *The dialectics of globalization: Regional responses to world economic processes – Asia, Europe, and Latin America in comparative perspective* (pp. 83–94). Boulder, CO: Westview Press.

Qu, B. Z. (2007). Mainland China–Hong Kong economic relations. In Y. M. Yeung (Ed.), *The first decade: The Hong Kong SAR in retrospective and introspective perspectives* (pp. 383–419). Hong Kong: Chinese University Press.

Singtao Daily. (2000, 23 June). Property tycoons to express their concerns on property market to President Jiang. A6 (in Chinese).

South China Morning Post. (2010a, 7 September). Hu heaps praise on Li Ka-shing as they meet for a one-on-one. EDT4.

South China Morning Post. (2010b, 7 September). Hu's meeting with tycoon positive for foreign firms. EDT5.

South China Morning Post. (2011, 5 March). "Two systems" doesn't trump "one country", Vice-President says. EDT5.

South China Morning Post. (2012, 26 March). Leung seeks unity after divisive poll. EDT1.

Sung, Y. W. (1997). Hong Kong and the economic integration of the China circle. In B. Naughton (Ed.), *The China circle: Economics and electronics in the PRC, Taiwan, and Hong Kong* (pp. 419–480). Washington, DC: Brookings Institution Press.

Ta Kung Po. (2001, 13 December). Zhang Gao Zai met Li Ka-shing in Shenzhen. A04 (in Chinese).

Wang, T., & Liang, H. (2004). Economic integration between Hong Kong SAR and Mainland China. In E. Prasad (Ed.), *Hong Kong SAR: Meeting the challenges of integration with the Mainland* (pp. 3–10). Washington, DC: International Monetary Fund.

Wen Wei Po. (2002, 9 May). Li Ka-shing greeted Zhang Gao Zai under the burning sun. B01 (in Chinese).

Wen Wei Po. (2005, 17 January). Xi Jinping led Zhejiang business delegation to Hong Kong. A01 (in Chinese).

Yep, R. (2007). Links with the Mainland. In W. M. Lam, P. L. T. Lui, W. Wong, & I. Holiday (Eds.), *Contemporary Hong Kong politics: Governance in the post-1997 era* (pp. 245–264). Hong Kong: Hong Kong University Press.

Yep, R. (2009). Accommodating business interests in China and Hong Kong: Two systems, one way out. In K. H. Mok, & R. Forrest (Eds.), *Changing governance and public policy in East Asia* (pp. 185–205). New York: Routledge.

Yep, R. (2010). One country, two systems and special administrative regions: The case of Hong Kong. In J. H. Chung, & T. C. Lam (Eds.), *China's local administration: Traditions and changes in the sub-national hierarchy* (pp. 86–109). New York: Routledge.

Young, S. N. M., & Cullen, R. (2010). *Electing Hong Kong's chief executive.* Hong Kong: Hong Kong University Press.

Part V

Rethinking Hong Kong's governance under Chinese sovereignty

From an opposition-centred explanation to a critical analysis of governing coalition building

9 Conclusion
Rethinking the governance crisis in post-1997 Hong Kong

As part of the post-1997 governing strategy of the Chinese government in Hong Kong, the state–business alliance was adopted and consolidated as the foundation of the HKSAR political order. The wishful thinking of Beijing leaders was that the post-colonial state shall be, as in the British colonial past, able to maintain effective governance with the political support of its coalition partner – the business sector.

However, the political developments in the post-1997 period indicate that things did not turn out as anticipated by Beijing's leaders. The discussions in the preceding chapters have illustrated that the state–business alliance as engineered by Beijing has been operated in a completely different political and socio-economic environment after 1997, and therefore not only fails to live up to its original function in serving as the organizational machinery for supporting the post-colonial state, it even provides fertile ground for breeding new governance problems. These political and socio-economic changes after 1997, including fragmentation of agents of business interests, growing disconnection of business elites from the community, institutionalization of business power under the HKSAR political system and the business sector's increased access to the sovereign state, have eventually plunged the post-colonial state into a political quagmire of pervasive public discontent and distrust and resulted in the lingering of the governance crisis after 1997.

In this concluding chapter we are going to adopt the *integrated conceptual framework*, known as "state capacity as governing coalition building", with a view to articulating an alternative theoretical perspective on the post-1997 governance crisis. This chapter will also highlight the theoretical implications of our research study by discussing its original contribution to literature and the future research agenda. Is the post-1997 governance crisis caused by the strengths of the democratic opposition, the vulnerability of the post-colonial state and its governing coalition, or both? Is the implementation of universal suffrage a comprehensive solution to the governance problems in Hong Kong? Is Hong Kong's experience unique in any sense when compared with other East Asian hybrid regimes? In this chapter we are going to discuss the theoretical implications of this book by answering these important questions.

234 *Rethinking Hong Kong's governance*

A new theoretical explanation on the governance crisis in post-1997 Hong Kong: the failure of the state–business alliance

> The leadership of the Hong Kong SAR government is finding it increasingly difficult to take action. To be sure, the fact that it is not a popularly elected government undermines its legitimacy. But equally important is that it has not yet built up its own governing coalition. As a result, it is constantly exposed to criticism from all fronts so that it finds it difficult to develop new initiatives to address issues and problems that require a longer-term framework and state commitment to solve.
>
> (Lui & Chiu, 2009, p. 126)

In this section we are going to articulate our alternative theoretical explanation to post-1997 Hong Kong's governance crisis. The major theoretical propositions of this alternative explanation could be summarized by the following three-step argument: (1) crisis of state embeddedness, (2) crisis of state autonomy and (3) failure of the state–business alliance.

First, because of the fragmentation of agents of business interests and the growing disconnection of the business sector from the community, the intermediary role of co-opted business elites has been significantly eroded and the linkages between the state, business and society have become fragmented after 1997. As a consequence, the post-colonial state is facing growing challenges in re-embedding itself with major socio-economic actors and therefore it struggles to forge societal acceptance for delivering policy changes.

Second, because of the institutionalization of business power under the HKSAR political system and the business sector's increased access to the sovereign state in Beijing, the business sector has developed considerable power leverages vis-à-vis the post-colonial state after 1997. As a consequence, the post-colonial state's relative autonomy is facing growing challenges from the business sector and therefore it struggles to maintain its role as the arbitrator of class interests.

Third, under the combined effects of crises of state embeddedness and of state autonomy, the enabling conditions that endowed a viable state–business alliance in the colonial time have been seriously eroded after 1997. Instead, the post-colonial state is neither embedded nor autonomous and it is facing severe governance challenges on two major fronts: because of the crisis of state embeddedness, the post-colonial state is struggling hard to steer policy changes and finds it increasingly difficult to produce sound policy outputs to sustain public satisfaction; Because of the crisis of state autonomy, the post-colonial state struggles to maintain its role as arbitrator of class interests and it can no longer hold the proper balance between business interests and public interests. The lingering of the crisis of state embeddedness and crisis of state autonomy have undermined the popular support base of the HKSAR political order, plunging the post-colonial state into a political quagmire of persuasive public discontent and public distrust.

The crisis of state embeddedness: the erosion of intermediary role of co-opted business elites and the fragmented linkages between the state, business and society

State capacity theorists have generally agreed that the ability of the state in steering the economy and society hinges on its ability to embed itself into the socio-economic structures by engaging in institutionalized cooperation with major economic and societal constituents. The significance of state embeddedness lies in its strategic importance in enabling the state to maintaining effective coordination of different interest groups and establish widespread societal acceptance for the policy initiatives of the state (e.g. Evans, 1995, 1997; Weiss, 1998). In this connection, the *integrated conceptual framework* indicates that the notion of state embeddedness is a necessary enabling condition for effective governing coalition building, under which the existence of institutionalized negotiation channels and encompassing intermediaries will enable the state to embed itself with the major socio-economic constituents in the decision-making process.

In application of this *integrated conceptual framework* into the analysis of the dynamics of the state–business alliance in Hong Kong before and after 1997, we put forth this theoretical proposition: when compared with its colonial predecessor, the post-colonial state is facing a crisis of state embeddedness in the post-1997 period. There is a widening gap between the post-colonial state and the major socio-economic constituents, and it struggles to forge societal acceptance for delivering policy changes.

In the British colonial period, because of the dominant position of British capital in the local economy and the leadership of local Chinese capitalists in the community before 1997, the British capitalists and the local Chinese capitalists represented the two major socio-economic forces in the colonial period. Therefore, by incorporating the representatives of major British hongs and prestigious local Chinese capitalists into the dense networks of advisory bodies and committees, the co-opted business elites had effectively performed the role of encompassing intermediaries between state, business and society. The major British hongs assumed an important bridging role between the colonial state and the business sector, while the prestigious local Chinese capitalists played the mediating role between the colonial state and the Chinese population. As a consequence, these unique enabling conditions endowed the colonial state with a considerable degree of state embeddedness so that it could embed itself into the socio-economic power structures of the colonial time. On the foundation of such state embeddedness, the colonial state had successfully established a solid political support base in both the economic and social arenas for consolidating its governance (see Chapter 3). However, the post-colonial state does not have such a luxury anymore and its political gap with the major socio-economic constituents has been widening as a consequence of the fragmentation of agents of business interests and the growing disconnection of co-opted business elites from the local community in the post-1997 period.

236 *Rethinking Hong Kong's governance*

After 1997, while the business elites have been extensively incorporated in the HKSAR political establishment, as in the colonial past, the post-1997 business representation system does not function smoothly when compared with the British colonial period. In colonial Hong Kong, the business representation system was not simply about co-option of individual business elites, but it actually featured the incorporation of highly centralized and encompassing British business groups. Such a traditional business representation system was, however, based upon Hong Kong's unique colonial history and political-economic order, where the dominant position of the British capital in the local economy and the closed political system provided the foundation for the major British business groups to fulfil the role of encompassing intermediaries between the colonial state and the business sector. But since the 1980s such a business representation system has already broken down because of the changing configurations of economic and political structures. The downfall of the major British business groups during the transitional period, together with the rise of local Chinese and Mainland capital, has resulted in the growing diversity of Hong Kong's business sector and has finally put an end to the vital role of encompassing intermediaries previously performed by the British hongs. Coupled with the implementation of democratic reforms to the Legislative Council, the political-economic foundations of the traditional business representation system have been shaken since the transitional period. However, because of the underdevelopment of business-oriented political parties after handover, such a vital missing link between the post-colonial state and the business sector has not been effectively filled up and there is a general lack of encompassing agents of business interests to perform the role of encompassing intermediaries. The fragmentation of agents of business interests after 1997 (including business-oriented political parties, non-affiliated pro-business legislators, major business associations and individual corporations) pointed to the fact that there exists no overarching political organization to represent business interests in the political arena and the Executive Council no longer functions as an institutionalized negotiation mechanism between the post-colonial state and the business sector. As a consequence, the post-colonial state finds it increasingly difficult to rely on the co-opted business elites to consult and mediate business interests and struggles to consolidate the support of the business sector for its policy agenda, despite the fact that business elites have been extensively incorporated into the HKSAR political establishment, as in the colonial past. The post-colonial state has been trapped in the paradox of "strong business representation, weak political support" (see Chapter 5).

On the other hand, the rise of civil society activism in recent years has posed important challenges to the state–business alliance. As a consequence of the emergence of the civil society, social activists are now ready to challenge the state–business alliance through social movements. However, in the face of the increasing level of state–society conflicts, the business-oriented political parties and the co-opted business elites are generally powerless in assisting the post-colonial state to overcome the challenges of the civil society due to their lack of community networks, the growing public mistrust of business elites and erosion of its ideological weapon of economism. As a consequence of their growing disconnection from the local community, the co-opted business elites generally lack the necessary community networks and public credibility to mobilize sufficient societal support for defending the post-colonial state in times of serious state–society conflicts. The political divide between the state–business alliance and the civil society has become a huge gap that the post-colonial state struggles to stride across (see Chapter 6).

All of the above structural changes have far-reaching implications for the functioning of the state–business alliance after 1997 and have severely undermined the embeddedness of the post-colonial state. Due to the fragmentation of agents of business interests and the absence of an overarching political organization to fulfil the role of encompassing intermediaries in the post-1997 period, there is a vital missing link between the post-colonial state and its business allies and therefore the post-colonial state is encountering growing difficulties in consolidating the support of its business allies in the policy process. On the other hand, because of their growing disconnection from the community, the business-oriented political parties and the co-opted business elites are not capable of bridging the political gap between the post-colonial state and the civil society. The political consequence of these structural problems is that the co-opted business elites could no longer perform the role of encompassing intermediaries between state, business and society after 1997 and therefore the post-colonial state is encountering growing challenges in re-embedding itself into the post-1997 socio-economic structure. As a consequence, there are fragmented linkages between the state, business and society after 1997 and the post-colonial state is struggling to forge societal acceptance for delivering policy changes, resulting in a "crisis of state embeddedness".

The crisis of state embeddedness is closely connected to erosion of policy-making effectiveness of the post-colonial state, i.e. the first major indicator of the post-1997 governance crisis (Chapter 1). Because of the widening political gap between the post-colonial state and the major socio-economic constituents, in the process of policy-making and implementation both the Tung Chee-hwa and Donald Tsang Yam-kuen Administrations have been exposed to political challenges from all fronts, including its traditional allies in the business sector and those newly emerged civil society groups. Facing serious challenges in gaining the cooperation of major socio-economic constituents, the post-colonial state struggles to forge societal acceptance for delivering policy changes (see Table 1.2).

The crisis of state autonomy: the business sector's growing challenge to the relative autonomy of the post-colonial state

State capacity theorists have long recognized that state autonomy, which can be defined as the capacity of the state to resist pressure of capture by powerful socio-economic actors within its external environment, is an important

238 *Rethinking Hong Kong's governance*

institutional prerequisite for building up state capacity. The significance of state autonomy lies in its strategic importance in enabling the state to pursue a public policy agenda broader than the interests of any particular interest group and achieve an appropriate balancing of different interests in the wider society (e.g. Evans, 1995; Miliband, 1969, 1977; Nordlinger, 1981; Skocpol, 1985; Weiss, 1998). In this connection, the *integrated conceptual framework* indicated that the notion of state autonomy is one of the necessary enabling conditions for effective governing coalition building, under which the state's holding of significant power leverages and sanctioning powers will enable it to resist the undue demands from its powerful coalition partners and reconcile different interests in society.

In application of this *integrated conceptual framework* into the analysis of the dynamics of the state–business alliance in Hong Kong before and after 1997, we put forth this theoretical proposition: when compared with its colonial predecessor, the post-colonial state is plunging into a crisis of state autonomy in the post-1997 period. Since the handover of sovereignty, the business sector has developed considerable power leverages vis-à-vis the post-colonial state, seriously undermining its relative autonomy. As a consequence, the post-colonial state's relative autonomy is facing growing challenges from the business sector and there is serious erosion of its role as the arbitrator of class interests.

In the British colonial time, the colonial Governor had maintained a transcendent position vis-à-vis the business sector under the colonial political system (as a result of the independent selection process of Governors and his monopoly powers of political patronage) and the relationship between the capitalist class and the sovereign state in London was largely distant (as a result of the lack of a common political-economic agenda and absence of institutionalized communication channels between the business sector and London, and also the absence of strong local presence of the London government in Hong Kong). All these unique enabling conditions had endowed the colonial state with a considerable degree of state autonomy so that it could maintain significant power leverages vis-à-vis its powerful business allies. On the foundation of such state autonomy, the colonial state successfully resisted the pressures of business capture and performed its role as arbitrator of different class interests if and when it saw the need (see Chapter 3). However, the post-colonial state does not have such a luxury anymore and its relative autonomy vis-à-vis the business sector has been severely undermined after 1997 as a consequence of the institutionalization of business power under the post-1997 political system and the business sector's increased access to the sovereign state in Beijing in the post-handover period.

After 1997, the power of the business sector has been institutionalized in both the executive branch and legislative process through the Chief Executive Election Committees and the functional constituency system. By virtue of their predominant control over the majority of seats in the Chief Executive Election Committees, the business sector has established an influential "king-making power" and been equipped with important institutional leverage when bargaining with the Chief Executive. On the other hand, the dominant position of the business sector over the legislative process is guaranteed by their exclusive

Conclusion 239

representation through the functional constituencies as well as their constitutional privilege to veto the legislative proposals sponsored by the majority of Legislative Councillors under the voting-by-group system. All these structural changes in the political system have provided the business elites with unprecedented power bases and equipped them with important power leverages vis-à-vis the post-colonial state. When compared with its colonial predecessor, the post-colonial state could no longer effectively exercise its power of political patronage to sanction and subdue the business elites, who now have their own institutionalized power bases under the Basic Law. Because of such a fundamental shift in the balance of power between the post-colonial state and the business sector, the business elites have become more aggressive in advancing their own interests and bargaining for policy concessions by making use of their own power bases and political privileges (see Chapter 7).

The business sector nowadays enjoys increased political and economic access to the sovereign state by virtue of their overwhelming representation in the Hong Kong delegations to the National People's Congress and the National Committee of the Chinese People's Political Consultative Conference, their close relationship with the Central Liaison Office and their intricate economic links with the Mainland authorities. Because of the closer political and economic relations between the business sector and the sovereign state, Beijing's leaders – rather than the HKSAR Chief Executive – have become the de facto power centre of the state–business alliance after 1997. Therefore, unlike its colonial predecessor, the post-colonial state can hardly be regarded as the final arbitrator of the state–business alliance and the ultimate power holder in the territory. From this perspective, the business sector's privileged access to the sovereign state have provided them with an unprecedented power leverage vis-à-vis the post-colonial state because they can now advance their own interests and agenda by means of circumvention activities (see Chapter 8).

All of the above structural changes have far-reaching implications for the functioning of the state–business alliance after handover and have severely undermined the relative autonomy of the post-colonial state. While the institutionalization of business power under the HKSAR political system and the extensive co-option of business elites by the Chinese government were deliberately designed to consolidate the post-colonial state's political support base in the business sector and to perpetuate the state–business alliance after 1997, the post-1997 political developments indicate that these arrangements have produced entirely counter-productive political outcomes. Instead of consolidating business support to the Chief Executive, these rules of engagement have only equipped the business sector with considerable power leverages vis-à-vis the post-colonial state so that they could make use of these channels of political influence to challenge the governing authority of the HKSAR Chief Executive and to bargain for policy concessions. The political consequence of these structural problems is that the post-colonial state's relative autonomy is facing growing challenges from the business sector and it struggles to maintain its role as the arbitrator of class interests, resulting in a "crisis of state autonomy".

240 *Rethinking Hong Kong's governance*

The crisis of state autonomy is closely connected to the erosion of the post-colonial state's role as the arbitrator of class interests, i.e. the second major indicator of the post-1997 governance crisis (Chapter 1). Because of the growing pressure of business capture, the post-colonial state's transcendence above the powerful business interests has become increasingly untenable. Unlike its colonial predecessor, the post-colonial state struggles to maintain its leadership and control over its powerful business allies, therefore undermining its governing authority as the guardian of public interests. On the one hand the post-colonial state is under greater pressure to provide various forms of financial support to the business sector; on the other hand it is not quite capable of mitigating social contradictions and encounters greater difficulties in overcoming business opposition in pursuing policy reforms (see Tables 1.3 and 1.4).

From failure of the state–business alliance to governance crisis: the political quagmire of pervasive public discontent and public distrust

State capacity theorists have highlighted the importance of forging coalitions with external socio-economic constituents as a means of mustering state capacity for governance. The strategic importance of governing coalition building is that it is an important means of providing the state with an organizational machinery for vanquishing its opponents and consolidating its rule. From this perspective, governing coalition building is essential to the survival of all political leaders no matter whether they are in authoritarian regimes or democratic systems (Bueno de Mesquita, Smith, Siverson & Morrow, 2003; Peters, 1995; Pierre & Peters, 2000; Slater, 2010). In this regard, the *integrated conceptual framework* indicated that the notions of state autonomy and state embeddedness are the two necessary enabling conditions that endowed the state with the capacity to engineer a viable governing coalition. On the foundation of state embeddedness, the state could embed itself with the major socio-economic actors and mobilize the required societal support for its governance and policies. On the foundation of state autonomy, the state could develop a considerable degree of relative autonomy to resist the undue demands from its powerful coalition partners and formulate policies that serve the broader collective interests. Such a governing coalition will then function as an organizational machinery for the state to balance, negotiate and reconcile the different societal interests and provide it with a stable political support base for maintaining governance. In this light, the essence of the *integrated conceptual framework* is that the different notions of "state autonomy", "state embeddedness" and "governing coalition building" are strategically linked and correlated with each other when accounting for governance and state capacity.

In application of this *integrated conceptual framework* into the analysis of the dynamics of the state–business alliance in Hong Kong before and after 1997, we put forth this theoretical proposition: the changing political and socio-economic environments after 1997 have eventually plunged the post-colonial state into the crisis of state embeddedness and crisis of state autonomy. As a result, after the

Conclusion 241

handover the state–business alliance not only fails to function as an organizational machinery for supporting the post-colonial state, it even provides fertile grounds for breeding new governance problems, finally plunging the post-colonial state into a political quagmire of pervasive public discontent and distrust, resulting in the lingering of the governance crisis after 1997.

In the British colonial time, the colonial state simultaneously combined the notions of "state autonomy" with "state embeddedness" in the process of "governing coalition building". By incorporating the senior executives of the major British hongs (who played the role of encompassing intermediaries between the colonial state and the business sector) and the prestigious local Chinese capitalists (who played the role of encompassing intermediaries between the colonial state and the Chinese community) into its advisory system (the Executive Council, Legislative Council and various advisory bodies), the colonial state successfully engaged in institutionalized cooperation with major socio-economic constituents and forged widespread societal acceptance for its governance. By holding significant power leverages and sanctioning powers vis-à-vis the business sector (the colonial Governor's transcendent position and monopoly power of political patronage and the relatively distant relations between the business sector and the sovereign state in London), the colonial state successfully resisted the pressures of business capture and performed its role as arbitrator of different class interests if and when it saw the need. In other words, these unique enabling conditions for state embeddedness and state autonomy had helped the colonial state to maintain a precious political balance in the process of governing coalition building, enabling it to consolidate its governance by mobilizing the support of the business sector while preventing the state–business alliance from degenerating into clientelism and cronyism. On the basis of the smooth functioning of such a viable state–business alliance, the colonial state had successfully command a decent level of public satisfaction and public trust for much of the colonial era. On the one hand the colonial state had made successful use of the extensive economic and social networks of its business allies to steer policy-making, thereby sustaining a relatively high level of public satisfaction toward its performance. On the other hand the colonial state had also minimized any possible fallout from the public for government–business collusion, maintaining public confidence in its impartiality and commanding a decent level of public trust (Chapter 3). The post-colonial state does not have such a luxury because after 1997 the functioning of the state–business alliance has been overshadowed by the crises of state autonomy and state embeddedness.

Under the combined effects of crises of state embeddedness and state autonomy, the state–business alliance is facing severe challenges on two fronts after 1997. On the one hand, the fragmentation of agents of business interests (as a result of the underdevelopment of business-oriented political parties) and the powerlessness of co-opted business elites in mediating challenges from civil society (as a result of growing disconnection of the co-opted business elites from the community) have plunged the post-colonial state into a crisis of state embeddedness, making it difficult to re-embed itself with the major socio-economic

242   *Rethinking Hong Kong's governance*

actors and to forge societal acceptance for delivering policy changes. On the other hand, the institutionalization of business power under the HKSAR political system (as a result of the installation of the Chief Executive Election Committee and the functional constituency system in the Legislative Council) and the business sector's increased access to the sovereign state (as a result of the closer political and economic relations between the Chinese government and the business elites) have plunged the post-colonial state into a crisis of state autonomy, resulting in growing challenges from the business sector and the erosion of its role as the arbitrator of class interests.

As a consequence of the crisis of state embeddedness and crisis of state autonomy, the state–business alliance as engineered by Beijing has been operated in completely different political and socio-economic environments after 1997. Unlike the British colonial time when the colonial state had made successful use of the state–business alliance to consolidate its governance while still maintaining its leadership and control over the vested business interests, the post-colonial state is facing a completely different scenario. On the one hand, the post-colonial state could not rely on the co-opted business elites to mediate its relationship with the major socio-economic constituents and to mobilize societal support for its governance and policies, resulting in the erosion of its policy-making effectiveness and growing public dissatisfaction with its performance (Figures 1.2–1.4). On the other hand, the post-colonial state's relative autonomy is facing growing challenges from the business sector and it struggles to maintain its role as the arbitrator of class interests, resulting in the deterioration in the level of public distrust and increasing public suspicions of government–business collusion (Tables 1.4–1.6; Figure 1.5). In other words, as a consequence of the crises of state embeddedness and state autonomy, the post-colonial state is neither embedded nor autonomous and it is facing severe governance challenges on two major fronts. Due to the crisis of state embeddedness, the post-colonial state is struggling hard to steer policy changes and finds it increasingly difficult to produce sound policy outputs to sustain public satisfaction. Due to the crisis of state autonomy, the post-colonial state struggles to maintain its role as arbitrator of class interests and it can no longer hold the proper balance between business interests and public interests. The lingering of the crises of state embeddedness and state autonomy have undermined the popular support base of the HKSAR political order, plunging the post-colonial state into a political quagmire of pervasive public discontent and distrust.

To conclude, after 1997 the state–business alliance not only fails to function as an organizational machinery for supporting the post-colonial state, it even provides fertile ground for breeding new governance problems such as intra-elite conflicts within the governing coalition, increasing public suspicions of government–business collusion and aggravation of class conflicts. The failure of the state–business alliance points to the fact that the post-colonial state does not have a viable organizational machinery to maintain effective governance and to thwart the challenges of the democratic opposition. Given the vulnerability of the state–business governing coalition, the post-colonial state has always been exposed to political challenges from all fronts in the policy process and has lurched from one governance crisis to another since the handover. On many occasions, the post-colonial state is encountering severe political challenges on two fronts: at its back, the post-colonial state struggles to consolidate the political support of its business allies and encounters their growing challenges to its relative autonomy; at the front the post-colonial state and its business allies are too vulnerable and powerless to thwart the challenges from the democratic opposition and the civil society. Under such circumstances, the political support base of the post-colonial state has become too fragile and vulnerable and therefore it has usually been trapped in the crossfire of contending political challenges in the process of governance after 1997. As a consequence of the changing political and socio-economic environments after 1997, the old way of maintaining governance through a state–business alliance does not work (Table 9.1). To restore effective governance in the HKSAR, it is time for the realignment of a new governing coalition in Hong Kong.

Rethinking Hong Kong's governance crisis under Chinese sovereignty: legitimacy deficit or failure of governing coalition building?

> In many of these cases, regime outcomes were rooted less in the character or behaviour of opposition movements than in incumbents' capacity to thwart them. Where incumbents possessed a powerful coercive apparatus and/or party organization, even well-organized and cohesive opposition challenges often failed. By contrast, where incumbents lacked the organizational blocs needed to steal elections, co-opt opponents, or crack down on protest, transitions occurred even when oppositions are weak.
>
> (Levitsky & Way, 2010, p. 25)

When accounting for the governance problems and political instabilities in hybrid regimes, much of the pre-existing literature focused on the role of opposition challenges and assumed that societal push is the major driving force that contributes to the democratic transition of authoritarian regimes (e.g. Beissinger, 2002; Bratton & van de Walle, 1997; Collier, 1999; Diamond, 1999; Fish, 1995; Wood, 2000). However, the most recent studies on hybrid regimes demonstrate that such an opposition-centred explanation gives disproportionate attention to the societal side of the story but pays too little and insufficient attention to the varying abilities of authoritarian regimes in accommodating the pressures for democratization (Levitsky & Way, 2010, p. 54). Emerging literature on authoritarianism has already indicated that strong states and robust governing-party organizations are critical to the stability and survival of authoritarian regimes when facing opposition challenges (e.g. Brownlee, 2007; Slater, 2010; Smith, 2005). Levitsky and Way's latest cross-national studies further confirmed that the organizational power of authoritarian incumbents is central to their capacity to resist opposition challenges and it is the primary factor that determines regime

Table 9.1 State–business alliance before and after 1997

	Before 1997	After 1997
State embeddedness Intermediaries between the state and the business sector	The colonial political-economic order gave rise to highly centralized and encompassing British hongs, who effectively fulfilled the role of encompassing intermediaries between the colonial state and the business sector. Through co-option of senior executives of British hongs, the Executive Council functioned as an institutionalized platform for mediating major business interests.	Because of the underdevelopment of business-oriented political parties after 1997, there is a general lack of encompassing agents of business interests to fill in the missing link between the post-colonial state and the business sector. The fragmentation of agents of business interests has made it difficult for the post-colonial state to mediate and consult major business interests.
Intermediaries between the state and the society	Because of the underdevelopment of the civil society, the business sector was the dominant societal force and the state–business alliance was largely immune from any political challenges from the civil society. As the natural leaders of the Chinese community, the prestigious local Chinese capitalists played the mediating role between the colonial state and the Chinese population.	The rise of civil society activism has brought about growing citizen participation in the policy process, posing important challenges on the state–business alliance. However, the co-opted business elites are powerless in assisting the post-colonial state to overcome the challenges of the civil society, making the whole state–business alliance too vulnerable amidst increasing levels of state–society conflicts.
Degree of state embeddedness	As a result of the incorporation of encompassing British hongs and prestigious local Chinese capitalists, the colonial state had successfully engaged in institutionalized cooperation with major socio-economic constituents. It was on these foundations the colonial state could embed itself into the socio-economic structures and establish a stable political support base for its governance and policy initiatives.	As a result of the erosion of the intermediary role of co-opted business elites between the state, business and society after 1997, the post-colonial state is facing growing challenges in re-embedding itself with the major socio-economic constituents, pushing it into a "crisis of state embeddedness". As a result, the post-colonial state struggles to forge political consensus for delivering policy changes.

Balance of power between the state and the business sector under the political system	The Governor's transcendent position and monopoly power of political patronage had furnished the colonial state with significant political leverage and sanctioning powers over the business sector.	The business sector has developed unprecedented power bases as a result of the installation of the Chief Executive Election Committee and functional constituencies. There is a shift in the balance of power between the post-colonial state and the business sector.
Relationship between the business sector and the sovereign state	The relatively distant political and economic relations between the business elites and the sovereign state in London discouraged the circumvention activities of business elites, preserving the colonial state's autonomy vis-à-vis the business sector and upholding its authority as the ultimate power holder in the territory.	The business sector enjoys increased access to the sovereign state in Beijing by virtue of their overwhelming representation in Hong Kong's delegations to the National People's Congress and National Committee of the Chinese People's Political Consultative Conference, closer relations with the Central Liaison Office and intricate economic links with various Mainland authorities. There is a growing tendency of the business sector to influence local politics by directly lobbying the Mainland authorities.
Degree of state autonomy	As a result of the transcendent position of the Governor in the colonial political system and the distant relationship between the capitalist class and the sovereign state in London, the colonial state had maintained significant political leverages vis-à-vis its powerful business allies. It was on these foundations that the colonial state could maintain its considerable degree of state autonomy, thereby successfully resisting the pressures of business capture and performing its role as arbitrator of different class interests if and when it saw the need.	As a result of the institutionalization of business power under the HKSAR political system and the business sector's increased access to the sovereign state in Beijing, the business sector has developed considerable political leverages vis-à-vis the post-colonial state, pushing it into a "crisis of state autonomy". As a result, the post-colonial state's relative autonomy is facing growing challenges from the business sector and therefore it struggles to maintain its role as the arbitrator of class interests.

continued

Table 9.1 Continued

	Before 1997	*After 1997*
Governing coalition building		
The governing coalition of the state and its effectiveness	By simultaneously combining the notions of "state autonomy" with "state embeddedness", the colonial state had engineered and maintained a viable state–business alliance. The existence of such a viable state–business alliance enabled it to consolidate its governance by mobilizing the support of the business sector while preventing the state–business partnership from degenerating into clientelism and cronyism.	Under the combined effects of crisis of state autonomy and crisis of state embeddedness, the state–business alliance has been operated in completely different political and socio-economic environments after 1997. The post-colonial state not only fails to count on its business allies to forge a stable political support base for maintaining its governance, it bears notoriety for collusion with the business sector. The failure of the state–business alliance after 1997 has undermined the popular support base of the HKSAR political order, plunging the post-colonial state into a political quagmire of pervasive public discontent and distrust.

Conclusion 247

outcomes. Incumbents with high organizational power could govern effectively and thwart strong opposition movements through their powerful governing-party organizations, while incumbents with weak organizational power will lack the necessary governing machinery to accommodate even moderate or weak opposition challenges (Levitsky & Way, 2010, p. 25). In this light, the emerging literature calls for a greater appreciation for analysis of governing coalition building so as to develop a more comprehensive understanding of the governance, survival and democratic transition of hybrid regimes.

The above theoretical discussions on hybrid regimes are illuminating to our understanding of the governance crisis in post-1997 Hong Kong. Currently, the *legitimacy deficit thesis* is the most popular explanation adopted by most local political scientists when accounting for Hong Kong's governance crisis after 1997 (e.g. Cheung, 2005a, 2010; Li, 2001; Ma, 2007a; Scott, 2005, 2007; Sing, 2001, 2003, 2009; Tang, 2008). Such a mainstream explanation highlights that the challenges of the democratic opposition have undermined the political legitimacy of the post-colonial state and plunged it into serious governance crisis. To use the words of Levitsky and Way, the *legitimacy deficit thesis* is an opposition-centred explanation which paid too much attention to the role of societal factors but largely overlooked the relevance of organizational weaknesses of the post-colonial state when explaining the governance crisis after 1997. In this sense, the principal limitation of the *legitimacy deficit thesis* is that it has overstated the political influences of the democratic opposition, but in reality the mobilization power of the democrats has actually been restricted by its fragmentation, internal fighting and factional rivalries (Ma, 2007b, 2011) and therefore the opposition movements in post-1997 Hong Kong could not in any way be considered as strong and robust.

If the democratic opposition could only pose moderate political challenges to the post-colonial state, then why does the post-colonial state fail to consolidate its governance and resist the challenges of the democrats? As argued by Levitsky and Way, if the opposition challenges are not strong enough, then the utility of opposition-centred explanation should be quite limited in accounting for regime outcomes and it is more important to examine the issue by looking at the robustness of the state (Levitsky & Way, 2010, p. 56). In this regard, this book had made an important original contribution to local political literature by going beyond the existing opposition-centred explanation as emphasized by theorists of legitimacy deficit and offers an alternative theoretical perspective to broaden and enrich our understanding of the governance crisis in post-1997 Hong Kong.

Building upon the *governing coalition thesis* as pioneered by Lau Siu-kai (Lau, 2000, 2002) and drawing upon the contemporary literature on governance and state capacity (Evans, 1995, 1997; Pierre & Peters, 2000; Weiss, 1998), this book develops an *integrated conceptual framework*, which is termed as "state capacity as governing coalition building", to re-examine Hong Kong's governance crisis under Chinese sovereignty. The central contention of this book is that the origin of the post-1997 governance crisis goes deeper and beyond the *legitimacy deficit thesis* because the failure of the post-colonial state to organize a viable governing coalition has already set the scene for the governance crisis.

248 *Rethinking Hong Kong's governance*

The empirical findings of this book showed that as a consequence of the crisis of state embeddedness and crisis of state autonomy, the state–business alliance as engineered by the Chinese government has been operated in completely different political and socio-economic environments after 1997 and it has already become more of a political burden than a political asset for the post-colonial state. The failure of the state–business alliance pointed to the fact that the post-colonial state does not have the necessary organizational machinery to resist the relatively moderate opposition movements of the pro-democracy camp. Because of its failure to engineer a viable governing coalition that could maintain elite cohesion, mediate different socio-economic constituents and accommodate opposition challenges, the post-colonial state has always been exposed to political challenges from all fronts in the governing process and finds it difficult to forge a stable political support base for maintaining effective governance.

While this book has highlighted the importance of governing coalition building for understanding Hong Kong's governance under Chinese sovereignty, we are not entirely denying the significance of the opposition-centred explanation currently adopted by theorists of legitimacy deficit. By emphasizing the concepts of political legitimacy and democratization, the *legitimacy deficit thesis* has made important contributions in accounting for the implications of constitutional reforms and local democratic movements since the 1980s. Its major limitation is that it has overstated the political challenges of the democratic opposition but under-explored the vulnerability of the post-colonial state. Instead of just focusing on opposition-centred factors, this book project has broadened the scope of existing local literature by examining the vulnerability and fragility of the post-colonial state in the contexts of changing state–business and state–society relationships. From this perspective, the theoretical conclusion of this book is that the post-1997 governance crisis cannot be purely explained in terms of democratic transition and legitimacy deficit – a critical analysis of governing coalition is equally, if not more, important in understanding Hong Kong's governance under Chinese sovereignty. In order to provide a more comprehensive account of the hybrid politics of the HKSAR, the critical analysis of governing coalition building should be combined with the opposition-centred explanation so as to examine the changing balance of powers between the post-colonial state and the democratic opposition.

The way out for Hong Kong's governance: in search of a new political order

> [T]he state's policy capacity has deteriorated in postcolonial Hong Kong due to the gradual deinstitutionalization and disarticulation of the political system, which has seriously weakened the SAR regime's capacity to steer society and the economy.... Rebuilding this capacity will require political legitimation through constitutional reform and the re-establishment of strategic linkages through inclusive governance.
>
> (Cheung, 2005b)

Conclusion 249

The alternative theoretical explanation put forth by this book not only offers novel interpretations of the governance crisis in post-1997 Hong Kong, it is also useful in shedding new insights on the possible solutions to the present political impasse.

Local political scientists generally agree that implementation of universal suffrage is the most effective way to rebuild Hong Kong's governance. Implicit in this contention is not only the moral expectations for establishing a full democratic regime in Hong Kong, but also its close connection with the *legitimacy deficit thesis*: the legitimacy crisis induced by the challenges of the democratic opposition is regarded as the principal factor that undermines the governing capacity of the post-colonial state and such a crisis could only be resolved completely by implementing universal suffrage for both the Chief Executive and the Legislative Council elections (e.g. Cheung, 2010; Ma, 2007a; Scott, 2007; Sing, 2009).

While there is no doubt that the implementation of universal suffrage is conducive to restoring its political legitimacy, the post-colonial state may not be able to ride out of the present governance crisis unless it could simultaneously re-establish a viable governing coalition to enhance its governing capacity. Conceptually, while the level of political legitimacy may shape the governing capacity of modern states, political scientists are of the view that it is necessary for both the democratic and authoritarian states to establish a strong political support base for consolidating its governance by forging a viable governing coalition with the major socio-economic actors (e.g. Bueno de Mesquita *et al.*, 2003, pp. 49–55; Pierre & Peters, 2000, pp. 98–100). From this perspective, it will be overly simplistic for us to assume that once universal suffrage for the Chief Executive and Legislative Council elections have been implemented the post-colonial state could re-establish strong and effective governance automatically, because the introduction of popular elections alone could not in any way guarantee that a viable governing coalition will also be put in place. Given our contention that the post-1997 governance crisis does not emanate merely from legitimacy deficit but was also contributed by the failure of the state–business alliance, rebuilding Hong Kong's governance needs fundamental reforms on both the fronts of implementing universal suffrage[1] (for restoring the political legitimacy of the post-colonial state) and governing coalition building (for re-engineering the strategic linkages between the post-colonial state and major socio-economic constituents).

In this connection, the existing state–business alliance, which originated in the colonial time and was adopted by the Chinese government during the transitional period, has become increasingly incompatible with the new political and socio-economic environments in Hong Kong today. As Hong Kong has evolved into a pluralistic polity (Fong, 2008), in order to consolidate its governing capacity the post-colonial state is increasingly required to forge a new governing coalition which is not just focused on the narrow business-professional interests but should also be encompassed by a wider range of political and socio-economic constituents. Therefore, the most imperative governance challenge

250 *Rethinking Hong Kong's governance*

facing the post-colonial state is how to purse a more inclusive style of governance by forging coalitions not only with its traditional business allies but also with newly emerged institutional and societal stakeholders. In order to re-engineer such a new governing coalition for supporting its governance, fundamental reforms are necessary to strengthen both the state autonomy and state embeddedness of the post-colonial Hong Kong state.

Strengthening state embeddedness: rebuilding the institutionalized negotiation mechanism and encompassing intermediaries

One of the structural problems of the existing state–business alliance is that the post-colonial state fails to engage in institutionalized negotiation and cooperation with the major socio-economic interests in its policy-making process, thus the post-colonial state has become continually embroiled in conflicts with different stakeholders when putting forward its policy agenda. As illustrated in this book, the erosion of the embeddedness of the post-colonial state after 1997 is closely connected to the fragmentation of agents of business interests and the growing disconnection of co-opted business elites from the local community.

The first important way to strengthen the state embeddedness of the post-colonial state is to re-organize the Executive Council as the core "institutionalized negotiation mechanism" between the post-colonial state and the major political and socio-economic constituents. During the British colonial time, the Executive Council had effectively functioned as the most important platform for mediating business interests and was the foundation of the state–business alliance. After the handover, business elites still occupy the majority of seats in the Executive Council, symbolizing the political alliance between the post-colonial state and the business sector. In accordance with Articles 55 and 56 of the Basic Law, members of the Executive Council should be appointed by the Chief Executive from among principal officials, legislators and social leaders and the government shall consult the Executive Council before making important policy decisions and introducing legislative proposals to the Legislative Council. The constitutional design of the Executive Council therefore provides the potential for it to develop into a core platform for forging a more broad-based governing coalition between the post-colonial state and the major stakeholders. By appointing not just business elites and leftist figures but also representatives from major political parties and civil society (including pro-democracy parties and organizations) as members of the Executive Council and formulating its policy agenda together with its coalition partners before introducing it to the Legislative Council, the Executive Council shall be able to resume its function as an institutionalized negotiation mechanism.

Another important way to strengthen the state embeddedness of the post-colonial state is to cultivate political parties to fulfil the role of "encompassing intermediates" between the state and the major socio-economic interests. In the colonial era, the effective functioning of the Executive Council as the foundation of the state–business alliance was facilitated the existence of major British

Conclusion 251

hongs, which acted as the encompassing intermediaries bridging the gap between the colonial state and the business sector. After 1997 the fragmentation of agents of business interests has already made it difficult for the post-colonial state to articulate and reconcile business interests, while other political parties are also underdeveloped and weak in terms of their representativeness, resources and mobilization power (Ma, 2007b). For comparative theorists, political parties play the essential role of interest articulation and are critical to the stability and smooth functioning of both democratic and authoritarian regimes (Levitsky & Way, 2010, p. 25). From this perspective, no matter whether Hong Kong could put in place an institution of popular elections and an overarching governing party,[2] development of party politics is necessary because more mature political parties could help fill in the missing link between the post-colonial state and the major political and socio-economic constituents. Reforming the proportional representation electoral system,[3] enacting party law and providing more generous public funding could all help nurture political parties in Hong Kong. If the existing fragmented political parties could be re-constituted into three or four major parties and a "coalition government" could be established by appointing the representatives of these major parties into the Executive Council, it will enable the post-colonial state to re-embed itself into the socio-economic structure and foster its institutionalized cooperation with the major political and societal constituents.

Strengthening state autonomy: rebuilding the governing authority of the Chief Executive

Another major structural problem of the existing state–business alliance is that the post-colonial state struggles to preserve its relative autonomy and resist the undue demands of its business allies, thus the post-colonial state's impartiality and transcendence above the powerful business interests have become increasingly untenable in the post-1997 period. As illustrated by this book, the erosion of the autonomy of the post-colonial state after 1997 is closely connected to the institutionalization of business power under the HKSAR political system and the business sector's increased access to the sovereign state in Beijing.

In this connection, the implementation of universal suffrage for the Chief Executive and Legislative Council elections is undoubtedly important, because it will prevent the business sector from exercising undue influence over the post-colonial state through the Chief Executive Election Committee and the functional constituencies. Yet, the introduction of popular elections is necessary but not sufficient to restore the relative autonomy of the post-colonial state vis-à-vis the business sector. On the one hand, it is comprehensible that the business sector may still manipulate the nomination of Chief Executive candidates for popular elections by virtue of their dominant position in the future Chief Executive Nomination Committee. On the other hand, the close partnership between Beijing and the local capitalists may continue to provide a more direct and privileged channel for the business elites to challenge the governing authority of the

252   *Rethinking Hong Kong's governance*

post-colonial state. Thus, even if universal suffrage could be fully implemented in the future it is inconceivable that the post-colonial state could effectively maintain a cohesive governing coalition if its coalition partners are still given some sort of "king-making powers" through the future Chief Executive Nomination Committee as well as the opportunity to resort to their sympathetic ears either in Beijing or in the local Central Liaison Office. From this perspective, the reduction of the nomination threshold in the Chief Executive Nomination Committee as well as reconstitution of the relationship between Beijing and the business sector are of paramount importance so that the Chief Executive can restore its role as the final arbitrator of Hong Kong's affairs and make himself the real power centre of any possible governing coalition in the territory.

Governing coalition building in the new era: where is the window of opportunity for the new political order?

The above discussions point to the conclusion that the implementation of universal suffrage is a necessary but insufficient solution to the governance crisis facing the post-colonial state. What Hong Kong needs is a complete overhaul of its existing political order so that the post-colonial state could not only re-establish its political legitimacy through popular elections, but could also re-engineer a new governing coalition to cope with the different governance challenges under the present-day political and socio-economic environments.

However, it is comprehensible that the window of opportunity to revamp Hong Kong's political order, in particular re-engineering a new viable governing coalition, remains remote in the foreseeable future. The answer is obvious: the pre-existing state–business alliance is closely connected to Beijing's interpretation of Hong Kong affairs and its governing strategy in the HKSAR, and therefore any realignment of a new governing coalition requires a fundamental review of Beijing's policy towards Hong Kong. For example, the reorganization of the Executive Council as the institutionalized negotiation mechanism between the post-colonial state and the major political and societal stakeholders needs to obtain the blessing of Beijing on having some forms of power-sharing with those pro-democratic political parties and civil society groups, who the Chinese government today still considers as hostile political forces. The further development of party politics (e.g. the establishment of a coalition government between the Chief Executive and the major political parties) requires a drastic change in Beijing's leaders' attitude towards political parties and executive–legislative relations. The re-instatement of the Chief Executive's role as the final arbitrator of local Hong Kong affairs also requires the Chinese government and its local agencies to refrain themselves from intervening in the local issues in the HKSAR and to fully respect the principle of the "high degree of autonomy" that Hong Kong should have enjoyed under the framework of "one country, two systems".

As a consequence, unless there are material changes to some basic principles of the Chinese government's Hong Kong policy, it is inconceivable that the pre-existing state–business alliance as well as the whole post-1997 political order

Conclusion 253

could be revamped in the near future. If this is the case, it is quite likely that Hong Kong will continue to be trapped in a crisis of governance in the years to come.

Comparing Hong Kong with other East Asian hybrid regimes: lessons from the case of Hong Kong and future research agenda

> [T]he hybrid regime category contains two fundamental and readily distinguishable sub-types: liberal authoritarianism and electoral authoritarianism.... Hong Kong's politics approximate liberal authoritarianism, with civil liberties mostly respected, but electoral competitiveness tightly restricted, especially for the topmost office chief executive.
>
> (Case, 2008)

"Hybrid regimes", which can be defined as political systems combining both democratic and authoritarian elements, have attracted the attention of Western political scientists in recently years (Diamond, 2002). This new wave of scholarly attention and academic debate are attributable to the fact that many hybrid regimes do not evolve in the direction of full democratization as previously predicted by political scientists, but have remained stable over a very long period of time. There are generally two types of hybrid regimes: liberal authoritarianism refers to political regimes where civil liberties are to a large extent respected but competitive electoral system are generally absent; electoral authoritarianism refers to political regimes where a system of regular multiparty elections has been put in place, but civil liberties and opposition activities are largely suppressed by the government (mCase, 1996, 2008; O'Donnell & Schmitter, 1986). Comparative theorists have long recognized that hybrid regimes are intrinsically unstable because the coexistence of democratic and authoritarian elements within a single political system would usually be an inherent source of political conflicts.

In the context of comparative political studies, Hong Kong is an interesting example of a hybrid regime. With a high degree of civil liberties but limited electoral franchise (only half of the seats in the legislature is elected by popular elections, but the head of the executive is hand-picked by the Chinese government), Hong Kong is a special type of liberal authoritarian regime featuring some electoral authoritarian elements (Case, 2008).

This book has re-examined the governance crisis in post-1997 Hong Kong within the theoretical construct of hybrid regimes. As a typical case of hybrid regime, the empirical findings of this book have certain theoretical implications for the study of contemporary hybrid regimes. First of all, the case study of Hong Kong speaks to the emerging literature on hybrid regimes. The latest literature on hybrid regimes has demonstrated that the robustness of the states and their governing-party organizations will largely determine whether the authoritarian incumbents could survive and consolidate their rule amidst opposition

254 *Rethinking Hong Kong's governance*

challenges (e.g. Brownlee, 2007; Levitsky & Way, 2010; Slater, 2010; Smith, 2005). From this perspective, this book has provided another good case study to validate the analysis of such emerging literature. Despite the fact that the challenges from the democratic opposition and civil society groups are only moderate, the failure of the state–business alliance in the post-1997 period has made the hybrid regime in Hong Kong increasingly vulnerable and ungovernable. In this sense, the study of hybrid politics in Hong Kong has made a contribution to the emerging literature and has illustrated the utility of its theoretical propositions in the East Asian contexts. Second, this book project has presented a new *integrated conceptual framework* (which is termed as "state capacity as governing coalition building") for examining and interpreting the governing coalition building under hybrid regimes. By drawing upon the contemporary literature on governance and state capacity (Evans, 1995, 1997; Pierre & Peters, 2000; Weiss, 1998), the *integrated conceptual framework* has highlighted the strategic linkages of state autonomy, state embeddedness and governing coalition building. This *integrated conceptual framework* has therefore offered a new theoretical perspective to examine the functioning and robustness of governing coalitions under hybrid regimes.

The above theoretical discussions have pointed to a new research agenda on comparing Hong Kong with other East Asian hybrid regimes. East Asia is a region where different types of non-Western democratic regimes could be found, including flawed democracies (Indonesia, Thailand and the Philippines), communist states (China, Vietnam and Laos), absolute monarchy (Brunei), military governments (Burma) and also hybrid regimes (Singapore and Malaysia). The existing local political literature has seldom compared Hong Kong with other East Asian states in the contexts of hybrid politics or authoritarian stability.[4] As far as academic research is concerned, comparative studies on the hybrid regimes of Hong Kong and other East Asian states is a relatively new area awaiting further intellectual exploration and development.

From this perspective, it would be particularly useful to compare the hybrid politics of Hong Kong, Singapore and Malaysia (Table 9.2). As this book demonstrates, Hong Kong's hybrid regime has become increasingly vulnerable and ungovernable after 1997 because the post-colonial Hong Kong state could only rely on a vulnerable state–business alliance to maintain its governance. As a consequence of the failure of the state–business alliance, the post-colonial state lacks the necessary organizational power to thwart the opposition challenges and has been embroiled in continuous challenges from all fronts in the governing process. Unlike Hong Kong, the hybrid regimes in both Singapore and Malaysia have demonstrated much stronger capacity in consolidating governance and resisting opposition challenges. It is comprehensible that the robustness of the hybrid regimes in Singapore and Malaysia is closely connected to their stronger governing-party organizations, i.e. the People's Action Party in Singapore and the National Front in Malaysia (the multi-ethnic party coalition formed by the United Malays National Organization, the Malaysian Chinese Association and Malayan Indian Congress). Both the People's Action Party and the National

Table 9.2 A brief comparison of the hybrid politics in Hong Kong, Singapore and Malaysia

	Hong Kong	*Singapore*	*Malaysia*
Type of hybrid regime	Liberal authoritarianism (with limited electoral franchise)	Electoral authoritarianism	Electoral authoritarianism
Degree of competitive election	The electoral franchise is limited, with only half of the seats in the legislature elected by popular elections. The Chief Executive is hand picked by the Chinese government.	Competitive elections are held regularly, but opposition parties have been suppressed by the incumbent through media control, law suits and manipulation of electoral rules.	Competitive elections are held regularly, but opposition parties have been seriously hobbled by the incumbent through media control, dirty tricks and manipulation of electoral systems.
Degree of civil liberty	There exists a vibrant civil society and high degree of civil liberty.	Civil participation has been strictly regulated by the government.	Certain liberal participations are permitted but debates on sensitive issues are still restricted
Governing coalition building	The state relies on a non-cohesive alliance with the business sector to maintain its governance.	The state is supported by the People's Action Party which is an institutionalized party with mass organizations and close connections with bureaucratic and military apparatuses.	The state is supported by the The National Front (Barisan Nasional), which is a multi-ethnic party coalition formed by the United Malays National Organization, the Malaysian Chinese Association and Malayan Indian Congress.
State of governance	The state has been trapped in governance crisis after 1997 and exposed to challenges from all fronts in the policy process.	The state has managed to maintain stable governance and control opposition challenges, despite the growing public grievances about economic inequalities in recent years.	The state has managed to consolidate its governance and resist opposition challenges, despite the emergence of the Reformasi Movement in recent years.

256   *Rethinking Hong Kong's governance*

Front have furnished their authoritarian incumbents with the necessary organizational power to consolidate their governance despite the increasing challenges of the opposition parties in recent years (Dayley & Neher, 2010; Lee & Nesadurai, 2010).

Obviously, a thorough comparison of hybrid politics of Hong Kong and other East Asian countries goes beyond the scope of this book and indeed it should be an important future research agenda for political scientists. In particular, it is worth examining the enabling conditions that contribute to the relatively smooth functioning of the People's Action Party in Singapore and the National Front in Malaysia and comparing these experiences with the failure of the state–business alliance in Hong Kong. From this perspective, this book not only promotes more theoretical reflections about the state of governance in Hong Kong, but also paves the way for the further development of comparative studies on East Asian hybrid regimes.

Conclusion

This chapter summarizes the central arguments of this book by articulating our alternative theoretical perspective to post-1997 Hong Kong's governance crisis. In applying the *integrated conceptual framework* we have made a three-step argument. First, as a result of the fragmentation of agents of business interests and the growing disconnection of co-opted business elites from the community, the post-colonial state is plunging into a crisis of state embeddedness and it struggles to forge societal acceptance for delivering policy changes. Second, because of the institutionalization of business power under the HKSAR political system and the business sector's increased access to the sovereign state in Beijing, the post-colonial state is plunged into a crisis of state autonomy and its relative autonomy is facing growing challenges from the business sector. Third, under the combined effects of crises of state autonomy and state embeddedness, the post-colonial state has been plunged into a political quagmire of pervasive public discontent and distrust, resulting in the lingering of the governance crisis in the post-1997 period. As a consequence, after 1997 the state–business alliance not only fails to function as an organizational machinery for supporting the post-colonial state, it provides fertile ground for breeding new governance problems.

Since the colonial time, the political order of Hong Kong has been built upon the foundation of a state–business alliance. The effective functioning of the colonial state–business alliance prompted the Chinese government to believe that it could adopt the same political formula to govern Hong Kong after 1997. By keeping the configuration of the state–business alliance largely intact, the Beijing leaders have ignored the fact that the effective operation of the state–business alliance in colonial Hong Kong was actually built upon the unique political and socio-economic environment before 1997.

In the British colonial time, the high concentration of economic powers, the closed nature of the colonial political system and the underdevelopment of civil society were all important structural factors that made the major British hongs

Conclusion 257

and the prestigious local Chinese capitalists the dominant societal force. As a consequence, it would not be difficult for the colonial state to forge a solid political support base for its governance by forming a political alliance with these major economic constituents. In addition, the colonial Governor's unrivalled political authority, monopoly of patronage powers and its authority as the ultimate power holder in the territory had all helped make sure that the colonial state's transcendence over different interests would not be challenged by its powerful business allies. These were all unique enabling conditions that made the formula of governing through state–business alliance workable in colonial Hong Kong.

Unfortunately, when they crafted the post-1997 political order during the transitional period, Beijing's leaders had generally overlooked that Hong Kong has been undergoing political and socio-economic transformation since the 1980s and the various enabling conditions that allowed a viable state–business alliance in the colonial time had been gradually changed. As a consequence of the growing diversification of the business sector, the gradual opening up of the political system and rising civil society activism, the HKSAR Chief Executive could no longer govern Hong Kong by simply co-opting individual business and professional elites into his governing coalition as in the colonial past. To maintain effective governance in present-day Hong Kong, the post-colonial state needs a more organized political machinery to consolidate the support of its business allies and to overcome the possible challenges of the democratic opposition and civil society. Ironically, the post-1997 state–business alliance not only fails to function as an organizational machinery for supporting the post-colonial state, it even creates new governance problems such as intra-elite conflicts, increasing public suspicion of government–business collusion and aggravation of class conflicts.

To conclude, the state–business alliance the post-colonial state has inherited is a product of outdated and conservative political thought, which was derived from Hong Kong's mode of governance during the heyday of British colonial rule. As illustrated by this book, although the formula of state–business alliance was once a solution for the colonial state in the past, it is now a problem for the post-colonial state. To restore effective governance in Hong Kong the whole political order in the territory has to be revamped so as to enable the post-colonial state to rebuild its governing capacity. Without a realignment of a new governing coalition in the HKSAR, the post-colonial state will continuously be trapped in a crisis of governance in the years to come.

Notes

1 It is worth noting the implementation of universal suffrage may not completely resolve the legitimacy deficit of the post-colonial state. While the Standing Committee of the National People's Congress has decided a "timetable for universal suffrage" in December 2007 (i.e. Hong Kong may implement universal suffrage for Chief Executive election in 2017 and for Legislative Council election in 2020), there are suspicions within the democratic camp and the society that the Chinese government may "manipulate"

258　*Rethinking Hong Kong's governance*

the popular elections of Chief Executive by screening candidates from the democracy camp through the mechanism of a nominating committee under Article 45 of the Basic Law. In the event that the Chinese government only allow Hong Kong to implement a universal suffrage devoid of substance, it is likely that the introduction of popular elections will not bring about a full democratic regime and Hong Kong will only be evolved from a "liberal authoritarian regime with limited electoral elements" into an "electoral authoritarian regime" (see Levitsky & Way, 2002, 2010; Schedler, 2002). If this is the case, while the formal democratic institutions may exist in Hong Kong after 2017, the Chinese government will make the playing field heavily skewed in favour of pro-Beijing political forces and the inherent political tensions and legitimacy deficit under the hybrid regime may remain unresolved.

2 It is well-known that the Chinese government does not want to see vibrant party politics in Hong Kong and has always been unfavourable towards the formation of a governing party (Ma, 2007b). For Beijing's leaders a strong ruling party with mass support and deep roots in society would be difficult to control and might nurture populist local politicians who can confront the central authorities by mobilizing public support in Hong Kong. Rather, the Chinese government is more inclined to a bipartisan Chief Executive who brokers interests between various local political forces (Ma, 2007a, p. 141). In line with Beijing's leaders' anti-party stance, the Chief Executive Election Ordinance stipulates that the Chief Executive could not be a member of a political party. It is comprehensible that even if the Chinese government introduces universal suffrage to Hong Kong, it may not allow the Chief Executive to develop an overarching governing party.

3 Research indicates that the existing proportional representation electoral system has resulted in the fragmentation of political parties. Adopting the Largest Remainder Formula and the Hare Quota, the existing proportional representation system encourages smaller parties and independents to run and forces the large parties to split their lists in order to increase their chance of winning the last seat. All of these in effect weakened instead of increasing party centralization (Ma, 2007a, p. 145).

4 An important exception is William Case's article in 2008 which compared the hybrid politics of Hong Kong and Singapore (Case, 2008).

References

Beissinger, M. R. (2002). *Nationalist mobilization and the collapse of the Soviet State.* New York: Cambridge University Press.

Bratton, M., & van de Walle, N. (1997). *Democratic experiments in Africa: Regime transitions in comparative perspective.* New York: Cambridge University Press.

Brownlee, J. (2007). *Authoritarianism in an age of democratization.* New York: Cambridge University Press.

Bueno de Mesquita, B., Smith, A., Siverson, R. M., & Morrow, J. D. (2003). *The logic of political survival.* Cambridge, MA: MIT Press.

Case, W. (1996). Can the 'halfway house' stand? Semidemocracy and elite theory in three Southeast Asian countries. *Comparative Politics, 28*(4), 437–464.

Case, W. (2008). Hybrid politics and new competitiveness: Hong Kong's 2007 Chief Executive Election. *East Asia, 25*(4), 365–388.

Cheung, A. (2005a). Hong Kong's post-1997 institutional crisis: Problems of governance and institutional incompatibility. *Journal of East Asian Studies, 5*(1), 135–167.

Cheung, A. (2005b). State capacity in Hong Kong, Singapore and Taiwan: Coping with legitimation, integration and performance. In M. Painter & J. Pierre (Eds.), *Challenges to state policy capacity: Global trends and comparative perspective* (pp. 225–254). New York: Palgrave Macmillan.

Cheung, A. (2010). In search of trust and legitimacy: The political trajectory of Hong Kong as part of China. *International Public Management Review, 11*(2), 38–63.

Collier, R. B. (1999). *Pathways toward democracy: The working class and elites in Western Europe and Latin America.* New York: Cambridge University Press.

Dayley, R., & Neher, C. D. (2010). *Southeast Asia in the new international era* (5th ed.). Boulder, CO: Westview Press.

Diamond, L. (1999). *Developing democracy: Toward consolidation.* Baltimore, MD: Johns Hopkins University Press.

Diamond, L. (2002). Thinking about hybrid regimes. *Journal of Democracy, 13*(2), 21–35.

Evans, P. B. (1995). *Embedded autonomy: States and industrial transformation.* Princeton, NJ: Princeton University Press.

Evans, P. B. (1997). Government action, social capital, and development: Reviewing the evidence on synergy. In P. Evans (Ed.), *State–society synergy: Government and social capital in development* (pp. 178–209). Berkeley, CA: University of California at Berkeley.

Fish, M. S. (1995). *Democracy from scratch: Opposition and regime in the new Russian revolution.* Princeton, NJ: Princeton University Press.

Fong, B. (2008). An analysis of the 2003 "Zero-Three-Three" civil service pay reduction settlement in Hong Kong: A neopluralist perspective. *Asian Profile, 36*(6), 559–580.

Lau, S. K. (2000). The executive-dominant system of governance: Theory and practice. In S. K. Lau (Ed.), *Blueprint for the 21st century Hong Kong* (pp. 1–36). Hong Kong: Chinese University Press (in Chinese).

Lau, S. K. (2002). Tung Chee-hwa's governing strategy: The shortfall in politics. In S. K. Lau (Ed.), *The first Tung Chee-hwa administration* (pp. 1–39). Hong Kong: Chinese University Press.

Lee, H. G., & Nesadurai, H. E. S. (2010). Political transition in Malaysia: The future of Malaysia's hybrid political regime. In M. Caballero-Anthony (Ed.), *Political change, democratic transitions and security in Southeast Asia* (pp. 95–123). New York: Routledge.

Levitsky, S., & Way, L. A. (2002). The rise of competitive authoritarianism. *Journal of Democracy, 13*(2), 51–65.

Levitsky, S., & Way, L. A. (2010). *Competitive authoritarianism: Hybrid regimes after the Cold War.* New York: Cambridge University Press.

Li, P. K. (2001). The executive–legislature relationship in Hong Kong: Evolution and development. In J. Y. S. Cheng (Ed.), *Political development in the HKSAR* (pp. 85–100). Hong Kong: City University of Hong Kong.

Lui, T. L., & Chiu, S. W. K. (2009). *Hong Kong: Becoming a Chinese global city.* London: Routledge.

Ma, N. (2007a). *Political development in Hong Kong: State, political society and civil society.* Hong Kong: Hong Kong University Press.

Ma, N. (2007b). Democratic development in Hong Kong: A decade of lost opportunities. In J. Y. S. Cheng (Ed.), *The Hong Kong Special Administrative Region in its first decade* (pp. 49–74). Hong Kong: City University of Hong Kong Press.

Ma, N. (2011). Hong Kong's democrats' divide. *Journal of Democracy, 22*(1), 54–67.

Miliband, R. (1969). *The state in capitalist society.* New York: Basic Books.

Miliband, R. (1977). *Marxism and politics.* Oxford: Oxford University Press.

Nordlinger, E. A. (1981). *On the autonomy of the democratic state.* Cambridge, MA: Harvard University Press.

260   *Rethinking Hong Kong's governance*

O'Donnell, G., & Schmitter, P. C. (1986). *Transitions from authoritarian rule: Tentative conclusions about uncertain democracies*. Baltimore, MD: Johns Hopkins University Press.

Peters, B. G. (1995). Introducing the topic. In B. G. Peters, & D. J. Savoie (Eds.), *Governance in a changing environment* (pp. 3–22). Buffalo: McGill-Queen's University Press.

Pierre, J., & Peters, G. (2000). *Governance, politics and the state*. New York: St. Martin's Press.

Schedler, A. (2002). The menu of manipulation. *Journal of Democracy, 13*(2), 36–50.

Scott, I. (2005). *Public administration in Hong Kong: Regime change and its impact on the public sector*. Singapore: Marshall Cavendish International.

Scott, I. (2007). Legitimacy, governance and public policy in post-1997 Hong Kong. *Asia Pacific Journal of Public Administration, 29*(1), 29–49.

Sing, M. (2001). The problem of legitimacy for the post-1997 Hong Kong government. *International Journal of Public Administration, 24*(9), 847–867.

Sing, M. (2003). Legislative–executive interface in Hong Kong. In C. Loh, & Civic Exchange (Eds.), *Building democracy: Creating good government for Hong Kong* (pp. 27–34). Hong Kong: Hong Kong University Press.

Sing, M. (2009). Hong Kong at the crossroads: Public pressure for democratic reform. In M. Sing (Ed.), *Politics and government in Hong Kong: Crisis under Chinese sovereignty* (pp. 112–135). Hong Kong: Hong Kong University Press.

Skocpol, T. (1985). Bringing the state back in: Strategies of analysis in current research. In P. B. Evans, D. Rueschemeyer, & T. Skocpol (Eds.), *Bringing the state back in* (pp. 3–37). Cambridge: Cambridge University Press.

Slater, D. (2010). *Ordering power: Contentious politics and authoritarian leviathans in Southeast Asia*. Cambridge: Cambridge University Press.

Smith, B. (2005). Life of the party: The origins of regime breakdown and persistence under single-party rule. *World Politics, 57*(3), 421–451.

Tang, J. (2008). Hong Kong's continuing search for a new order: Political stability in a partial democracy. In C. McGiffert, & J. T. H. Tang (Ed.), *Hong Kong on the move: 10 years as the HKSAR* (pp. 18–36). Berkeley, CA: University of California at Berkeley.

Weiss, L. (1998). *The myth of the powerless state: Governing the economy in a global era*. Cambridge: Polity Press.

Wood, E. J. (2000). *Forging democracy from below: Insurgent transitions in South Africa and El Salvador*. New York: Cambridge University Press.

Epilogue

Hong Kong's governance in the aftermath of the 2012 Chief Executive election: governing coalition built on sand

After 15 years of governance under the Tung Chee-hwa and Donald Tsang Administrations, the 2012 HKSAR Chief Executive election turned a new page in Hong Kong's politics. The election was an unprecedented three-way race with the two pro-government candidates – the former Chief Secretary Henry Tang Ying-yen and the former Convenor of the Executive Council Leung Chun-ying – fighting fiercely against each other, and the no-hoper Albert Ho Chun-yan from the pro-democracy camp running to press for constitutional reforms (*The Standard*, 2012a, 1 March). The result of the election held on 25 March 2012 was seen as a "divisive poll": within the 1,200-member Chief Executive Election Committee, Leung Chun-ying received 689 votes, Henry Tang received 285 votes, Albert Ho received 76 votes and 82 papers were declared invalid (*South China Morning Post*, 2011a, 8 April).

Leung Chun-ying's electoral victory over Henry Tang was certainly unexpected by many politicians and political pundits in Hong Kong. At the beginning of the electoral contest, Henry Tang was the forerunner because he had been groomed by the Chinese government for the position of Chief Executive for decades.[1] Henry Tang was also seen as the favourite candidate of the major business tycoons and the senior civil servants and is the icon of the existing state–business alliance (*Bloomberg*, 2011, 28 September). It was comprehensible that the original plan of the Chinese government was to hand-pick Henry Tang as the next HKSAR Chief Executive (*South China Morning Post*, 2011b, 20 September), while Leung Chun-ying was only allowed to enter the race for the purpose of creating a stronger sense of competition in the electoral process (*Ming Pao*, 2011, 24 September).

Unexpectedly, the Chinese government was forced to revisit its succession plan when Henry Tang's popularity ratings and creditability were severely undermined by an unauthorized building works scandal.[2] As a consequence of the scandal, the Chinese government found it politically infeasible to stick to its original plan to hand-pick Henry Tang because to choose a scandal-plagued candidate as the Chief Executive would only result in widespread public anger in Hong Kong (*Reuters*, 2012, 22 February). Given that Henry Tang had already become an unelectable candidate and scuttling the poll would only create further political uncertainty,[3] the remaining option for the stability-obsessed Chinese

262 *Rethinking Hong Kong's governance*

government was to throw its support behind Leung Chun-ying, who commanded a higher level of popular support in various public opinion polls.[4] In making its final decision to hand-pick Leung Chun-ying instead of Henry Tang as the next HKSAR Chief Executive, the Chinese government seemed to be opting for damage control rather than seeking deliberately to change its longstanding policy to govern Hong Kong through the state–business alliance.[5]

Against this background, after the Chief Executive election Beijing leaders have immediately called for "grand reconciliation" (*Da Hejie*) within the pro-government camp. Obviously, the Chinese government wanted the new Chief Executive Leung Chun-ying, similar to his two predecessors Tung Chee-hwa and Donald Tsang, to continue to govern Hong Kong through a political alliance of business elites, senior civil servants and pro-Beijing leftists. The intention of Beijing's leaders was clearly reflected in the organization of Leung Chun-ying's governing coalition. As in the past, Leung Chun-ying's political team is a mixture of political ministers of the former administration, senior civil servants, business elites and professionals (Table E.1), while the unofficial members of its Executive Council mainly comprises business leaders, professionals and representatives of major pro-government political parties (Table E.2). In other words, Leung Chun-ying is expected to continue to govern Hong Kong through a political alliance dominated by business elites and senior civil servants while the pro-Beijing leftists continue to serve as minority partners.

Unfortunately, the Chinese government's game plan suffered another setback because the post-election developments clearly demonstrate that Leung Chun-ying's governing coalition is a much more vulnerable and incohesive governing

Table E.1 Background analysis of political officials under the Leung Chun-ying Administration

Occupational background	Leung Chun-ying Administration	
	No.	%
Political ministers of former administration	14	34.1
Civil service and public organizations	8	19.5
Politicians	2	4.9
Business	2	4.9
Profession	5	12.2
Higher education	3	7.3
Social services	4	9.8
Labour	0	0.0
Media and culture	3	7.3
Total	41	100.0

Source: Author's own research based on the background information of the political appointees announced by the HKSAR government.

Note
This background analysis covers those political ministers (i.e. Senior Secretaries, Secretaries, Under Secretaries and Political Assistants) appointed by Leung Chun-ying from July 2012 to December 2013.

Epilogue 263

Table E.2 List of unofficial members of the Executive Council appointed by Leung Chun-ying in 2012

Name	Occupation background
Lam Woon-kwong (Convenor)	Chairperson of the Equal Opportunities Commission
Bernard Charnwut Chan	President of Asia Financial Holdings Co. Ltd.
Cha Shih May-lung	Former Vice Chairman of the China Securities Regulatory
Chow Chung-kong	Chairman of the Hong Kong General Chamber of Commerce
Cheung Chun-yuen	Chairman of the Hong Kong Mercantile Exchange
Cheng Yiu-tong	Honorary President of the Hong Kong Federation of Trade Unions
Cheung Chi-kong	Executive Director of One Country Two Systems Research Institute
Cheung Hok-ming	Legislative Councillor
Li Kwok-cheung	Emeritus Professor of Surgery of Chinese University of Hong Kong
Liao Cheung-sing	Senior Counsel
Law Fan Chiu-fun	Hong Kong Deputy to the National People's Congress of the People's Republic of China
Lam Fan-keung	Former Senior Portfolio Manager at UBS Global Asset Management
Lee Wai-king	Legislative Councillor
Wu Hung-yuk	Management consultant

Source: Information Services Department (2012), *ExCo Membership Announced*, Press Release on 29 June 2012 (www.info.gov.hk/gia/general/201206/29/P201206290526.htm).

coalition when compared with his two predecessors. Not the favourite candidate of the major business tycoons and the senior civil servants, Leung Chun-ying so far has failed to repair rifts within the state–business alliance. On the one hand, the Leung Chun-ying Administration conflicts openly with the business sector on issues such as the introduction of stamp duty measures for addressing the overheated property market.[6] On the other hand, Leung Chun-ying and his supporters have been embroiled in a series of quarrels with bureaucrat-turned-political ministers and senior civil servants on budget allocations[7] and public appointments.[8] Even for the pro-Beijing leftists, who usually refrain from openly challenging the Chief Executive, publicly opposed the Leung Chun-ying Administration on a number of policy initiatives such as the expansion of landfills.[9] Despite Beijing's leaders' repeated calls for unity and support for the new government, Leung Chun-ying's governing coalition is proving to be built on sand (*South China Morning Post*, 2012, 23 February).

If the state–business alliance was proved to be an "ineffective" governing coalition under the two former Chief Executives, Tung Chee-hwa and Donald Tsang, from 1997 to 2012, the situation facing Leung Chun-ying is much worse given that under his administration the state–business alliance is not only "ineffective" but is even gradually "disintegrating". Governing through a loose and incohesive governing coalition, the Leung Chun-ying Administration is

264 *Rethinking Hong Kong's governance*

particularly vulnerable to the challenges of the democratic opposition and the civil society. Coupled with a series of scandals that have plagued his governing team,[10] unlike his two predecessors Leung Chun-ying did not enjoy any honeymoon period (Figure E.1) and his administration has been plunged into a political quagmire of pervasive public discontent and distrust almost from the first day of its inauguration (Figures E.2–E.3).

The governance problems facing the Leung Chun-ying Administration once again demonstrated that the origin of the post-1997 governance crisis goes deeper and beyond the *legitimacy deficit thesis* because the failure of the post-colonial state to organize a viable governing coalition has already set the scene

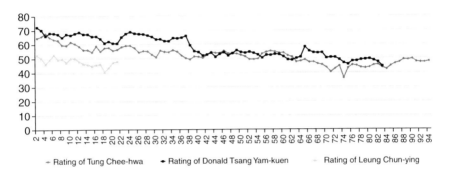

Figure E.1 Comparison between the public ratings of Tung Chee-hwa, Donald Tsang Yam-kuen and Leung Chun-ying (source: University of Hong Kong's Public Opinion Programme (http://hkupop.hku.hk)).

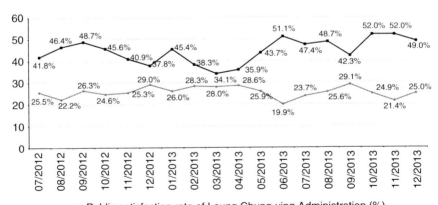

Figure E.2 The level of public dissatisfaction towards the Leung Chun-ying Administration (July 2012–December 2013) (source: University of Hong Kong's Public Opinion Programme (http://hkupop.hku.hk)).

Note
This figure excludes respondents who answered "Half–half" and "Don't know/Hesitate to say".

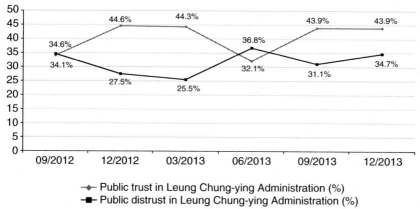

Figure E.3 The level of public trust towards the Leung Chun-ying Administration (September 2012–December 2013) (source: University of Hong Kong's Public Opinion Programme (http://hkupop.hku.hk)).

Note
This figure excludes respondents who answered "Half–half" and "Don't know/Hesitate to say".

for the governance crisis. To use the words of Levitsky and Way (2010), in order to provide a comprehensive account of the hybrid politics of the HKSAR, the opposition-centred explanation should be combined with a critical analysis of governing coalition building so as to examine the changing balance of powers between the post-colonial state and the opposition forces.

Notes

1 As a businessman-turned-politician, Henry Tang was groomed by Beijing for the position of the Chief Executive for decades. He was appointed by the Chinese government as the Secretary for Commerce, Industry and Technology in 2002 and took up the positions of Financial Secretary in 2003 and Chief Secretary for Administration in 2007. Henry Tang's father, Tang Hsiang-chien, a textile industrialist from Shanghai, developed ties with former Chinese President Jiang Zemin and Henry Tang's election bid was seen as being supported by the Shanghai faction (*The China Post*, 2011, 1 March).

2 On 13 February 2012, *Ming Pao* reported that there was an unapproved basement extension at Henry Tang's home at No. 7 York Road, Kowloon Tong. Henry Tang initially said the unauthorized works was located at his home at No 5A York Road, which is a canopy above the garage and digging works were carried out to deepen the garage for storage (*The Standard*, 2012b, 14 February). However, on 15 February 2012 *Sharp Daily* published a set of floor plans indicating that the unauthorized structure was a 2,400-square-foot illegal basement comprising store room, fitness room, cinema and wine-tasting room (*Sharp Daily*, 2012, 15 February). On 16 February 2012, Henry Tang's wife took responsibility for the unauthorized works and Tang apologized for mishandling the issue. The scandal seriously damaged the credibility of Henry Tang and opinion polls showed that the majority of respondents called for

Henry Tang to quit the Chief Executive race (*South China Morning Post*, 2012, 23 February).

3 When Henry Tang was embroiled in the scandal some business elites argued that members of the Election Committee should cast a blank vote collectively so that neither Leung Chun-ying nor Henry Tang would have a clear majority to win. To do so would force a new round of campaigning in early May and provide enough room for the business sector to identify another more credible candidate to replace Henry Tang. However, the idea of scuttling the poll alarmed Beijing's leaders who believed that it would only make it more difficult to control the electoral process and also cause serious damage to Hong Kong's stability (*Yazhou Zhoukan*, 2012).

4 Throughout the election Henry Tang had been trailing Leung Chun-ying in various opinion polls. Between the periods of October 2011 to March 2012, Leung's support ratings steadily stood above the 40 per cent line and usually led Henry Tang by more than 20 percentage points. For details, see the website of the Public Opinion Programme, University of Hong Kong: http://hkupop.hku.hk.

5 Anonymous interviewee.

6 In October 2012 the Leung Chun-ying Administration introduced the Buyer's Stamp Duty and the enhanced Special Stamp Duty to cool down the overheated property market. In February 2013, the Leung Administration further announced the increase of ad valorem stamp duty for residential and non-residential properties. In this connection, the Leung Administration introduced the *Stamp Duty (Amendment) Bill 2012* and the *Stamp Duty (Amendment) Bill 2013* in January 2013 and April 2013, respectively, with a view to enacting these stamp duty measures by legislation with retrospective effect. Pro-business legislators and business chambers severely criticized the two legislations as intervening with market operation and they pressurized the Leung Administration to introduce different kinds of exemptions during the legislative process (*South China Morning Post*, 2013a, 14 June). At the time of writing, these two bills are still in gridlock with the Legislative Council.

7 In July 2013, Ronnie Chan Chi-chung, Chairman of the Hang Lung Properties and also a strong supporter of Leung Chun-ying, severely criticized John Tsang Chun-wah, the bureaucrat-turned Financial Secretary, as a "big sinner" for his supposed tight-fisted approach to government spending. Although both Leung Chun-ying and John Tsang immediately clarified that they are on good terms with each other, Ronnie Chan's outburst was widely regarded by political pundits as exposing the tension between Leung and Tsang over the budget allocations, as the former tends to increase government spending on various social policy initiatives while the latter insists the traditional principle of financial prudence of the civil service (*The Standard*, 2013, 18 July).

8 In May 2013 the Leung Chun-ying Administration proposed to the Finance Committee of the Legislative Council the expansion of the three strategic landfills in Tseung Kwan O, Tuen Mun and Ta Kwu Ling. However, the funding proposals of the Leung Chun-ying's Administration met with strong opposition from the pro-Beijing leftists from the Hong Kong Federation of Trade Unions and those from the Democratic Alliance for the Betterment and Progress of Hong Kong had been vague over its leanings. Without enough votes to push it through, the Leung Administration was forced to withdraw the funding proposal for the Tseung Kwan O landfill in late June 2013. One month later, the Leung Administration suffered another setback as pro-government parties and pro-democracy parties joined hands to pass a motion deferring the scrutiny of the proposals for expanding landfills in Tuen Mun and Ta Kwu Ling to the next legislative session. As a consequence, the funding proposals for expanding the three landfills all ended in failure (*South China Morning Post*, 2013b, 14 July).

9 In November 2012 there were reports that Sophia Kao Ching-chi, full-time member of the Central Policy Unit, was given the power by the Chief Executive to screen and identify candidates for advisory and statutory bodies. Such an arrangement effectively

changed the established practice for policy secretaries and senior civil servants to identify suitable people for advisory bodies under their bureaus and created unease among the civil service. The internal government emails showing the details of Kao's power were subsequently revealed in local newspapers and political pundits read into the information leakage the silent opposition from civil servants (*The Standard*, 2012c, 30 November).

10 The public scandals included the illegal structures found at Leung Chun-ying's homes on The Peak, the arrest, resignation and prosecution of Secretary for Development Mak Chai-kwong for abusing civil service housing allowances, the resignation of Barry Cheung Chun-yuen as Executive Councillor following police investigation of the Hong Kong Mercantile Exchange, the resignation of Franklin Lam Fan-keung as Executive Councillor as a result of his alleged attempts to make use of insider information to sell flats ahead of stamp duty measures, the resignation of Henry Ho Kin-chung as Political Assistant for failing to declare his family's stake in land on Kwu Tung site (*South China Morning Post*, 2013c, 1 July; 2013d, 3 August).

References

Bloomberg. (2011, 28 September). China's Hong Kong succession takes shape as Tang steps down. Retrieved 1 January 2013 from www.bloomberg.com/news/2011-09-28/hong-kong-chief-secretary-henry-tang-said-to-resign-announcement-planned.html.

Levitsky, S., & Way, L. A. (2010). *Competitive authoritarianism: Hybrid regimes after the Cold War*. New York: Cambridge University Press.

Ming Pao. (2011, 24 September). Giving more time to Tang and Leung. A01 (in Chinese).

Reuters. (2012, 22 February). China frets as choice for Hong Kong leader strays off script. Retrieved 1 January 2013 from http://in.reuters.com/article/2012/02/22/hongkong-china-election-idINDEE81L07E20120222.

Sharp Daily. (2012, 15 February). The under-palace in Tang's house. A01 (in Chinese).

South China Morning Post. (2011a, 8 April). Unhappy campers take on "superman". City1.

South China Morning Post. (2011b, 20 September). Beijing "prefers Tang as new boss". EDT1.

South China Morning Post. (2012, 23 February). 66pc of public want Tang to pull out of race. EDT1.

South China Morning Post. (2013a, 14 June). Lawmakers warn of stand against stamp duty move. BIZ4.

South China Morning Post. (2013b, 14 July). Plans to expand all landfills will go back to Legco. EDT5.

South China Morning Post. (2013c, 1 July). Leung's year of fading expectations. EDT4.

South China Morning Post. (2013d, 3 August). Exco loss sparks talent pool fears. CITY3.

The China Post. (2011, 1 March). Tang confirms bid to be next Chief Executive of Hong Kong despite scandal. Retrieved 1 January 2013 from www.chinapost.com.tw/china/local-news/hong-kong/2011/11/27/324198/Tang-confirms.htm.

The Standard. (2012a, 1 March). It's a three-way race. P04.

The Standard. (2012b, 14 February). Tang "sorry" for illegal garage canopy. P04.

The Standard. (2012c, 30 November). Lam denial in doubt as Kao power revealed. P08.

The Standard. (2013, 18 July). "Sinner" jibe leaves Tsang feeling down. P01.

Yazhou Zhoukan. (2012). The crisis of scuttling the Chief Executive Election. *Yazhou Zhoukan*, 26(10), 28–29 (in Chinese).

Appendix
Interview guidelines

In order to gain primary understanding of the functioning of the state–business alliance before and after 1997, arrangements were made to conduct face-to-face interviews with a number of influential political players. The interviewees include government officials, legislators, business leaders, public affairs consultants, civil society leaders, academics and experts who are considered as having

Table A.1

Background of the interviewee	Date of interview
(I) Government officials	
1 Former head of a high-level policy unit of the HKSAR government	16 August 2011
2 Former Director of Bureau of the HKSAR government	3 August 2011
3 Former Secretary of Department of the HKSAR governent	30 November 2011
(II) Pro-business politicians	
4 Founding Chairman of a business-oriented political party	19 July 2011
5 Legislative Councillor of a business-oriented political party	10 August 2011
6 Legislative Councillor of a business-oriented political party	17 August 2011
7 Chairman of a business-oriented political party	15 November 2011
(III) Pro-Beijing politicians	
8 Hong Kong delegate to the National Committee of the Chinese People's Political Consultative Conference	7.9.2011 and 5 April 2012
(IV) Business leaders	
9 Chairman of a major chamber of commerce	7 July 2011
10 Non-official Executive Councillor with business background	8 August 2011
(V) Civil society leaders	
11 Social movement activist	29 July 2011
12 Chairman of a policy think-tank	16 August 2011
(VI) Public affairs consultants	
13 Public affairs consultant	18 August 2011
14 Public affairs consultant	24 August 2011
(VII) Academics and experts	
15 Academic specializing in colonial Hong Kong studies	7 July 2011
16 Hong Kong-based China observer	23 August 2011

Appendix 269

first-hand information about state–business relations and governance in Hong Kong. In order to protect the identities of the interviewees, their names will not be directly quoted and published.

The interviews were conducted in the form of face-to-face interviews. A standard list of proposed interview questions had been set to provide some guidelines for the interviews and several common questions were to be asked to collect the interviewees' general comments on the dynamics of the state–business relations before and after 1997. Nevertheless, because each interviewee has unique knowledge and experiences in different areas, special and tailor-made questions were also asked in each interview.

Table A.2

Standard list of interview questions

1 The business sector had been widely considered as major coalition partners of the Hong Kong government in both colonial and post-1997 Hong Kong. How would you comment on the changing dynamics of government–business relations both before and after 1997?

2 Business-oriented political parties have been underdeveloped and fragmented in the post-1997 period and they are generally unable to function as an effective agent of business interests. Do you think the underdevelopment of business-oriented political parties in Hong Kong has brought about any implications for government–business relations after 1997?

3 As a result of the emergence of civil society activism in recent years, there are increasing public criticisms against government–business collaboration. Do you think the rise of civil society activism has brought about any implications for government–business relations after 1997?

4 The power of the business sector has been institutionalized under the post-handover political system through the Chief Executive Election Committee and the functional constituency electoral system in the Legislative Council. Do you think the design of the post-1997 political system has brought about any implications for government–business relations after 1997?

5 The business sector has developed increased access to the sovereign state in Beijing after 1997 as a result of the closer political and economic relations between the Chinese government and the business elites. Do you think the closer relations between the business sector and the sovereign state have brought about any implications for government–business relations after 1997?

6 Do you think the business sector has provided strong political support to the HKSAR government in the process of governance and policy-making? If not, what are the reasons behind this?

Index

Page numbers in *italics* denote tables, those in **bold** denote figures.

administrative bureaucracy, in Hong Kong 75
agents of business interests, fragmentation of 142–54, 234, 236; Nutrition Labelling Scheme 149–53; West Kowloon Cultural District 153–4
Almond, Gabriel A. 51
American Bankers' Association 132
American Chamber of Commerce 149–52
anti-Communist legislators 197
anti-corruption movement 164
anti-Godber movement 164
Asian Financial Crisis (1998) 19, 61
Asia-Pacific Economic Co-operation Forum 53

balance of power 40, 204–6, 223, 239, 248, 265
Basic Law 23, 29, 105, 183–4, 239; Annex I of 186–7; Annex II of 196–7, 199; Article 45 of 43n18; Article 55 of 250; Article 56 of 250; Article 74 of 27, 44n21; Basic Law Consultative Committee (BLCC) 113, 116, 184; Basic Law Drafting Committee (BLDC) 112–13, 116, 184; corporatist design instituted by 201; distribution of power under 196; drafting process of 184; legal foundation of 206n1; as mini-constitution of the future HKSAR 113; objectives of 184; post-1997 constitutional system under 196; provisions under 186; for selection of Chief Executive 186; "two ups and two downs" process 184; voting-by-group arrangement in 196
Beijing's strategy, for state–business alliance: background analysis of

members of China-appointed bodies *114*; business representation system 122; co-option of the business sector and 106–12; features of 106; Hong Kong people ruling Hong Kong, principle of 105; policy of incorporating local capitalist class as majority 113; political co-option, pattern of 113; politics of transition and post-1997 political order 104–6; post-1997 state–business alliance, making of 106–12; Sino-British Joint Declaration on the Question of Hong Kong (1984) 104, 112; support of the co-opted business elites 161; traditional business representation system, end of 122–31
British and Chinese merchants, emergence of 76–9
British business groups 85, 122, 131; British hongs, end of the era of 123–9; Hutchison-Whampoa 123, 126; Jardine Group 85, 107, 123, 126–7, 129, 131, 155; market capitalizations of 125, **127**; position of British capital in Hong Kong 123; predominant position of 125; Swire Group 77, 123, 126; Wheelock 123, 126; *see also* Chinese business groups
British capital in Hong Kong economy, decline of 125
British capitalist class 76–8, 83, 235
British Chamber of Commerce 152
British colonial administration 73–4, 76, 105, 109, 126, 129, 197, 204; evaluation of performance of *96*; public satisfaction and public trust, levels of 96
British colonial system of governance *see* British colonial administration

British Empire, dissolution of 90, 92
British hongs 85, 95, 107, 122–3, 127–9, 131, 147–8, 155, 235–6, 241, 256; co-option of 154; end of the era of 123–9
British Taipans 123, 127
budget allocations 263
bureaucratic polity, concept of 75
business associations: formation of 142; in Hong Kong *143*; in Western democratic countries 132–3
business elites: British colonial practice of co-opting 162; circumvention activities by 221–5; communication channel for 213; co-option into HKSAR political establishment 121, 210, 213–15; endorsement of 172; erosion of intermediary role of 235–7; influences in the legislative process 204; power in bargaining with the Chief Executive 196; public mistrust of 237; representation in advisory bodies 160–2; state–business alliance, incorporation in 161
business leaders, public perceptions of *171*
business power, institutionalization of 36, 238; in executive branch 185–96; under HKSAR political system 201–5; in legislative process 196–201
business representation system, traditional 122, 127; appointment of senior executives 131; breakdown of 134; British-dominated economy, transition from 123–9; economic and political structures since the 1980s 122–31; electoral politics and 129–30; features of 129; new political economy in Hong Kong 130–1; political-economic foundations of 123; princely hongs, end of the era of 123–9
Business Roundtable, USA 133
business sector post-1997, Hong Kong: direct access to Beijing 223; direct access to sovereign state 221–5; diversification of 123–9, 257; economic links with the Mainland authorities 218–21; economism, notion of 172; financial resources and talents 136; implications of growing disconnection of 168–74; institutionalized access to the sovereign state 211–13; under modern capitalist economies 132–4; overseas experiences 132–4; patterns of prganization of 132; power bases for 201–5; privileged position in legislative process 199–201; and relative autonomy

of the post-colonial state 237–40; representation of 131–42; selected circumvention activities by *226*
business-oriented political parties: business elites, involvement of 137; community networks of 170; development of 134; establishment and sponsorship of 132; factional rivalries within 137; historical review of 134–6; lobbying for government officials 137; organization of 132; rise and fall of 134–6; role in organizing and representing business interests 133; structural constraints on 136–42; underdevelopment of 121, 131–42, 169

Canton 77
Canton–Hong Kong Strike-Boycott (1925) 87, 99n9
capitalist system 9, 103, 105, 107, 111–12, 115
catalytic states 61
Central Liaison Office 187, 199, 210–11, 213–15, 222–3, 225, 239, 252
Central People's Government (CPG) 23, 186, 214
Central Policy Unit 161; analysis of part-time members in *165*; function of 175n4
Cheung, Anthony 75
Cheung Kong-Hutchison Group 126
Chief Executive 7, 249; appointment of 183; case of the 2007 election of 190–6; dual leadership roles 185; Election Committees *see* Chief Executive Election Committees; Election Ordinance 186; methods for selecting and appointing 186; as power centre of the state–business alliance 223; powers of political appointment and patronage 186, 205; rebuilding the governing authority of 251–2; veto, power of 197, 239
Chief Executive Election Committees: appointment of 185; background analysis of members of *192–4*; business power, institutionalization of 185–96; composition of 186, *187*; decision-making process 196; dominant position of the business sector in 187–90; government policies, formulation of 195; king-making power 205, 238, 252; major sectors 187; powers of policy-making and implementation 186; register of electors for *188–9*; small-circle nature 199

272 Index

Chief Executive Nomination Committee 251–2
Chief Executive Selection Committee 190; background analysis of members of *191*
Chinese business groups: acquisitions of British companies 123; Cheung Kong-Hutchison Group 126; Hang Lung Group 126; Henderson Group 126; market capitalization of 125, **128**; New World Group 126; Sun Hung Kai Group 126; *see also* British business groups
Chinese capital in Hong Kong economy, emergence of 125
Chinese capitalist class 79, 83, 161, 235, 241; types of 78–9; *see also* British capitalist class
Chinese Communist Party (CCP) 211
Chinese constitution, Article 57 of 211
Chinese entrepreneurs 123–4
Chinese General Chamber of Commerce (CGCC) 79, 133
Chinese Manufacturers' Association of Hong Kong 133, 148–9, 215
Chinese People's Political Consultative Conference (CPPCC) 113, 210, 211–13, 222–3, 239; background analysis of Hong Kong members of *213*
Chinese tycoons, rise of 123
civic centre 87
civil liberties 3, 5, 7, 41n1, 253
civil society activism: challenges of 173; Express Rail Link, case of 173–4; growing waves of 167; protest rallies 166; rise of 160, 162–7, 236; state–business alliance, impact on 168; values and policy agenda 170
civil society organizations 5, 8, 53, 164, 167; development of 160; governance process, role in 34; number of *167*; policy agenda 167; political challenges of 160
Closer Economic Partnership Arrangement (CEPA) 20, 218
coalition, concept of 64
coalition government 251–2
collaborative colonialism 85
collective bargaining system 133
colonial bureaucracy 76, 80, 106
colonial Hong Kong: anti-colonial movements 87; British and Chinese merchants, emergence of 76–9; capitalist class, making of 76–9; Chinese capital, flow of 123; colonial state, nature of 73–6; conditions for

state autonomy in 87–94; District Watch Force 78–9; economic power, expansion of 78; encompassing intermediaries, incorporation of 83–7; establishment of 77; Executive Council 81, 83; governing coalition building in 82–97; institutionalized negotiation mechanisms 83–7; and leaders of the Chinese community 78–9; Legislative Council 81, 83, 89; political appointment and patronage 88–9; position of British capital in 123; princes of 76–8; public satisfaction and public trust, levels of 96; representative of the British Queen in 92; social disputes 78; state embeddedness, conditions for 83–7; state–business relations in 79–82; taxation policy 80; trade activities, development of 77; traditional business representation system in 122, 127; transcendent position and political autonomy of colonial Governor 87–94; treaty ports 77
colonial political system 75, 88, 92, 95, 98, 131, 204, 238, 256
colonial state, nature of 73–6
communication channels, institutionalized 92, 95, 213–14, 238
community networks, of major political parties *170*
Comparative Politics: A Developmental Approach (1966) 51
competitive authoritarianism *see* electoral authoritarianism
Competitive Authoritarianism: Hybrid Regimes After the Cold War (2010) 28
constitutional design, of post-1997 political system 183–5
constitutional reforms, politics of 43n19
consultative democracy 164
Convention on Extension of Hong Kong Territory (1898) 74
Cooperative Resource Centre 135
Council on Economic Planning and Development, Taiwan 59
Cyberport project 16, 42n12, 170

Dahl, Robert 5
decision-making 8, 56, 68, 75, 81–2, 183, 196, 204, 214, 235
decolonization, process of 131–2
democratic political parties 211, 252
democratic state, autonomy of 57–8

Deng, Xiaoping 104, 108, 112
directorships, held by individual directors *126*
District Watch Force 78–9
Donald Tsang Administration, Hong Kong 9, 11, 20; business regulatory initiatives under *12–14*

East India Company 77
economic globalization 52
Economic Planning Boards (South Korea and Singapore) 59
economic power structures, fragmentation and decentralization of 129
Economic Synergy 136, 144, 147, 170
economic thesis, notion of 19–20
economism, political discourse of *172, 174,* 237
electoral authoritarianism 5–7, 253
electoral politics, development of 129–30
embedded autonomy, of state: notion of 33–4, 50, 58, 65; state capacity and 58–9
encompassing intermediaries 60, 67–8, 83–5, 87, 95, 97, 122–3, 127, 129, 131–2, 134, 144, 153–5, 235–7, 241, 250–1
ethnic conflicts 7
ethnic minority groups 211
European Economic Community 90
Evans, Peter 33–4, 58, 64–5; embedded autonomy, notion of 60, 62; state–society synergy, theory of 63
Executive Council 81, 83, 250; effective functioning of 250; Express Rail Link project, approval of 173–4; institutionalized negotiation mechanism 252; reorganization of 252; representation of business interests in *150–1*; rule of confidentiality 195; unofficial members in *84, 86, 163*
executive-dominant governance system 8–9, 29, 31, 197
Express Rail Link (Guangzhou–Shenzhen–Hong Kong) project 173–4, 177n15

Federation of Hong Kong Industries 133, 148–9, 215
Food and Health Bureau 149, 152–3
food retailers and suppliers 152
food safety 149–50
foreign capital 107, 140, 221
foreign missionaries 164
forging coalitions 50, 65; state capacity as 64–5

forums of negotiations 60
free market capitalism 172
"Freedom of the World" survey 3, 41n1
Fukuyama, Francis 33
fully autonomous state 68
fully embedded state 68
functional constituencies: background analysis of legislative councillors returned by *200*; distribution of registered electors by *198*; electoral system 199, 205; institutional design of 196–9; list of motions rejected by *202–3*; number of motions rejected by *201*; voting-by-group system 199

genocides 7
governance crisis post-1997, Hong Kong 7–18; under Chinese sovereignty 243–8; economic thesis 19–20; legislative success rate *10*; legitimacy deficit and 18–27; limitations of legitimacy deficit thesis 26–7; people participating in protest rallies **16**; political leadership thesis 19, 21; public dissatisfaction, level of **15**, 240–3; public trust, level of **17**, 240–3; as result of poor economy/poor political leadership 18–21; social demonstrations, number of **16**; state capacity and 33; state–business alliance, failure of 234–43; state-centric perspective to 35–7; theoretical explanation on 234–43
governance, definition of 50, 52
governance system, executive-dominant 8–9, 29, 31, 197
governed interdependence (GI): concept of 34, 50, 59–60, 67; state capacity as 59–61
governing coalition building: in colonial times 82–97; failure of 243–8; importance of 248; opportunity for the new political order 252–3; state capacity as 65–8
governing coalition thesis 29, 32, 247; consequences of the failure of 36–7
government–business collusion 16, 97, 170, 257; public perceptions on *18*; transfer of interests 17
Grantham, Alexander 94

Hang Lung Group 126
Hang Seng Index 124–5
Harris, Peter 75
Henderson Group 126

274 *Index*

Hong Kong: A Study in Bureaucratic Politics 75
Hong Kong Affairs Advisers (HKAA) 113, 116
Hong Kong and Macau Work Committee (HKMWC) 214–15, 227n5
Hong Kong Bank 77, 79, 85, 107, 126–7, 129, 131, 155
Hong Kong Chinese Importers' & Exporters' Association 149
Hong Kong Club 77
Hong Kong General Chamber of Commerce (HKGCC) 77, 79, 133, 148–9
Hong Kong Jockey Club 78
Hong Kong people ruling Hong Kong, principle of 104–5, 112, 166, 214
Hong Kong Progressive Alliance 135–6; income and expenditure accounts of *138–9*
Hong Kong Retail Management Association 152
Hong Kong SAR Preparatory Committee (HKSARPC) 113, 116
Hong Kong Special Administrative Region (HKSAR) 7, 9, 11, 18, 22, 105; acquisition by Britain 77; channel of communication with London 222; civil liberties 7; during colonial rule *see* colonial Hong Kong; comparison with other East Asian hybrid regimes 253–6; co-option of business elites into 121; delegations to Beijing *224*; Donald Tsang Administration 9, 11–14, 20; economic integration with China 123; economic performance with public support *20*; establishment of 184; executive-dominant governance system 8–9; financial and business services 218; financial crisis (2008) 19; governance crisis after 1997 *see* governance crisis post-1997, Hong Kong; governing coalition, analysis of 27–32; as hybrid regime 7–18; institutionalization of business power in 206; inward direct investment by major countries *219*; new political economy in 130–1; number of regional headquarters in **140, 141**; outward direct investment of **220**; people's views on social harmony *19*; percentage of assets hold by **220**; political order 248–53; political systems of 184; state officials in China

visited by business delegations in *225*; status under Chinese sovereignty 7; total trade with Mainland China **219**; total trade with United Kingdom *91*
Hong Kong Suppliers Association 152
"horse-trading" 195, 207n7
Hu, Jintao 210
human development 62
Huntington, Samuel 3
Hutchison-Whampoa (British business group) 123, 126
hybrid regimes: challenges of democratic opposition under 18–27; competitive election, degree of **6**; democratic and authoritarian elements 5; growing scholarly attention on 3–6; in Hong Kong 3–18, *255*; importance of 3; Lau Siu-kai's theory and its limitations 29–32; Levitsky and Way's comparative studies on 28–9; in Malaysia *255*; notion of 3; number of "partly free" *4*; politics of 27–9; in Singapore *255*

income inequality 172
Individual Visit Scheme, Hong Kong 20
industrial bank, establishment of 93
institutional incompatibility 8
institutionalized negotiation mechanisms 68, 83–7, 148, 153–5, 250–2
instruments of power 64
interlocks per company, number of *125*
interlocutors 60, 67
inter-state cooperation and collaboration 53

Jardine Group 85, 107, 123, 126–7, 129, 131, 155
Jardine, William 77

Kooiman, Jan 54

labour protection, provision of 9, 93–5
labour unions 133, 214
labour-intensive production units 218
Legislative Council 7, 22–3, 26, 173, 183; Chief Executive Election Ordinance 186; composition of *89, 130*; democratic reforms, implementation of 130; democratization of 129; electoral college seats 129; electoral system of 197; factional rivalries with 137; functional constituency electoral system 196–201; introduction of elected seats into 129–30; political functions of 196;

representation of business sector in 204; unofficial members in *84*; veto, power of 196; voting-by-group system of 196–201

Legislative Councillors, background analysis of pro-business *145*

legislative success rates: of Hong Kong *10*; of post-colonial state 9

legitimacy deficit thesis 247, 249, 264; Lau Siu-kai's theory 29; limitations of 26–7; notion of 18–26

legitimacy, notion of 26

Letters Patent 74

Leung Chun-ying Administration, Hong Kong: background analysis of political officials under *262*; governing coalition 263; public dissatisfaction towards **264**; public trust towards **265**; unofficial members of the Executive Council appointed by *263*

Li, Ka-shing 210

Lianghui 213

liberal authoritarianism 5, 7, 22–3, 253

Liberal Democratic Federation 134; income and expenditure accounts of *138–9*; interlocking directorships of *146*

listed companies 123, 125–6

Lok Sin Tong 164

Mainland–Hong Kong economic integration, implications of 218–21

Man Mo Temple, construction of 78

Mann, Michael 51

manufacturing industries, growth of 123, 218

"market as magic bullet" model 62

market capitalization 124–6, 172

Marx, Karl 56; theories of relative autonomy of the state 56–7

mass mobilization 170

Mass Transit Railway Corporation 173

Matheson, James 77

mergers and acquisitions 123

Miliband, Ralph 56, 238

Ministry of International Trade and Industry (MITI), Japan 59

modern developmental states, effectiveness of 34, 58

multi-level governance, emergence of 52–3

Nam Pak Hong Association 78

Nanking, Treaty of 74

National Association of Manufacturers, USA 133

National Federation of Independent Business, USA 133

National Front, Malaysia 254, 256

National People's Congress (NPC) 113, 184, 210, 211–13, 222–3, 239; background analysis of Hong Kong deputies to *212*; functions of 211

natural leaders 85, 161–2, 169

New World Group 126

newly industrializing countries (NICs) 59

non-intervention, doctrine of 92–3, 97

Nordlinger, Eric A. 33, 57–8

Nutrition Labelling Scheme 149–53

O'Connor, James 9

"one country, two systems," framework of 45n23, 104, 112, 184, 215, 252

Opium War (1842) 74, 77

Patten, Chris 130, 156n3

peak associations 133–4, 156n5

Pei-chun, James Tien 135, 183, 190, 195

Pengfei, Ji 113

People's Action Party, Singapore 254, 256

Peters, Guy B. 35, 54, 64–5, 67

Pierre, Jon 35, 54, 64–5, 67

Po Leung Kuk (charitable organization) 79, 164

Policy Address and Legislative Programme, Hong Kong 9

policy making, by government: autonomy of democratic state in 57–8; corporatist model of 65; framework for 34–5; societal support to 168; *see also* public policy making

Political Action Committees 132

political attrition 9

political autonomy: of colonial Governor 87–94; definition of 55; notion of 33, 50, 55, 57, 65; state capacity as 55–8

political confrontation 7–8, 22, 24

"political deals" 195

political discourse of economism, public perceptions on *172, 174*

political leadership thesis, notion of 19, 21

political liberalization 5

political situations 8

polyarchies, theory of 5

post-colonial governing coalition, robustness of 29–32

post-colonial state and the society, widening gap between 168–74

Poulantza, Nicos 9

Powell, G. Bingham 51

276 Index

Preliminary Working Committee (PWC) 113, 115
property development sector, growth of 123
Protection of the Diaoyu Islands Movement 164
public appointments 263
public bureaucracy 59
public discourse, development of **171**
public dissatisfaction, toward Hong Kong government **15, 264**
public finances, management of 80
public health, protection of 149
public housing programme 93–4
public policy making: autonomy of democratic state in 57–8; subsidiary legislations for 84
public satisfaction, towards colonial administration 96
public sector reforms 25, 53
public trust, level of **17,** *97*
public–private partnership 62, 154; institutionalized 60; state-sponsored 61

Qing Empire, British invasions of 74

real estate hegemony: dominance of 17; notion of 43n15
relative autonomy, of state: Marxist theories of 56–7; notion of 33, 55
religious organizations 164, 211
Royal Instructions 74

Seamen's Strike (1922) 87, 99n9
Secretary of State for the Colonies 88, 90
self-employed business owners 132
semi-authoritarianism 5
semi-democracy *see* electoral authoritarianism
Severe Acute Respiratory Syndrome (SARS) 19
Shek Kip Mei Fire (1953) 93–4
Shenzhen Special Economic Zone 210
Sino-British Joint Declaration on the Question of Hong Kong (1984) 104, 112, 184, 211
Sino-British negotiation, over future of Hong Kong 103–4, 107, 166
Sino-British trade 77
Skocpol, Theda 33, 57–8, 67
small- and medium-sized enterprises 132; distribution of *142*
social capital 34–5, 62–3
social harmony, Hong Kong people's views on *19*

social imbalances, mitigation of 93
social inequalities 172
social pluralism, development of 166
social welfare, provision of 9, 79, 93, 167
"soft money" contributions 132–3
Star Ferry Pier episode (2006) 176n9
state autonomy 33, 35, 67–8, 92; conditions for 87–94; crisis of 36, 234, 237–40; significance of 238; strengthening 251–2
state capacity: building of 61; concept of 32; definition of 50–5; as embedded autonomy 58–9; as forging coalitions 64–5; and governance 32–5, 50–5; as governed interdependence 59–61; as governing coalition building 65–8; integrated conceptual framework on 67, 69, 83, 94, 233, 238, 240, 254; and notion of political autonomy 33; as political autonomy 55–8; and role in modern governance 33; as state–society synergy 61–3; theoretical approaches to *66*
state embeddedness 67–8; conditions for 83–7; crisis of 36, 234, 235–7; embedded autonomy, notion of 33–4; foundation of 96; strengthening 250–1
state–business alliance 29, 32, 36, 50, 58–9; before and after 1997 *244–6*; British-centred 112–13; business representation system 121; Chief Executive as power centre of 223; China-centred *see* Beijing's strategy, for state–business alliance; civil society activism and challenges to 168; in colonial Hong Kong 76, 79–82; and constitutional design post-1997 political system 183–4; contribution to effective governance in colonial Hong Kong 82–97; contributions of 96; dynamics of 204, 210, 222; failure of 35, 36, 234–43, 254; financial assistance 97; formation and evolution of 79–82; functioning of 94–7, 143; governing coalition 38; incorporation of business elites into 161; for maintaining effective governance 80, 94–7; new challenges for 162–7; pillars of 122; public challenges to 160
state-owned enterprises 221
state–society conflicts, 160, 169, 173–4, 236–7
state–society relations 32, 34, 38, 162; dynamics of 164
state–society synergy 59, 67; Evans' theory of 63; state capacity as 61–3

Index 277

strikes and social disturbances: Canton–Hong Kong Strike-Boycott (1925) 87; riots of 1967 87, 93, 99n10; Seamen's Strike (1922) 87, 99n9; Shek Kip Mei Fire (1953) 93–4
"strong business representation, weak political support" paradox 142–54, 236
Sui-kai, Lau 75
Sun Hung Kai Group 126
Swire (British business group) 77, 123, 126

Thatcher, Margaret 104
tourism industry, promotion of 195
trade associations 61, 85, 132–3, 152, 162
transfer of interests 17, 174
transgovernmental cooperation 53
transitional powers 23
transnational corporations 53
Tsang, Donald 11, 20–1, 38, 173, 190, 195, 237, 262
Tung Chee-hwa Administration, Hong Kong 9, 20, 30, 166; Policy Address (1999) 153; public satisfaction and public trust in 20
Tung Wah Hospital 79, 85–7, 164

United Democrats of Hong Kong 134–5

United Kingdom 90; Hong Kong channel of communication with 222; Hong Kong's total trade with *91*
urban planning projects 25
US Chamber of Commerce 132–3

value-added business 219
veto, power of 196–7, 239
voting-by-group system 27, 196–9, 239; list of motions rejected under *202–3*; number of motions rejected under *201*

Weber, Max 43n16, 51
Weberian bureaucratic insulation 34, 58–9
Weiss, Linda 34, 60–1, 64–5; theory of governed interdependence 61
West Kowloon Cultural District (WKCD) 16, 25, 149, 153–4, 170, 223
Western capitalist economies 132–4
Wheelock (British business group) 123, 126

Xu, Jaitun 105, 107, 111, 121, 134, 213, 215

Zhang, Gaoli 228n8

eBooks
from Taylor & Francis
Helping you to choose the right eBooks for your Library

Add to your library's digital collection today with Taylor & Francis eBooks. We have over 45,000 eBooks in the Humanities, Social Sciences, Behavioural Sciences, Built Environment and Law, from leading imprints, including Routledge, Focal Press and Psychology Press.

Choose from a range of subject packages or create your own!

Benefits for you
- Free MARC records
- COUNTER-compliant usage statistics
- Flexible purchase and pricing options
- 70% approx of our eBooks are now DRM-free.

Benefits for your user
- Off-site, anytime access via Athens or referring URL
- Print or copy pages or chapters
- Full content search
- Bookmark, highlight and annotate text
- Access to thousands of pages of quality research at the click of a button.

Free Trials Available

We offer free trials to qualifying academic, corporate and government customers.

eCollections
Choose from 20 different subject eCollections, including:
- Asian Studies
- Economics
- Health Studies
- Law
- Middle East Studies

eFocus
We have 16 cutting-edge interdisciplinary collections, including:
- Development Studies
- The Environment
- Islam
- Korea
- Urban Studies

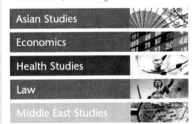

For more information, pricing enquiries or to order a free trial, please contact your local sales team:

UK/Rest of World: **online.sales@tandf.co.uk**
USA/Canada/Latin America: **e-reference@taylorandfrancis.com**
East/Southeast Asia: **martin.jack@tandf.com.sg**
India: **journalsales@tandfindia.com**

www.tandfebooks.com